Information Technology

Visit the IT & Applied Computing resource centre
www.IT-CH.com

IFIP – The International Federation for Information Processing

IFIP was founded in 1960 under the auspices of UNESCO, following the First World Computer Congress held in Paris the previous year. An umbrella organization for societies working in information processing, IFIP's aim is two-fold: to support information processing within its member countries and to encourage technology transfer to developing nations. As its mission statement clearly states,

> IFIP's mission is to be the leading, truly international, apolitical organization which encourages and assists in the development, exploitation and application of information technology for the benefit of all people.

IFIP is a non-profitmaking organization, run almost solely by 2500 volunteers. It operates through a number of technical committees, which organize events and publications. IFIP's events range from an international congress to local seminars, but the most important are:

- the IFIP World Computer Congress, held every second year;
- open conferences;
- working conferences.

The flagship event is the IFIP World Computer Congress, at which both invited and contributed papers are presented. Contributed papers are rigorously refereed and the rejection rate is high.

As with the Congress, participation in the open conferences is open to all and papers may be invited or submitted. Again, submitted papers are stringently refereed.

The working conferences are structured differently. They are usually run by a working group and attendance is small and by invitation only. Their purpose is to create an atmosphere conducive to innovation and development. Refereeing is less rigorous and papers are subjected to extensive group discussion.

Publications arising from IFIP events vary. The papers presented at the IFIP World Computer Congress and at open conferences are published as conference proceedings, while the results of the working conferences are often published as collections of selected and edited papers.

Any national society whose primary activity is in information may apply to become a full member of IFIP, although full membership is restricted to one society per country. Full members are entitled to vote at the annual General Assembly. National societies preferring a less committed involvement may apply for associate or corresponding membership. Associate members enjoy the same benefits as full members, but without voting rights. Corresponding members are not represented in IFIP bodies. Affiliated membership is open to non-national societies, and individual and honorary membership schemes are also offered.

Information Technology
Supporting change through teacher education

IFIP TC3 WG3.1/3.5 Joint Working Conference on
Information Technology: Supporting change through
teacher education
30th June – 5th July 1996, Kiryat Anavim, Israel

Edited by

Don Passey,
Senior Research Fellow,
Lancaster University,
Lancaster, UK

and

Brian Samways,
Education Officer,
Birmingham City Council,
Birmingham, UK

Published by Chapman & Hall on behalf of the
International Federation for Information Processing (IFIP)

CHAPMAN & HALL
London · Weinheim · New York · Tokyo · Melbourne · Madras

Published by Chapman & Hall, 2–6 Boundary Row, London SE1 8HN, UK

Chapman & Hall, 2–6 Boundary Row, London SE1 8HN, UK

Chapman & Hall GmbH, Pappelallee 3, 69469 Weinheim, Germany

Chapman & Hall USA, 115 Fifth Avenue, New York, NY 10003, USA

Chapman & Hall Japan, ITP-Japan, Kyowa Building, 3F, 2-2-1 Hirakawacho, Chiyoda-ku, Tokyo 102, Japan

Chapman & Hall Australia, 102 Dodds Street, South Melbourne, Victoria 3205, Australia

Chapman & Hall India, R. Seshadri, 32 Second Main Road, CIT East, Madras 600 035, India

First edition 1997

© 1997 IFIP

Printed in Great Britain by Athenæum Press Ltd, Tyne & Wear

ISBN 0 412 79760 7

A catalogue record for this book is available from the British Library

∞ Printed on permanent acid-free text paper, manufactured in accordance with ANSI/NISO Z39.48-1992 and ANSI/NISO Z39.48-1984 (Permanence of Paper).

CONTENTS

Preface

This volume records the proceedings of an IFIP International Working conference that was held in Israel during the summer of 1996. As is common for conferences like this one, the title and focus were chosen well over a year in advance. As the conference approached, it was clear that the selected themes were high on the list of contemporary concerns in many countries around the world. The atmosphere during paper sessions and the workshops reflected a shared view that issues of contemporary importance were being addressed.

Under-pinning the conference was a recognition that there are many examples around the world of how information and communications technologies can make a positive contribution to teaching and-learning at all levels of education. Indeed, it is clear that the range of possibilities shows every sign of continued growth. Against this background, however, there is the universally daunting challenge of preparing and sustaining teachers who are capable of making appropriate use of new technology to support both traditional and emerging educational objectives and who are also able to thrive in a climate of continuous change. The challenge is compounded by the implications of computer and communications based technologies for the fundamental roles of the teacher.

Within the framework of the conference, and through the sharing of experience gained in education systems around the world, delegates sought to identify critical issues and successful strategies that have led to effective support for pre-service and in-service teachers. This volume is testament to the high quality of the debate that took place and we hope that the thinking that is recorded here can be used to help others who are seeking to use their teacher education systems to further the effective and appropriate use of technology in teaching and learning.

Conferences are not just about academic deliberation! Our hosts at the conference provided us with a wonderful welcome and an excellent working environment which enabled old friendships to be renewed and new ones to be forged. We are most grateful to them for all that they did.

David Benzie
Chair of the Programme Committee

IFIP gratefully acknowledges the support of the following organisations in their sponsorship of this conference:
UNESCO
Aleph ad Taph Ltd.
Computerstore Ltd.
Bezek - Israel Telecommunications Company Ltd.
School of Education, Bar-Ilan University

IFIP Technical Committee for Education TC3

IFIP is a non-profit organisation, which has as its mission to be the leading, truly international, apolitical organisation which encourages and assists in the development, exploitation and application of Information Technology for the benefit of all people. Proceedings of IFIP Congresses and many of its Conferences are published and distributed world-wide and a complete list of the (approximately) 400 titles is available from the IFIP Secretariat. IFIP also publishes an annual Information Bulletin and a quarterly Newsletter describing its work which are available free of charge.

Each of its Technical Committees is composed of one representative from each IFIP Member organisation of which there are 57 representing 69 countries. One of the aims of IFIP is to promote information science and technology by encouraging education in information processing, and the Technical Committee for Education (TC3) was established in 1963 for this purpose.

TC3 arranges every 4 to 6 years a World Conference on Computers in Education (WCCE). The world of "Education and Information Technologies" is made visible to the professional informatics society through these conferences and through the quarterly TC3 journal of the same name. The Committee also offers consultancy in informatics education, often carried out in co-operation with UNESCO or other international organisations.

TC3 supervises seven Working Groups which deal with specialised aspects of education and informatics. These cover the following areas:

Secondary Education	Working Group WG 3.1
University Education	Working Group WG 3.2
Research into Education	Working Group WG 3.3
Professional/Vocational Education	Working Group WG 3.4
Elementary Education	Working Group WG 3.5
Distance Learning	Working Group WG 3.6
Educational Management	Working Group WG 3.7

Much of the real work within TC3 is carried out by the working groups, each of which consists of specialists who are individually appointed by their peers, independent of nationality.

IFIP Technical Committee TC3 and its Working Groups may be reached through:

IFIP Secretariat
Hofstrasse 3
A-2361 Laxenburg
Austria,

(Tel. +43 2236 73616, Fax +43 2236 736169, E-mail ifip@ifip.or.at)
(http://www.ifip.or.at)

IFIP TC3 Working Group 3.1 - Informatics in Secondary Education

Aims

The Working Group aims to develop effective communication among its members who come from many different countries. It seeks to gather the most recent information on research and practice related to informatics at the secondary level. This information is communicated through the Working Group's communication network, through working conferences and workshops. In this way the information is developed into a collective expertise, shared by the members of the Working Group. On the basis of this collective expertise prospective ideas about development and impact of informatics at the secondary education level are formed. The collective expertise is shared with others through open conferences, seminars and workshops, through publications and consultancy.

Scope

The themes of the work done within IFIP WG 3.1 concern all aspects of computers in secondary schools. Among the themes are:
- informatics education (or computer science education).
- informatics in other subjects.
- computer tools for teachers.
- computers as pedagogical tools in teaching and learning.
- influences of these tools on the contents and methods of teaching and learning.
- computer tools for management and administration of secondary schools.
- computers and teacher education.
- distance learning.
- local, regional and national policy.

Current Work: Guidelines of Good Practice

The accumulated knowledge and experience of IFIP Working Group 3.1 is synthesised in 'Guidelines for Good Practice'. In this work the group is aware of the fact that for good practice there is in general no unique solution, and that specific circumstances of people and countries must be taken into account. These Guidelines are a tradition in Working Group 3.1 and the first series of Guidelines appeared in the beginning of the seventies. Currently the following Guidelines for good practice have been or are being produced:
- H. Taylor, R. Aiken, and T. J. van Weert, *Guidelines for good practice: Informatics education in secondary schools*. IFIP Working Group 3.1, Geneva, 1992.
- F. Ruiz i Tarrago and T. J. van Weert (eds.), *Guidelines for good practice: Integration of information technology in secondary education: main issues and perspectives*. IFIP Working Group 3.1, Geneva, 1993.

- D. Tinsley and T.J. van Weert (eds.), *Guidelines for good practice : Tele-learning in Secondary Education*. IFIP Working Group 3.1, 1994.

IFIP Working Group 3.1 has also produced *Informatics for Secondary Education : a Curriculum for Schools* (UNESCO 1994).

Activities

Through working conferences, workshops and seminars, IFIP Working Group 3.1 seeks to develop and exchange the knowledge of informatics on the secondary phase between the working group members and other interested persons. Usually, the results of these activities are published as a book or as special issues of international journals. Examples of recent work include the following:

- Proceedings of the IFIP Open Conference *Informatics and Changes in Learning*. The conference, sponsored by WG 3.1 and 3.5, was held from June 7th to 11th 1993 at Gmunden, Austria.
- Proceedings of the IFIP Working Conference *Integrating Information Technology into Education*. This WG 3.1 conference was held in October 1994 at Barcelona, Spain.
- Proceedings of the IFIP World Conference WCCE '95 *Liberating the Learner*. The world conference, sponsored by IFIP TC3 (including WG 3.1) was held in July 1995 at Birmingham, UK.
- Proceedings of the IFIP Working Conference *Information Technology: Supporting Change Through Teacher Education*. This WG 3.1 and 3.5 joint conference was held from June 30th to July 5th 1996 at Kiryat Anavim, Israel.

How to become a member

Membership is open to those who have actively participated in at least two working group activities, and is subject to approval by the working group at the annual meeting. Members are selected for their expertise, and come from both IFIP member countries and non-IFIP member countries.

IFIP Working Group 3.1 may be reached through:

IFIP Secretariat
Hofstrassev 3
A-2361 Laxenburg
Austria

Tel. +43 2236 73616, Fax +43 2236 736169, E-mail ifip@ifip.or.at
Internet http://www.ifip.or.at

IFIP TC3 Working Group 3.5 - Informatics in Elementary Education

Introduction

IFIP Working Group 3.5 was formed in 1983 and its work since then has focused on issues associated with the role of ICT (Information and Communication Technologies) in elementary (including pre-school) education. At the time that the group was formed, little attention had been paid to the possible role that ICT could play in the early period of schooling despite wide acceptance of the premise that this phase of education provides the critical foundation for all that follows.

In the years since the group was formed, members from around the world have contributed to international debate of both pedagogical and strategic issues as they relate to the effective use of ICT to support teaching and learning. Issues associated with ICT and teacher education have been of particular concern.

Aims and Scope

- to study the problems arising in informatics education and the use of methods of informatics in the professional development of teachers, both pre and in-service, and teachers of teachers.
- to promote the development of informatics education material:
i)   for the primary/elementary school teachers, and
ii)   for the primary/elementary school curriculum, including, for example, the use of the methods of informatics in all disciplines and individualisation of education.
- to bring the problem of informatics education in primary/elementary schools to the attention of school management at all levels - school, regional and national.

Activities

The above aims have principally been realised through publications that have arisen from IFIP open and working conferences that have been sponsored by the group. These meetings have all provided an active forum for the discussion of ideas and experiences. They have been particularly effective in enabling lessons learnt in one country to be shared around the world. Recent publications include:

- Proceedings of the IFIP Open Conference *Informatics and Changes in Learning*. The conference, sponsored by WG 3.1 and 3.5, was held from June 7th to 11th 1993 at Gmunden, Austria.
- Proceedings of the IFIP Working Conference *Exploring a New Partnership: Children, Teachers and Technology*. This WG 3.5 conference was held from June 26th to July 1st 1994 at Philadelphia, USA.
- Proceedings of the IFIP World Conference WCCE '95 *Liberating the Learner*. The world conference, sponsored by IFIP TC3 (including WG 3.5) was held in July 1995 at Birmingham, UK.

- Proceedings of the IFIP Working Conference *Information Technology: Supporting Change Through Teacher Education.* This WG 3.1 and 3.5 joint conference was held from June 30th to July 5th 1996 at Kiryat Anavim, Israel.

How to become a member

Membership is open to those who have contributed to activities arranged by the working group. Prospective members are proposed and approved at the annual meeting of the working group.

IFIP Working Group 3.5 may be reached through:

IFIP Secretariat
Hofstrassev 3
A-2361Laxenburg
Austria

Tel. +43 2236 73616, Fax +43 2236 736169, E-mail ifip@ifip.or.at
Internet http://www.ifip.or.at

Editorial Introduction

A major strength of IFIP conferences is the valuable opportunity provided when practitioners, evaluators, lecturers, teachers, and researchers come together to share and discuss their experiences. For conference participants this is a joy; for editors it is less so! We, as editors, have been challenged with the opportunities afforded by the participants - to present to you, the reader, as coherent a picture as possible, from a rich but diverse range of accounts, case studies, research studies, positional papers, and reviews.

Previous recent IFIP conferences have focused upon a range of significant issues which have considered the ways in which new technologies and their applications are having effects and potential impacts upon the role and practices of those involved in education. This conference focused particularly upon the role of teacher education in supporting change with regard to the introduction, implementation and integration of new technologies for teaching and learning.

A number of common themes emerged from the conference, and it is clear to see that these themes, presented below and through these proceedings as section headings, are all highly pertinent to the contemporary subject of developing changes in IT practice for teacher education, and the ways in which support for teachers in both in-service and pre-service categories should be considered.

Information technology: supporting change through teacher education

A common agreement which emerges from any current discussion about the implementation of IT practice within teaching is that it is neither an easy thing to accomplish, nor something where there are a simple range of factors to consider. The features of change which contribute to this complexity, but which also enable practice and implementation to be considered, can be placed into four groups:
1. factors arise from a number of levels, and their relationships across those levels - change is affected by the levels within the educational system, which each play a part in systemic change;
2. perceptions of past and present successes and future potential - change is considered worthy and necessary due to either the successes that are recorded or the potential that is considered desirable;
3. factors which affect both failure and success - change is affected by a range of technological, political, pragmatic, and conceptual factors which create both barriers to success and levers to success; and
4. time - change works within a time frame which enables a continuous and successive wave of past reflections, present endeavours, and future ideals to be considered.

When support for change is being considered, factors come into play locally, but they are just as likely to arise from any one of the educational levels that influence teaching practice and learning requirements. For example, consider influences upon the teacher:
- at a national level, there can be an influence of national guidelines and national curriculum requirements;

- at a societal level, there can be an influence of community values and commercial considerations;
- at an institutional or school level, there can be an influence of developmental intentions and institutional policy;
- at the level of classroom organisation, there can be the influence of resource deployment upon access;
- at a teacher level, there can be an influence of individual pedagogical focus and curriculum intentions; and
- at a pupil level, there can be an influence that home use brings to bear upon classroom demands and expectations.

Within this multi-layered web of influence, the need for change, and the ways in which support for change can be considered, is set within a context that is often full of potential conflicts. For example:

- whilst change is considered a desirable outcome, teachers in practice are likely to feel supported through development rather than through their being asked to change;
- whilst integration of new practice is a future intention, a wider perspective often suggests that reformation or transformation are the desirable outcomes required;
- whilst the introduction of new technologies and the practices associated with them requires a level of highly exemplified detail that teachers can understand, a great deal of detail can mean that important and over-riding philosophies and concepts can be all too easily lost in an endeavour to satisfy the detailed skills laid down;
- whilst societal, national and international pressures determine the need for the new, there is still also the need to retain the traditional within some form of desirable balance; and
- whilst there is a need to learn and integrate new practice, there is also a need to retain a confidence and competence in teaching which is based upon a recognised knowledge of previous success rather than upon an uncertainty of developing practice.

Is it any wonder that the introduction of practices for using new technologies brings about a plethora of different solutions which emerge as the context itself changes? Is it any wonder that teachers introduce new practice in ways which range from the 'bolting on' of single activities, through insertion of a range of activities within a school year, to seamless use in lessons whenever and wherever practice seems appropriate? Is it any wonder that anyone involved or considering this field and its many topics is brought back to the questions: what are the purposes and philosophies of education? does the use of technology lead us to question these?

Reflections and futures

In order to grasp the challenges that development and change present, those who are involved in the field, either intellectually or as practitioners, are concerned with gaining understandings of what are perceived as the two major time poles which offer both potential and success, and restrictions and barriers. These time poles are, firstly, the past, which can offer reflective views and perceptions, and provide a contextual view of where development and change might need to move from, and, secondly, the future, which can be viewed through the insights of those who can inspire others with ideas of the ways in which future trends are taking us. The conference was fortunate indeed in being able to consider these two time poles through the contributions of, firstly, a keynote address from Jim Ridgway, whose analytical reflections enable current development and change practice to be considered in terms of past lessons, and secondly, a valuable paper contribution from Jan Visser and Manish Jain, who, from their work in UNESCO and elsewhere, offer ideas of the needs for future scenarios, and the implications that these have for the ways in which teachers and learners should be prepared.

Aspects and concepts of change, and the implementation of innovation

At least since the 1960s, it has been recognised, firstly through the needs of industry and commerce, and later, through the needs of education, that development and change have been a necessary domain to understand as fully as possible. Indeed, to integrate concepts, ideas, models and theories of change into the preparation and practice of those who will be the subject of development and change have also been recognised as being desirable, if not, essential. Three papers within the conference contribute particular perspectives in this domain. The paper from Gail Marshall offers ideas of some ways in which evaluation can identify particular and significant aspects and factors concerned with development and change which should be considered within present and future practice. Brent Robinson offered a review of literature on development and change, and argued the importance of integrating such ideas and concepts within the literature to both current and future practice. Zemira Mevarech, from her study of trainee teachers, offers a perspective of teacher development which allows a greater understanding of the ways in which trainee teachers adopt and integrate the use of information technologies into practice. These three papers enable both past and current conceptions of development and change to be related to the needs of the present and the future.

Defining the future curriculum at a national level

To enable appropriate teacher training to be put into place, it is necessary to understand at least two factors which will apply to the future of those teachers: firstly, the nature and extent of the curriculum which they will be asked to implement, and, secondly, the ways in which, at a national level, new conceptions will arise that they are asked to integrate into their teaching. Four papers address a range of issues which are concerned at a national level with these needs. David Benzie considers the concept that has been introduced into the national curriculum in England and Wales, termed information technology capability, and questions whether such a conception has been adequately, carefully or sufficiently defined. Márta Turcsányi-Szabó explains the way in which informatics is being considered for introduction into the curriculum in Hungary, and the implications for teachers. Harriet Taylor and Lajeane Thomas indicate how national standards are being considered and created for students in the United States, and what this means for teachers. Deryn Watson takes a longer term view of the range of initiatives within England and Wales which have been initiated and undertaken in efforts to integrate information technology into commonplace teaching practice, and considers some of the consequences of the shifts that have happened over at least a 15 year period in the ways in which information technology in teaching have been conceived.

Exploring potential implementation practices for teachers

It is widely regarded that a most significant key to the success of introducing and integrating information technology practice into teaching use is the approach that individual teachers make to the development and changes that they are presented with. The roles that IT can play in teaching and learning, attitudes taken towards computers, and the potential ways in which they can be used, are clearly significant within this discussion. Five papers within the conference offered perspectives on this topic. Margaret Cox considers a range of attitudinal and pedagogical concerns which confront teachers and schools when they use information technology in practice. Yaacov Katz reviews evidence concerning psychological and attitudinal features involved when teachers and pupils use or do not use computers, and argues that these features should be considered centrally when looking at the development and changes that are desirable in teaching and learning practices. Joyce Currie Little considers the role, problems and position of informatics education in curriculum and pedagogic practices for the future, while John Oakley and Anne McDougall consider the issues that teachers face and address when children are involved in programming activities. A detailed perspective from Peter Hubweiser, Manfred Broy and Wilfred Brauer considers how the use of information technology enables certain concepts for modelling information to be focused upon more centrally than the technology itself.

Support agencies and their roles

The role of external support agencies in helping teachers within schools to further their practice and implementation of information technology applications has been accepted widely as a necessity. Teachers in schools do not feel that they can develop new practices without adequate training and support, and often do not feel able to devote the time necessary for acquiring techniques and understanding. Having support personnel who can devote time to maintaining a developing understanding, on a continuous or semi-continuous basis, has been felt to avoid the necessity for all teachers to devote the time necessary for this. However, the focus and mechanisms which support agencies adopt differ widely - a fact that is in part, at least, due to the particular contexts in which they operate. Within the conference, four papers were presented which offered perspectives of the means that four different support agencies have adopted in four different nations. Wolfgang Weber identified the approaches and work undertaken in an advisory centre in Germany, David Passig detailed the approaches and successes of outcomes to date of a centre in Israel, Sindre Røsvik related the particular use of educational seminars in disseminating the development of practice in Norway, and Yvonne Buettner detailed the curriculum approaches, the conceptual framework adopted, and some outcomes to date of the work of an in-service centre in Switzerland.

Ways to support teacher education and teacher educators

As well as the need to consider the integration of support into in-service agencies for teachers already in practice, many educators have considered and continue to consider the needs of integration for pre-service and in-service education which is undertaken within educational training institutions. A number of studies have now been carried out on methods adopted in the past, and the outcomes of those studies are informing new practice being undertaken by educational training institutions. Five papers in the conference offered perspectives on this topic. Jean Underwood identified from a range of studies a range of factors which should be considered and addressed when constructing programmes for the professional development of teachers. Georges-Louis Baron, Eric Bruillard and Alain Chaptal consider, from a range of research studies in France, the role of the increasing personal use of information technology by teachers, and the implications that this has for future classroom use. Steve Kennewell considers, from research within the United Kingdom, the need and means to integrate practice through the professional development of appropriate decision making mechanisms for teachers. Phil Nanlohy describes the outcomes of research and its impact upon how the integration of educational computing is being addressed in a teacher training institution in Australia, while Qi Chen describes the outcomes of research and the means of integrating educational computing into a teacher training programme in an institution in China.

Case studies of teacher and school development when using information and communication technologies

Across a range of countries teacher and school development mechanisms in a variety of forms are either in place, in review, or in the process of being initiated. Five papers within the conference provide opportunities to view such developments in school situations in four countries. Bruce Rigby describes the background and means being undertaken to offer schools in one region of Australia the opportunities to undertake change through systematic school reform, while Anne McDougall and Jennifer Betts indicate the mechanisms adopted in one school in Australia through a provision of technology immersion. Pieter Hogenbirk details the outcomes and perceptions of school reform through a national developmental project within the Netherlands. Kay Rye describes an initiative in New Zealand to support teacher development, and Lisbeth Appelberg indicates the means and outcomes of a programme in Sweden to support the professional practices of both teachers and young children.

Considering the integration of information and communication technologies within subject teaching and within teaching methodologies

A consideration of the integration of information and communication technologies can be focused through the perspectives and needs of particular subject areas, and through the teaching methods that are used and adopted within those subjects. Five papers address ideas which are concerned with this theme. Menucha Weiss indicates how the use of videotaping can facilitate research methods in identifying teaching practices that are used by teachers of mathematics. Herbert Loethe indicates how the use of computers can be considered within the pre-service of teachers of mathematics, and Vincenzo Auricchio, Giuliana Dettori, Simonetta Greco and Enrica Lemut indicate how computer use can be considered by teachers of mathematics when equipment in deployed in particular ways, either within traditional classroom environments or within specialised computer laboratories. Beverly Ferrucci and Jack Carter indicate the means and outcomes of integrating a more specific technology to address more specific subject needs, in particular, the use of graphing technologies for algebra studies. David Squires offers a perspective in this area which identifies the need to consider the software used, and the potential for its integration, through appropriate evaluation mechanisms.

Cognition and the integration of information and communication technology uses for the pupil

The integration of information and communication technologies depends not solely upon the need to understand how the integration can be considered from the viewpoint of teaching method, but also from the viewpoints of the effects of those teaching methods upon the activities that are being set and undertaken by pupils in classrooms, and the ways in which those activities or tasks impact upon the cognitive abilities and needs of the pupils themselves. The interaction between teaching methods and cognitive abilities are addressed in three papers in the conference. Bridget Somekh addresses the needs that exist to consider the relationship between activities that are constructed using information and communication technologies and the ways in which pupils learn. Amos Dreyfus, Benjamin Feinstein and Janet Talmon consider this area through the focus of the subject of biology, and the needs for particular cognitive skills and abilities within that subject area. Whilst the relationship between these cognitive skills and abilities and the ways which information technology enables students to approach such learning is considered within this latter paper, Andreas Schwill addresses the area from another viewpoint, by considering and identifying the fundamental cognitive skills that computer science education offers.

The increasing need for focus upon cultural and social factors

The development of teacher education concerned with information and communication technologies is embedded within the context of a wider social development and change. As information and communication technologies become more widely used and adopted in areas of society, questions of the implications of such use and adoption begin to emerge. Social perspectives at this stage begin to contribute not only to our understanding of what is happening, but also to our understanding of some of the current and future barriers to desired change. Three papers in the conference offer different perspectives on this issue. Mícheál Ó Dúill considers the basic ways in which information technologies are constructed and operate, and argues that our use of them will depend not only upon this construction, but upon our adoption and acceptance of this writing rather than mathematical construction. Alnaaz Kassam and Ronald Ragsdale offer a sociological perspective on this issue, and indicate some of the sociological needs that must be addressed if information technology use is to be integrated into teacher professional development successfully in the future. Toni Downes indicates from a range of studies the impact that wider social access to information and communication technologies is beginning to have. These three papers were of particular significance within the conference as they identified what is likely to be an increasingly important area to consider and understand: the role of social and sociological factors in development and change that is driven by the need for technological use.

Future scenarios and the challenges they offer

Development and change, and the appropriate support for development and change, is driven by perceptions of the potential of uses for information and communication technologies, and the perceptions of the ways to provide support appropriately. Five papers within the conference offer perspectives which contribute to this issue. Michelle Selinger offers some ideas of the range of outcomes that can result when electronic communications are adopted to support teacher education. Similarly, Antonio Osorio indicates the ways in which one teacher education institution is currently undertaking this support. Hiroyuki Tanaka considers the new opportunities that multimedia provides, and the needs that this is likely to imply for use and authoring by teachers and pupils. Paul Nicholson and George Duckett offer a perception of the classroom construction and means that are likely to be possible in the future using technologies to create virtual classrooms. Bernard Cornu synthesises the means that are currently available and those which will develop, and offers a summary of the factors that must be included within teacher education currently and in the future in order to address the needs that exist already and that are likely to develop in the near future.

It is fortunate that a conference can offer such a wide range of complementary perspectives in an area of contemporary interest. This conference provided a complementarity of contribution of width and depth, which enables this book to provide what the editors believe to be a comprehensive account of current concerns, of current practices, and of current needs for those who wish to consider the support for teachers when integrating information and communication technology use.

The outcomes of the conference, which are in part reported through the chosen topics of the Focus Group Reports in this document, confirmed that the nature of current change should be considered to be: continuous (requiring regular and frequent need for review of past effects and future potentials); successive (requiring an analysis of the particular factors of influence at any given time); and in the form of successive waves or cycles (requiring the nature of the technological basis and educational implications of any particular wave or cycle to be understood). Outcomes from the conference pointed to the need for those supporting change through teacher education to include in their development considerations:

- reflections upon past practices, philosophies, purposes and outcomes;
- future potentials and practices that are implied and identified;
- the future scenarios and the challenges they offer;
- cultural and social issues and context;
- the involvement and contribution of concepts of development and change;
- the past weaknesses and successes in the implementation of innovation;
- the ways in which present and future curricula are defined at a national level;
- the ways in which shifts in pedagogical practices for teachers are implied;
- the effects described through current case studies of teacher and school development in a range of contexts when using information and communication technologies;
- the means to deploy and offer support via appropriate agencies, and their roles;
- the ways in which support for teacher education and teacher educators can be integrated into institutional practice;

- the implications for subject teaching and for teaching methodologies within particular subjects; and
- the need to understand effects as well as intentions upon pupil cognition for the integration of uses of information and communication technologies for the pupil.

In conclusion, we, the editors, would like to thank all those who have contributed to the creation of this volume. Without the depth and breadth of experience and expertise offered through these papers and reports, and without the patience and tolerance of the authors in preparing these contributions, we would be unable to offer you, the reader, such benefit. We hope that you value the contents of this volume, and hope that we have reproduced each contribution faithfully.

As a coda, it was with great sadness that we heard of Brent Robinson's death soon after this conference had concluded. Brent was recognised as a leading light in the early development of the use of IT in the teaching of English in the UK, both as a writer of software, and of books and articles. His interest in the use of electronic communications led to his creating an early 'writer-in-residence' project, which gave children access to professional writers via e-mail. Latterly, his interest and enthusiasm was directed towards ideas of concepts and models of change and development, and the ways in which they could be incorporated into the professional development programmes of those involved in the integration of new and innovative practice. This, like his other initiatives, was characterised by his willingness to direct into it both energy and advocacy, but with realism. Brent's contribution in this volume is concerned with this latter field, and we hope that it will remain as a continuous testament to the width of his involvement in the field of IT in education.

Don Passey and Brian Samways, Editors

Don Passey is a Senior Research Fellow in the Department of Psychology in Lancaster University working with the STAC Project. He has undertaken extensive research and development in the field of IT in education, particularly in elementary and secondary education, with regard to support, implementation and integration of development into practice. He has authored and co-authored a range of materials, papers and books on subjects relating to the integration of information technology through change and development in education. He has worked in individual schools, with local education authorities, government agencies, and with companies, in the UK and in other countries, in a consultancy and research capacity, and has undertaken a wide range of national evaluation studies in the UK. He is currently a member of the IFIP Working Group 3.5.

Brian Samways is the Director of Birmingham City Council's Education Department Information Systems Training Centre, which supports schools and the LEA in the administrative use of computer systems. Previously he was Director of the Birmingham Educational Computer Centre (BECC), and also worked as Associate Director at the University of Birmingham, creating the Central Institute for the regional in-service accreditation of teachers and lecturers, and as Research Officer at the Royal Society of Arts where he developed the RSA National Diploma in IT for teachers and trainers. He has taught at all educational levels, is a national external verifier for the RSA Examinations Board and was until recently external examiner to London Guildhall University. He is the UK representative and Chairman of IFIP Technical Committee for Education (TC3), has been a member of WG3.1 for 12 years, was Conference Chairman for the World Conference on Computers in Education (WCCE/95) and is joint editor of the international journal *Educational and Information Technologies*.

Section 1: Reflections and futures

1

Vygotsky, informatics capability, and professional development

Jim Ridgway
Department of Psychology
University of Lancaster, Lancaster LA1 4YF, UK

Abstract

Vygotsky asserted that intellectual tools such as writing and science change human cognition, and human cultures. Informatics is a new tool which promises new sorts of cognitive development, and has already produced a good deal of cultural change. How can we enculturate educational reform associated with informatics? In particular, how can we change classroom practice? This paper describes some approaches to professional development, and highlights their strengths and weaknesses. It argues that people need to be offered ways to change which are consistent with their current theories of personal and professional development; tools are needed which directly suit their current needs; and there is a need to engender a belief in lifelong development throughout the educational system. A set of criteria for evaluating attempts to support professional development is offered, and suggestions are made about how informatics itself, and IFIP, can support the process.

Keywords

Professional development, classroom practice, culture, information technology, pedagogy

1   VYGOTSKY'S IDEAS ON INFORMATICS CAPABILITY

This paper would have been easier to write had not Vygotsky died in 1934, a long time before the invention of the digital computer. His writings on cognitive development, however, can be of direct benefit to our understanding of the challenges of computers to education; we can also learn a good deal from the work that his ideas inspired in Russian education, after his death. Western readers will be familiar with Vygotsky's work on language development, and his theories about the roles of guidance in instruction - in particular, the notion of the Zone of Proximal Development. His theories have a far wider scope than this; this wider scope is of particular interest to our understanding of the processes of educational change associated with computers.

Vygotsky was centrally concerned with understanding how it is that children with roughly the same intellectual starting points in life in different cultures become completely enculturated over the course of their childhood. They learn to use physical tools such as chopsticks or forks, cars and bicycles; they learn to use intellectual tools like speaking and writing Russian or Chinese, and using mathematics. A key analogy which Vygotsky offers links physical and mental tools. A child's first approach to eating is to pick up food in the hand, and to transfer it (and everything else!) to the mouth. This involves some primitive pre-wired responses, and some practice. Things change dramatically when the child learns to use a spoon. A whole new sequence of movements has to be learned; the hand now approaches from the side, with a scooping movement; the final destination of the hand is the side of the mouth, so that the spoon, not the hand, reaches the mouth. Learning is done at a cost (in terms of time, effort, and wasted food) but results in considerable gains later in terms of the foodstuffs which can be accessed, and efficiency of eating. Learning is also a guided social act - the teacher is critical to the nature of the activities which are undertaken (so Chinese children learn to use spoons and chopsticks, and French children learn to use spoons and forks). The choice of tools is determined culturally, and tool use leads to a major reconfiguration of hand and arm movements. Intellectual tools such as language, reading and writing, and mathematics all work in similar ways - they derive directly from the culture into which a child is born, and they radically reorganise the child's mental structures. Language, literacy, science, and mathematics are not just things that people 'have' or 'do', they define the person in quite fundamental ways - in terms of their minds, in terms of the power they can exert over their environments, and in terms of their community membership.

The cultural processes associated with IT would be of great interest to Vygotsky. At the grand level of society, it is clear that IT is at the centre of a cultural vortex which is bringing about radical social change in terms of patterns of employment and methods of communication; at the level of intellectual discipline, IT has had a profound effect on the cultural practices associated with every academic discipline over the last 10 years. For example, imagine anyone doing research in literature who did not use a word processor; a statistician who did all calculations by hand; a scientist who logged their data after direct observation. Such people undoubtedly exist, but are the Zeppelins of their profession. At the level of individual development, it is clear that many students engage in a great deal of peer tutoring in home environments (for example, when playing games) with no outside input (Downes, 1996). In contrast, at the intermediate level of educational institutions, the culture has hardly begun to take on board appropriate uses of the new intellectual tool.

Next, consider Vygotsky's notion of intellectual development. Table 1 offers a breathtakingly brief account of his core theory. Vygotsky distinguishes between lower order and higher order mental functions. The key concept behind higher order mental functions is the idea of increasing integration of functions as development progresses. This is also the central idea of informatics capability - our educational goals are not just that students will be able to demonstrate piecemeal competence on particular IT related tasks ('Can use a spread sheet in mathematics, can use a word processor in English, can use a database in science, and therefore is IT literate'); rather, we want IT use to be a seamless part of students' intellectual abilities - something which permeates their thinking in the same way that language does, and that mathematics and science ought to.

Table 1 Vygotsky's Distinction between Lower and Higher Mental Functions

	LOWER	HIGHER
ORIGINS	Inherited	Via Learning
STRUCTURE	Unmediated	Mediated by signs and other tools (for example, reading and writing)
FUNCTIONS	Involuntary	Voluntarily controlled
RELATIONSHIP TO OTHER FUNCTIONS	Isolated	Connected with other functions in a system (i.e. no modules)

People who have developed Vygotsky's ideas in education - notably Davydov (for example, 1995) have adopted an educational philosophy which we can apply to IT. Rather than basing educational practice on formal structures (for example, introducing the concept of number by asking students to match a pair of cows with a pair of trees with a pair of houses etc. to support the emergence of the idea of 'two-ness' in accordance with Russell and Whitehead's formal definitions in Principia Mathematica) and formal operations like symbol manipulation (2+3=?), they advocate teaching which reflects the historical emergence of ideas, and which emphases the power which, for example, mathematics endows on its users. So mathematics should be introduced in terms of its origins. Numbers are useful because they facilitate: commerce - swapping goats for lengths of cloth is dramatically easier if a common system of measures is in place; agriculture - dividing land fairly is a real problem if you have no notion of measurement; planning future events can be difficult, too! and so on. Teaching proceeds by posing challenges to students which reveal the intellectual power of the new tool.

What is to be learned from this? If we want teachers to learn new informatics concepts, we should show how using these new intellectual tools lets them do things they really want to do, much more simply than by any other means.

Vygotsky has a number of important ideas for us:
- informatics will change thinking, and the ways that individuals see the world;
- informatics will take on a role of defining cultures;
- learning can begin in piecemeal ways, but informatics capability needs to be integrated with other intellectual tools before it becomes a higher order skill;
- teaching should focus on the power the new ideas give the users over situations.

Teacher educators undoubtedly face a difficult challenge - to help adults learn to think in new ways, and to enculturate IT into school communities which already have stable cultural practices which work quite well for teachers.

2   A GLOBAL CONTEXT OF CHANGE

National Curricula with strong informatics components have been introduced in Japan, Hungary, New Zealand, the UK, and elsewhere. In the USA, technology standards developed jointly by the International Society for Technology in Education, and the National Council for Accreditation of Teacher Education, are having a major impact on State policies (see Taylor, 1996); the same phenomenon can be seen in other federal systems (for example, Queensland, Australia).

Why is so much effort being devoted to curriculum development - particularly in mathematics, science, and technology - at present? Essentially:

*   many governments believe that school performance in teaching these subjects underpins economic success. The global economy is increasingly competitive, and the largest profits are to be made from products which derive from intellectual effort, such as microprocessor based products, rather than from the sale of raw materials. A scientifically and computer literate populace is seen as essential to world economic eminence;
*   students need to develop mathematical and scientific literacy in such a way as to support informed citizenship.

Informatics has additional, special, attractions:

*   as jobs change, there is a growing educational need to provide lifelong learning;
*   technology promises to solve problems that cannot be solved in other ways, such as providing learning opportunities on the scale that is likely to be required in the future.

It follows that curriculum reform associated with informatics will be an ongoing process for a long time to come, in most countries.

3   ON THE NATURE OF REFORM

All but the most superficial reforms require a reconceptualisation of:

*   the educational goals to be attained;
*   the best ways to get there; and (in the case of informatics)
*   the essential nature of the discipline.

A hallmark of every non-trivial reform is that consensus on the nature of the intended change is often at best fragile, and at worse, illusory. If it were not true, the reform itself would be hardly worthwhile. It is hard to introduce reforms which require a change of teaching style, or a reconceptualisation about what is valuable. For this to happen, individuals have to reconstruct their knowledge, not just rearrange their intellectual deck chairs. The problem is exacerbated in situations where the intended changes are described largely in words, without a detailed specification of tasks to be performed, without examples of classroom practice, and without assessment tasks and their associated marking schemes (as they so often are in national policy documents).

4   MODELLING TEACHER DEVELOPMENT

It will be helpful to ask how changes in classroom practice come about. Clarke and Peter (1993) offer a model which sets out to recognise the complexity of teacher development. Their model has several interesting features. For our purposes, we will focus on the assertions that:

- classroom behaviours are determined directly by teacher beliefs;
- classroom activities are the catalyst for professional growth;
- reflection mediates between experiences and subsequent beliefs;
- changes in beliefs regarding the efficacy of new practices depend upon teacher evaluations of the success or otherwise of the associated classroom events.

It follows from the model that it is essential for early experiences in some new teaching venture to be met with success - where success is defined to be good classroom experiences, as judged by the teacher, from their current viewpoint. In practical terms, this means that advocacy of new classroom activities needs two kinds of support: the first is an input which causes the teacher to want to make the change; the second is a set of activities which result in classroom success, as judged by the teacher.

5 SUPPORTING PROFESSIONAL DEVELOPMENT

5.1 All about Jim...

It is easy to be romantic about teacher professionalism, and to believe that teachers want to change, and that everyone who wants to change can do so. It is salutary to consider more representative members of the teaching profession, as our target audience for change. Here, we will focus on Jim.

Jim teaches mathematics in a secondary school:
- he has 20 years' experience (he has 1 year's experience, repeated 20 times);
- he is an autonomous professional (no one ever sees him teach);
- he has an integrated, coherent, and progressive curriculum (he uses a textbook);
- he regularly updates his professional skills (he goes for a day course to the university each year).

It is important that we do not dismiss the real skills that Jim brings to bear as a teacher, and to remember that Jim is functioning quite satisfactorily, by his standards, and also by the standards expected of him by his school. A second dimension to consider is that asking Jim to teach in different ways is asking him to expose his mathematics, his professional competence, his classroom credibility with children, and the respect which the school has for him. The costs to us of his classroom failure would be tiny; the costs to Jim might be very great indeed. If Jim were a gambler used to calculating expected utilities of different gambles, he would probably decide not to play 'curriculum reform'. A major challenge which we face is to support Jim's professional development, without demanding that he takes unacceptable risks.

5.2 Components of teaching knowledge

Teaching is a very complex activity, with a large number of component skills. A successful teacher is likely to have well developed knowledge about:
- their subject discipline;
- interacting with individuals;
- planning for others' learning;

- planning their own professional development.

Each of these areas of knowledge can be involved in curriculum reform. For example, if some new topic is to be taught, such as informatics-based statistics in geography, science or mathematics, then subject knowledge needs to be acquired. In the case of statistics, the concepts might be quite unlike much of the mathematics teachers already know, and teachers themselves might share many of the naive conceptions of their students, such as the gambler's fallacy, or an insensitivity to sample size when drawing conclusions about data.

A central concern is to ask how these changes in teacher knowledge can be brought about.

5.3   Traditional approaches to change - materials and INSET

A number of approaches to curriculum change are in common use. These include:
- development of new curriculum materials, for example, textbooks;
- professional development, for example, courses, teacher certification;
- compromise schemes, for example, 'quantum step' or 'box' approaches; and
- imposed better quality control, for example, of teachers or schools.

It is useful to contrast two extreme models - materials development and professional development - each in a relatively pure form.

The target audience for curriculum materials is 'all teachers'. This approach to curriculum change is particularly good for teachers who work exclusively from text books (who are in a large majority). Good curriculum materials can also be particularly useful to teachers at the start of their professional development (however many years they have been teaching!) As an approach to supporting curriculum reform, curriculum materials are good for widespread dissemination, supporting changes in content, and are usually associated with relatively low development costs. The approach is probably bad for inducing any changes which move teaching practice far from where it is at present, such as changes in process skills.

While the target audience for professional development is notionally 'all teachers' - it is particularly useful for teachers who have skills to share, and who wish to be involved in networks for professional development. As an approach to supporting curriculum reform, professional development potentially is good for bringing about deep changes in attitudes and beliefs, for developing process skills, and for establishing collegiality. It is often associated with high costs; it runs the risk of the dilution and corruption of designers' intentions (especially if cascade models are used); and it often has less effect on classroom practice than it seems (for example, Passey and Ridgway, 1992a, 1992b).

It suffers a number of other problems. Too often, it is: piecemeal; not linked to long term professional growth; not related to classroom practice; and is unrelated to rewards for teaching excellence.

This strategy of examining the strengths and weaknesses of 'straw men' leads to over-generalisations which most professionals would challenge. The virtue of the approach is that it leads to the articulation of some criteria against which attempts to promote professional development might be judged; these criteria can be helpful when planning professional development. This will be revisited, later.

5.4 Approaches to professional development

It is interesting to contrast a number of current approaches to teacher professional development.

Approach 1: Make the profession of teaching more like other professions
Darling-Hammond (1988) described some characteristics of professionalism. These include taking collective responsibility for the definition, transmittal, and enforcement of professional standards. Increased professionalism implies a clear professional voice (c.f. ISTE and NCTM in the USA) and a high level of interest in a whole range of professional activities such as self regulation, and a strong political voice which is proactive, rather than passive. This relates directly to the theme of 'the intended curriculum' raised earlier. Documents from professional organisations, of course, often seek to support changes in the 'implemented curriculum', too - but implementation changes will rarely overflow outside the classrooms of teachers already committed to change.

A major problem with teacher professional development has been that career progression has meant that skilled teachers get out of the classroom, and move into managerial positions. One can contrast this situation with professional development practices common in medicine, the law, and engineering. There, professional development is seen as a lifelong activity; while a number of career paths are available, it is common for doctors, lawyers, and engineers to practice their profession throughout their whole careers, without moving into administrative roles. Such moves - where classroom teachers can be paid as much as head teachers (as in some Australian States) promise to celebrate and preserve excellent classroom practice.

Approach 2: identify and develop skills (atomism)
The essential challenge that advocates of these approaches define for themselves is to develop an appropriate set of teacher skills. There is usually a supposition that these skills are either known, or knowable.

Lampert (1988) has offered a clear explication of this approach, applied to mathematics education. She suggests the following sequence of activities:

* identify the learning we want to produce;
* ask what kind of teaching might produce that kind of learning;
* ask what kind of knowledge (conceived broadly) teachers need to teach in appropriate ways;
* decide what kind of educational experiences teachers need to acquire such skills.

Teachers might need to develop: their informatics skills; a richly interconnected knowledge base; knowledge of difficulty levels; ideas of common student conceptions and misconceptions, and their remediation; ideas on ordering experiences; procedural skills; classroom management skills; and personal confidence.

A whole range of educational experiences might be offered to teachers to help them acquire such skills: reading; attending lectures; use of off-the-shelf materials; in-class observations; visits by a support teacher; practice with a small group of children; analysing videotape; in-class experimentation; peer group discussions; and the like.

What are the inherent virtues and vices of an atomistic approach?
- it can offer useful seeds for thinking about teaching; and in particular, about some of the component skills;
- checklists may be very useful to probationary teachers;
- components of skill can form the basis for teacher appraisal;
- it raises interesting questions about how particular component skills can best be learned;
- conversely, teaching skills are complex and interrelated, and there is no best single way to slice things up;
- the issue of skill integration also needs to be considered;
- several atomistic approaches assume that teaching skills are generic rather than subject specific. This assumption is extremely dubious, and needs to be explored empirically.

A helpful set of components of teaching skill can be found in the work of the Stanford Teacher Assessment Project (see Shulman et al, 1988). Here again, there is an effort to describe teaching skill in terms of component competencies, but these competencies are closely related to teaching behaviour, in the ways described by Lampert (1988). Schulman's list includes: topic sequencing; explaining algorithms; explaining teaching decisions; analysis of a textbook; evaluation of students' work; working in a group to develop materials; and analysing a videotape of a classroom event.

Approach 3: support reflective practice
Supporting the development of reflective practice often means providing support for people whose educational values one does not necessarily share. There is usually a supposition that by encouraging discussion about particular events, common values will emerge. One attempts to use a constructivist approach to develop knowledge structures (for example, Ridgway and Passey, 1991).

This approach commonly bases teacher development on shared experiences directly related to the teaching process, such as team teaching, or classroom observation. This seems an obvious starting point, and it is surprising that it is not the major vehicle used to support teacher development. One of the major failings of the organisation of education is that there is still very little observation of teaching by teachers.

Approach 4: apprentice models
These are characterised by an expert working alongside a novice in some way. A major virtue of apprentice models is that knowledge development can take place at many different levels. It is natural to ask questions at an instrumental level, as part of collaborative working, as well as about knowledge structures, and about educational philosophies. Several examples can be offered.

In the UK, there has been a government funded scheme to allow experienced teachers to work alongside others in the same subject areas, in the role of "guide on the side, not sage on the stage". These support teachers are referred to as Advisory Teachers (see Ridgway and Shone, 1990, for an account of some working practices). Evaluations of their effectiveness in changing classroom practices have been positive.

Apprentice models can founder because of pressures on time, and the expense of providing experts. Peer tutoring can avoid some of these problems, but some sort of external input will be essential to provide guidance on the sorts of support which is effective, to monitor progress, and to offer provocative questions which will lead professional development forward.

Approach 5: peer tutoring models

These are characterised by the organisation of teacher groups so as to provide mutual support for professional development by sharing experiences of teaching. Examples of peer tutoring are provided by the work of Barnett and Tyson (1993) supporting teacher groups which discuss case studies, and by the California Renaissance Project, where teachers discuss videotapes they have made of their own teaching. Peer tutoring models are expensive in terms of time, and often need high levels of external input to maintain their momentum.

Approach 6: local teacher assessment

The approach to teacher appraisal in England might be described as 'Unstructured Reflection'. Teachers have an interview with a more senior member of staff about a range of different aspects of their work. The discussion should cover:
- self appraisal of current strengths and weaknesses;
- planning targets for future development;
- action in class;
- a review of progress.

While the appraisal does not take place in class, there is a clear attempt to promote staff development by supporting reflective practice (see Passey and Ridgway, 1991, for practical guidance on self evaluation).

Approach 7: teacher portfolios

Teacher portfolios are being explored in different places, for different purposes (see Wolf's annotated bibliography, 1991). Teacher portfolios are analogous to student portfolios, and can comprise video, exemplary lessons, student reports, case histories, and the like. Portfolios can be used to support long term teacher development by:
- celebrating excellent practice;
- making instrumental knowledge explicit;
- offering windows on each teacher's view of teaching and learning;
- supporting reflection and analysis of current practices;
- providing a focus for conversations about professional development;
- imposing a broad set of attainments when assessing teachers.

If we believe in supporting the development of reflective practice, we must find ways to support its emergence. Valuing teacher constructions locally, and exploring their validity more widely, is an important part of this development.

6   WHAT CAN THE IFIP COMMUNITY DO TO SUPPORT PROFESSIONAL DEVELOPMENT?

An elementary analysis of the number of teachers in need of informatics skills, and the capacity of most educational systems to provide professional development likely to have any effect upon classroom practice, shows that we are set to fail, unless a more radical approach is taken to professional development. The essential tension we face is that surface reforms in terms of content can be brought about on a large scale by the introduction of new curriculum materials, while deep changes of attitude, belief, and educational ambitions, and changes in the processes of teaching seem to depend upon human interactions, and are therefore expensive in terms of resource provision (for example, Gilmore, 1994; Hogenbirk, 1996). The challenge we face is to provide professional development in ways that support more fundamental changes, without incurring massive costs.

We need to problematise the change process. There are too many cosy assumptions made by politicians that change in classroom practice is easy to bring about once the political will is there, and resources are brought to bear. The debate on the sorts of changes that are desirable, how they might be instigated, and how they can be monitored and acted upon, needs to be promoted.

A second major theme is to promote the idea of extended professional development over the working lives of teachers, and to move the organisation of the education system to accommodate such development (Cornu, 1996). In some areas of health care, professional registration is renewed at intervals, and renewal depends on evidence of attendance at courses which update professional skills. If applied to education, this would have implications for teachers' time, and the ways they view their professional practice, with shifts towards more professional networking, and more action research. It will certainly require the development of new sorts of ways to document and improve professional practice.

6.1 Informatics as a vehicle for change

The medium of informatics promises to be a valuable source of support for professional development; CD-ROM frees us from the static 2D world of paper, and allows classroom events to be observed, re-observed, annotated and discussed.

Recordings of individual students, or classroom processes, can exemplify particular styles of tutoring, teaching, classroom management, and the like, so that educational ambitions are well understood (for example, Welch, 1993). Understanding is an essential step to rejection of the changes being advocated, as well as to their acceptance.

Informatics offers the potential to provide local tutorial and peer support for materials which are produced centrally. Recent developments in supporting local groups via electronic conferences (Appelberg, 1996; Passig; 1996) will be followed with interest.

Informatics is also capable, in principle, of providing learning opportunities on the scale that is likely to be required in the future; an example of this is the recent proposal to broadcast the UK's Open University materials which support professional development to India via satellite; and to adapt their undergraduate degree courses so that they can be provided via the Internet.

It is important to be sceptical about the nature of the changes that are brought about, and not to assume that the conceptual problems we face can be solved via a quick technological fix. It is also important to address the day to day reality of school - access to the Internet is very restricted (it will be interesting to observe the effects of linking schools to broad band information networks - see Osorio, 1996); even time for a group of teachers to watch and discuss a clip of a classroom in action will involve a good deal of co-ordination.

When considering educational change, it is useful to distinguish between:

- the intended curriculum (set out in policy documents, textbooks, or as reflected in teacher intentions - see Benzie, 1996; Cox, 1996; Dunn and Ridgway, 1994);
- the implemented curriculum (what happens in class); and
- the attained curriculum (what students can do at the end of these activities).

Each of these is quite distinct; each is an essential target for the reform movement. In many countries, the process has gone well at the rhetorical and political level - fine policy statements (often associated with resources) are in place. The most difficult challenges are yet to be faced - changing teacher beliefs and knowledge, changing classroom practice, and student attainment. The teacher is the only person who makes change happen at these levels.

6.2 Informatics and the intended curriculum

National and local statements of educational policy need to endorse the use of informatics in teaching. An obvious starting point is to emphasise the unique contribution of informatics to intellectual development, and to argue for broadly based reforms which promote particular uses of informatics, not just generic teaching skills. There is a good deal of evidence that teacher conceptions of informatics in education are highly restricted, and are not likely to be conducive to fundamental pedagogic change (see Ridgway and Passey, 1995a, 1995b). It is our responsibility to communicate better!

To support the rhetoric of change, we need vivid examples of:

- uses of informatics;
- uses of informatics in school to support different curriculum activities;
- a wide variety of classroom practices to liberate conceptions of what teaching using informatics can involve.

We also need a set of warnings about what is NOT desirable. Concepts only take on meaning when examples from outside their class are given. In this case, we need examples where informatics leads to poor educational experiences. Vivid examples include: the use of word processing to create 'best' pieces of work from hand-written scripts; the use of CD-ROMs to support 'browsing' - often uncritical page turning; essays made up of encyclopaedia entries which have been assembled by a student; use of a computer as a scarce resource which dominates the lesson plan.

These examples can all be provided via CD-ROM. Different interpretations of the intended reforms - teaching about informatics versus the development of informatics capability across the curriculum, for example - are best understood by considering concrete examples.

Examples of student work might be included here to demonstrate some long term curriculum ambitions.

6.3 Informatics and the implemented curriculum

CD and the Internet can be used to provide resources which teachers and teacher educators can access when introducing some classroom change (for example, Weber, 1996). Resources include: print; exemplary lessons; clips of classroom activities, and perhaps some annotation from teachers and students about things that are going on (Rigby, 1996); schemes of work that integrate informatics activity; and examples of student work.

Electronic conferences can be used to support local groups (Selinger, 1996). These have the potential to improve central provision by providing feedback to authors on topics which are seen to be difficult, by analysis of frequently asked questions, and so on.

Systems to support the development of teacher portfolios have considerable potential benefits; so too do postgraduate courses with a strong informatics base (for example, Carss, 1996).

All of these provisions are likely to require centres which collate materials from a wide variety of sources, test them locally, then distribute them widely.

In the initial stages of professional development, it is important to engage teachers in activities which are educationally worthwhile, which relate directly to the curriculum they teach, which are difficult to do without informatics support, yet which do not demand high levels of informatics capability (see Cox, 1996; Passey and Ridgway, 1992c).

6.4 Informatics and the attained curriculum

Any attempt to document the attained curriculum requires sample informatics based tasks; examples of student work at different ages, in different subjects; and a variety of scoring schemes, which show how different aspects of performance might be rewarded.

The Toronto video bench marks provide an example of ways to exemplify student's attainment levels in a number of mathematical domains; similar resources should be developed for informatics. Video and CD provide an excellent way to demonstrate different levels of attainment. Systems of student portfolios can help document the development of student informatics capability across curriculum areas. The Balanced Assessment Project has developed a large collection of tasks in mathematics which can be used to create systems of assessment which match the educational ambitions of users. Many of these are based on technology. It is important to develop and test tools which can allow us to judge the match between the intended curriculum and the attained curriculum. The gaps between intention and attainment can then be the focus for future work.

7   CRITERIA FOR COMPARING MODELS OF PROFESSIONAL DEVELOPMENT

This section poses questions which every plan to promote professional development on a wide scale should consider.

Realism 1 - attending to the major phases: how does the proposed plan for change affect: the intended curriculum; the implemented curriculum; and the attained curriculum?

Realism 2 - breadth and depth: does it have a wide target audience?; what kinds of changes might it effect?

Realism 3 - costs: what are the development costs?; what is the investment of your time in each teacher?; how long would it take to influence every school within 10 kilometres?; within 100 kilometres?; in the whole country?; what are the costs associated with each phase of dissemination?; what are the costs to teachers? (see Passey and Ridgway, 1992c)

Realism 4 - dilution and corruption: what kinds of corruption are likely to occur when it is widely used?; what mechanisms are in place to ensure that classroom practices bear some resemblance to what you hoped would happen?

Realism 5 - supporting professionalism: how does it support professional development?; a culture of collegiality, and co-operation within and across schools?

Realism 6 - systems and stakeholders: any functioning education system requires the combined efforts of a large number of people, who play a variety of different roles; the interests and goals of these people are often different, as are their rewards for different educational outcomes (Ridgway and Passey, 1993a); what stakeholders have been considered (students; parents; teachers; departmental heads; school heads; administrators; politicians)?; why should they support the reform?

8   INFORMATICS: BEYOND PRAGMATISM

In the midst of these detailed ideas on how we might support professional development, it is important to ask questions about the long term effects of different approaches to teaching and learning. The challenges posed by Lampert (1988) to our knowledge of how to teach particular teacher skills are relevant here, and it is clear that we need some empirical validation of different approaches to teacher development - do they really develop teacher skills in the ways we imagine?

If we are to learn how to develop reflective teacher practitioners, convinced of the value of lifetime learning, we must start with some explorations of teachers' informal theories of a wide range of educational issues, and the impact these theories have upon their classroom practices. We need to use these ideas as springboards for their professional development.

We need to elicit and explore formal and informal theories, and to test their practical utility. These theories need to range across:

- theories about the nature of teaching;
- theories of learning;
- theories of knowledge;
- theories of educational change;
- theories of personal development and motivation.

The paper began with an account of some ideas from a white European male who died over 60 years ago. Vygotsky's ideas are still useful to us, both at a practical level - as a source of ideas to support professional development - and at a grander, conceptual level. Informatics is a new tool; tools increase our powers over the environment (and often over each other); tools (such as writing and science) change the ways we think; human cultures can be defined by their tool uses and artefacts. As a group promoting the widespread use of this new tool by young people, we have a responsibility to promote uses which are likely to have positive effects upon human cultures at local, national, and international levels.

9　REFERENCES

Appelberg, L. (1996) Communication - learning - information technology applied examples, in D. Passey and B. Samways (eds.) *Information Technology: Supporting change through teacher education*, Proceedings of the IFIP TC3 WG3.1 and 3.5 Conference in Kiryat Anavim, Israel.

Barnett, C. and Tyson, P. (1993) Case Methods and Teacher Change: Shifting Authority to Build Autonomy, in B. Atweh, C. Kanes, M. Carss and G. Booker (eds.) *Contexts in Mathematics Education*: Proceedings of the Sixteenth Annual Conference of the Mathematics Education Research Group of Australasia. MERGA, Brisbane.

Benzie, D. (1996) Information technology capability: is our definition wide of the mark? in D. Passey and B. Samways (eds.) *Information Technology: Supporting change through teacher education*, Proceedings of the IFIP TC3 WG3.1 and 3.5 Conference in Kiryat Anavim, Israel.

Carss, M. (1996) Documents sent to the author on postgraduate courses offered by a consortium of universities in Queensland, Australia.

Clarke, D. and Peter, A. (1993) Modelling Teacher Change, in B. Atweh, C. Kanes, M. Carss and G. Booker (eds.) *Contexts in Mathematics Education*: Proceedings of the Sixteenth Annual Conference of the Mathematics Education Research Group of Australasia. MERGA, Brisbane.

Cornu, B. (1996) Teachers and teacher education facing information and communication technologies, in D. Passey and B. Samways (eds.) *Information Technology: Supporting change through teacher education*, Proceedings of the IFIP TC3 WG3.1 and 3.5 Conference in Kiryat Anavim, Israel.

Cox, M. J. (1996) Identification of the changes in attitude and pedagogical practices needed to enable teachers to use information technology into the school curriculum, in D. Passey and B. Samways (eds.), *Information Technology: Supporting change through teacher education*, Proceedings of the IFIP TC3 WG3.1 and 3.5 Conference in Kiryat Anavim, Israel.

Darling-Hammond, L. (1988) Accountability and Teacher Professionalism. *American Educator*, Winter, **8-13**, 38-43.

Davydov, V. V. (1995) The Influence of L. S. Vygotsky on Education Theory, Research, and Practice. *Educational Researcher,* **24**, 3, 12-21.

Downes, T. (1996) The computer as a toy and tool in the home - implications for teacher education, in　D. Passey and B. Samways (eds.) *Information*

Technology: Supporting change through teacher education, Proceedings of the IFIP TC3 WG3.1 and 3.5 Conference in Kiryat Anavim, Israel.

Dunn, S., and Ridgway, J. (1994) What CATE did - An Exploration of the Effects of the CATE Criteria on Students' use of IT During Teaching Practice. *Journal of Information Technology for Teacher Education*, **3**, 1, 39-50.

Ericsson K. A. and Smith, J. (1991) *Towards a General Theory of Expertise: prospects and limits*. Cambridge University Press, Cambridge.

Gilmore, A. M. (1994) Information Technology in the Classroom: an evaluation of professional development for teachers. *New Zealand Journal of Educational Studies*, **29**, 1, 21-36.

Hogenbirk, P. (1996) The Pit-Project: a teacher networking approach for broad-scale use of information and communication technologies, in D. Passey and B. Samways (eds.) *Information Technology: Supporting change through teacher education*, Proceedings of the IFIP TC3 WG3.1 and 3.5 Conference in Kiryat Anavim, Israel.

Lampert, M. (1988) What can research on teacher education tell us about improving quality in mathematics education? *Teaching and Teacher Education*, **4**, 2, 157-170.

Mevarech, Z. R. (1996) The U-curve process that trainee teachers experience in integrating computers in the curriculum, in D. Passey and B. Samways (eds.) *Information Technology: Supporting change through teacher education*, Proceedings of the IFIP TC3 WG3.1 and 3.5 Conference in Kiryat Anavim, Israel.

Osorio, A. J. (1996) Research on telematics for teacher education, in Passey, D. and Samways, B. (eds.) *Information Technology: Supporting change through teacher education*, Proceedings of the IFIP TC3 WG3.1 and 3.5 Conference in Kiryat Anavim, Israel.

Passey, D. and Ridgway, J. (1991) *Building on Success: Evaluation and Self-Evaluation for Advisory Teachers*. National Council for Educational Technology, Coventry.

Passey, D. and Ridgway, J. (1992a) *Effective In-Service Education for Teachers in Information Technology: A Set of Case Studies and Notes for their Use*. Northern Micromedia, Newcastle.

Passey, D. and Ridgway, J. (1992b) *Effective In-Service Education for Teachers in Information Technology: A Resource for INSET Providers*. Northern Micromedia, Newcastle.

Passey, D. and Ridgway, J. (1992c) *Co-ordinating National Curriculum Information Technology: Strategies for Whole School Development*. Framework Press, Lancaster.

Passig, D. (1996) A knowledge based model of a networked teachers' training centre for in-service training with information and communication technology, in D. Passey and B. Samways (eds.) *Information Technology: Supporting change through teacher education*, Proceedings of the IFIP TC3 WG3.1 and 3.5 Conference in Kiryat Anavim, Israel.

Ridgway, J. and Passey, D. (1991) Constructivist Approaches to Educational Computing. *Australian Educational Computing*, September, 4-9.

Ridgway, J. and Passey, D. (1993a) An International View of Mathematics Assessment - through a glass, darkly, in M. Niss (ed..) *Investigations into Assessment in Mathematics Education*. Kluwer, London.

Ridgway, J. and Passey, D. (1993b) Teacher Informatics Capability: the key to changes in learning, in A. Knierzinger and M. Moser (eds.) *Informatics and Changes in Learning*, Proceedings of the IFIP Open Conference, Gmunden, Austria.

Ridgway, J. and Passey, D. (1995a) What is IT about? On plural perceptions and a plethora of practices, in Y. Katz (ed.) *Computers in Education: Pedagogical and Psychological Implications*. IFIP, Bulgarian Academy of Sciences.

Ridgway, J. and Passey, D. (1995b) Integrating IT: How to Use Existing Evidence About Individual Teacher Evolution to Plan Systemic Revolution, in D. Tinsley and D. Watson (eds.) *Integrating Information Technology into Education*. Blackwell, London.

Ridgway, J. and Shone, M. (1990) *The Roles and Deployment of Advisory Teachers with special reference to Information Technology.* National Council for Educational Technology, Coventry.

Rigby, B. (1996) Networking educational change: meeting the challenge of systematic school reform, in D. Passey and B. Samways (eds.) *Information Technology: Supporting change through teacher education*, Proceedings of the IFIP TC3 WG3.1 and 3.5 Conference in Kiryat Anavim, Israel.

Sandoval, J. (1995) Teaching in Subject Matter Areas: Science. *Annual Review of Psychology,* **46**, 355-374.

Selinger, M. (1996) Learning to teach at a distance: exploring the role of electronic communication, in D. Passey and B. Samways (eds.) *Information Technology: Supporting change through teacher education*, Proceedings of the IFIP TC3 WG3.1 and 3.5 Conference in Kiryat Anavim, Israel.

Shulman, L.S., Haertel, E. and Bird, T. (1988) *Towards Alternative Assessments of Teaching.* Teacher Assessment Project, School of Education, Stanford University.

Taylor, H.G. (1996) The TTACOS Project - laying the foundation for national technology standards for Students in the United States, in D. Passey and B. Samways (eds.) *Information Technology: Supporting change through teacher education*, Proceedings of the IFIP TC3 WG3.1 and 3.5 Conference in Kiryat Anavim, Israel.

Vygotsky, L.S. (1981) The genesis of higher mental functions, in J. Wertsch (ed.) *The concept of activity in Soviet psychology*. Sharpe, New York.

Weber, W. (1996) Advisory centre for new technologies - an addition to teacher training, in D. Passey and B. Samways (eds.) *Information Technology: Supporting change through teacher education*, Proceedings of the IFIP TC3 WG3.1 and 3.5 Conference in Kiryat Anavim, Israel.

Welch, M. (1993) Establishing Educational Partnerships With Strategic Interventions Through Video-Mediated Staff Development. *Journal of Educational and Psychological Consultation,* **4**, 3, 267-273.

Wolf, K. (1991) *Teaching Portfolios.* Far West Laboratory for Educational Research and Development, San Francisco.

10   BIOGRAPHY

Jim Ridgway is a Reader in Psychological Aspects of Education in the Department of Psychology at Lancaster University. He is the director of the Centre for the Study of Advanced Learning Technologies (CSALT) and director of the Supporting Technology Across the Curriculum Project (STAC). He has undertaken extensive research into the areas of change and innovation involving IT in education, is recognised internationally for his work in this field, and has authored and co-authored a range of books, articles and papers in this field. He is internationally recognised for his work on the assessment of mathematics, and is currently involved in a major innovation programme within the United States, which is concerned with the adoption and implementation of innovation and change to support assessment practices in mathematics.

2

Towards building open learning communities: re-contextualising teachers and learners

Jan Visser and Manish Jain
Learning Without Frontiers Coordination Unit
UNESCO, Paris, France

Abstract

This paper seeks to situate ICTs and their application in the domain of teacher education within the broader construct of "open learning communities." It attempts to use the opportunity of discussing ICTs to (1) raise fundamental questions about the ends and means of teaching and learning within a broader social, political, economic and cultural context, and (2) explore alternative approaches to building increasingly dynamic learning environments that are consistent with and responsive to the needs, interests and aspirations of individual learners and their local contexts/communities.

Keywords

Teacher education, distance learning, communications, culture, implications, open learning

1   INTRODUCTION

"Our vision of the coming century is of one in which the pursuit of learning is valued by individuals and by authorities all over the world not only as a means to an end, but also as an end in itself. Hence, much will be expected, and much demanded, of teachers, for it largely depends on them whether this vision can come true."

Learning: The Treasure Within, Delors Commission Report (1996)

The emergence of powerful new information and communication technologies (ICTs), such as those based on the use of computers and multimedia, digital compression and switching techniques, satellites, fibre-optics and wireless networks, artificial intelligence, and virtual reality, dramatically expand our options for engaging in teaching and learning at the individual, community, and societal levels. ICTs provide opportunities for greater flexibility, interactivity and accessibility. They help visualise applications such as interactive radio and television, videoconferencing, teletext, Internet-based environments of dialogue (ranging from the chatroom to academic discussion circles), Web publishing, and individualised CD-ROM tutorials. Although the future is still only dimly imaginable, one can sense that we are at the edge of something potentially very exciting, extremely big and, quite frankly, truly overwhelming. Discussion around these new technologies thus tends to stir up a whole range of emotions - sometimes rather naive ones - ranging from optimism and hope to uneasiness and anxiety. The reason for this is that, in addition to expanding current delivery options, the emergence of these new technologies present us with the opportunity (some would say force us) to question fundamental assumptions, to re-think existing approaches, to collectively conceptualise and generate new ideas and community-based alternatives and even sometimes, albeit more rarely, to catalyse social and institutional change.

However, to unlock the potential of such technologies, it is critical to revive an age-old discussion over *means* and *ends*. Technology, however sophisticated and inspiring to the imagination of technologists, will not automatically result in the benefits that are sometimes forecast by its advocates. The history of technology shows a disappointing repetition of instances of predicted revolutions that subsequently failed to materialise. In the majority of these cases of stunted growth, the attention to the means overshadowed the concern with the ends. The pursuit of ever more hi-tech forms of technology and increased access to technology can only be justified by our expectations about their potential contribution to a better world. Just chasing after the hottest technologies is a shallow pursuit and not worth the excitement it often generates. The overriding questions are: *What are our goals, how do these goals relate to creating a better world, and how do the technologies we pursue help achieve our goals?*

In the domain of education, a greater level of complexity surrounds these questions. Not only are the emerging technologies affecting the means by which we facilitate learning, they are also influencing the ends themselves. As they both provoke and facilitate the shift from an "industrial" model of society to a post-industrial information society, they are, in fact, implicitly re-defining the fundamental nature of learning and teaching. For example, the overwhelming amounts of rapidly changing information (and questions about the integrity of much of that information) makes it no longer possible nor relevant to learn - and thus to teach - in the same ways that we used to.

This paper seeks to situate ICTs and their application in the domain of teacher education within the broader construct of "open learning communities." It attempts to use the opportunity of discussing ICTs to (1) raise fundamental questions about the ends and means of teaching and learning within a broader social, political, economic and cultural context and (2) explore alternative approaches to building increasingly dynamic learning environments that are consistent with and responsive to the needs, interests and aspirations of individual learners and their local contexts/communities.

We begin by discussing evolving notions of learning within a world in transition, characterised by the increasingly rapid pace at which things become outdated. Learning is a critical element in responding to this situation. Secondly, we try to lay out an expanded vision of teachers and teaching that stimulates and enhances a variety of mediated learning environments. Finally, the paper concludes by positing an alternative conceptualisation of teacher education within the broader framework of building and sustaining open learning communities. We argue that simply layering ICTs as technological quick-fixes on top of existing institutions and processes is not enough. Rather, they must seek to create and sustain social and institutional change. It is their success in achieving this which will ultimately determine whether the new ICTs live up to their revolutionary hype.

2   LEARNING IN A CHANGING WORLD

2.1 Changing perspectives of learning and teaching in the information society

There is an intimate link between developments in the world of learning and those that pertain to the information society. This relationship will be analysed in more detail in the sections that follow. The learning side of the equation will be tackled first. Two perspectives will particularly be highlighted: the recognition that learning is an innate ingredient of our very humanity; and the ensuing concern that conventional learning environments are not well-suited for meeting society's learning objectives.

2.2 Learning for life... it takes a lifetime

We live in a time that learning is taking on a distinctly enhanced meaning. It is a time when changes in the learning environment, which have been advocated for decades if not centuries, are becoming necessary rather than merely desirable. Learning is an essential basis for both action and reflection and thus for creativity and problem solving. Learning is a pursuit in its own right which goes beyond the utilitarian conceptions that have for a long time related it almost exclusively to the world of work. In developing and industrialised nations alike, change, and consequently the need to respond and adapt to change and to manage ensuing conflict, are fundamental ingredients of life. Learning is the mechanism through which human beings cope with - and in turn contribute to - change. The possibility to engage in learning throughout one's life and across multiple dimensions of life is thus essential for survival as well as a condition for a continual quality of life. The traditional perceptions regarding education, based on the assumption that learning is the prerogative of the young, and that adult learning is at worst a response to failure and at best a marginal supplement, an exception rather than the rule, are becoming rapidly outdated. Learning is increasingly seen as a *lifelong* and *life-wide* requirement. This is contrary to the notion of learning as a mere preparation *for* life - with a discrete beginning and end - but not as an integral part *of* life.

To be a productive and participating member of society, one needs to be able to continue to learn, to grow with changes in the environment and to respond to the availability of different opportunities. For example, the increasing emphasis on informal sector activities as well as changing patterns of employment cause linear career paths to be replaced by career networks in which people find themselves exploring distinct environments and moving into divergent directions at various stages of their lives. Inherent in the emergence of the information society is also the need to rethink the priorities accorded to work-related activities *vis-à-vis* activities not directly related to the world of work. This is particularly relevant considering that in many societies people now spend decreasing proportions of their active life on what traditionally would be called 'work' and increased proportions of it on activities that would traditionally have been seen as pertaining to 'leisure'. Quality of life, then, becomes less a function of self-realisation in the (formal and informal) work environment and more a dimension of, for instance, social, cultural and political participation in society. The boundaries between work, leisure and learning start gradually to disappear and learning becomes a dimension of a work/learning/leisure merger. Learning for work, learning for leisure, and learning for learning are all valid options within that context.

The above conceptualisation requires us to rethink traditional learning goals, such as literacy. Literacy has long been seen as a gateway to the world of learning. However, its definition as the ability to describe and interpret the world in terms of alphanumeric symbols is no longer adequate. There are many literacies and, consequently, illiteracies. Technological illiteracy, political illiteracy, ecological illiteracy, intercultural illiteracy, and so many other ways in which people are hindered in their ability to act and reflect upon their environment are just as important as the inability to read and write. Across these various literacies there is a growing problem of information overload which threatens to paralyse us. The inability to process and critically analyse information is increasingly a concern. Learners must develop the ability to access and process huge volumes of information so as to create meaning and generate new knowledge.

2.3 Limitations of conventional learning environments

A second important perspective on learning is the question of unmet learning needs. The world has known unmet learning needs as long as education has been a conscious concern of societies. What is new now is that such unmet learning needs can no longer be seen as isolated phenomena within the boundaries of particular countries or distinct parts of the world. The world is increasingly becoming a global society and a learning place in its own right. The extent to which the world will be able to learn, will condition its survival and its ability to make the planet an acceptable, and hopefully desirable, place to live. Global learning depends on the ability of societies to turn themselves into learning societies and of communities within societies to constitute themselves as learning communities. In turn, learning communities exist to the extent that their individual members are learning individuals.

But what is the global reality? As we approach the end of the second millennium, there are still more than 900 million illiterate people in the world. New illiterates emerge every day as the result of inadequate school systems, inappropriate curricula, and insufficient conditions to prevent relapse into illiteracy once people have become literate. More than 130 million school-age children world-wide do not go to school. The millions that do go to school often fall victim to the diploma disease, ending up with learning achievements that do not relevantly relate to their immediate needs nor guarantee that learning sustains throughout their lives.

School systems, as we know them, reflect the requirements of the formal economy and, besides their obvious role in serving the learning needs of new generations, they also serve as channels for the socialisation of human beings into the pre-existing socio-economic hierarchies pertaining to the formal system. They are ill-equipped to respond to the learning challenges and opportunities of the future. Schools are burdened with a great deal of pressure due to increasing demand. In the past, they served a smaller and less diverse clientele, often already in many ways pre-selected. Today's schools are expected to carry out the almost impossible task of meeting the diverse needs of many more students. In its advice to UNESCO's Executive Board, the 'Ad Hoc Forum of Reflection on UNESCO's Role in the Last Decade of the Twentieth Century' concluded in 1993 that "education is increasingly necessary and less and less possible, due to its cost."

Furthermore, many schools are weakened by outdated structures which constitute an impediment to learning. Among these barriers are the continued reliance on the artificial separations between levels of education, such as primary, secondary and tertiary, or between socio-economically biased different tracks of learning, such as academic and vocational or technical. Equally inappropriate are often the ways in which human knowledge has become compartmentalised in stale curricula and presented in ways that are relevant, if at all, only for portions of society. Furthermore, these curricula tend to narrowly concentrate only on a small portion of the intelligence spectrum. During the 1980s various researchers (for example, Sternberg and Detterman, 1986; Sternberg and Wagner, 1986) reviewed and broadened the concept of intelligence. Howard Gardner (1983), for example, identifies at least seven different human intelligences that allow us to engage in learning in order to make sense of the world: (1) language; (2) logical-mathematical analysis; (3) spatial representation; (4) musical thinking; (5) the use of the body to solve problems or to make things; (6) an understanding of other individuals; and, (7) an understanding of ourselves.

An additional problem is the lack of responsiveness to the varying needs and circumstance of learners. This applies, for instance, to individual differences in styles and pace of learning. It also applies to the way schools often restrict learning to a narrow daily time block and the requirement on learners to be available on a year-long basis, thus creating incompatibilities for important groups of learners who are subject to expectations not taken into account by such constraints.

Mainstream schools sometimes have difficulty in acknowledging other learning environments, other partners, or other systems of knowledge. They are furthermore limited - and are at great risk to rapidly grow almost totally out of touch with developments in society at large - often continuing to rely heavily on teachers as the main source of knowledge and information. With the changes taking place in society, schools are in dire need to de-formalise and re-constitute themselves as components of learning environments that facilitate people's mobility across a wide range of options to participate in society at large as well as in their local communities.

3   TOWARDS OPEN LEARNING COMMUNITIES: THE TEACHER AS LEARNER AND THE LEARNER AS TEACHER IN MEDIATED ENVIRONMENTS

3.1   A shift from the traditional conception of the teacher

Teaching is essential to the learning process. However, conceptions about teaching and teachers have lagged behind and, as a result, often run counter to the changes required in response to the situations discussed above. The emphasis of the teaching process has been centred around the teacher rather than the learner. In recent history, the tendency has been to view the teacher as an impersonal "expert" in the classroom whose only role is to transmit knowledge, facts, skills to the "empty" learner. This section attempts to challenge such limited conceptions of teaching and teachers by raising three basic questions: (1) what is the role of the teacher?; (2) who is the teacher?; (3) where does learning take place? We ask these questions today with a firm belief that in the future, because of the changing nature of learning (by some referred to as nothing less than a paradigm shift) the role of teaching and teachers will be more complex, more demanding and perhaps more essential than it already is.

3.2 What is the role of the teacher?

The teacher is someone who intervenes in the learning process of others. The process can be seen as providing prompts for engaging, stimulating, structuring, and encouraging learning in individuals and communities. While transmission of some types of knowledge and skills is part of this process and will continue to be important, the complexity of society and demands made on the problem-solving capacity of human beings will require that teaching be seen as fundamentally going-beyond the transmission of information. In the world of the future, we envision that the teacher will be responsible for carrying out several inter-connected roles, as briefly described below.

Facilitation
Facilitating learning entails building, accessing and validating a variety of activities, frameworks, information, and experiences for the learner to connect to. It should be clarified that facilitation implies more than simply providing access to new information or technologies; rather, it involves enabling understanding and creating meaning. This means raising the capacity of learners to ask questions rather than focusing on the provision of answers to predetermined questions. The teacher must challenge the thoughts and ideas of learners and stimulate them to engage in critical thinking and self-reflection. Essential to the process of facilitation is the ability of the teacher to link the appropriate set of interactions with the individual learning styles, interests and experiences of each learner as well as with the profiles of the communities that the learners perceive themselves as being part of.

Curriculum innovation
Centralised curricula around the world have often been unable to take into account the rich diversity in society, and suffered from lack of imagination, flexibility and relevance. The result is that many learners find themselves "lost" in the learning process. Given the broad range of learning styles, needs, interests, backgrounds, and aspirations of learners, teachers must adapt and develop new curricular approaches, content and language to ensure that curricula are, on one level, linked to the daily life of the learner but, on another level, push the learners to explore beyond the mundane aspects of their daily lives into undiscovered possibilities. The movement towards decentralisation provides an opportunity for allowing teachers greater control over the curricula. However, with curriculum innovation, there must be greater efforts to conduct decentralised and participatory field research in order to understand the strengths and weaknesses of different strategies. Engaging in such research allows teachers to interact constructively and flexibly with the curriculum on a continual basis.

Connection of learners and communities
While learning is an individualised effort, it is also a social activity. Teaching must be conceived of in terms of a larger social exercise of connecting learners (and, in the process, building communities) to each other and to the world around them. The process of connecting learners involves creating dialogue among diverse groups of learners that allow them to understand and appreciate the differences as well as the similarities that bond us as human beings. This means that teachers must be committed to understanding their learners and the communities that they come from. As part of this on-going process, they must also be willing to question their own internal biases and stereotypes.

Complementing/supplementing other channels

In addition to the traditional teacher, many other additional "channels" currently exist and are emerging, such as textbooks, newspapers, and magazines, educational radio or TV broadcasts, computers, audio or video tapes, the surrounding physical and human environment, libraries, specialised work areas such as to perform science experiments or for creative expression. Teaching becomes a process of integrating these resources so that they complement, supplement and enhance each other. This demands a sensitivity to the inherent strengths and weaknesses of each of the channels and how they satisfy different styles of learning and different types of content. Teachers can also play a role in introducing these new media into communities where there is often fear or resistance to change.

Motivational support

The teacher must play a critical role in providing motivational support through constructive feedback and encouragement to the learner, responding to a broad range of motivational needs that vary over time and across learners. Learning is a process that is filled with success and failure - oftentimes involving great struggle and perseverance on the part of the learner. In many cases, failure can lead to great disappointment and withdrawal. However, if well managed, failure can also be turned into an important prompt to learning and thus can become the basis for success. It is the role of the teacher to provide positive inspiration at critical junctures of the learning process to ensure that learners stick with the laborious task of learning. However, the teacher should not take on this role in isolation, but rather seek to build a learning community in which other learners provide motivational support to each other as well.

Learning

A good teacher is a continual learner. In order to be effective, the teacher must remain connected with changing societal frames of reference (economic, cultural, political, social, technological, etc.) as well as with changing needs and interests of learners. They must be able to learn from their environment. But more importantly, they must be able to learn from their learners. This involves constantly trying to understand how learners react to, interpret and create meaning from different activities. It also involves a willingness to experiment with and adapt new approaches. In addition, the process of teaching involves modelling a love of learning. This love is something that one cannot fake. If the teacher demonstrates a dedication to learning, there is a high probability that the learners will "catch" that spirit of learning.

3.3 Who is a "teacher"?

We are all teachers just as we are all learners. The implications of the discussion in the previous sections points to a situation in which teaching can no longer be considered the sole jurisdiction or responsibility of the traditional classroom teacher. The teacher in the institution we call 'schools' still has an important role to play in supporting the learning process. However, we must seek to break down the barriers that have supported the historical isolation of teachers in schools from other "teachers" in society. In order for continuous learning to occur, the responsibility for teaching must be distributed and integrated with other institutions and individuals throughout society. We thus posit three broad categories of "teachers":

1) *Human beings*

This category includes the teacher in the classroom. But it also includes a wider range of individuals in society who are informally called upon to play equally important roles in complementing/supplementing the classroom teacher. These "teachers" build alternative learning environments and mediate access to diverse and valuable bodies of knowledge, traditions, information, skills, experiences, etc. The profound teaching contributions made by such groups as parents, family members, friends; community and religious leaders; literacy, community health, agricultural extension workers; tutors in different distance learning settings; journalists, artists, actors, musicians; media people (program producers, editors); and, artisans, craftsmen, farmers, traders, should be validated. In addition, we should recognise that learners are oftentimes teachers when they are called upon to contribute to the learning of others.

2) *Media*

The "teacher" should also be seen as including a variety of media for the learner to connect to. Such media-constructed environments include those that are built around technology and take the form of print, television, radio, computers, etc. It also includes learning that is prompted by socio-cultural activities such as community service activities, meditation/prayer, internships/apprenticeships, etc. In addition, one cannot overlook the learning that takes place when one is able to connect with the natural environment. We must clarify, however, that while the human "teacher" will be a medium among the other media, the human teacher is still distinct from these other media with roles and attributes that cannot be substituted by them, particularly in the sense that only the human teacher is capable of engaging in learning him or herself.

3) *Life experience*

Finally, we are also taught by life experiences. This includes spontaneous processes such as love and death, that cannot be easily structured or planned in a conscious way. It also includes processes that are determined, at least to an extent, by choice or by the dynamics of the human environment the individual is part of. It is thus a crucial task of human as well as mediated teachers to connect learners to such important channels of learning, helping them to reflect on and value their experience, and to integrate life experience with the curriculum.

3.4 Where does learning take place?

Learning is a natural human process that occurs wherever human beings interact with each other and with their environments. Much of society's effort to create the conditions for learning concentrate on the school system. However, learning can take place in formal as well as informal settings. It is not uncommon that some of the best instances of learning occur outside a formal setting as the learners tend to be more at ease and learning tends to be more contextualised within a relevant socio-cultural setting. For learning both within and outside the formal context to become optimally effective, it is thus important that artificial barriers between the two environments be reduced. Different media can play an important role in bridging the gap.

4 TEACHER EDUCATION: THE LEARNER/TEACHER AND TEACHER/LEARNER IN A MEDIATED LEARNING ENVIRONMENT

To this point, we have focused our discussion around the *ends* of education exploring implications and demands for learning in the context of a changing world and with it the need to incorporate an expanded view of teaching, the teacher and the spaces where learning occurs. Inherent in the discussion has been a re-discovery of the duality of learning and teaching - the teachers must be learners ("teacher/learner") and the learners must be teachers ("learner/teacher"). This is an essential element of the idea of open learning communities. Recognising this duality and supporting it requires that we reformulate many existing (and outdated) institutions, approaches and processes which were conceptualised along linear roles and relationships. At this juncture then, it is appropriate to shift the discussion to the *means*. Rather than placing all of our hope on blind chance, how do we actively facilitate this shift in thinking about learning and teaching?

The area of teacher education provides a natural starting point for initiating this process of change. However, as we will highlight hereafter, it should be clear from the onset that teacher education is an integrated part of a broader conception encompassing the education of both learners *and* teachers for their new roles in open learning communities. In this section, then, we will discuss points of intervention into teacher education, particularly focusing on how information and communication technologies can be used to facilitate the process of change. But first it is necessary to reframe a few key conceptions around teacher education. The emergence of new ICTs provides an opportunity and a necessity for pursuing this exercise.

The distinction between pre-service and in-service education is no longer a useful one

This is particularly the case if we begin to conceive of teacher education in terms of a more continuous and fluid process. In this context, pre-service teacher education is best to be seen as a preparation not only for a pre-determined role as teacher but particularly also for effective interaction with a continued learning-teaching process. The new ICTs help negotiate a hybridisation between formal and distance education. Face-to-face teaching is no longer only for pre-service education, and distance education is no longer only reserved for in-service education. Throughout the teacher education process, there should be a strong integration of both face-to-face and distance learning approaches.

Distance education is no longer a valid category

Perraton (1986) defines distance education as "an educational process in which a significant proportion of the teaching is conducted by someone removed in space and time from the learner." However, such a definition begins to rapidly lose its meaning if we situate it within the broader construct of learning and teaching discussed previously. The more it becomes an established notion that the teacher engages in learning and the learner is a teaching agent, the less relevant it becomes to focus on the separation in space and time of the two roles. The relationship between teaching and learning is fundamentally a dialectical one, based on a partnership between human beings to jointly create meaning (see, for instance, Dervin, 1981; Chieuw and Mayo, 1995; Visser, 1995). This partnership is no longer solely dependent on the physical proximity of its constituent members, nor is its quality necessarily determined by it. Separation in space and time is a mere matter of option, in many cases based on convenience or appropriateness in context rather than sheer necessity. What matters, and what needs to be validated, is simply the quality of the dialogue between partners - "teachers" and "learners" in the traditional sense of the word, but also other members of the learning community.

A corresponding "learner education" is required

"Teacher/learners", as they emerge from their traditional roles, must now first of all learn to become good learners. Being a good learner is not an easy task - it requires a great deal of discipline, patience, resourcefulness, inquisitiveness, open-mindedness, creativity and flexibility. This implies that teacher education must put greater emphasis on developing in "teacher/learners" the skills required to become better learners. In addition to encouraging teachers to become learners, teacher education must also support the process of "learner/teachers" in becoming teachers, both in terms of how they can teach each other and how they can teach the teacher. Thus, teacher education may seek to involve "learner/teachers" in parts of the process.

The new ICTs must not be viewed as replacing the human element in teacher education

There is increased frustration with the existing process of teacher education. ICTs are sometimes seen as a means of "fixing" this problem, particularly as they allow bypassing - or doing away altogether with - the assumed weak link, the traditional teacher trainer. This view, however, is erroneous. It was argued above that, in a context of different media, including the human being as one of them, the most striking characteristic which distinguishes the human medium from non-human ones, is the capacity to learn. "Teacher/learners" can thus best be prepared for their new roles in an environment which models the behaviours they are expected to acquire. Such an environment should therefore be profoundly human and humanising and technologies need to be incorporated in it so as to enhance, rather than to detract from, this human aspect.

4.1 Points of intervention in teacher education

Many attempts at improving the quality and motivation of "teacher/learners" through teacher training schemes have resulted in disappointment. Evaluations point, among other weaknesses, to the cascade model and its inherent transmission loss as well as to the gap between what is learned in the training situation and the realities of the field. The use of information and communication technologies within a distance learning context is often advocated as a way to overcome such weaknesses. Excitement has been generated around new ICTs as it is assumed that they can 'bring the best expert directly to the teacher' and facilitate two-way communication between the teacher and learner. Unfortunately, these are very narrow applications of the ICTs and we do not foresee them resulting in any significant shifts in learning and teaching as they are simply extensions of existing approaches and processes. These "benefits" only serve to reinforce the teacher-over-learner hierarchies. However, the ICTs, if properly applied, possess the ability to unleash revolutionary changes in the field of teacher education. We suggest the following focal points for application of the new ICTs to teacher education.

Participatory teacher education

Teacher education should be geared towards building a link between the various "teacher/learners" in society. Selected joint training sessions may be organised to do this with ICTs being utilised to facilitate greater communication, collaboration and reflection among the various partners. Initial sessions could start with discussions on how to work together, sharing of roles, and ensuring overlap (for reinforced learning). Such a process of dialogue should be geared towards discovering a basis for partnership in building open learning communities, i.e. identifying strengths and weaknesses of each partner, formulating an understanding of the needs and interests of various learners, negotiating points of compromise, and team building. More importantly, it should be focused on developing a shared consensus around learning and how it relates to broader objectives of social change and development.

In addition, the ICTs provide an interesting opportunity for involving "learner/teachers" in selected teacher education activities. They can play a role in facilitating increased communication and sharing between "teacher/learners" and "learner/teachers." The ICTs potentially provide a way for not only the "learner/teacher" to understand the "teacher/learner" better, but also for the "teacher/learner" to understand the "learner/teacher" and for the "learner/teachers" to understand each other, and sometimes even themselves, better.

Flexible training for specific needs of teachers

One of the strengths of the ICTs is that they facilitate moving away from generic teacher education models with relatively little relevance to the lives and daily problems of the "teacher/learner." The ICTs allow for the development of specific training models that are sensitive to the different needs, working conditions, learning styles, language and backgrounds of individual "teacher/learners." Such individually-tailored approaches of teacher education are better geared towards addressing issues of motivation and morale. However, this should not be taken to mean that a group of centralised training designers try to design hundreds of specialised training programs, but rather that they should utilise the ICTs to support a process in which "teacher/learners" take on a greater role in generating and designing their own training programs.

Teacher education conceived of as on-going and in the learning environment

The ICTs allow the potential for teacher education to be moved out of centralised training institutions and into the "teacher/learner's" own working environment. In addition, they open up the opportunity to think of teacher education as a career-long career-wide activity rather than as a pre-service phase with bouts of in-service training merely for refresher purposes. Such an emphasis on on-going training is essential to allowing the "teacher/learners" to continually reflect on critical aspects of their own teaching as well as critical aspects of their own learning.

Overcoming the dichotomy between subject matter and pedagogy/andragogy

The ICTs allow us to rethink the content of teacher education. Traditionally there has been an artificial dichotomy between mastery of subject matter and pedagogical/andragogical skills, sometimes with a tendency for teacher education to emphasise the subject matter aspect of the content. Teacher education content should be re-oriented to focus on learning and learners with subject matter and pedagogical/andragogical elements integrated around this focus. In addition, the ICTs should be used to make teacher education more consistent with the pedagogical/andragogical concerns being advocated, such as active learning, critical thinking, collaborative processes and creativity.

Interacting with different media

Noting the expanding role the new media are already playing in the provision of education, and cognisant of how this role will undoubtedly expand, it is critical to recognise the importance of media literacy among "teacher/learners." Such media literacy requires a strong understanding of the strengths and limitations of each medium and familiarity with strategies to reinforce the effect one medium can have on learning through the use of other media. However, the idea of media literacy should be conceived beyond the glitzy hi-tech schemes available on the market. "Old" technologies such as print, radio, television will no doubt continue to make great contributions to the development of open learning environments worldwide, particularly if integrated in supporting community contexts. Furthermore, the "teacher/learner" should be encouraged to venture beyond them and also to make improved use of relatively unexplored media of popular expression such as puppet shows, local dances and music. Teacher education should ensure that teachers interact and experiment with these various media and creatively reflect upon how they can best be used in different learning environments. This should be more than a mere theoretical exercise and actually involve hands-on experience.

5 TAKING ON THE CHALLENGE

Technology in and of itself does not change the world. Human beings do. They do so by using technologies in creative and critical ways, opening up important new opportunities to respond to existing and emerging problems. The challenge is there to be met.

In this paper we have argued that learning and teaching need to change fundamentally. We have also argued that a good starting point to provoke such change is by re-conceptualising the roles of teachers and learners. Technology has been posited as an opportunity to create processes that encourage teachers to become learners and learners to become teachers. This is a major shift, the realisation of which entails overcoming equally major obstacles.

The question that remains is how to facilitate this shift. The complexity of the situation does not allow for simple blueprint approaches. However, we have two powerful tools available. First and foremost is our capacity to learn. Second is the power of the ICTs themselves to enhance such learning. We must thus seek to take advantage of these tools by building, in our own environment, similar roles and relationships as the ones advocated in this paper. This calls for a commitment to view ourselves not only as experts but also as learners who must, while implementing change, actively engage in a process of continuous interaction, reflection, redefinition of positions and informed risk taking. The starting point for effective change thus lies in our willingness to change ourselves.

6   REFERENCES

Chieuw, S.F. and Mayo, J.K. (1995) The conceptual foundations of multichannel learning, in S. Anzalone (ed.) *Multichannel learning: Connecting all to education.* Education Development Center, Washington, D.C.

Dervin, B. (1981) Mass communication: Changing conceptions of the audience, in R.E. Rice and W.J. Paisley (eds.) *Public communication campaigns.* Sage, Beverley Hills, CA.

Gardner, H. (1983) *Frames of the Mind: The Theory of Multiple Intelligences.* Basic Books, New York.

Perraton, H. (ed.) (1986) *Distance education: An economic and educational assessment of its potential for Africa.* World Bank, Washington, D.C.

Sternberg, R.J. and Detterman, D.K. (eds.) (1986) *What is intelligence? Contemporary viewpoints on its nature and definition.* Ablex, Norwood, New Jersey.

Sternberg, R.J. and Wagner, R.K. (eds.) (1986) *Practical intelligence: Nature and origin of competence in the everyday world.* Cambridge University Press, New York, NY.

The International Commission on Education for the Twenty-first Century, UNESCO (1996) *Learning: The Treasure Within.* UNESCO, Paris, France.

Visser, J. (1995) Can new technologies lower the barriers to quality education for all? in S. Anzalone (ed.) *Multichannel learning: Connecting all to education.* Education Development Center, Washington, D.C.

7   BIOGRAPHY

Dr. Jan Visser is an eclectic craftsman and scientist. In the mid-1960s, he worked in Europe and Israel as a theoretical physicist, combining research with teaching. Struck by the intricacies of human learning, and fascinated with the human condition and how it can be changed through human development, he became an educationalist. He has worked throughout the world, particularly in Africa. In the 1980s he became interested in instructional systems design with a focus on issues of motivation. Dr. Visser also has extensive experience as a manager, having performed duties as dean of faculty, office director and program co-ordinator, and having been trained in this field. In addition, he is a musician (who builds his own instruments), film-maker, writer, and avid walker.

Manish Jain is currently a member of the Learning Without Frontiers Coordination Unit in UNESCO. Prior to joining LWF, he worked as an educational consultant in the areas of planning, policy analysis, research and media/technology in Africa, South Asia, and the former-Soviet Union with several international development agencies, governments and NGOs. He is a strong proponent of South-South co-operation. Mr. Jain has also worked as an investment banker with Morgan Stanley during which time he focused his attentions on the high technology and telecommunications industries. He holds a Master's degree in education from Harvard University and a B.A. in economics, international development and philosophy from Brown University.

The views represented in this paper are solely those of the authors, and do not necessarily reflect the views of the United Nations Educational, Scientific and Cultural Organization.

Section 2: Aspects and concepts of change, and the implementation of innovation

3

Time for change: critical issues for teacher educators

Gail Marshall
Gail Marshall and Associates
2393 Broadmont Ct., St. Louis, MO, USA

Abstract
Changes in classrooms provoked by technology do not necessarily translate into significant improvements in teaching and learning. We must ask what changes in pedagogy have occurred as a result of equipping classrooms with technology, how those changes have produced improvements in students' learning, and what conditions promote successful changes in pedagogy.

Keywords
Classroom practice, cognition, evaluation/formative, evaluation/summative, policy, problem solving

1   INTRODUCTION

In spite of technology, teaching has changed little since the days when students heard the prophets' words or roamed as scholar adventurers. Most research in technology settings, with the notable exception of studies such as the ImpacT Report (1993), has failed to determine what teaching acts actually occur with regularity in technology settings, what impact, if any, those teaching acts have on students, and how changes in teaching have been initiated and sustained. To remedy this situation, we must scrutinise our work and change our perspectives. The revolution in software evaluation (Squires and McDougall, 1994), shifting from an emphasis on mechanistic evaluation instruments to rubrics assessing what teachers and students can know and do with technology, points the way.

An examination of the sources and effects of change in teaching practices must acknowledge the impact of teachers' underlying beliefs about the teaching/learning process on their decisions (Marshall, 1993; Benzie, 1995). Questions framed in a behaviourist perspective often fail to inform us of what is actually happening in classrooms, why specific teaching acts were chosen, and what happens as a result of the choices. As long as our questions are rooted in behaviourist conceptions of teaching and learning, we will not move forward in our understanding of the complex relation between teaching and students' understanding and action.

Progress has been made in specifying the differences between behaviourist and constructivist methods (Murphy and Moon, 1989), but the educational technology community has paid scant attention to the manifold interconnections between teaching and learning within the different frameworks.

2   THE PROBLEM OF CHANGE AND CRITICAL ISSUES

Issue 1. What, if anything, has changed in teaching since the introduction of technology into classrooms? And if there are changes, are those changes consistent with good pedagogical practice?

We must not assume that all teachers embrace the same vision of what changes in classroom practice ought to result from technology use, or that the majority of teachers will change their methods as they incorporate technology.

Consider that sales of drill and practice software constitute the largest sales of educational software in the United States. This is consistent with many American teachers' beliefs in the efficacy of behaviourist teaching methods. Can we say that teaching has changed because technology now delivers lessons where the teacher previously used cardboard flashcards or workbooks filled with drill exercises?

Consider an illustration that is only one step removed from the electronic flashcard-type of pedagogy. In many classrooms where students have access to relatively complex problem-solving software, the software is used in ways that undercut the pedagogical intent of the developers. One example is classrooms where students work with *Hot Dog Stand*, a program that can operate on at least three levels: (1) buy and sell hot dogs and see how much money you make; (2) buy and sell hot dogs based on a 'good consumer' model and see how much money you make; (3) adopt hypotheses about what types of purchases generate the highest revenue and play out a series of games testing those hypotheses. In the majority of classrooms I visit, teachers, apologetically but routinely, leave students to their own devices with the software assuming that 'something' will be learned.

Many teachers, if they monitor the students' activities at all, seem content with this use of the software. A constructivist would say that the teacher's role here is to generate some dissonance. If the students have not arrived at the stage of routinely testing hypotheses, the teacher should structure the lesson so that hypothesis testing becomes a focal point, and model, if students do not understand hypothesis-testing techniques, strategies for testing hypotheses. But many teachers are unsure of how to weave together hardware and thoughtware.

Teachers working from a behaviourist perspective tend to emphasise learning content over learning process so they use technology either to teach the same content they taught previously but at a faster pace or to teach more content in the same time period. Are we satisfied with this approach?

Constructivist teachers tend to be less concerned with students' performance on standardised tests and more concerned with students' ability to engage "fundamental ideas", so they tend to regard technology as a tool for teaching topics that might have been difficult to teach in pre-technology days. They use technology for problem solving, for working with geometric constructions at earlier grade levels than they did before the advent of technology, and/or for providing opportunities for students to create projects based on Internet access or videodisk use.

But what of the depth of those lessons? How often have we seen superficial 'cut and paste' productions? What have students learned from collecting a series of images stored somewhere and pasted into their reports? Are the reports more insightful? Do they provide a heightened learning experience for students who might otherwise not have understood the ideas and processes supposedly provoked by the activity?

In the absence of models or criteria for conducting technology-based instruction, many teachers begin to assume that merely using technology will enhance students' learning. We must help teachers analyse their work, and help them make the connection between what they do with technology and how those actions contribute to students' performance.

Issue 2. Can we say that changes occurring since the introduction of technology have been productive for students?

Empirical data about the effects of technology use by students are sadly lacking, and most impact studies have been conducted in the behaviourist tradition. We do have anecdotal reports of benefits derived from technology use, but the criteria applied to judge the effectiveness of these lessons are sketchy at best.

Here again, the fundamental split between two opposing epistemological traditions comes into play. If you adhere to a behaviourist tradition, the fact that students' skills seem to be enhanced by the use of drill programs will lead you to say that the use of technology has been an important addition to classrooms. The constructivist would question such complacency, saying technology may not have been responsible, the skills may not be important skills, and may not be integrated into the students' repertoire of performances.

From a constructivist perspective we have reason to be pessimistic about what changes have occurred as a result of technology's role in today's classrooms. Let us consider an example.

Let us say that Hypercard is used for a project called 'Our Visit to the Zoo.' Students collect all sorts of information about animals - their eating habits, their size, their countries of origin, the gestation period, rate of growth, etc., and record the data. After the zoo visit, students collect more data, check the data, and obtain pictures of the animals. Then they manipulate the stacks to group together all the animals with similar gestation periods. From these data different types of graphs and charts can be made. The creation of those graphs and charts can lead to still more questions about the relations between variables. Students may ask if animals with long gestation periods produce animals that at adulthood are larger than animals with shorter gestation periods. Sorting and resorting allows students to work at key skills of classifying, sorting, and searching. Those are activities that can lead to cognitive reorganisation.

But we do not have many studies to check if such technology-related manipulations of data occur or produce changes in students' thinking. In fact, we have ignored or been cautious about setting specific criteria for how students' thinking should be shaped from technology use. Our failure to consider what we want students to learn from working with technology often leads us to accept activity for the sake of activity.

Issue 3. What conditions lead teachers to successfully initiate and sustain technology use, and are those changes productive for learning?

If we look back to the introduction of classroom-based technology use, I think we would be well advised to think that, like Moses leading the Israelites through the wilderness, we may have had an idea of our destination but little notion of what might happen along the way. We have been less than rigorous in our definitions or demands about what constitutes appropriate levels of change. Similarly, we have not been vigilant about charting the connection between change and the conditions that promote change.

Is it truly a change if a teacher shifts from using workbooks to using electronic flashcards? Is it truly a change if a teacher supplies problem-solving software for students, but fails to monitor students' learning in those situations? Is it truly a change if teachers fail to determine if students have opportunities to apply what they've learned in technology settings to other classroom activities? Is it truly a change if teachers fail to look at technology's ability for recursion, iteration, for random generation, and fail to model the thinking strategies needed to work with these processes? Is it a change if teachers neglect to build those capabilities into explicit lessons - both with and without the use of technology?

Do we know what changes are difficult for teachers to make but worth making in terms of productive growth for students? Here again, the difference in belief systems shows its impact. It is relatively easy for a behaviourist teacher to change from being a non technology-user to a frequent technology-user. Granted changes in scheduling must occur and maybe students must double up, but the classroom will look pretty much the same as before.

But the change for a constructivist teacher might be more difficult. Where do manipulatives fit with computer use? Do we model problem solving to the entire class or small groups? Does every student work with the same piece of software? At the same time? If not, are different skills addressed? How is the curriculum reorganised to accommodate all these solutions?

Similarly, the criteria behaviourist teachers may apply to judge the success of their work will differ from criteria judged acceptable by teachers working within a constructivist framework, so it may be simpler for a behaviourist teacher to be satisfied by technology use. But we have little data on the ways teachers conduct evaluations of students' work in technology settings, nor do we know what use is made of the evaluative data, so these questions are not easily answered.

3   CONCLUSION

Change can happen serendipitously. An unexpected insight leads to a change in behaviour. Change can happen because of a plan when we know what we want to do and act to achieve that plan. Change can happen haphazardly. Do we know anything about the course of technology-based pedagogical change? Is serendipity fruitful? Does planned change work and, if not, what do teachers do when planning fails? Do they revert to previous pedagogical practices or rework their attempts at change? Do we know anything about the stability or permanence or generalisability of technology-related change?

If we work with a set of criteria, we know what we want to do, what impact our actions should have, and what the level of acceptable attainment would be. In the absence of criteria can we say that technology-using teachers have met our expectations? Can we tell how difficult it will be to attain our goals? Can we say what strategies work in reaching those goals?

It is time to assess what types of change have occurred, what types of change have been difficult and why, and what the implications of change mean for students. Three major questions might form the basis of our work: How should technology-based teaching and learning be conceptualised? How do teachers adapt technology-based teaching practices in ways that are consistent with the specific features of technology? How do technology-based classroom activities acknowledge the ways learning occurs? These questions, posed in order to provoke a re-examination of pedagogical practices, may help us set an agenda for stable, generalisable, and attainable change.

4   REFERENCES

Benzie, D. (1995) The impact of our questions on Information Technology policy and practice, in J.D. Tinsley and T. van Weert (eds.) *World Conference on Computers in Education IV: WCCE '95 Liberating the Learner*. Chapman and Hall, London.

Marshall, G. (1993) Informatics and changes in learning: The American dilemma and opposing epistemological perspectives and unanswered questions, in D.C. Johnson and B. Samways (eds.) *Informatics and Changes in Learning*. Elsevier Publishers, Amsterdam.

Murphy, P. and Moon, B. (1989) *Developments in learning and assessment*. Hodder and Stoughton, London.

Squires, D. and McDougall, A. (1994) *Choosing and using educational software: A teacher's guide*. The Falmer Press, London.

Watson, D.M. (ed.) (1993) *The ImpacT report: An evaluation of the impact of Information Technology on children's achievements in primary and secondary schools*. King's College, London.

5   BIOGRAPHY

Gail Marshall has observed classrooms and analysed the impact of teaching as an evaluator of state and federal programs for the St. Louis Public Schools, St. Louis, MO and as a member of the evaluation team of the Comprehensive School Mathematics Program and the Midwest Regional Exchange at CEMREL, Inc. With a doctorate in Child Development from Washington University, St. Louis, MO, she has conducted research studies on children's thinking strategies. She currently serves as International Editor for *Leading and Learning with Technology*, a publication of the International Society for Technology in Education and conducts evaluations for school districts and state departments of education.

4

Getting ready to change: the place of change theory in the information technology education of teachers

Brent Robinson
University of Cambridge
17 Trumpington Street, Cambridge CB2 1QA, UK

Abstract

This paper argues that information technology training and support for teachers has traditionally focused on issues of hardware, software and pedagogy, neglecting to identify, analyse or shape the nature of the processes of change which accompany technological innovation. The paper therefore examines the nature of computers as an educational resource and discusses the consequent changes in knowledge, skills, attitudes and behaviour required of teachers who use information technology. The paper also addresses the skills and knowledge required for teachers to be effective change agents beyond their classrooms, to support their own use of technology and to act as catalysts for organisational change. The paper refers to concepts and techniques from the literature on change theory which have already impacted on school development in order to help educators understand and locate their place within processes of technological innovation and equip them to exploit opportunities for bringing about improvements. The concluding section of the paper argues that an understanding of the phenomenology of information technology innovation in schools and of educational change in general ought to be required of every computer using teacher. Teacher educators must acquire this knowledge to understand better the nature of the task facing their students and so provide these students with relevant support and training.

Keywords

Professional development, teacher education, information technology, innovation

1   INTRODUCTION

It is likely that we have much to gain from the application of change theory to the introduction of IT in education....Teacher educators should consider the need for pre-service and in-service teachers to understand and master change processes alongside their IT development. *(Final Report of Professional Group on IT in Teacher Education, World Conference on Computers in Education, 1995).*

1.1 The 3 phases of information technology innovation

Early information technology (IT) initiatives in schools were essentially technology centred. The principle seemed to be that 'as long as the facilities are available and teachers are trained in computing, adoption... is inevitable' (Anderson et al, 1979, p. 229). But it soon became evident that access to hardware and software alone were insufficient to ensure successful uptake. Learning how to use information technology in the classroom involves more than training in hardware and software use. It requires pedagogic understanding of what computer assisted learning applications are trying to do and of what the hardware and software are capable of doing. In consequence, later initiatives tended to focus on pedagogic rather than technical concerns. Still, however, the uptake of information technology in schools has been patchy and in the search for more effective technological innovation, those involved have come to realise that human factors are important variables in the change process. Increasing attention is therefore being paid to human and institutional as well as to technological and pedagogic issues. For example, in the United Kingdom, schools themselves and educational support agencies have increasingly turned to the personal and institutional factors involved in technological change. The National Council for Educational Technology (1993) noted in its medium term plan for 1993-6 that: 'case studies from commerce and industry show that effective use of IT is accompanied by personal and organisational change' and in the last 5 years there have been many publications which focus on organisational and human issues in relation to information technology innovation. (For examples, see NCET, 1995; Passey and Ridgway, 1992; Eraut et al, 1991.)

The histography of IT development resonates with current theories of educational change. The attention which has been paid successively in teacher training (both pre-service and in-service) to hardware and software, then to pedagogy and now to human factors in IT use in schools mirrors Fullan's (1991) belief that educational innovation requires a change of teaching resources, teaching strategies and beliefs. Fullan observes that most change efforts have concentrated on changes which overlooked people (behaviour, beliefs, skills) in favour of things (regulations, materials) and this is essentially why innovation has failed more times than not; people are much more difficult to deal with than things but also more necessary for success (p. 249).

Information technology poses an enormous, possibly unique, challenge as a resource to the teacher because its use demands considerable shifts on **all** fronts. Numerous authors accept that the use of information technology may be changing the way teaching is conducted (see, for example, Sheingold and Hadley, 1990). The fundamental change required to use computers for teaching is to teachers' existing conceptions of the teaching learning process and to their conceptions of their pedagogic role within it. Such authors as the above identify among computer using teachers, a shift from teacher directed teaching to student centred learning, often socially dynamic, in environments that are complex and interactive. In this, it is not just new skills and competencies that are required. Computer use in schools also requires changes to educational ideology (Wild, 1993). Faced with the scale and complexity of such changes, it becomes clear that we must ensure we help colleagues to respond positively to the profound changes required of them, to consider such changes critically, to accept them where appropriate and to manage the transition process effectively.

2   TEACHERS AND CHANGE

In order to accommodate information technology in their teaching, teachers require not only knowledge of the changes required and the skills to accomplish them but also in relation to the processes of change itself. In order to master and guide technology innovation in schools, teachers require a procedural and conceptual knowledge of change. They need to understand the process of change, be able to locate their place in it and then be able to act.

2.1   Attitude

Whilst some teachers can cope adequately with large scale change, others are far more conservative in nature. In fact, with regard to the adoption of computers, it has been found that teachers as a professional group are highly conservative (Adkisson, 1985; Gillman, 1989). Many teachers enjoy stability, see change as a threat and shun problems as undesirable. Yet it is a recurrent theme of change theories that change should be viewed positively and confidently. This is not to say that change is not uncomfortable: 'Almost every important learning experience we have ever had has been stressful' (Block, 1987, p. 191) and Schon (1971) reminds us that all real change involves passing through zones of uncertainty - the situation of being at sea, of being lost, of confronting more information than you can handle (p. 12). Despite all this, however, change theorists argue that the teacher can, and should, adopt a positive attitude to change and learn to accept it as a valuable part of professional development: 'The anxieties of uncertainty and the joys of mastery are central to the subjective meaning of educational change' (Fullan, 1991, p. 32). Teachers must also learn to accept that 'Conflict is fundamental to any successful change effort...success in school change efforts is much more likely when problems are treated as natural, expected phenomena, and are looked for' (Fullan, 1991, p. 27). Eraut's (1988) study of the uptake of information technology in schools found computer using teachers who exhibited typically positive attributes - teachers who possess confidence, seek out opportunities for change, enjoy risk taking and are willing to work with new methods of learning. Teacher educators should help teachers to develop confident, positive, proactive attitudes so that they may cope more effectively with the challenges of technological innovation in schools.

2.2   Action

If teachers are to use information technology successfully in schools, they need to become effective change agents. An effective change agent is a teacher who can take responsibility and action to exploit the many opportunities in a school for bringing about improvements (Fullan, 1991, p. xiv). Teachers must have the capacity to know **when** and **how** to pursue and implement certain change possibilities. While many goals may be identified as desirable, not all are attainable. There must be a critical assessment of whether or not action is desirable in relation to certain goals and whether or not the action is implementable - in brief, whether or not it is worth the effort. Teachers need to weigh carefully the strengths and weaknesses of their plan - searching for opportunities and evaluating their merit, identifying obstacles and threats and assessing whether or not they may be surmounted or obviated. The most responsible act may be to reject goals and actions that are bound to fail and to work earnestly at those that have a chance of success (Fullan, 1991, pp. 103-4).

It is important for the teacher to know how to cope with policies, programmes and constraints that are imposed upon him or her (Fullan, 1991, p. xiii). Much depends not just on the individual but on the organisational context within which the individual is working. It is rarely possible for a single teacher's desire to use IT in his or her teaching not to be affected by wider policy, timetable, curricular and resource issues within a school. The IT using teacher will therefore often need to effect change elsewhere in the institution. Moreover, many teacher change agents will see whole school change in relation to IT to be a highly valued goal in itself, not just in relation to the realisation of their own teaching needs. But schools, like individuals, can be conservative places. Many researchers (Cuban, 1984; Kerr, 1989; David, 1991; Papert, 1993) have indicated that schools have changed very little in the last century. What appears to some individuals as a straightforward professional improvement can, to an organisation, be felt as undesirably disruptive if it means that the culture must change its values and habits in order to accommodate the alteration. Change agents should be aware of a natural resistance to individual or organisational change in schools and understand that this might play an important part in shaping the institution's response to any use of information technology.

In order to facilitate their own teaching with IT and/or to move the school forward technologically, teachers require strategic problem solving and evolutionary planning models which are based on knowledge of the change process and which emphasise organisational issues (see Louis and Miles, 1990). For example, recent work by MIT which looked at the process of IT innovation within industry has been used by the UK National Council for Educational Technology (1995) as the basis for a 5 stage model of technological change in schools which can provide a framework for action. The model identifies characteristics of a learning organisation at successive stages of technological development and so provides a means for locating the present state of institutional development together with targets which imply action.

Ultimately, the goal must be to establish schools which are effective 'learning organisations' - that is, institutions which are responsive and proactive environments, manifesting a flexible and adaptable culture in the face of desirable or necessary technological change. Such institutions will acknowledge the role of individuals as agents in the change process and support their empowerment. Staff must be supported by a culture where it is constantly possible to learn, where visions are shared and which essentially encourages risk taking and the possibility of change by creating a safe climate of innovation.

3   THE ROLE OF TEACHER EDUCATION

There is little evidence to date that these 'learning organisations' already exist or that we are preparing individual teachers to create them or to function optimally within them. In initial teacher education, problems of personal change or institutional innovation are rarely considered explicitly (Fullan, 1991, pp. 300-1) despite the need for student teachers to create immediate situations where they can practice using IT, let alone embark upon the career long process of ongoing professional development through change. Fullan carried out a national Canadian survey in which only 15% of teachers and teacher educators felt that their programmes were preparing teachers to any great extent to have the perceptions and skills to implement changes. Grunberg and Summers (1992) conducted a lengthy review of the growing wealth of literature on the subject of technological innovation and concluded that computer innovation in schools is not a topic of any great priority in initial teacher training. They argued:

"In initial teacher education the emphasis should be on developing classroom competence with information technology and encouraging student teachers to think critically about its role in teaching and learning. Problems of institutional innovation and change are far more likely to be the concern of school principals, senior managers, regional or national advisers, curriculum development agencies, and government ministers." (p. 272)

Yet if teachers at the beginning of their careers are to develop the personal and professional skills to use information technology in their teaching, it must be recognised that they are likely to experience considerable personal change and frequently encounter a need or desire to effect organisational change also. Problems of change and innovation should not be ignored in initial teacher education. Nor, at in-service level, should they be considered only the province of senior educational managers.

Many of the barriers to the adoption of microcomputers in schools are specific examples of barriers to change in general (Cox and Rhodes, 1989). It is time that we looked at the increasing corpus of literature on technological innovation in schools (see Grunburg and Summers, 1992) and reflected on what we could do better to prepare teachers for the innovation we ask them to embark upon. As we move away from a technocentric view of technological innovation, we should look also at the substantial body of wider literature which exists concerning educational change in schools (see Wu, 1988). Teacher educators must acquire a better understanding of technological innovation and hence the enormous challenge facing the teachers they educate. All teachers should be helped towards an understanding of the phenomenology of technology innovation and of educational change so that they might better plan for their own professional development and for the development of the organisations within which they teach.

4   REFERENCES

Anderson, R., Hansen, T., Johnson, D. and Klassen, D. (1979) Instructional computing: acceptance and rejection by secondary school teachers. *Sociology of Work and Occupations*, **6**, 227-250.

Adkisson, J. (1985) *A Study of Policy Issues Concerning the Instructional Uses of Microcomputers and a Survey of the Policies of Selected Boards of Education.* Doctoral dissertation, The George Washington University. (Dissertation Abstracts International, 46, 25A). ERIC Clearing House on Educational Management, University of Oregon, Eugene, Oregon.

Block, P. (1987) *The Empowered Manager.* Jossey Bass, San Francisco.

Cox, M. and Rhodes, V. (1989) *The Uptake and Usage of Microcomputers in Primary Schools with Special Reference to Teacher Training.* ESRC Research Report, InTER/8/89, Lancaster.

Cuban, L. (1984) *How Teachers Taught: constancy and change in American classrooms, 1890-1980.* Longman, New York.

David, J. L. (1991) Restructuring and technology: partners in change. *Phi Delta Kappan,* **73,** 1, 37-40 and 78-82.

Eraut, M, Pearce, J., Stanley, A. and Steadman, S. (1991) *Whole School IT Development.* Kent IT in Schools Support Team, Sittingbourne.

Fullan, M. (1991) *The New Meaning of Educational Change.* Teachers College Press, New York.

Gillman, T. (1989) *Change in Public Education: a technological perspective* (Trends and Issues, Series No. 1). ERIC Clearing House on Educational Management, University of Oregon, Eugene, Oregon.

Grunberg, J. and Summers, M. (1992) Computer innovation in schools: a review of selected research literature. *Journal of Information Technology for Teacher Education,* **1,** 2, 255-276.

Kerr, S. T. (1989) Technology, teachers. and the search for school reform. *Educational Technology Research and Development,* **37,** 4, 5-17.

Louis, K. and Miles, M. (1990) *Improving the urban high school: What works and why.* Teachers College Press, New York.

NCET (1993) *Medium Term Plan.* National Council for Educational Technology, Coventry.

NCET (1995) *Managing IT.* National Council for Educational Technology, Coventry.

Papert, S. (1993) *The Children's Machine: rethinking schools in the age of computers.* Basic Books, New York.

Passey D. and Ridgway J. (1992) *Co-ordinating National Curriculum IT: Strategies for Whole School Development.* Framework Press, Lancaster.

Schon, D. (1971) *Beyond the stable state.* Norton, New York.

Sheingold, K. and Hadley, M. (1990) *Accomplished teachers: integrating computers into classroom practice.* (Report No. IR 014 677). Center for Technology in Education, Bank Street College of Education, New York. (ERIC Document Reproduction Service No. Ed 322 900).

Wild, M. (1995) Pre-service teacher education programmes for information technology: an effective education? *Journal of Information Technology for Teacher Education.*

Wu, P. (1988) Why Change is Difficult? Lessons for Staff Development. *Journal of Staff Development,* **9,** 2, 10-14.

5   BIOGRAPHY

Brent Robinson is the University Lecturer in Information Technology in Education and a Fellow of Hughes Hall at the University of Cambridge where his major teaching and research interests are in the field of teacher education. He is the editor of two journals - the *Journal of Information Technology for Teacher Education* and *Computers and Education* - and Vice President of the Society for Information Technology and Teacher Education.

5

The U-curve process that trainee teachers experience in integrating computers into the curriculum

Zemira R. Mevarech
Bar-Ilan University
School of Education, Ramat-Gan, Israel

Abstract

Professional development programs, whether they focus on computer environments or on non-computer environments, are assumed to play an important role in professional growth. Typically, designers of such programs anticipate that the main outcome will be improvement in teachers' pedagogical knowledge and practice. To what extent have professional development programs experienced unfavourable outcomes? Are such negative outcomes unavoidable? The present paper addresses both issues. Based on research in the areas of cognitive psychology and professional development in education, this study questions the widely accepted assumption that gaining expertise is a linear developmental process. Instead, the study shows that integrating computers into the curriculum is a U-curve process that involves a negative side of decline in performance followed by a positive side of overcoming difficulties and reconstructing teachers' pedagogical content knowledge. The U-curve model consists of the following stages: survival, exploration and bridging, adaptation, conceptual change and invention. Unfortunately, however, only a few teachers move into the invention stage; others drop out at one stage or another of the U-curve process.

Keywords

Professional development, teacher education, innovation, learning models, future developments, Logo

1   INTRODUCTION

Until recently, the main research foci in the area of computer education were (and still are) the software and the students, with little attention (relatively speaking) devoted to the teachers (for example, Katz and Offir, 1996; Mevarech and Netz, 1991). Several reasons may explain this phenomenon. First, it is possible that, explicitly or implicitly, researchers have assumed that computers can replace the teacher and thus there is no need to focus on the teacher. Second, having access to friendly software has led researchers to believe that teachers would know what to do with it, without being explicitly trained in doing so. Finally, since professional development in education started to flourish much after computers had been introduced into schools, researchers have not utilised the growing knowledge in this area.

Yet, current research has shown that teachers face considerable difficulties in integrating computers into the curriculum (for example, Ingvarson and Mackenzie, 1988). These findings raise the need to examine the stages that teachers pass through when they teach with the aid of computers. The present paper addresses this issue. In particular, the study examines the following questions: To what extent have professional development programs regarding computer learning environments unfavourable outcomes? Are such negative outcomes unavoidable? And if they are, how can teachers cope with these difficulties? My main thesis is that professional development in education is not a linear process that involves a continual growth in teachers' pedagogical knowledge, skills, and beliefs, but rather a U-curve process that involves "a negative side of decline in performance and attitudes followed by a positive side of overcoming the difficulty and reconstructing teachers' pedagogical-content knowledge" (Mevarech, 1995a, p. 151).

Evidence supporting the U-curve phenomenon is obtained from a series of observations and interviews with experienced teachers who were teaching in two kinds of co-operative computer learning environments emphasising metacognitive processes: Application-Based Computer (ABC) course (Mevarech, 1995b) and Logo-Stat (Mevarech and Kramarsky, 1992; 1993). These two courses were selected for several reasons. First, both courses emphasise general strategies and thus recruit teachers from many disciplines. Second, both courses introduce innovations in technology and instructional methods. Finally, since both courses exert positive effects on students' cognitive and metacognitive components as well as on social relationships (Mevarech and Kapa, in press; Mevarech and Kramarsky, 1992; 1993), it would be interesting to examine how successful programs affect teachers' professional development.

2   THE U-CURVE MODEL

Stage A: Survival
The first stage is characterised by "survival behaviours". During the first weeks of working in a new computer learning environment, many teachers, even experienced teachers, behave as if they are first-year teachers. They swing from permissiveness to excessive strictness, are concerned with discipline and management problems, and focus only on physical changes in classroom organisation. In our interviews, many teachers express their concerns by raising a series of "what if" questions: "What if there will be a bug in the software?" "What if there will be a short circuit or another unexpected problem?" " What if a student will ask a question for which I will not have an answer?" Hall et al (1975) described this stage as: "mechanical use of the innovation -- state in which the user focuses most effort on the short term day-to-day use of the innovation with little time for reflection ... [At this stage] teachers solicit management information about such things as logistics, scheduling techniques, and ideas for reducing amount of time and work required of the user" (p. 8).

Although most of the teachers we observed and interviewed were experienced teachers, when a problem arose they seemed to forget their rich pedagogical knowledge schema. When these teachers planned their lessons they strictly followed the suggestions offered in the teacher guidance and did not base their decisions on their pedagogical schema. When they ask for help, it always relates to technical questions such as: which key to push in order to get ..., how much time to allocate for ..., or how to handle discipline problems. Interestingly, any problem that arose in the classroom was immediately interpreted as related to the new technology. When the mentors asked the teachers to plan a student-teacher-computer activity, many teachers responded that they "cannot interfere with the computer work". As Riding (1984, p.1) described: "teachers conceive the computers as yet one of seven-world wonders, which if ignored will go away:"

Why do experienced teachers behave like novices when they start working in a new computer learning environment? According to current theories in cognitive psychology, prior knowledge is a major factor in influencing all aspects of information processing, from perceptions and encoding of cues, through levels of information processing, to retrieval, problem solving, and metacognitive functioning. Furthermore, cognitive researchers have indicated that when the new and prior knowledge are in accord, the new knowledge may be easily assimilated with the existing schema; when, however, the new and prior knowledge contradict each other, the old knowledge often interferes with the new knowledge and causes a decline in performance, as seen in learning to use a new keyboard that is slightly different from an old one. This is probably what happens when a teacher is exposed to a new computer learning environment: the rich pedagogical knowledge base interferes with the encoding and processing of cues provided in the new environment and causes discipline problems, rigid behaviour, decline in performance, and the use of traditional teaching methods. Indeed, Dawyer et al (1991) and Mevarech and Netz (1991) reported that teacher who used for the first time application-based computer systems or CAI programs replicated traditional instructional and learning activities, almost never interacted with other teachers sharing the same problems, were mainly engaged with technical problems, and showed no change in professional self-esteem.

Stage B: Exploration and bridging

Not all teachers survive the entry stage. Many drop out of the project. Yet, those who do survive move into a stage of exploration and bridging. They start to approach the new learning environments more positively, although they are still hesitating and probing. At this stage most teachers are preoccupied with themselves (Hall et al, 1975). In the interviews they express their concerns by asking: "How can *I* cope with the innovative method/software/learning environment?". The emphasis here is on the teachers themselves rather than on the students. Exploring and bridging often results in a smooth implementation of the innovative software with less stress and minimal management problems. Teachers at this stage usually report that implementation is going fine with few if any problems, yet no reflective responses are observed. On the contrary, teachers use the new software routinely, but pay little attention to ways of adapting the innovation to the needs of their students.

Stage C: Adaptation

The adaptation stage is characterised by reflective use of the innovative learning environments. At this stage, teachers know the requirement, they can cope with "technical" problems" and they are pretty much aware of the pros and the cons of the innovation. Teachers' mental energy is, therefore, devoted to reflective integration of the computers in the curriculum. They frequently discuss pedagogical problems with their colleagues and often show self-confidence in applying their own pedagogical knowledge schema in solving problems. Teachers at this point are not preoccupied any more with themselves but rather with their students. They often ask questions such as: "How can my *students* learn graphing with computers?"

Another change in teachers' behaviour concerns their planning behaviour. Whereas in previous stages, planning relates to moment-to-moment problems and short-term outcomes, at this stage planning is based on seeing the entire unit. Teachers use their knowledge about children's developmental characteristics, and they base their teaching on learning theories. For example, teachers using the ABC course expressed feelings that even low-achieving children can function at a very high cognitive level by utilising the computerised tools and learning co-operatively with other children.

Stage D: Conceptual change and invention

The progression from survival, through exploration and bridging, to adaptation builds a readiness for conceptual change. At this stage, teachers use the innovation in a reflective and dynamic way, and they often provide evidence showing that they have experienced conceptual change regarding the learners and the learning processes.

In our interviews, many teachers start talking in constructivistic terms rather than in "knowledge transmission" terms. They emphasise creative thinking, hypothesis testing, and problem solving. As one teacher said: "Before I was exposed to the ABC course I thought that school depressed students' creativity. I thought that only high achieving students could be creative. Now I think that there is still some hope and school can enhance creativity, including creativity of "weak" students. Instructional activities at this point focus on the cognitive and psychological objectives of the unit and how they can be achieved. In the interviews teachers were not concerned any more with technical problems. Instead, they were concerned with long term effects of the programs such as how to avoid misconceptions, how to share instructional activities with their colleagues, and how to enrich their theoretical knowledge. Dawyer et al (1991) indicate: "The most important change in this phase was an increasing tendency of teachers to reflect on teaching, to question old patterns, and to speculate about the causes behind changes they were seeing in their students" (p. 50).

Conceptual change may be followed by invention - some teachers may suggest new ways of integrating computers into the curriculum. Naturally, invention is suggested only after teachers had experienced conceptual change and only by a small number of teachers. For example, several ABC teachers who attained conceptual change have designed an interdisciplinary course for junior high school students based on a variety of application software. The teachers defined new learning objectives, developed all the learning activities that are appropriate for attaining these purposes, and exposed the students to a large number of different application software.

The U-curve model may have important implications for designers of in-service training programs, teachers, principals, and practitioners. First, anticipating immediate improvement in professional development and being unaware of the difficulties may increase frustration and lead many teachers to drop the innovation under different kinds of excuses. Changing teachers' expectations by introducing the notion of the U-curve model may facilitate the integration of computers into the curriculum. Second, it is well known that staff development programs must be combined with intensive support. The U-curve model may specify the kind of support that has to be provided at each stage. Third, involving teachers in school level decisions regarding the integration of computers into the curriculum may increase teachers' responsibility and facilitate the transition through the stages. Finally, discussing with teachers the expected difficulties, while reflecting upon their technical and pedagogical knowledge may be a powerful means in enhancing professional development. Since sometimes the feeling of frustration observed in the survival stage is intertwined with feelings of "discovery" and enthusiasm (Huberman, 1989), the positive feelings have to be utilised to facilitate the move to the next stage. Positive evidence showing the beneficial effects of learning co-operatively at the computer (Mevarech and Light, 1992) indicated that computers can be used not only for mastery of basic skills, but also for enhancing higher order thinking processes and social relationships between students. Similar techniques may be used for training teachers. Since the role of the teacher is crucial in integrating computers into the curriculum, the U-curve model merits future research.

3   REFERENCES

Dawyer, D.C., Ringstaff, C. and Sandholz, J.H. (1991) Changes in teachers' beliefs and practices in technology rich classrooms. *Educational Leadership*, **48**, 45-52.
Hall, G.E., Loucks, S.F., Rutherford, W.L. and Newlove, B.W. (1975) Levels of use of the innovation: A framework for analyzing innovation adoption. *Journal of Teacher Education*, **26**, 52-56.
Huberman, M. (1989) On teachers' careers: Once over lightly, with a broad brush. *International Journal of Educational Research*, **13**, 347-362.
Ingvarson, L. and Mackenzie, V. (1988) Factors affecting the impact of inservice courses for teachers: Implications for policy. *Teaching and Teacher Education*, **4**, 139-155.
Katz, Y. and Offir, B. (1996) The teacher and integrating computers in the curriculum, in Z. Mevarech and N. Hativa (eds.) *The computer in school*. Shoken Press, Tel-Aviv.
Mevarech, Z.R. (1995) Teachers' paths on the way to and from the professional development forum, in T. Guskey and M. Huberman (eds.) *Professional Development in Education*. Teacher College Press, New York.
Mevarech, Z.R. (1995b) Information Processing Technologies: What do students learn and how? in Y.J. Katz (ed.). *Computers in Education: Pedagogical and Psychological Implications*. IFIP and Bulgarian Academy of Sciences, Sophia.
Mevarech, Z.R. and Light, P. (eds.) (1992) Cooperative Learning with Computers. Special issue of *Learning and Instruction*, **2**.
Mevarech, Z.R. and Kramarsky, B. (1992) How and how much can cooperative Logo environments enhance cognitive performance and interpersonal relationships? *Learning and Instruction*, **2**, 259-274.

Mevarech, Z.R. and Kramarsky, B. (1993) Vygotsky and Papert: Social cognitive interactions with Logo environments. *The British Journal of Educational Psychology*, **63**, 96-109.

Mevarech, Z.R. and Kapa, E. (in press) The effects of a problem solving based Logo environment on children's information processing components. *British Journal of Educational Psychology*.

Mevarech, Z.R. and Netz, N. (1991) Stability and Change in affective characteristics of teachers. Can computer environment make a difference? *British Journal of Educational Psychology*, **61**, 233-239.

Riding, J. R. (1984) *Computers in the primary school: A practical guide for teachers*. Open Books, London.

4 BIOGRAPHY

Zemira R. Mevarech is Associate Professor in the School of Education and the Institute for the Advancement of Social Integration in Schools, Bar-Ilan University, Israel. A graduate of the University of Chicago, Dr. Mevarech was a visiting professor and a visiting researcher in various universities and research institutes. Her primary research interests are: computer learning environments, mathematics education, and the development of instructional methods for enhancing higher order thinking processes. Currently, Prof. Mevarech and her team are carrying out a large scale study with more than 30 junior high schools which investigates the impact of IMPROVE - an innovative instructional method for teaching mathematics in heterogeneous classrooms. In addition, they are investigating various aspects of integrating computers into schools, particularly Logo-Stat and Application Based Computer courses.

Section 3: Defining the future curriculum at a national level

6

Information technology capability: is our definition wide of the mark?

David Benzie
College of St Mark and St John
Derriford Road, Plymouth, PL6 8BH, UK

Abstract

The introduction of a National Curriculum for UK schools in the late 1980s was accompanied by a definition of pupil IT capability. That definition places a strong emphasis on pupils' ability to use IT tools and information sources to analyse, process and present information. This definition has proved to be durable in that it has, in essence, remained intact even though the National Curriculum as a whole has been modified.

The practical consequence of this definition is that classroom activity has focused on teaching pupils how to use *particular* IT tools to carry out *particular* tasks. IT activities for trainee teachers and for teachers on in-service courses have followed a similar pattern.

In this paper it is argued that a change of emphasis is needed. Teaching pupils to focus on the particular produces learning that is "brittle". In other words, it is not the type of learning that will prove to be durable in a rapidly changing domain even though that is exactly what is needed given the general characteristics of IT.

The paper proposes a revised definition of IT capability which is designed to foster learning that has a focus on pupils' own ability to identify situations where IT can be effectively deployed and, significantly, on their ability to adopt learning strategies that enable them to acquire the practical skills that could lead to the realisation of possibilities.

Keywords

Elementary education, secondary education, basic skills, classroom practice, computer literacy, pedagogy

1   INTRODUCTION

Definitions matter. The reason that they matter is because the act of defining initially creates and then confines the scope of legitimate discussion about an entity. Definitions that remain un-contested for long periods of time often come to underpin notions of orthodoxy and when that orthodoxy becomes pervasive it can be difficult and painful to challenge, even when it can be shown that there is a strong case for so doing.

Although IT (Information Technology) is still a recent phenomenon in education it has always been associated with an intense debate whose aim is to define both the role and the significance of IT in this context. During the 1980s alternative conceptions of the computer as teaching machine and the computer as tool both featured in the discussion (see, for example, Watson, 1987 and Taylor, 1980) but by 1989 a broad consensus which placed a strong emphasis on the latter emerged in the UK. The defining document that simultaneously captured the state of debate at the time and provided the framework for developments in the following years was produced by HMI in that year (HMI, 1989).

One consequence of the debate in the late 1980s was an attempt to define the concept of IT capability. It was at this time that a National Curriculum was being introduced into the British education system and one aspect of this was a definition of IT capability (DES, 1990) for school-age pupils. The definition proved to be un-contentious (in the UK) and so, despite a number of major upheavals to the National Curriculum, it has remained largely intact. IT capability is currently defined in the following way by the National Curriculum:

> "Information technology (IT) capability is characterised by an ability to use effectively IT tools and information sources to analyse, process and present information, and to model, measure and control external events. This involves:
> * using information sources and IT tools to solve problems;
> * using IT tools and information sources, such as computer systems and software packages, to support learning in a variety of contexts;
> * understanding the implications of IT for working life and society."
> (DfE, 1995)

The detail of the HMI (1989) report points to activities such as active exploration and self-managed learning (see, for example, paragraphs 11, 15 and appendix 5b) and so, to a certain extent, does the revised National Curriculum (DfE, 1995) through phrases such as "..become discerning in their use of IT", "..develop a greater responsibility for their use of IT" and "..learn to operate unfamiliar systems". However, these concepts do not find explicit expression in either the main statement or in the detailed requirements of what pupils should be taught. Indeed, the main consequence of the definition that we have is that IT activities in school have tended to focus on showing pupils how to do a particular task or to use a particular IT tool in ways that are typified by the range of exemplar activities described by SCAA (1995). This focus on the particular is echoed by NCET (1995b) when they discuss progression in IT capability in the following way: "Pupils acquire new skills in response to the needs of an activity...consolidation of skills...leads to IT Capability." In other words, the focus is firmly on the skill and not on the mechanism by which it is acquired.

In another context, the DES (1989) produced the most significant attempt to define IT capability in higher education, but that attempt only related to trainee teachers and its influence was short lived. Within three years all that remained was the requirement that trainee teachers, should be able to "demonstrate ability to select and use appropriate resources, including Information Technology" (DfE, 1992). In the absence of guidelines it is hardly surprising that the development of student IT capability (in higher education) has lacked a clear focus.

2   IT CAPABILITY AND WIDER EDUCATIONAL AIMS

Educationally focused political headlines have, for a number of years, been dominated by calls for a "back to basics" campaign but away from that rhetoric there are widely held views that force a consideration of other objectives. NCET, for example, express a commonly held view when they say:

"Constant change will be a continuing feature of our lives. Much of that change is a result of the progress of technology. Schools and colleges will need to prepare learners to work confidently with the new technologies. More importantly, they must prepare learners for a working environment characterised by changing skills requirements and changing work patterns." (NCET, 1995a)

The critical issue here is constant change and, in particular, change associated with technology. It is this issue that points to a key problem associated with current definitions of IT capability. Those definitions say nothing about change or about how to help pupils and students to manage change even though it is a defining characteristic of the technology.

Indeed, it is argued that the problem is even more acute than it first appears. As we have seen, the current definitions of IT capability focus on teaching pupils how to use *particular* IT tools to carry out *particular* tasks. It is highly likely that the results of that process will prove to be very "brittle" - in other words, they are not transferable and they lack the flexibility that facilitates durability in the face of change.

This problem must also be seen against the background of developments in our understanding of how humans learn, of the significance of preparation for adult learning and of the characteristics of effective learners.

We have already seen that an acceptable definition of IT capability must recognise the dynamic of continual change and this implies that learning and re-learning are implicitly associated with IT capability. If we also take the view that human cognition is socially grounded (Crook, 1994) it also becomes clear that what is learnt in that particular social setting must be seen, in part, as preparation for becoming an effective learner in the social settings that will be met post-school.

Learning is now a lifelong issue. Claxton (1996) echoes many others when he says "Learning can no longer be seen as a task for people in the first quarter of life. And what it is that needs to be learnt, and the level of flexible understanding that is required, is also undergoing a profound change." Knowles (1990) reminds us that adult and child learners differ in important respects - for example, in the degree to which they are able to identify learning goals and the extent to which they can use past experience as a key resource, but it is also important to remember that an increasingly important function of school (and university) education is to foster the skills and attitudes in learners that will enable them to play an active role in managing their own life-long personal development. Candy (1990) identifies a number of traits of autonomous learners and whilst he suggests that we should be wary of attempts to develop autonomous learning as a generalised capability he does identify characteristics such as the ability to engage in deep-level learning and the ability to make intelligent guesses about items of information that are missing that can be directly applied to the context of the development of pupils' IT capability.

So we are now faced with the issue that pupils and students need to be prepared for lifelong learning and it is schools that have the first responsibility for laying the foundations. The concrete expression of that preparation must be found in the nature of the educational goals set by the National Curriculum and in the fine detail of its requirements. The current definition of IT capability is part of the fine detail, but it is providing a focus that is, in some important respects, inconsistent with key educational aims.

3   AN ALTERNATIVE VIEW OF IT CAPABILITY

When proposing change there is always a tension between the desire to argue for dramatic change that would (perhaps!) lead to a radical change in practice and the alternative of suggesting incremental change on the grounds of a pragmatic assessment of the likelihood of effecting something real. Marshall (1994) provides us with a grim catalogue of innovations that have failed because their underlying philosophy is too far removed from current practice and from this it is clear that an incremental approach that provides bridges from the known is more likely to bear fruit. In Vygotskian terms, we are more likely to make progress if attention is focused on the zone of proximal development (Vygotsky, 1978) with proposals for change providing cues that are accessible to and achievable by teachers (and others) given their current understanding.

This approach does not always sit comfortably with articulate pleas for substantial change. In his discussion of technological literacy Beynon (1993), for example, mounts a persuasive argument that technology is over-vocationalising education. He goes on to propose that teachers (the focus of the discussion) should develop the ability to "read technology" but whilst the argument is extremely persuasive in terms of its desirability it is also clear that underlying concepts are some distance (in cognitive terms) from where most teachers are. The real issue, then, must be to provide definitions, and by implication guidance, that link current practice to more desirable goals.

Somekh and Davies (1991) through a discussion of pedagogy for Information Technology provide us with a very helpful list of learner (i.e. school-age children) competencies that, they argue, we should seek to encourage. Phrases such as "..increasing independence of thinking and self-sufficiency..", "..purposefully to select and use available resources..", "..take risks...and learn from mistakes.." and "..take responsibility for their own learning.." all occur in the argument and these are consistent with the goal of equipping pupils with the skills required for effective life-long learning. When these ideas are linked with the insights that Kennewell (1995) gives us into the cognitive processes associated with the development of IT capability, a clearer picture begins to emerge of how we might move forwards. The issue that neither address, however, is the ability of individuals to identify opportunity and to manage the process of acquiring the skills that are necessary in order to translate mere possibility into actuality. And it is this ability which is key for adult learners.

Taking these ideas together, an alternative to the current definition of IT capability could be:

IT capability is characterised by the ability to identify situations where IT tools can be deployed to good effect and by the ability to manage the acquisition of the practical skills that are required for that effect to be realised.

Pupils who posses an IT capability will be able to:
- use IT tools and information sources to analyse, process and present information;
- use IT tools and information sources to solve problems;
- make focused explorations of and with IT tools, thus extending their own skills and understanding;
- demonstrate an understanding of the implications of IT for society.

Note, in the new definition, that IT capability is separated out from the use of IT in teaching and learning. This is quite deliberate. It has been effectively argued by others (NCET, 1995a) that IT can be used to improve the quality of teaching and learning but we must not confuse this use of IT with the development of a personal IT capability. Students at all levels regularly make highly effective use of IT based learning materials and that is to be applauded, but we must not make the mistake of, for example, equating the manipulation of a small number of variables in a complex population model with the development of serious IT capability.

So what difference would this definition make in practice? One consequence would be a new focus on personal qualities (willingness to explore, inquisitiveness, taking responsibility and organising personal learning) that transcend vocationalism (thus meeting some of Beynon's objectives) and an increased emphasis on strategic issues along the lines of those suggested by Somekh and Davis (1996).

More specifically, classroom activities to encourage IT capability might include:

- An increase in the discussion of analogues of computer activities with the aim of helping pupils to develop robust mental models of computer functionality.
- Pupils should be encouraged to explore a new item of software and to find out all they can about it. Following explorations, they should be encouraged to reflect on how they organised the exploration and to discuss alternative approaches with others.
- Pupils should be encouraged to identify connections and spot patterns in the way that computer systems work. Those patterns provide powerful clues when new situations and problems are met.
- When problems are met by pupils, teachers should, where possible, resist the temptation to provide a "quick fix". With hands in pocket, the teacher should use normal questioning techniques to lead pupils to solutions by helping them to relate the immediate problem to their existing knowledge.
- An active classroom discussion of the range of strategies that can be adopted when problems occur. The premise should be that facing and overcoming technical problems is normal and there are both high and low level strategies that can be used to overcome them.

- Many computer programs provide readily accessible facilities that are either partially or totally incomprehensible - for example, many spreadsheet programs can produce a dazzling array of graphs but none of them are universally appropriate. At one level there is the issue of teaching pupils to select a graph that is appropriate to the data but for the learner (and it is acknowledged that this is particularly demanding) this is only a particular instance of the general problem of finding out how to make good use of a readily available, powerful but mysterious tool. Strategies for coping with this type of situation should be discussed and pupils given the opportunity to practice them.
- When pupils are engaged in (non-IT focused) learning activities they should be encouraged to discuss and identify the role that IT could play. They could then identify what they could do given their current skills and beyond that they could identify the IT skills that they would need for the full potential to be recognised and plan for the acquisition of those skills. On occasions they should follow the process through.
- Getting help is a critical issue. Classroom discussion of how we can best help each other and how we can get the most from books, teachers, manuals, on-line help and other sources will help pupils to acquire a key skill for long term independent learning.

Few of these activities will involve a radical departure from current practice but they do require change. Principally, that change involves a greatly reinforced emphasis on the strategic issues of learning and on an explicit identification and discussion of them.

4   CONCLUSIONS

The current (UK) definition of IT capability for pupils provides a solid base for classroom activity but we have seen that it lacks a key dimension if our goal is to achieve something that is durable in the long term and which also stimulates the acquisition of skills that are transferable to other areas.

The proposal for a revised definition is based on the need to equip pupils with the skills and insights to manage a dynamic technology where simple knowledge of the particular is of little long term benefit. There is, however, also the recognition that implied new activities must be within reasonable cognitive distance for most teachers if there is to be any likelihood of their widespread adoption.

5   REFERENCES

Beynon, J. (1993) Technological literacy: where do we go from here? *Journal of Information Technology for Teacher Education*, 2, 1, 7-35.

Candy, P.C. (1991) *Self-Direction for Lifelong Learning: A Comprehensive Guide to Theory and Practice*. Jossey-Bass, San Francisco.

Claxton, G. (1996) Integrated learning theory and the learning teacher, in G. Claxton, T. Atkinson, M. Osborn and M. Wallace (eds.) *Liberating the Learner: Lessons for Professional Development in Education*. Routledge, London.

Crook, C. (1994) *Computers and the Collaborative Experience of Learning.* Routledge, London.

Department for Education and Science (1989) *Information Technology in Initial Teacher Training.* HMSO, London.

Department for Education and Science (1990) *Non-Statutory Guidance: Information Technology Capability.* HMSO, London.

Department for Education (1992) *Initial Teacher Training (Secondary Phase). Circular 9/92.* Department for Education, London.

Department for Education (1995) *Information Technology in the National Curriculum.* HMSO, London.

HMI (1989) *Information technology from 5 to 16: Curriculum Matters 15.* HMSO, London.

Kennewell, S. (1995) Information Technology capability - how does it develop? in J.D. Tinsley and T.J. van Weert (eds.) *World Conference on Computers in Education VI: WCCE '95 Liberating the Learner.* Chapman and Hall, London.

Knowles, M. (1990) *The Adult Learner: A Neglected Species.* Gulf, Houston.

NCET (1995) *Information Technology and Learning: Problem or Solution? NCE Briefing: New Series 8.* National Commission on Education, London.

NCET (1995) *Approaches to IT Capability: Key Stages 1 and 2.* NCET, Coventry.

Marshall, G. (1994) Cautionary verses: prospects and problems in achieving the aims of the computer revolution, in J. Wright and D. Benzie (eds.) *Exploring a New Partnership: Children, Teachers and Technology.* North Holland, Amsterdam.

Somekh, B. and Davies, R. (1991) Towards a pedagogy for information technology. *The Curriculum Journal,* **2**, 2, 153-170.

Somekh, B. and Davis, N. (1996, in press) Getting teachers started with IT and transferable skills, in B. Somekh and N. Davis (eds.) *Using IT Effectively in Teaching and Learning: Studies of Pre-service and In-service Teacher Education.* Routledge, London.

Taylor, R.P. (1980) *The Computer in the School: Tutor, Tool, Tutee.* Teachers College Press, New York.

Vygotsky, L.S. (1978) *Mind in Society.* Harvard, Cambridge, Mass.

Watson, D. (1987) *Developing CAL: Computers in the Curriculum.* Harper and Row, London.

6   BIOGRAPHY

David Benzie teaches at a College of Higher Education where a major focus of activity is the in-service and pre-service training of teachers. His teaching is mainly focused on in-service teacher training and he has responsibility for a masters degree programme in information technology. He is also responsible for supporting colleagues who wish to introduce and develop information technology based components on their courses.

7

Present role of informatics teachers in view of applications

Márta Turcsányi-Szabó
Loránd Eötvös University
Department of General Computer Science, 1088 Budapest,
Múzeum krt. 6-8., Hungary

Abstract

Six years after major political changes, and following many years of heated discussions, the Hungarian National Curriculum was finally created in the latter part of 1995. The new regulation identified a compulsory curriculum for informatics, specifying basic requirements at different school levels, as well as the use of applications in other curriculum areas to support learning skills, thinking, self education, exploration and problem solving. Seeking to match the general requirements of the National Curriculum with regards to application systems, this paper describes the goals for informatics teacher training planned through some topics of taught courses.

Keywords

Elementary education, secondary education, teacher education, curriculum development, informatics as a study topic, national policies

1 INTRODUCTION

According to the 130/1995 (Hungarian Gazette 1995 No. 91) government decree, our new National Curriculum has finally been agreed and produced. The new regulation was much awaited, for it was anticipated that it would provide a more flexible background for the development of individual school curricula, breaking away from the line of centralised regulations of the past. It states only those requirements that will provide an equal minimal base, both in terms of content and proportion, for all national schools (irrespective of different school type). On the other hand it allows a great deal of freedom for developing differentiated individual curricula, adjusted to particular circumstances and aimed at the pedagogical values of schools, parents, and students.

2   GUIDELINES

The flexible requirements are achieved through the following guidelines:
- The total requirements are formulated to enable schools within average settings to fulfil the tasks in 50-70% of the total time prescribed in the educational regulation, allowing complementary activities according to individual choice and values.
- The contents and requirements are formulated in terms of general cultural fields and sub-fields rather than by subject, to facilitate schools in developing and grouping the contents of their subjects individually.
- Requirements are not defined by grades, but build on the characteristics of age groups who require different teaching-learning strategies, divided accordingly into periods which end in the 4th, 6th, 8th, and 10th grades, thus providing guidance towards the requirements of the basic cultural knowledge examination at the end of the 10th grade.

The new National Curriculum not only allows the use of different educational books and materials, but encourages the individual preparation of such aids by schools.

The cultural fields and sub-fields specified in the National Curriculum can be seen in the table below. These fields and sub-fields can be grouped into subjects in several ways, according to the amount of compulsory and non-compulsory course hours in individual school policies. Hence, the hours required in each field can only be expressed in approximate proportions (see Table 1).

Table 1 Required hours for different cultural fields

Cultural field	school grades (value in %)			
	1-4	5-6	7-8	9-10
Native language and literature (Hungarian language and literature; language of ethnic minorities and literature)	32-40	16-20	11-13	11-13
Living foreign languages	-	11-15	9-12	9-13
Mathematics	19-23	16-20	10-14	10-14
Man and society	4-7	5-9	10-14	10-14
Man and nature (science experience; physics; chemistry; biology and health education)	5-9	8-12	16-22	15-20
Our earth and surroundings	-	-	4-7	4-7
Arts: music; dancing; drama; visual culture, movie and media culture	12-16	12-16	9-12	9-12
Informatics: computer science; library use	-	2-4	4-7	4-7
Life style and practical knowledge: technical; domestic science and management; career orientation	4-7	5-9	6-10	5-9
Physical training and sports	10-14	9-13	6-10	6-10

The National Curriculum states requirements by dividing them into three categories:
- material to be taught to master and develop particular skills;
- requirements for the development of competencies;
- minimal requirements for passing specified grades.

Table 2 Material to be taught within specified periods

	Till end of 6th grade	Till end of 8th grade	Till end of 10th grade
Basics of computer science	Computers and their surroundings. Introduction to basic issues of informatics. Using calculators. The sense of orders of magnitude.	Handling computers and accessories. Basic issues about informatics. Historical review of computers. Informatics in Hungary.	Types and characteristics of hardware equipment. Tools of textual and graphical man-machine interaction. News, information, and data types.
Use of operating system		Use of operating systems: Basic knowledge of operating systems used in schools. Use of utilities.	Use of operating systems: Solving problems on the level of the operating system; use of utilities. Getting acquainted with the role of networks. The basics of networks.
Running programs		Use of computers in learning and acquiring knowledge through educational programs.	
Converting to algorithms	Composing algorithms in text and diagrams, and understanding them.	Developing algorithms through text and diagrams. Coding a simple algorithm.	Developing algorithms and coding. Knowledge of a few commands in a programming language.
Computer aided problem solving		Logical games. Simulating random events. Modelling simple natural and economic events.	Modelling processes. Optimisation. Fine-tuning existing programs in order to solve problems.
Constructing, editing text and pictures		The meaning of text and picture construction, editing. The basic handling of a word processor and a drawing tool.	A more thorough view of the functions of word processing and picture editing. Knowledge of the main functions of a word processor and a picture editor.
Databases and spreadsheets		Introduction to databases and spreadsheets: Simple search problems. Connection between data.	Function of spreadsheets. Entering and editing data. Basic ideas of functions, graphs, diagrams, histograms, connections and differences. Problems of searching and queries in databases. Maintenance of databases.

For convenience, the table of requirements presented here (in Table 2) encompasses a short abstract of the first categories only. The field to be investigated is that of informatics, including the ability to access, process, and transmit information, as well as the legal and ethical issues of information handling.

Educators of all subjects have to use materials, taking several common concepts into consideration - among others, the craft of learning, thinking, self education, exploration and problem solving using all available tools. Most of the information that reaches us today is transmitted not by natural means, but through artificial channels. Students have to master the ability to sort out the important pieces from the mass of information poured on them. The field of informatics thus represents a major part in education, even if the proportion in the table does not reflect this emphasis. The versatility of the computer in itself, and as part of a wide network, provides a new tool that is increasingly available, thus having to be accounted for in sophisticated problem solving that is of concern to various fields.

The main source of today's learning is centred in modern libraries, thus the importance of searching, finding, abstracting, and handling information according to needs has to be mastered through the sub-field of library informatics.

With younger age groups, the main issues of traditional library use are investigated: printed and non-printed document types and their characteristics; tools used for direct and indirect orientation; writing up on a theme using library materials and documents; information centres, libraries, databases; the ability of using libraries to search for information; main steps and methods in independent information acquisition; and the need for proper form and ethical references.

With older age groups, the tools for orientation in libraries have to include knowledge about: data storage and advanced forms and techniques of information processing; computerised catalogues, bibliographies and other library related databases; techniques of intellectual work, independent acquisition of knowledge, acquiring and deepening knowledge about library use and its complex role in problem solving.

3   BACKGROUND OF TEACHER TRAINING IN HUNGARY

There are three other universities besides Loránd Eötvös University (ELTE) in Hungary that are involved in the training of secondary school teachers: Attila József University of Arts and Sciences (Szeged), Lajos Kossuth University of Arts and Sciences (Debrecen), and the University of Veszprém (Veszprém). There are five colleges in Hungary that are involved in training elementary school teachers: Gyula Juhász College of Education (Szeged), Dániel Berzsenyi College of Education (Szombathely), György Besenyei College of Education (Nyiregyháza), Károly Eszterházy College of Education (Eger), and the Teacher Training College-Level Faculty at ELTE (Budapest).

Continuous consultations and coordination over the past few years led to two systems for the development of graduation requirements being equally accepted and put in place recently (one at university level and the other at college level). The next step in this co-ordinated system should look at how attained credit levels in subjects can facilitate the mobility of students, enabling them to complete part of their studies in one university and part in another.

At present, the number of informatics/computer science teachers who have already graduated or are presently studying is about 2,800 to 2,900. Among these, 1,710 students graduated from the Loránd Eötvös University and Lajos Kossuth University and the number of students presently studying there is about 800. At Attila József University, the University of Veszprém and at the teacher colleges, the graduation of informatics teachers goes back historically only two years, with a very small number of students graduating each year (between 15 and 30 per year). The first informatics teachers graduated about 10 years ago. Since then 2 to 3 generations of computers have changed in schools, not to mention the changes of software. About 2 to 3 informatics teachers per school is the target aimed at, which means that about 10 to 15 thousand teachers of informatics are necessary, far more than can be trained in the near future.

Another possible path to provide for an adequate IT application in education is through teachers of subjects other than informatics. Librarian informatics is a new subject that can be chosen only very recently, thus the graduation of such teachers can only be realised in the future. Basic IT education for other teachers is in an even worse situation.

4   CONCEPTS IN TEACHING APPLICATION SYSTEMS

Concentrating on basic IT concepts, the aim of teaching lies in its uses in everyday life. Thus the tools of IT, both hardware and software, have to be considered as a single unit, providing a solution for a targeted job. Their possibilities and limits of use reflect the value of their application. This value, however, does not mean the range of technical tricks attainable, but the path of possible solutions regarding the problem itself (Turcsányi-Szabo, 1995). A teacher of informatics looks upon application systems with a technical mind and not through the emerging problems that life produces, so, the inner values of solving the problem proper are not thought about. But teachers dealing with an individual subject and its underlying philosophy could see a more realistic solution for adoption, deepening subject knowledge through sophisticated means. Let us investigate a few examples.

Transmitting information
Computer related tools help in transmitting visual and verbal information through artificial channels to humans. The dimension of information and its information content determines its value. The form of the message determines primarily the emotional value of perception (Moles, 1958). Regardless of the final form of presentation (paper or electronic), readability and formal emphasis adds great value to the interpretation of information.

The most general form of transmitting messages is through writing. Developing written information incorporates all functions, starting from the emergence of need to the achievement of the final version, including composition, checks, formulation, and illustration (Williams, 1991). Tools should provide a flexible environment for development, while methods should involve a deeper insight into composing and representing information, including: sophisticated techniques of composition; aesthetics of the final product; illustrations; the ability to emphasise information properly; the techniques of accessing, searching, selecting, processing electronic information in databases, arranging, sorting documents, and making one's way through the vast amount of information available.

Linguistic structures

The use of spelling, language, and stylistic checkers can only be valued realistically if the underlying mechanism of the tool is well understood. The modelling of language helps in understanding our own language structures as well as understanding the boundaries of interactive question-and-answer systems and programming languages (Turcsányi-Szabo, 1993).

Drawing and picture editing

The choice and use of the proper drawing tool, be it either bit or vector based, does not primarily require the mastering of the techniques of software, but the understanding of visual perception and the aesthetics of development. Graphical user interfaces help manoeuvring within systems, electronic books, accessing information and invoking events, which require the basic understanding of symbols, icons, and pictograms.

Spreadsheets, and the visualisation of quantitative information

The visualisation of quantitative information through spreadsheets and graphing tools might not only need the techniques of how to use the software, but the understanding and proper use of visual symbols and aesthetics of representation (Tufte, 1983).

Multimedia

Voice addition enhances user interfaces and multimedia products, adding a new dimension of value. Voices and tones play a large role in non-verbal communication. Thus, it is necessary to become acquainted with the forms of symbolic expression through sounds. It is likely that animation adds a great deal to a presentation, giving dynamism by changing pictures parallel to sound effects. The animation of processes helps the understanding of aspects otherwise unexpressed.

Modelling

Developing models through a simple programming language facilitates the understanding of computer mechanisms, as well as a means of accepting the boundaries and possibilities of its extension.

5   CONCLUSION

Teachers of informatics should not only look upon application systems with a technical mind, but also with an eye for the emerging problems that life offers, providing inner purpose for solving a problem proper. Teacher training programs in subject areas other than informatics are urged to include IT usage, to deepen subject knowledge. Meanwhile, the mission of informatics teachers should be extended to developing their knowledge for other teachers in schools.

6   REFERENCES

130/1995 Government Regulation the National Curriculum, in Hungarian Gazette, Official Paper of the Republic of Hungary 1995, No. 91.

Moles, A.A. (1958) *Théorie de l'information et perception esthétique*, Flammarion.

Turcsányi-Szabo, M. (1993) *Where to place LOGO in teacher training*, in Proceedings of the Fourth European Logo Conference, University of Athens, Department of Informatics, pp. 201-209.

Turcsányi-Szabo, M. (1995) *Learn to Apply*, in Proceedings of the 6th National Conference on IT Applications, Siófok, Hungary, pp. 364-372.

Tufte, E. R. (1983) *The Visual Display of Quantitative Information*. Graphics Press.

Williams, N. (1991) *The Computer, the Writer, and the Learner*. Springer-Verlag.

7   BIOGRAPHY

Márta Turcsányi-Szabó received both B.S. and M.S. degrees in Computer Science from Loránd Eötvös University (Budapest, Hungary). She started working on research before graduation in 1979, and since then has gone on to teach as well. Devoted to the use of Logo since 1982, she has written several educational materials and programs on the subject. Her present research field includes application systems, educational use of computers, and design of educational programs. Her research area is focused on developing educational microworlds for children which give motivation to the study of different subjects.

8

The TTACOS Project - laying the foundation for national technology standards for students in the United States

Harriet G. Taylor
EDAF - 111 Peabody Hall, Louisiana State University
Baton Rouge, LA 70803-4121, USA

Lajeane G. Thomas
Louisiana Tech University
P. O. Box 3161, Ruston, LA 71272 USA

Abstract

The International Society for Technology in Education (ISTE) is collaborating with professional organisations to develop technology standards for pre-college students. In the first phase of the project, basic assumptions and broad categories for the standards have been identified and distributed for public input. A key part of the process was the TTACOS Project in which educators across the nation provided their ideas about technology standards on-line. The standards project, including TTACOS, is one of a series of initiatives by ISTE to produce formal guidelines for technology teachers and learners in the United States. These efforts are described, with an emphasis on the multi-year standards project and the framework developed through the TTACOS Project.

Keywords

Information technology, national policies, standards

1 INTRODUCTION

As computers and information technology become part of most American schools, the need for national standards for the use of technology in education increases dramatically. National standards that define what all students should know about and be able to do with technology lay a foundation for the integration of technology into education at all levels.

The International Society for Technology in Education (ISTE) has provided leadership in the United States in the field of educational technology. In 1993, ISTE began an initiative to develop technology standards for all students. Since technology touches virtually all students and subjects, ISTE formed an extensive partnership network with the major professional educational societies. At the same time, ISTE sought funding for the project from a variety of national sources and private foundations.

ISTE also began the TTACOS Project. TTACOS, or Teachers, Technology, and Children On-Line Standards Project, was a project to solicit ideas for standards from classroom teachers. The TTACOS Project provided valuable data that helped to categorise the technology standards. The framework and domain classifications that were developed are the foundations of the effort to develop national standards that will be recognised for their validity and utilised across the nation as benchmarks for all students in K-12 education.

2   BACKGROUND

2.1 National emphasis on standards

In recent years, national policy makers have begun to emphasise equality and quality of educational opportunities for all students and to link legislation and funding to recognised standards for student achievement. The recent Goals 2000: Educate America Act has been a major contributor to the standards movement, particularly in the area of technology (Donovan, 1994). Funding for technology is tied to state and district technology plans, which often must include indicators linked to existing curriculum area standards.

Professional organisations within the United States have developed standards for a variety of curriculum areas. In many cases, the standards have had a significant impact on educational practices and assessment. For example, the mathematics standards (NCTM, 1989) have been the major catalyst for mathematics reform within the United States. Thus, there is a mandate for technology standards that meet the national goals and support the existing standards movements in all subject areas.

2.2 Previous ISTE initiatives

In 1989, ISTE formed an alliance with the National Council for Accreditation of Teacher Education (NCATE) and began an extensive project to develop standards for teacher preparation programs. ISTE developed standards for 4 programs to prepare technology specialists for schools (Thomas, 1993). These standards underwent an extensive validation process before adoption by NCATE (Taylor, 1993; Thomas, 1994). They are now utilised in the evaluation (Abramson, 1993) of teacher preparation programs within the United States.

Embedded within the ISTE/NCATE standards are a set of Foundations for All Teachers (Friske et al, 1995) specifying reasonable technology competencies to prepare all teachers. In an effort to create more dramatic impact on teacher education, ISTE lobbied to create changes within the NCATE professional unit standards (NCATE, 1995). These are standards that are applied to the entire professional education unit, not just the technology speciality programs. They include indicators for faculty and student development, technology infrastructure and support, and curricula. ISTE was gratified when the NCATE produced its first unit standards revision in more than a decade and included many of the technology indicators suggested by ISTE (Thomas, 1995).

2.3 ISTE standards project

Four phases
The standards project was broken into phases for implementation and funding purposes. These include the development of the following standards over a three to four year period:
• Technology Foundations Standards.
• Standards for Using Technology in Learning and Teaching.
• Educational Technology Support Standards.
• Standards for Student Assessment and Evaluation of Technology Use.

In the first phase of this federally funded project, assumptions and broad categories of standards for what students should know about and be able to do with technology were identified and sent for public review. Initial drafts advocate establishment of learning environments that facilitate communication skills, creativity, collaborative learning, problem-solving, and informed decision-making. They are aimed at providing students with fundamental technology skills learned through practice in meaningful settings, and developing responsible, ethical attitudes towards technology and learning.

Partners
ISTE has joined with other major professional educational organisations in the development of technology standards. These include:
• American Federation of Teachers (AFT).
• Association for Supervision and Curriculum Development (ASCD).
• Council of Chief State School Officers (CCSSO).
• National Association of Secondary School Principals (NASSP).
• National School Boards Association (NSBA).
• National Education Association (NEA).
• Software Publishers Association (SPA).

Curriculum liaisons will lead in the development of technology standards for their subject areas. The materials developed will be distributed by professional organisations through print media, conferences, teleconferences, town meetings, and the World Wide Web.

3   TTACOS PROJECT

3.1 Overview

To start the standards project, ISTE inaugurated the TTACOS Project. TTACOS, or Teachers, Technology, and Children On-Line Standards Project, was developed to solicit ideas for standards from classroom teachers in the United States. Unlike the previous accreditation project which started with a research base and then moved to practitioners, this project began with brainstorming with educators to develop initial models for the standards.

TTACOS first targeted teachers in two states, Florida and Texas, known for progressive support of technology in their schools as well as for well-developed state networks that reached virtually all of the teachers. TTACOS went on-line for three months in 1994 and 1995. Educators were asked to provide three items that should be standards for students in their grade and or subject area. In addition, they were encouraged to describe a favourite classroom technology activity for inclusion in an anthology of classroom practice.

The two test states, Texas and Florida, each contained large state technology organisations which conducted national conferences in the spring of 1995. To reach a broader cross-section of the population, the ISTE committee conducted live sessions at these conferences to determine additions and refinements to the data collected on-line.

3.2 Domains

The TTACOS survey instrument was free-format. Often data sent in was in activity form rather than competency format. This data proved quite valuable, however, because the same key topics and ideas were repeatedly mentioned by virtually all of the teachers. These included phrases such as keyboarding, word processing, databases, content specific tools, creating presentations, problem solving, telecommunications, and resource acquisition. For the live sessions, these were categorised into four broad areas, and sample competency examples at 4 different developmental ages were presented for each area. This was done to define and illustrate the scope of the possible standards for the educators at the live sessions and to allow them to input suggestions for changing the framework on a more concrete level.

About six months were spent analysing, refining, and categorising the data collected in the various TTACOS activities. This produced a set of underlying assumptions and also resulted in an initial framework of knowledge and skills domains for the technology standards (Thomas et al, 1996). The domains included Basic Operations and Concepts; Social, Ethical, and Human Issues; Productivity Tools; Technology Tools for Communications; and Technology Tools for Research, Problem-Solving and Decision-Making.

Basic operations and concepts
Includes areas such as operation of systems, basic concepts and terminology, limitations and uses of technology, connectivity and compatibility, attitudes towards

technology, adaptive/assistive technologies, and collaborative and personal productivity strategies.

Social, ethical, and human issues

Includes areas such as historical and societal impact of technology, issues related to automation and retraining, evaluation of technology usefulness for tasks, hardware/software requirements and resources, becoming technology consumers, privacy, copyright, and intellectual property rights, responsible and ethical decisions and behaviour.

Productivity tools

Includes areas such as word processing, databases, spreadsheets, utility programs, telecommunications, multimedia use (graphics, animation, video, sound, presentation), emerging technologies and collaborative process tools.

Technology tools for communications

Includes areas such as traditional and emerging library skills, remote information resources, electronic communications, distance learning and teleconferencing, networking and research skills, management of information.

Tools for research, problem-solving, and decision-making

This involves a higher-order use of many of the tools and skills identified in the previous domains and includes areas such as combining tools to solve problems, utilisation of specialised productivity tools, self-monitoring of effectiveness, collaborative skills, critically consuming information, construction of knowledge environments.

4 THE FUTURE

The TTACOS domains document and structure is being developed into a survey instrument which will be administered by the national partners. Funds for meetings of partners and a national initiative to conclude the first phase have been generated. Efforts continue to seek funding for the other stages and to move the process forward. These efforts have been heightened by an impatient public, which is now demanding the standards. The current plan is to produce useful products within the year to meet the national demands as phase one of the project. The final versions of the standards will be disseminated in a variety of ways, including the ISTE World Wide Web page http://isteonline.uoregon.edu.

5 CONCLUSIONS

The International Society for Technology in Education has undertaken an initiative to develop standards for students and technology. These standards reflect a movement from the traditional teacher-dominated classroom environments to restructured learning environments. They feature student-centred instruction, multi-modality stimulation, multimedia, collaborative work, information exchange, exploration and inquiry, critical thinking, and informed decision making. Technology is intertwined in the fabric of learning at all levels.

Standards outlining what students should know about and be able to do with technology provide a vision for the future. The TTACOS Project has produced an ambitious range of domains and basic assumptions. The challenge now is to work as a nation to produce standards to reflect our national goals and needs and ensure that resources are provided so that all learners may meet these goals through quality education and lifelong learning.

6   REFERENCES

Abramson, G. (1993) Technology and the teacher education accreditation process. *Educational Technology Review*, Autumn/Winter, 27-30.

Donovan, F. and Sneider, C. (1994) Setting and meeting the national standards - With help from technology. *Technology and Learning*, **15**, 1, 40-48.

Friske, J., Knezek, D., Taylor, H., Thomas, L. and Wiebe, J. (1995) ISTE's technology foundation standards for all teachers: Time for a second look? *Journal of Computing in Teacher Education*, **12**, 2, 9-12.

NCATE (1995) *Standards, Procedures, and Policies for Accreditation of Professional Education Units*. NCATE, Washington, D. C.

NCTM (1989) *Curriculum and Evaluation Standards for School Mathematics*. National Council of Teachers of Mathematics, Reston, Virginia.

Taylor, H., Thomas, L. and Knezek, D. (1993) The development and validation of NCATE-approved standards for computer science teacher preparation programs. *Journal of Technology in Teacher Preparation,* **1**, 4, 319-333.

Thomas, L. (ed.) (1993) *Curriculum Guidelines for Accreditation of Educational Computing and Technology Programs* (2nd edition). ISTE, Eugene, Oregon.

Thomas, L. (1995) NCATE releases new unit accreditation guidelines: Standards for technology are included. *Journal of Computing in Teacher Education*, **11**, 1, 5-7.

Thomas, L., Taylor, H. and Knezek, D. (1996) New learning environments for the 21st century: Technology standards for K-12 education. *Proceedings of the International Conference on Technology in Education*, New Orleans, pp. 323-325.

Thomas, L., Wiebe, J., Friske, J., Knezek, D., Sloan, S. and Taylor, H. (1994) The development of accreditation standards in computing/technology education. *Journal of Computing in Teacher Education*, **10**, 4, 19-28.

7   BIOGRAPHY

Harriet G. Taylor is Associate Professor of Education at Louisiana State University. She is currently a member of the ISTE Board and the ISTE Accreditation and Professional Standards Committee. She is active in several international initiatives and is an elected member of the IFIP Working Group 3.1 on Secondary Education.

Lajeane G. Thomas is a Distinguished Professor in the College of Education at Louisiana Tech University. She is currently on special assignment serving as Project Administrator for the Goals 2000/LaNIE Program and the Louisiana Technology Learning Challenge Grant. She is a past president of ISTE and is the chair of the ISTE Accreditation and Professional Standards Committee.

9

A dichotomy of purpose: the effect on teachers of government initiatives in information technology

Deryn M. Watson
School of Education, King's College London
Waterloo Road, London SE1 8WA, UK

Abstract

One perspective on the last twenty years, which has seen the introduction of computers in education in the UK, is that it has been an enormously successful and dynamic time. An alternative perspective which I propose here, is that this period has been characterised by a confusion of purpose and lack of clarity of objectives. A chronology of national initiatives indicates conceptual confusion as to the role of Information Technology (IT) within schools, a dichotomy of purpose, and the shifting climate from Computer Assisted Learning (CAL) to IT skills. These initiatives have also shifted their focus away from software development, to in-service training and support through a number of short-lived agencies each with changing foci for implementation. I believe this has inhibited the success of in-service and explains the relatively infrequent use of IT by teachers in schools.

Keywords

Secondary education, curriculum policies, implications, information technology, innovation, national policies

1   INTRODUCTION

The growing interest for over twenty years in the role of computers in education in the UK is evidenced by a sequence of national initiatives.

1. National Development Programme in Computer Assisted Learning (NDPCAL) 1973-7: 35 different projects developing and evaluating CAL materials.
2. Microelectronics in Education Programme (MEP) 1980-86: projects in curriculum development; regional centres established for training and resourcing/information.
3. Micros in Education Support Unit (MESU) 1986-8: software development, teacher training and resourcing/information support, but in different bases.

4. National Council for Educational Technology (NCET) from 1988: absorbed an older advisory body (CET) and MESU to act as the agency for a new government initiative, IT in Schools.

5. Information Technology in Schools from 1987: a new government strategy replacing national projects with various grants focused on hardware upgrades and the development of training support for teachers, advisers and trainers.

6. IT in the National Curriculum 1989-95: IT became the only "cross-curricular" subject to be incorporated into the enacted orders of the new National Curriculum (1988). At first IT was part of Technology (DES, 1990), but following the Dearing review in 1994 it was eventually identified as a separate subject (DFE, 1995).

A biennial series of statistical bulletins shows that the number of computers in schools has grown over the same period. However research suggests that IT use is not commonplace, and that there are still a number of barriers to the incorporation of IT into the syllabus.

2 ABSENCE OF CONSISTENCY AND DIRECTION

2.1 Confusion of role

NDPCAL worked with a clear pedagogic definition of Computer Assisted Learning (CAL)(Hooper, 1975), that is, using 'computers as a learning resource', and he stated that there was a distinct difference between teaching people with computers, and teaching people about computers.

MEP identified two different areas of territory to be covered. First, the investigation of the most appropriate ways of using the computer as an aid to teaching and learning, maintaining the perspective of CAL. In principle software could be developed for computer based learning across the curriculum, but the programme gave priority to applications in mathematics, the sciences, craft/design technology, geography and courses related to business and clerical occupations. The second area was the introduction of new topics in the curriculum, either as separate disciplines, or as new elements in existing subjects. These included microelectronics in control technology, electronics, computer studies, computer linked studies such as computer aided design, data logging and data processing, word processing, and the use of computers as a means of information retrieval from databases (Fothergill, 1981).

During the period 1980-88 there was a proliferation of courses in computer science and computer studies for pupils at both 14 and 16+. Teaching about the computer gained attention, and made increasing demands upon the availability of hardware. In contrast came the publication of a series of reports from subject associations, commissioned by the DES to identify the role of IT for each subject area. These universally espoused the value of CAL for their discipline. But it was a growing separation of CAL from other aspects of learning about and with the technology that I believe heralded the confusion of purpose that is apparent in subsequent curriculum documents.

2.2 Developing IT concepts

This apparent confusion of purpose was reflected in the documents that lie at the core of current national perspectives of IT that now influence schools. An examination of three key documents enables me to chart shifts in the definition and role of IT.

Information Technology from 5 - 16

This document reflects the dual perception as it 'sets out to help schools devise a coherent strategy for making effective use of IT, both in the enrichment of existing subjects and in learning about the technology itself'. Under the aims, it states clearly that 'Although IT is only one of a host of important factors affecting society and schools today, it is unusual among current agencies of change in that it impinges directly on the learner at all ages; on the nature and content of study; and therefore on the curriculum and the teacher' (HMI, 1989). It continues by laying out a clear framework of purpose for the use of IT in schools.

'Through the use of IT in the curriculum, schools will also be helping pupils become knowledgeable about the nature of information, comfortable with the new technology and able to exploit its potential. The aims of working with IT are:
i. to enrich and extend learning throughout the curriculum, using the technology to support collaborative learning, independent study and re-working of initial ideas as well as to enable pupils to work at a more demanding level by obviating some routine tasks;
ii. to help young people acquire confidence and pleasure using IT, become familiar with some everyday applications and be able to evaluate the technology's potential and limitations;
iii.to encourage the flexibility and openness of mind necessary to adjust to, and take advantage of, the ever-quickening pace of technological change, while being alert to the ethical implications and consequences for individuals and society;
iv. to harness the power of technology to help pupils with special educational needs or physical handicaps to increase their independence and develop their interests and abilities;
v. to help interested pupils undertake detailed study of computing and to design IT systems for solving problems.'
(HMI, 1989)

There are two distinct approaches incorporated here, with a pedagogic role at first being followed by vocational and somewhat technocentric aspects in two and three. These aims are supported by a detailed list of objectives and translated into specific issues that can be addressed. Geography, for instance. is described as 'one useful model of how IT concepts can be related to activities in various subject studies'. The aims were converted into 'IT concepts and objectives', listed as communicating, data handling, modelling etc. These, by the end of the document, have become central, and a subject is demoted to being merely a context for delivery. Thus IT concepts and skills are defined as being separate from CAL for subject-based learning.

Information technology in the National Curriculum

The dichotomy noted above continues in the National Curriculum Technology document (DES, 1990); teachers are exhorted to take both approaches, but at different stages one message appears to be more important than the other.

IT is defined thus:

'Pupils should be able to use Information Technology to :
• communicate and handle information.
• design, develop, explore and evaluate models of real or imaginary situations.
• measure and control physical variables and movement.
They should also be able to make informed judgements about the application and importance of information technology, and its effect on the quality of life.'
(DES, 1990)

These are in effect a condensed form of the IT concepts the HMI document identified. The related programmes of study are then defined:

'In each key stage pupils should develop information technology capabilities through a range of curriculum activities which will:
• develop confidence and satisfaction in the use of information technology;
• broaden pupils' understanding of the effects of the use of information technology;
• encourage the flexibility needed to take advantage of future developments in information technology;
• enable pupils to become familiar with the computer keyboard;
• encourage the development of perseverance;
• enable pupils to take greater responsibility for their own learning, and provide opportunities for them to decide when it is appropriate to use information technology in their work.' (DES, 1990)

Although related to the HMI aims, the vocational aspects are dominant and increasingly technocentric. It is difficult to relate many of these capabilities to a subject-centred curriculum learning purpose. In the Teachers' Notes on IT in the National Curriculum (NCC, 1991) IT is referred to as a tool in the curriculum with 'a number of functions'.

Rewriting the National Curriculum

By 1994 it was apparent that the attempt to maintain the dual role of IT as a tool to deliver the curriculum and as a subject with a conceptual and skills basis in its own right was under substantial strain. In the Dearing review, IT is separated from Technology (DFE, 1995):

'IT capability is characterised by an ability to use effectively IT tools and information sources to analyse, process and present information, and to model, measure and control external events. This involves:
• using information sources and IT tools to solve problems;

- using IT tools and information sources, such as computer systems and software packages to support learning in a variety of contexts;
- understanding the implications of IT for working life and society.

Pupils should be given opportunities, where appropriate, to develop and apply their IT capability in their study of National Curriculum subjects.' (DFE, 1995)

So following the familiar list of IT concepts and skills, the role of a tool to support subject-based learning has been reduced to a mere recommendation.

2.3 Dichotomy of purpose

Thus it would appear that the notion of CAL has been made more diffuse by the increasing notion of separate concepts and skills of IT. It is, I believe, this which has made for problems of misunderstanding the role of IT within specific subjects. Where geography teachers may chose to use a data base to encourage pupils to pose and test hypotheses about, for example, population growth, at the same time they are being asked to teach about data retrieval and ensure that a specific and measurable IT capability is delivered. At every stage a teacher using IT has added complexity and potential conflict of purpose. Although the documents espouse the role of computers to support learning and teaching, the phrase CAL has almost completely disappeared.

It seems to me that the increasing interest in the notion of IT skills, and the shift to support the use of commercially based IT packages, is geared to prepare pupils for the world of work, and thus is more related to a vocational than a pedagogic rationale (Hawkridge, 1990). Elsewhere this has been referred to as the 'commodification' of education.

2.4 Disjointed teacher training

Since 1980 in-service education has been a part of the national strategy for bringing about the IT revolution in schools. But as with the articulation of the purpose of educational computing, every few years the style and means of implementation has changed.

In MEP teacher training was focused on initial awareness courses to be followed by longer (up to one week) and further (up to three months) specialist courses. The majority of these were to be delivered through new regional centres, not existing institutional bases. A large numbers of teachers attended awareness courses, and the director of MEP, Fothergill, claimed that a quarter of all teachers in UK had been on an MEP in-service training (INSET) course and used computer based learning materials. But it is clear that the impact of their training was minimal. Indeed, Her Majesty's Inspectorate (HMI) reported that 'too late in the day, did they address a major need: to see the role of the new technology through the eyes of the uncommitted classroom teacher and assess the likely contribution which IT was observed to be making to learning in ordinary lessons' (1987). Although there had been successes, these 'need to be seen against a background where the majority of pupils and teachers rarely used microcomputers'. HMI commented on the 'cascade' approach to INSET: 'some teachers were unable to obtain sufficient time on return to school to cascade'. During any school visit, HMI also found that where teachers were using or teaching about the new technology, their initial training had in only rare instances provided a foundation in IT work.

In MESU the dissemination mechanism changed. Working directly with Local Education Authorities (LEAs) and higher education institutions, the focus shifted on 'training the trainers' rather than engaging directly with teachers in schools. The software development component rapidly shifted to the development of courses and training materials for advisory teachers. In 1988 the new IT in Schools initiative was announced, as a 'major new strategy on new technology in schools'. MESU was closed; the central thrust of the strategy to be serviced by NCET, focused almost exclusively on in-service training. Software development was not mentioned, which heralded the subsequent emphasis on the role of general purpose, commercially designed packages for curriculum delivery. Different course materials were produced which replaced the earlier ones with the curriculum emphasis.

By the late eighties there was an increasing perception that the training provision, both in-service and pre-service, had been piecemeal and ineffective. A survey of IT use in schools (DES, 1989) showed that although half the teachers in secondary schools had been on initial awareness training, less than 25% reported to have made significant use of computers, except those in computer and business studies, and on average less than 10% reported that IT made a substantial contribution to teaching and learning. The Trotter Report (1989) painted a woeful picture, claiming that most aspects of the initial teacher training system were not equipped to keep pace with and make a proper contribution to the developments in IT use in schools. The Parliamentary Office for Science and Technology report (POST, 1989) was critical of aspects of policy and in particular a lack of clarity of objective and consistency of strategy.

A substantial proportion of the IT in schools grants initiatives in the mid-nineties still focus on training courses and materials, in recognition of the failures of the last fifteen years. The changing perception of a role for IT in the curriculum has created a confusing pattern in which classroom teachers find themselves exhorted to use the new technologies.

3   THE REALITY IN SCHOOLS

The effect of this confusion and ever-shifting perceptions may be one reason for the evidence of relatively little take-up and regular use of CAL or IT skills in schools. The latest statistical bulletin, (DFE, 1995) shows still less than 10% of teachers (apart form those of computer and business studies) reported IT making a substantial contribution to teaching and learning; little change in the last six years.

ImpacT was a major national research project, 1989-1992, that engaged in a longitudinal in-depth research study on the role of IT in pupils' learning (Watson, 1993). Despite extensive monitoring of resources and use, little discernible difference in effect was established between classes with widely different resourcing. The effects of IT use on pupils' learning was only clearly established in two subjects, mathematics and geography. The overall message from the ImpacT project was that while some valuable IT work was taking place in subject classrooms, this was not happening widely. Where it was happening, the role and perceptions of the teacher, above all other variables, was critical.

The case study component of the project enabled a more detailed exploration of the motivations behind those teachers who did use IT. It was the keen IT users who managed, despite considerable organisational difficulties, to obtain access to resources and who were flexible in their approach to its use. Often it was only their interest which persuaded schools to take advantage of hardware purchase schemes. In particular it was these teachers who recognised and enjoyed the pedagogic potential of IT because it related to their own philosophical underpinnings about teaching, and the nature of their subject. Few of these teachers had been on any in-service courses associated with the national initiatives. They were at home with CAL; they 'taught with computers' rather than 'delivered IT'.

But the schools themselves and their colleagues did not display such confidence. Rather they reflected all the confusions of national policy on the ground. Headteachers and school prospectuses extolled the virtues of computers to enhance subject learning. But in these same schools the computer rooms were almost universally booked for business information skills, and basic IT skills courses. Pupils would 'do' a term of word processing, but not then use the application again for any normal curriculum work. Recent OFSTED (1995) inspection reports confirm that IT has barely impacted upon the work of teachers and pupils. Following the Dearing review there is a real danger that IT will become the domain of specialist teachers.

While there are strong economic and social pressures for incorporating IT into schooling, there are also resistances. Skillbeck (1975) distinguishes between curriculum change that may be planned by the participants who wish to change the situation for their own satisfaction, and change which is haphazard, which the participant may chose to accept or reject. He draws a further distinction between change that builds upon the established system, and change which by being more disruptive and comprehensive provides genuine innovation. The fact that the introduction of IT can be defined as both hazardous and disruptive contributes to the problems of incorporating it into the school curriculum.

It is my contention that the range of government initiatives has simply made the process more complex and haphazard. The confusion over the role and purpose is mirrored in schools; the piecemeal and inconsistent in-service provision appears to have left little impact upon the profession itself. There is a role for both computer assisted learning and the developing of IT skills and concepts in the curriculum. But it is still only those teachers who have a clear personal professional commitment to using computers for their own pedagogic ends who have brought about the only real change discernible in schools.

4   REFERENCES

DES (1989) *Survey of Information Technology in Schools:* Statistical Bulletin. DES, London.

DES (1990) *Technology in the National Curriculum.* HMSO, London.

DFE (1995) *Information Technology in the National Curriculum.* DFE, London.

DFE (1995) *Survey of Information Technology in Schools:* Statistical Bulletin. DFE, London.

Fothergill, R. (1981) *Microelectronics Education Programme: The Strategy.* DES, London.

Hawkridge, D. (1990) Who needs computers in schools, and why? in M. Kibby (ed.) *Computer Assisted Learning: selected proceedings from the CAL '89 Symposium.* Pergamon, Oxford.

HMI (1987) *Aspects of the Work of the Microelectronics Education Programme* . DES, London.

HMI (1989) *Information Technology from 5 to 16: Curriculum Matters 15.* HMSO, London.

Hooper, R. and Toye, I. (eds.) (1975) *Computer Assisted Learning in the United Kingdom: Some case studies.* Council for Educational Technology, London.

NCC (1991) *Information Technology in the National Curriculum: Teachers' Notes.* NCC, York.

OFSTED (1995) *Information Technology: a review of inspection findings, 1993/94.* HMSO, London.

POST (1991) *Technologies for Teaching: The Use of Technologies for Teaching and Learning in Primary and Secondary Schools* . Parliamentary Office of Science and Technology, London.

Skilbeck, M. (1975) School-based curriculum development and the task of in-service education, in E. Adam (ed.) *In-service education and teachers' centres.* Pergamon, Oxford.

Trotter, J. (1989) *Information Technology in Initial Teacher Training.* DES, London.

Watson, D.M. (ed.) (1993) *The ImpacT Report: An Evaluation of the Impact of Information Technology on Children's Achievements in Primary and Secondary Schools.* King's College, London.

5   BIOGRAPHY

Deryn Watson is a Senior Lecturer in Educational Computing. Since the mid-1970s she has been actively involved in the research and development of CAL materials in the humanities and languages, writing on both models of software development and the potential for interactive learning. She has researched into the impact of IT on children's learning; her current research is on those teachers who do use IT and the potential role of telematics.

Section 4: Exploring potential implementation of practices for teachers

10

Identification of the changes in attitude and pedagogical practices needed to enable teachers to use information technology in the school curriculum

Margaret J. Cox
School of Education, King's College London
University of London, Waterloo Rd., London SE1 8WA, UK

Abstract

Many different countries have been coping with the difficult decision of whether to include the teaching of information technology (IT) as a separate subject or to encourage the use of IT across the curriculum, within all traditional school subjects. Nations and individual schools which adopt the policy of teaching IT as a separate subject only have to persuade and effect the change in pedagogical practice of a small minority of teachers within a school, whereas if the policy is to effect an integration of IT right across the school curriculum, then the majority of teachers within a school have to change their pedagogical practice to make appropriate use of IT within their lessons.

Substantial research, based on the work of Fullan and others, has shown that a change in pedagogical practice not only depends upon the willingness of the individual teacher but on the policies and practices of the institution as a whole, and of the culture within that institution. Research at King's College into the uptake of computers in schools, the impact of teacher training, and the pedagogical practices in the classroom has provided evidence that the regular use of computers in the classroom is related to the attitude of the headteacher (principal), the attitude of the teachers to IT, their expectations of the learning impact of the technology, the responses of the pupils and the teachers' understanding of the role of the computer within the subject being taught.

This paper reviews the findings reported in the literature and more recent results being gathered from research into the uses of experienced and inexperienced IT teachers, being undertaken at King's College. This range of research results is used to support a theoretical framework relating the changes in pedagogical practices to the training needs of the class teacher. Consideration in this review will be given to the two approaches of using IT across the curriculum and teaching IT as a separate subject. It is argued that in order to bring about the necessary permanent changes in individual teachers' pedagogical practices, teacher trainers must regard the whole school as a living evolving organism which needs to be nurtured through training to become dependent upon IT and its ever changing environments for its future health and success.

Keywords
Teacher education, attitudes, classroom practice, integration, pedagogy, research

1   INTRODUCTION

For more than a decade there have been discussions in the international literature and amongst policy makers about whether computers in education (Information Technology in education) should be taught as a separate subject and/or integrated across the curriculum. This difficult decision has been influenced by national resource implications, the nature of hardware and software made available to schools, the pedagogical practices and national curriculum policies, and the level of expertise amongst the existing teacher profession. In spite of sustained government efforts through national programmes to establish regular integrated use of IT in schools there is still substantial evidence of the lack of successful integration as reported, for example, by the International Association for the Evaluation of Educational Achievement (Pelgrum and Plomp, 1991), in a study of the use of computers in education in 19 education systems, and in the recent IFIP working conference on Integrating Information Technology into Education (Watson and Tinsley, 1995).

In the UK there have been national programmes as long ago as 1973 to promote the use of computer assisted learning in education (Cox, 1983) and in recent years since the introduction of the National Curriculum in 1988 it has been government policy that IT should be used across the curriculum in all subjects wherever it was considered to be appropriate. However, in spite of these requirements which include the recent addition of IT as a separate subject, the IT practice and focus varies significantly from school to school. Evidence from research such as the Impact project (Watson, 1993) and the STAC project (Ridgway and Passey, 1995) has shown that not only does the level and nature of use depend upon the resource provision, access and particular curriculum requirements but that the majority of teachers involved in these studies lacked sufficient pedagogical skills to be able to use IT advantageously in their lessons and they were unaware of the substantial contribution IT can make to pupils' learning.

Although research has shown that the majority of teachers make insufficient effective use of IT, there is substantial research evidence over the past 20 years to show that using computers in education can enhance the learning of concepts, the development of process skills, and can promote a positive attitude towards learning. The work of Cox and Elton (1974), the Organisation for Economic Co-operation and Development (1987), Millar (1991), the Tools for Exploratory Learning Project (Bliss et al, 1992), Cox (1992), the Impact Project (Watson, 1993) and Nicholson (1993) are a few examples of many research studies which have shown positive gains in learning promoted by the use of IT in education.

Given that there are national requirements or programmes in many countries to promote the use of IT in schools and given that there is overwhelming evidence for the benefits which IT use can provide, why is there such resistance to change and what are the barriers which prevent the adoption and integration by teachers in the classroom? This paper provides evidence from two small scale research projects to support the research findings of others described above regarding these frequently raised questions.

2   USES OF INFORMATION TECHNOLOGY IN EDUCATION

To consider the changes in attitude and pedagogical practices needed to enable teachers to use IT in the school curriculum, firstly it is important to clarify the nature of IT use in educational establishments. The uses of IT in education broadly embrace four types of uses, as is shown in figure 1.

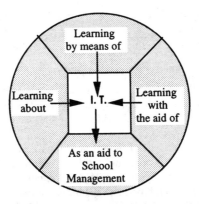

Figure 1 Interrelation among four different areas of Information Technology use

Van Weert (1986) defined these four areas of use as follows:
(i) Learning *about* information technology, which covers the learning about the social impact of IT; developing skills in the use of applications; learning the principles of programming; and of software and machinery structure.
(ii) Learning with *the aid of* information technology refers to a further aid to the learning process, such as a CD-ROM encyclopaedia, a graphics calculator, or sensors for collecting data; in all such cases the computer is used as a support or a resource, but does not provide the teaching modality.
(iii) Learning by *means of* information technology, as defined by van Weert, includes both Computer Assisted Learning (CAL) such as science and geography simulations and computer based modelling; and Computer Managed Learning (CML) referring to computer based programme management of a pupil's learning progress through a particular course.
(iv) Information technology as an aid to school *management,* refers to the use of IT for carrying out tasks related to the school management and to store information related to the students' learning progress.

From the research referred to earlier it is clear that to promote educational uses of IT to enhance learning in all subjects then it would be desirable for all teachers to achieve (ii) and (iii) above. However, a common way of promoting the use of IT in schools, in many countries, is to expect the teacher to teach about IT (i) and possibly to use IT for administration (iv). Several reasons are given for this restricted use: lack of resources, lack of trained teachers, insufficient time, and inappropriate software. What is rarely stated by policy makers is that to use IT as a means of enhancing learning often requires a substantial change in pedagogical practice, and that this change in pedagogy is closely related to the nature of the IT task. Even if innovative teachers can make this change the level of support through their institution may help them sustain this change or alternatively in many cases prevent successful integration taking place.

3   ATTITUDES TO USING IT IN EDUCATION

In a longitudinal study of IT use across the curriculum, Cox and Rhodes (1989) investigated the sustained integration of computer use in primary schools and the relationship between long term integration and the attitudes of the teachers in the schools. The research methodology used was qualitative, gathering evidence through a range of methods, including structured teacher interviews. Recent extensive analysis of the earlier data collected from 160 primary teacher interviews, 60 classroom observations, headteacher interviews, teacher trainer interviews and observations of six teacher training courses provided evidence of the teachers' attitudes towards the value of IT use in their schools.

Teachers were interviewed with different questions according to their use of IT in their classrooms. From observations and teachers' reported use over three years and their decision to attend further professional development courses, the teachers were grouped into categories: enthusiasts; dabblers; conformists; marginalists and disenchanted (Rhodes, 1996). Headteachers were classified according to the grouping by Bliss, Chandra and Cox (1986) as democratic, autocratic, and laissez-faire. Analysis of the data showed that where the head-teacher had a positive attitude to IT in education, and a democratic style of leadership, every teacher in the school had a positive attitude towards the use of IT and were classed as either enthusiasts or dabblers.

Where the headteacher had an indifferent or negative attitude towards the value of IT in education, then there were disenchanted non-users and marginalist lone users in their schools. If the headteacher had also a laissez-faire style of leadership then there was little growth in the use of IT in the school. Where the headteacher had an autocratic leadership style IT was introduced without the support of the staff and significant resentment was expressed by the class teachers about having to use IT.

Although this was not a large scale quantitative study using conventional attitude questionnaires, the extensive qualitative responses of the teachers and evidence of their IT use (or lack of it) indicates that both the leadership style and the attitudes of the headteacher to IT in education can be a major influence on the successful integration of IT use by the teacher in the classroom.

Evidence from this study reported earlier (Cox and Rhodes, 1989) also showed that the teacher's ability to integrate IT use in the lessons depended upon the type of educational software used. A second longitudinal study involving regular observations of two teachers using IT in a secondary school provides further evidence to support this finding.

4   PEDAGOGICAL PRACTICES

In a recent longitudinal project (Pittaway, 1996) two secondary school teachers were observed in their use of IT over a period of more than two years, involving classroom observations and teacher interviews. The teachers were chosen for the stages in their development of IT use. One teacher was the IT co-ordinator for the school and had been using IT for six years in mathematics, the other was a teacher enthusiastic but new to IT use who was also using it in mathematics with 13-14 year-old pupils. Extensive observations of the types of software chosen by these two teachers and the pedagogical practices in the classroom showed that the experienced IT teacher made careful preparation of the educational activities to be completed by the pupils using the software and also monitored their progress throughout the lessons regarding the content and relevance of the activities. She had developed a facilitating role with the pupils and was able to promote individualised learning and innovative uses of the software.

The inexperienced teacher, who for her non-IT lessons prepared class activities and questioned pupils regularly, discarded these pedagogical practices when using educational software and restricted herself entirely to technical advice on using the software. The teacher showed no inclination to supervise the educational aspects of the IT based lessons. This supports the findings of others that teachers get distracted by the technology and need to pass through this phase to obtain an appropriate change in pedagogical practice.

In the case of the inexperienced teacher she had only reached the first innovation stage of school IT development as indicated in Ridgway and Passey (1995). However, what is interesting here is that there was no evidence that either of these teachers had to make a significant change in their pedagogy. In the case of the experienced teacher she showed evidence over several years that innovation and change were part of her pedagogical practice and the inexperienced teacher had succeeded in using IT regularly but had avoided having to make any fundamental challenges to her values and class practice by marginalising herself from the educational activities of her IT lessons.

5   FRAMEWORK FOR THE INTEGRATION OF IT

The research reported here supports the work of others in developing plans for the successful integration of IT, however there are three particular aspects not often considered which are particularly relevant when considering different national priorities.

Teaching IT as a separate subject
If the decision is to teach IT only as a separate subject ((i) on Van Weerd's model) then the problems of headteacher support and co-operation amongst teachers of the institution as a whole does not arise since a small core of specialised teachers can deliver this curriculum. There is also less cost for in-service education of teachers. However, if as some countries are planning, the aim is to use such specialist teachers to train others in the school at some later stage then all the other issues described below will need to be addressed .

Evidence from research has also shown that it is possible to teach IT as a separate subject with little change in pedagogical practice other than organising the uses of the equipment and software.

One of the major dangers of adopting the policy of only teaching IT as a separate subject is that pupils will be deprived of the enhancements which IT use can bring to the learning of other subjects, and that those pupils not learning IT will be deprived of the opportunities to develop the very necessary range of IT skills for the workplace.

Integrating IT across the curriculum

The research described here has shown that if IT use is to be integrated across the curriculum that this implies not only that most of the teachers in the school will need adequate training and support but that if pupils are to use it regularly in any one subject then that subject teacher will need to use it every day in order to enable all pupil groups to use it even once every two weeks.

The implications in terms of resourcing and teacher education for IT across the curriculum are dependent upon many institutional factors described by Ridgway and Passey, such as the support of the senior management, in-service education, resources policy, etc. Extensive studies by Fullan (1991) on effective innovation in schools has shown that the three aspects, technological, cultural and political need to be addressed for institutionalisation of an innovation to be sustained. Evidence from a research project of Rosenholtz (1989) on teachers' communications in schools found that the majority of teachers were isolated from each other and there was a lack of collegiality and a lack of collective enterprise amongst teachers in a school. In a recent literature review by Grunberg (1996) of research into innovation in schools it was shown that a lack of collegiality within schools was a major factor in preventing innovation to be sustained.

Therefore, in order to deliver IT across the curriculum it is necessary to engage the whole school in the process of change. Using IT in lessons does not necessarily mean there is the required change in pedagogical practice. It is argued that in order to bring about the necessary permanent changes in individual teachers' pedagogical practices, teacher trainers must regard the whole school as a living evolving organism which needs to be nurtured through training to become dependent upon IT and its ever changing environments.

6   CONCLUSIONS

From the literature and the research reported here it is evident that there will be different teacher education requirements for teaching IT as a separate subject and integrating the use of IT across the curriculum. More than 20 years research has shown however that the use of IT across the curriculum enhances individual pupils' understanding, therefore the decision to teach IT as a separate subject without also including it across the curriculum may require less investment of resources and teacher education in the short term, but may well lead to a deprivation for the pupils and serious disadvantages to such an education system in the long term.

It cannot be assumed also that IT teachers will be able to train other teachers within a school since the whole issue of institutional culture and politics may mitigate against any fundamental change for the rest of the teachers. The question is really not can we afford to teach IT across the curriculum but can we afford not to?

7 REFERENCES

Bliss, J., Mellar, H., Ogborn, J. and Nash, C. (1992) *Tools for Exploratory Learning,* Technical Reports 1-5. King's College London.

Bliss, J., Chandra, P.A.J. and Cox, M.J. (1986) The Introduction of Computers into a School. *Advances in Computer Assisted Learning.* Pergamon, Oxford.

Centre for Educational Research and Innovation (1987) *Information Technologies and Basic Learning: Reading, Writing, Science and Mathematics.* Organisation for Economic Co-operation and Development, Paris.

Cox, M.J. and Elton, L.R.B. (1974) Solving Schrödinger's Equation with a Desk Calculator and Plotter. *American Journal of Physics,* **42,** 340-341.

Cox, M.J.(1983) Case Study of the Application of Computer Based Learning, in N.J. Rushby (ed.) *Computer Based Learning - State of the Art Report.* Pergamon, Oxford.

Cox, M.J. and Rhodes, V. (1989) *The Uptake of Computers in Primary Schools: Implications for Teacher Training.* Economic and Social Research Council, Ref. No. C 00232359.

Cox, M.J. (1992) The Computer in the Science Curriculum. *International Journal of Educational Research,* **17,** 1, 19-34. Pergamon Press, Oxford.

Fulham, M. (1991) *The new meaning of educational change.* Cassell Educational, London.

Millar, R. (1991) Why is science hard to learn? *Journal of Computer Assisted Learning,* **7,** 2, 66-74. Blackwell Scientific Publications, Oxford.

Nicholson, P. (1993) Facilitating Changes in Learning with Electronic Communications, in A. Knierzinger and M. Moser (eds.) *Informatics and Changes in Learning.* Proceedings of the IFIP Open Conference, June 7-11, Gmunden, Austria. Institute for School of New Technology, Linz, Austria.

Pelgrum, W.J and Plomp, T. (1991) *The Use of Computers in Education World-wide. Results for the IEA 'Computers in Education Survey of 19 Education Systems.* International Association for the Evaluation of Educational Achievement, Pergamon Press, Oxford.

Pittaway (unpublished, 1996) *The pedagogical practices of using IT in the classroom - and the changing advisory teacher's role.*

Rhodes, V. (unpublished, 1996) *The uptake of computers in school - implications for teacher training.* PhD Thesis.

Ridgway, J. and Passey, D. (1995) Using evidence about teacher development to plan systemic revolution, in D. Watson and D. Tinsley (eds.) *Integrating Information Technology into Education.* Chapman and Hall, London.

Rosenholtz, S. (1989) Effective Schools: Interpreting the Evidence. *American Journal of Education,* **93,** 3, 352-388.

Van Weert, T. (1986) A model syllabus for literacy in information technology for all teachers, in R. Ennals, R. Gwyn and Zdravchev (eds.) *Information Technology and education: the Changing School.* Ellis Horwood Ltd.

Watson, D. and Tinsley, D. (eds.) (1985) *Integrating Information Technology into Education*. Chapman and Hall, London.

Watson, D.M, (ed.) (1993) *The Impact Report - An Evaluation of the Impact of Information Technology on children's achievements in primary and secondary schools*. King's College, London.

8   BIOGRAPHY

Margaret Cox is currently a senior lecturer in educational computing at King's College London. She was co-ordinator for CAL at Surrey University for 10 years before taking up the post as Director of the Computers in the Curriculum Project in 1982 (to 1991) at Chelsea (now part of King's College). She was co-director of the UK government's ImpacT project from 1988 to 1991, director of the MODUS (Computer Based Modelling) Project from 1986 to the present, and the ESRC project (1985-1990) on the uptake of computers in primary schools. Her main research interests are the impact of IT on teaching and learning, CBL, modelling for learning, and the factors promoting the integration of IT in schools.

11

The centrality of affective variables in the implementation of a national strategy for teacher and pupil information technology suitability in elementary schools

Yaacov J. Katz
School of Education
Bar-Ilan University, Ramat-Gan 52900, Israel

Abstract

Empirical studies dealing with the relationship between personality and attitudinal variables on the one hand and computer related variables on the other have consistently indicated that not all teachers or pupils relate in the same positive way to the use of Information Technology (IT) in the educational situation. It appears that certain personality traits and attitudinal sets characterising teachers and pupils are related to positive computer related attitudes whereas other personality variables or attitudinal constructs are connected to less positive computer related attitudes.

A national strategy of introducing computers into the educational system should take personality and attitudinal variables of both teachers and pupils into consideration in order to achieve as efficient and as cost-effective a utilisation of computers in the classroom as possible. It is also postulated that different personality and attitudinal constructs will be related to differential attitudes towards the various hardware and software packages available for instruction and learning.

Keywords

Attitudes, instruction (CAI), pedagogy

1 INTRODUCTION

Modern society is becoming increasingly more dependent on information technology in general and on computers in particular in order to solve its daily problems. The educational system is becoming aware of the importance of computers in the teaching and learning domains and there is cautious optimism that the growing use of computers in schools may well bring about the long dreamed of educational revolution for teachers and pupils alike. The modern day educational system is attempting to rise to the challenges posed by computers, and it appears that computers have the potential to contribute to improved teacher skills and performance. Robinson (1989), in summing up almost twenty years of experience regarding the use of computers in the educational system, declared that it is now commonly accepted that computers should play a central role in education.

Other commentators, however, recognise that the educational impact of computers within the classroom has not as yet been efficiently maximised. The computer has not as yet become the potent force in the educational system as confirmed by Dunn and Ridgway (1991). These researchers put the lack of efficiency in computer use in the educational system down to the fact that not all teachers and pupils have the personality and attitudinal profiles necessary for the effective use of computers in the instructional and learning processes.

2 TEACHERS

One of the three main areas in which the computer can bring about positive change within the educational system is that of instruction (the other two being administration and auxiliary specialisations). Thus teachers are in the forefront of the technological revolution that is overtaking the educational system and have the potential to increase efficiency within the teaching process by effectively utilising the computer for Computer Assisted Instruction (CAI) which can include the use of drill and practice, the use of generic software for pupil-computer interaction, the use of databases and spreadsheets, as well as the use of individualised software programs for the benefit of heterogeneous learning groups. Schools are under increasing pressure to respond to the rapid changes occurring in modern society and as a result teachers will have to play an increasingly central role in utilising computers for the benefit of their pupils.

It appears that there is a significant correlation between teacher personality and the acceptance of computers as an effective instructional aid. Chandra, Bliss and Cox (1988) indicated that the attitudinal and personality sets of teachers seem to be important factors in their decisions to use (or disregard) computers in CAI, thus emphasising the centrality of teacher personality to positive computer oriented attitudes.

Offir and Katz (1990) indicated that teachers characterised by the ability to accept innovation and change are more willing to use computers as an instructional aid within the framework of CAI than teachers who prefer traditional teaching methods. In addition they confirmed that teachers who, by their very nature, are risk-takers in their personal and professional lives are more likely to have positive computer oriented attitudes than teachers who are cautious and fear taking risks. In a study which examined the personality attributes significantly correlated with positive computer oriented attitudes on the basis of the Eysenck Personality Questionnaire (Eysenck and Eysenck, 1975), Katz and Offir (1991) found that positive extraversion which includes loudness, boisterousness, and sociability; inverse neuroticism which includes calmness, flexibility, social adjustment and self-confidence; and positive psychoticism which includes impulsiveness, craving of change, as well as stimulus- and sensation-seeking are significantly related to positive attitudes of teachers towards the use of computers for instruction in the classroom situation.

Although Katz and Offir (1991) conducted their study using the Eysenckian personality model in Israel, a series of personality studies (Levin and Montag, 1987) have indicated a high level of similarity between the personality constructs and attitudes held by Israeli subjects, and those held by Western European, North American and Asian samples. Therefore it may be inferred that the personality attributes related to computer oriented attitudes in the sample of Israeli teachers could conceivably be correlated with computer linked orientations among teachers in other societies.

Evans, Katz and Francis (1995) indicated that, contrary to popular belief, there are no significant gender differences regarding positively oriented computer related attitudes among teachers. These results confirm earlier studies conducted by Hunt and Bohlin (1993) and Kay (1989) which intimated that no differences exist between male and female teacher trainees regarding computer attitudes. Evans, Katz and Francis (1995) further showed that teachers, familiar with computers as a result of home use or because they voluntarily attended computer courses, had a lower level of computer anxiety and more positive attitudes towards computers as instructional tools than teachers lacking basic computer experience.

There is no doubt that the chain of findings presented in this paper indicate that personality traits and attitudinal constructs are primary factors to be taken into consideration when deciding the suitability of the individual teacher to computer use in the instructional process, despite the almost universal familiarity with computers that has developed in modern society.

3   PUPILS

Katz and Offir (1993) stated that the computer has the potential of increasing the effectiveness of the learning process, is able to supply both individualised and controlled instruction, is capable of gathering and storing a wealth of information, can rapidly execute complex learning tasks, and can easily present pupils with accurate evaluations and other educational outputs. Although many schools have acquired computers and use them in the instructional process, it is not yet clear whether a majority of pupils are in fact able to efficiently use computers for Computer Assisted Learning (CAL). One of the issues apparently related to positive computer attitudes as well as efficient computer use in the classroom, is that pertaining to pupils' personality profiles (Kulik, Bangert-Drowns and Williams, 1983). An examination of studies conducted to ascertain personality and attitudinal traits of pupils engaged in CAL indicates that certain personality and attitudinal variables are significantly correlated with pupils' computer related attitudes. Empirical evidence intimates that certain personality and attitudinal traits are related to more positive computer related attitudes than others.

It appears that positive attitudes toward CAL are related to higher levels of self-recognition, self-confidence and locus of control of elementary school pupils (Woodrow, 1991). Katz and Offir (1990) found that positive computer oriented attitudes are related to social image and school satisfaction. Pupils with a positive social image prefer study through the medium of CAL as do pupils who express dissatisfaction with teachers who use traditional and older established teaching methods.

Katz (1993) indicated that pupils characterised by creativity and originality have more positive CAL related attitudes than those not typified by the same factors. In addition, personality traits, such as impulsiveness, stimulus-seeking, sensation-seeking, creativity, and the craving of change, significantly characterise pupils who have positive computer related attitudes. On the other hand, pupils typified by anxiety, depression, tension, irrationality, shyness, moodiness, dependency, emotionality, guilt feelings, low self-esteem, and need of social acceptance, hold less positive computer related attitudes.

Regarding the issue of gender, Harvey and Wilson (1985) and Martin, Heller and Mahmoud (1992) indicated that no sex differences were found between male and female elementary school pupils regarding their computer related attitudes. These findings contradict popular opinion that boys hold more positive computer related attitudes than girls.

The above mentioned studies dealing with computer related attitudes clearly indicate the existence of a significant relationship between pupils' personality and attitudes and the will to use computers in the educational setting. It appears that certain personality and attitudinal constructs promote the adoption of positive computer related attitudes whereas other personality and attitudinal variables mitigate against the formation of positive attitudes toward the use of computers in the educational setting.

4   CONCLUSION

The growing body of evidence presented above indicates that personality and attitudinal variables are related to positive computer related attitudes of teachers. It is suggested that a screening process, based on personality and attitude examination is adopted by school authorities or school principals in the decision-making process regarding the employment of teachers who, in their instructional roles, are expected to use computers. It is advised that teachers' basic personality and attitudinal attributes are examined so as to evaluate their suitability to effective computer usage. The computer may well bring about the long dreamed about educational revolution, and more specifically, the teaching revolution. If the teachers using computers for CAI possess the personality attributes which promote positive computer oriented attitudes, then the chances of achieving the dream of an educational revolution through the use of information technology may finally be realised.

A similar screening strategy based on examination of personality and attitudinal constructs is recommended for implementation regarding the selection of pupils suited to computer assisted learning tasks. It appears that learning self-image, and social self-image, in addition to other attitudinal variables such as school satisfaction, and motivation for study have a bearing on the formation of pupils' attitudes towards the use of computers in the learning process. It is becoming increasingly apparent that, for psychological reasons, not all pupils have positive attitudes towards learning with computers. Thus it is tentatively suggested that some type of elementary psychological screening and adaptation take place before pupils are introduced to CAL so that all pupils may be initiated into differential computer learning that suits their own particular personalities or attitudinal profiles. A national screening strategy, such as that suggested above, may conceivably contribute to added effectiveness of outcomes when using computers in the learning process.

5   REFERENCES

Chandra, P., Bliss, J. and Cox, M. (1988) Introducing computers into a school - management issue. *Computers and Education*, **12**, 1, 57-61.

Dunn, S. and Ridgway, J. (1991) Computer use during primary school teaching practice: a survey. *Journal of Computer Assisted Learning*, **7**, 7-17.

Evans, T.E., Katz, Y.J. and Francis, L.J. (1995) Psychometric properties of the Hebrew version of the Francis Attitude Towards Computers Scale. *Psychological Reports*, **77**, 1003-1010.

Eysenck, H.J. and Eysenck, S.B.G. (1975) *Manual of the Eysenck Personality Questionnaire*. Hodder and Stoughton, London.

Harvey, T.J. and Wilson, B. (1985) Gender differences in attitudes towards microcomputers shown by primary and secondary school pupils. *British Journal of Educational Technology*, **3**, 183-187.

Hunt, N.P. and Bohlin, R.M. (1993) Teacher education students' attitudes toward using computers. *Journal of Research on Computing in Education*, **25**, 487-497.

Katz, Y.J. (1993) Achievement level, affective attributes and computer oriented attitudes: a profile of a successful end-user, in A. Knierzinger and M. Moser (eds.) *Informatics and changes in learning*. IST Press, 13-15 (Section VII), Linz, Austria.

Katz, Y.J. and Offir, B. (1990) Computer assisted instruction and students' social orientations. *Proceedings of 5th Jerusalem Conference on Information Technology*. IEEE Computer Society Press, 660-664, Los Alamitos, CA.

Katz, Y.J. and Offir, B. (1991) The relationship between personality and computer related attitudes of Israeli teachers. *Education and Computing*, **7**, 249-252.

Katz, Y.J. and Offir, B. (1993) Computer assisted learning and cognitive abilities: hardware and software implications, in A. Knierzinger and M. Moser (eds.) *Informatics and changes in learning*. IST Press, 11-13 (Section I), Linz, Austria.

Kay, R.H. (1989) Gender differences in computer attitudes, literacy, locus of control and commitment. *Journal of Research on Computing in Education*, **21**, 307-316.

Kulik, J.A., Bangert-Drowns, R.L. and Williams, G.W. (1983) Effects of computer-based teaching on secondary school students. *Journal of Educational Psychology*, **75**, 19-26.

Levin, J. and Montag, I. (1987) The effect of testing instructions for handling social desirability on the Eysenck Personality Questionnaire. *Personality and Individual Differences*, **8**, 163-167.

Martin, C.D., Heller, R.S. and Mahmoud, E. (1992) American and Soviet children's attitudes toward computers. *Journal of Educational Computing Research*, **8**, 155-186.

Offir, B. and Katz, Y.J. (1990) Computer oriented attitudes as a function of risk-taking among Israeli elementary school teachers. *Journal of Computer Assisted Learning*, **6**, 1-2, 168-173.

Robinson, B. (1989) Computer assisted learning: automatons or thinking individuals, in W. Tulasiewicz and A. Adams (eds.) *Teachers' expectations and teaching reality*. Routledge, 232-246, London.

Woodrow, J.E.J. (1991) Locus of control and computer attitudes as determinants of the computer literacy of student teachers. *Computers and Education*, **16**, 237-245.

6 BIOGRAPHY

Dr. Yaacov J Katz serves as the Deputy-Director of the School of Education and Head of Educational Sciences at the Bar-Ilan University. He also serves as the Chairman of the School of Education's Graduate Studies Program and is the Director of the Institute of Community Education and Research. His main teaching and research interests focus on attitudinal research in the school system with particular emphasis on computer related attitudes of teachers, pupils and students. Dr. Katz has edited a book on the impact of pedagogical and psychological variables on computers in education and has published numerous scholarly articles in internationally recognised academic journals.

12

Informatics education as a new discipline

Joyce Currie Little
Department of Computer and Information Sciences
Towson State University, Towson, MD 21204 USA

Abstract

After presenting some characteristics of evolving disciplines, this paper gives background information on the evolution of informatics as a discipline. A discussion of how informatics can be extended into a program of informatics education supported by the various informatics departments follows. Arguments for the advancement of informatics education as a new discipline include some suggestions about how topics from the informatics body of knowledge can be incorporated into all levels of pre-college education, over all subjects.

Keywords

Computer literacy, informatics as a study topic, information technology

1   THE EVOLUTION OF NEW DISCIPLINES

As a new discipline evolves, the body of knowledge becomes identified and enters the mainstream of study for preparing for work in that discipline. As formal study gains recognition and is required for employment, the subject matter becomes more refined. As entry-level jobs begin to require formal study for entry into work, the discipline begins to mature. Individuals will begin to form associations. Codes of ethics and standards of practice will arise. Program accreditation for college study will often follow. New disciplines may initially be classified as a craft or an art; they may begin as a trade rather than as a profession. Often, overlap with other more well established programs will cause difficulties of ownership. Opportunities for individuals to become recognised by obtaining a credential will sometimes lead to licensing.

Some of the characteristics identified with a profession include: "full-time activity in the performance of certain tasks on the job; the establishment of training programs or courses appropriate to the job; the creation of a national professional association; hard competition with neighbouring occupations, especially at the beginning; political agitation in order to gain legal support for the protection of job territories; and the use of rules and ideals established by means of formal codes of ethics" (Habenstein, 1970). Some of the advantages of professionalising an occupation or discipline include: a higher level of quality of competency of the employee, more predictable and reliable results of workplace activity in uncertain and complex situations, and a reduction of bureaucracy within the organisation. As more of the routine tasks are taken over by automated processes, the highly skilled, problem-solving worker is needed for the organisation to have more adaptability, especially during times of change (Benveniste, 1987).

Typical of new disciplines are difficulties with terminology and vocabulary, not the least of which is what to call it. There are many varieties of programs related to computing, and the names and definitions are not yet precisely defined, nor are they consistent across universities, much less across the international boundaries of the world today. For the purposes of this paper, the term 'informatics' will be used to denote all programs related to the computing and information sciences discipline.

2   THE EVOLUTION OF INFORMATICS PROGRAMS

The preparation of guidelines for computing-related programs at the baccalaureate level were initiated in the 1960s by the Association for Computing Machinery (ACM, 1965), with a recent revision in conjunction with IEEE-Computer Society (Tucker, 1991). Guidelines for baccalaureate and graduate programs in Information Systems have been prepared separately by ACM and DPMA, with the first in the 1970s and the most recent version done in co-operation (Couger, 1995). Curriculum reports in software engineering were produced by the Software Engineering Institute at both undergraduate and graduate levels (Gibbs, 1989). Recent program innovations called informatics blending some aspects of other programs have been studied (NSF, 1994).

Recommendations for two-year programs in informatics for job preparation and/or later transfer to four-year colleges were produced both by ACM and DPMA. The most recent ACM report addressed four different programs, as well as the separate issue of computing for other disciplines. Most of these models recognise the needs of individuals who seek a job after no more than two years of post-secondary education; such programs are classified as 'vocational-technical' programs in the United States.

Recommendations and guidelines for programs for pre-college study have also been produced. Guidelines for courses in secondary schools were published by a committee of ACM (1993). Later, an international working group produced recommendations for computer literacy, for a vocational program, for a more advanced professional program, and for the use of informatics in other disciplines (UNESCO, 1994). Both these reports advocate study about informatics in pre-college education.

There has been some work to incorporate informatics instruction into grades lower than secondary level, although the heaviest use of computers at those levels is to support other learning activities (Anderson, 1992). Recommendations for change in programs at this level often include a reference to 'technology.' Project 2061 recommends some instruction about technology for K-12 students (AAAS, 1989). Informatics topics are proposed as a subject for middle school children in the Maryland Collaborative for Teacher Preparation project (MCTP, 1995).

3   THE IMPACT OF INFORMATICS ON SOCIETY

The impact of information technology has already been noted in educational institutions, governments, corporations, the marketplace, and society as a whole. This impact has global proportions. Information about such impact is often taught in introductory courses as well as in advanced courses in computer-related programs. It should be a part of the education of students at all levels. It can be included in all courses and all subjects, at all levels, as it crosses all disciplinary boundaries. Materials are now being made available by ImpactCS, a project supported by the National Science Foundation (Martin et al, 1996).

4   COMPUTING LITERACY AND INFORMATION LITERACY

In the 1960s, computer literacy meant learning how to do computer programming. Later, it meant learning about how to use electronic spreadsheets, databases, and word processors with a personal computer. Today, it means learning about computing and information technology, its terminology and its impact, along with some use of applications software on a personal computer or local area network, as well as how to use electronic communications, newsgroups, and the Internet. Such computing literacy is also recommended for the entire workplace. "With increasing access to technologies, creating a literate, well-trained and skilled workforce for an increasingly competitive world becomes top priority for many nations" (Charp, 1996).

The 'information literacy' movement promotes the use of technology for access to information (Shapiro and Hughes, 1996). Many such courses provide information on how to use the Internet, how to do electronic publishing, and how to use electronic communications to gain access to information. It does not refer to computer literacy (Ratteray and Simmons, 1995).

Computing literacy and information literacy can both be taught across disciplines in several ways. Some colleges require a computing literacy course. The 'Computing Across the Curriculum' movement, patterned after 'Writing Across the Curriculum,' is sometimes used as a paradigm for incorporating such a requirement. Students take service courses offered by one or more of the informatics departments, followed by an advanced course in computing applications in their discipline offered by their own faculty, resulting in a higher depth of informatics knowledge for all majors, including teacher education majors.

5   THE ROLE OF CREDENTIALS

One of the characteristics of a profession is the move toward the acceptability of a method to recognise those qualified to practice in the field. The practice of 'credentialing' teachers is accepted by most countries, by means of some type of 'teacher certification,' usually in a discipline (Gal-Ezer, 1996). Over half the states in the US have some type of certification requirement for informatics teachers at some level of education (Duncan, 1992). The National Council for Accreditation of Teacher Education has adopted standards for informatics for teacher education programs (Thomas et al, 1992).

Professional certification is available in informatics through the Institute for Certification of Computing Professionals (ICCP), a non-profit organisation formed by several computer associations. The credential, called the Certified Computing Professional (CCP), has identifiable specialities, such as Software Engineering (Little, 1996). Vendor-specific certification is becoming popular for those who want recognition of their capability in the use of certain software products (Reilly, 1996).

6   IMPROVEMENT OF PROFESSIONAL PRACTICE

Improvement in the professional practices of informatics personnel is important and needed. Many efforts are simultaneously underway to improve the quality of programmes being offered. An improved process for the professional practices of informatics personnel seems to be a major goal. Examples of improvement projects include the Capability Maturity Model, developed by the Software Engineering Institute, and the ISO 9000 standards model. Such improvements would have positive impact on education and training, which can benefit all the informatics industries.

One ongoing improvement effort is the work of the joint Task Force of representatives from IEEE-CS and ACM, now working to define Software Engineering as a profession. Work is now being done to define the body of knowledge. Upon its completion, several sub-committees will address other issues, including curriculum recommendations and ethical practices.

7   PROBLEMS FACING INFORMATICS EDUCATION

The tools used in informatics continue to change rapidly, both in hardware and software. The practices used to apply the tools to problems in need of solution are also continuing to change. It is almost impossible for corporations in industry to maintain a current state in their computing environment, and it is even more difficult for schools. In addition to maintaining current hardware and software, good technical and managerial support is also needed, to co-ordinate, manage, acquire, maintain all the systems being acquired. Staff are needed to carry out the work required to sustain the many new applications being run on computers and communications today.

From where do colleges and schools get the support they need? In many cases, such support is being solicited from private industry, from organisations which provide grants, and from community contributions. As a result, the National Information Infrastructure which will provide computing and information technology to the schools is now tied to corporations, to industry, to grants from governments, to colleagues in institutions of higher education, to parents of students, and to the general public at large. The Telecommunications Reform Act of 1996 calls for the establishment of a National Educational Technology Funding Corporation to offer assistance to states for the funding of services to schools and libraries (Charp, 1996). The ability to get and keep such an infrastructure is dependent on such collaborative relationships. "Information technology has emerged as a permanent, respected, and increasingly essential component of the college experience" (Green, 1996).

8   INFORMATICS EDUCATION AS A NEW DISCIPLINE

Although the computing disciplines are evolving toward the definition of a profession, informatics education has not evolved as far. Although recommendations for programs have been available for some time (ACM, 1985), long term progress has been slow. Some new ways to approach curricular change may be needed, such as those which look across boundaries of other more-established disciplines and across all levels of education. Some suggestions for enhancement are:

- Promote good practice in the profession of informatics by working towards having computer specialists as professionals in the office as computer specialists, on the staff as computing co-ordinators, in the classroom as teachers.
- Integrate technical topics of informatics as a subject with other sciences, anywhere science appears in K-12.
- Incorporate instruction about the technology into the student's use of it as a tool. When students use computers to communicate via the Internet, for example, teach them something about computing literacy too.
- Mesh topics of informatics and its applications into all other subjects, such as the arts, or in the study of animals, etc.
- Include topics of the impact of technology on humankind in every discipline, as that discipline is taught. Encourage an appropriate usage of technology in the future.

With an interdisciplinary approach to subject matter, informatics can serve as a bridge between and among disciplines. The informatics discipline, through its faculty, could promote and support informatics education in the way that some other disciplines have done. To make progress, it is critical to have co-operation between informatics departments and teacher education programs.

9   CONCLUSION

The informatics discipline, in all its many flavours, needs to provide strong support for the creation of informatics education. By broadening the content of informatics to include all aspects of computing and communications literacy, by promoting the practice of using computing across all curricula, and by working towards giving students capability in computing applications in every field - student outcomes at all levels can be enhanced. Teacher education for the discipline of informatics can and should make it possible to prepare all students to function well in an information age.

10   REFERENCES

AAAS (1989) *Science for all Americans*. American Association for the Advancement of Science, Washington.
ACM (1965) An undergraduate program in computer science - preliminary recommendations. *Communications of the ACM*, **8**, 9, 543-552.

ACM (1985) *Curricula recommendations for secondary schools and teacher certification.* New York.

ACM (1993) *ACM Model High School Computer Science Curriculum.* New York.

Anderson, R. (ed.) (1992) *Computers in American schools.* IEA Computers in Education Study, University of Minnesota, Minneapolis.

Benveniste, G. (1987) *Professionalizing the organization: reducing bureaucracy to enhance effectiveness.* Jossey-Bass, San Francisco.

Charp, S. (1996) Technological literacy for the workplace. *T.H.E. Journal*, **23**, 8, 6.

Charp, S. (1996) Telecommunications and Networking. *T.H.E. Journal*, **23**, 9, 6.

Commission on Higher Education (1995) *Information literacy in higher education: a report on the middle states region.* Philadelphia.

Couger, J. D. et al (1995) IS '95: guidelines for undergraduate information systems curriculum. *MIS Quarterly*, **19**, 3, 341-359.

Duncan, D. (1992) Qualifications of information technology teachers: the role of education and certification. *Journal of Information Systems Education*, **4**, 1, 2-5.

Gibbs, N. E. (1989) The SEI education program: the challenge of teaching future software engineers. *Communications of the ACM*, **32**, 5, 594-605.

Gal-Ezer, J. (1996) Computer science teachers' certification program. *Computers and Education*, **25**, 3, 163-168.

Green, K. (1996) The coming ubiquity of information technology. *Change*, **28**, 2, 24-31.

Habenstein, R.W. (1970). Occupational Uptake: Professionalizing, in *Pathways to Data.* Aldine Publishing, Chicago, 99-121.

Little, J.C. (1996) Certification through ICCP. *ACM SIG3C Online*, New York, 14.

Martin, D.D., Huff, C., Gotterbarn, D., Miller, K. and Project ImpactCS Steering Committee (1996) Curriculum guidelines for teaching the consequences of computing, in *Proceedings of the ACM SIGCAS Symposium on Computers and Quality of Life*, Philadelphia.

MCTP (1995) *Materials from the Center for Mathematics and Sciences Education.* Towson State University, Towson.

Shapiro, J.J. and Hughes, S.K. (1996) Information Technology as a Liberal Art. *Educom Review*, **31**, 2, 31-35.

National Science Foundation (1993) *Education for the next generation of information specialists: a framework for academic program in informatics.* Washington.

Ratteray, O.M.T. and Simmons, H.L. (1995) *Information literacy in higher education: A report on the middle states region.* Commission on Higher Education, Philadelphia.

Reilly, V. A. (1996) A new wave in software certification. *ACM SIG3C Online*, **3**, 2, New York.

Thomas, L., Friske, J. et al (1992) Standards for accrediting computer education teacher programs in the United States, in *Proceedings of the Ninth International conference on technology and education*, Paris, 486-488.

Tucker, A.B. et al (1991) *Computing Curricula 1991: A report of the ACM/IEEE-CS Joint Curriculum Task Force.* IEEE Computer Society Press.

UNESCO (1994) *Informatics for Secondary Education: A Curriculum for Schools.* Paris.

11   BIOGRAPHY

Joyce Currie Little is Professor and former Chair of the Department of Computer and Information Sciences, at Towson State University in Baltimore, Maryland USA. She has been active in the computer field for over twenty-five years. She was awarded the Distinguished Services Award by ACM in 1993 for her service to the computing community, became an ACM Fellow in 1994, and was made an AAAS Fellow in 1995. Joyce is interested in informatics education, software engineering, computing personnel research and the societal impact of technology on society.

13

Issues in the preparation of teachers of programming for children

John Oakley
Faculty of Education, Charles Sturt University
Bathurst, NSW 2795, Australia

Anne McDougall
Faculty of Education, Monash University
Clayton, Vic. 3168, Australia

Abstract

This paper outlines issues that warrant attention in the professional development of teachers of programming to young children.

To teach programming well, teachers must themselves have a good understanding of, and confidence in using one or more programming environments appropriate for young learners. Curriculum policy and intentions are important. Much of the successful work in children's programming has occurred in settings where an integrated approach to curriculum is taken. Pedagogical techniques for teaching of programming need to be considered. Successful approaches generally show a balance between guidance and discovery, with apprenticeship, consultation, collaboration and other techniques working well in various situations. Teachers of programming need to understand the development of skills of collaboration and consultation. This is important in continuing their own professional development as well as in fostering the collaborative working strategies supported by programming in classrooms. Discussion of programming's relationship with more general problem solving, possibilities of transfer of learning from programming to other areas of the curriculum, changes in learners' attitudes to errors, the encouragement of learners' reflection and thinking about thinking, and effects on learners' self confidence and feelings of empowerment in learning, are also important components of teacher preparation in this area.

Keywords

Teacher education, classroom practice, computing, curriculum development, programming, teaching methods

1   INTRODUCTION

This paper draws on the literature on children's learning of programming, and on interviews with successful teachers of programming at elementary school level, to outline issues that warrant attention in the professional development of teachers of programming to children.

2   KNOWLEDGE OF PROGRAMMING

To teach programming well teachers need knowledge and experience sufficient to have understanding of, and confidence in, one or more programming environments appropriate for young learners. Johanson (1988) relates the best of programming instruction with teacher knowledge of programming concepts such as recursion. This view is supported by Pea, Kurland and Hawkins (1987) and Leron (1985) who stress the importance of teachers having intensive training in the programming language being taught, avoiding teacher expectations being limited to drills on language features (Dalbey and Linn, 1986). Leron also warns that poorly prepared teachers tend to concentrate on the language and its syntax, ignoring the instrumental, instructional, and social environments postulated by Kurland, Clement, Mawby and Pea (1987). Subject knowledge and teaching skill are thus essential qualities of the teacher of programming. Pea and Kurland (1984a) emphasise that it is by interactions with skilled teachers that skill in problem solving and planning develops.

Teachers of programming to young children need to be competent programmers at a level sufficient to guide their pupils and to set challenges for more advanced pupils. This requires sufficient knowledge to be able to recognise challenges, and to provide whatever intervention might be necessary. It is highly unlikely that these attributes will be acquired in traditional teacher education learning environments. Depth of knowledge is best achieved in context and when there is a recognised need to gain further insights into programming and, importantly, into teaching strategies that encourage children to become independent learners. Teachers and student teachers must be able to choose and establish programming contexts that will foster new types of relationships among children, their teacher and subject matter (Papert, 1980).

Pea acknowledges the importance of a supportive culture in the implementation of the Logo language in schools and emphasises the importance of teachers being able to create a culture that fosters the development of thinking skills through a judicious use of examples, student projects, and direct instruction (Pea, 1984). Likewise, Johanson (1988) and Glaser (1986) exhort teachers to develop a complex school culture in which computers play significant roles in helping students to engage in higher-order thinking. Papert, Pea, Johanson, and Glaser all emphasise the development of a culture where higher order cognitive skills can be fostered in association with programming activities.

3   CURRICULUM POLICY AND INTENTIONS

The teaching of programming must take place in the context of curriculum policy and intentions. Papert (1985) advocates a method of teaching programming that is guided by curricular intentions different from the norm. Traditional methods of teaching programming are inconsistent with the curricular aims associated with Logo. Walker and Schaffarzik (1974) suggest that failure to achieve intended outcomes may relate to the possibility that programming instruction did not embody specified objectives of the wider curriculum. They also note that mastery of syntax and programming principles dominates instructional time and thus effectively dominates the curriculum. Similarly, Clements (1986) notes that it was curricular intentions embodied in Logo instructional procedures that accounted for the effects found. Johanson (1988:15) argues that, not only must there be curricular intent, but that programming should be significant in its attachment to bodies of content.

Our studies reveal that integration of programming into traditional subject areas (for example, mathematics, science, social science) is much favoured by the teachers of programming and the wider body of teaching staff. It is considered that integration of programming across the total school curriculum not only establishes a relevant context for programming activities but also provides a sharp focus for the children and enhances the range of learning experiences. This suggests that explicit curricular intentions, particularly with respect to metacognition and refinement of thinking, are a likely cause of the effectiveness, or otherwise, of instruction in programming languages. Research since the early 1980s indicates that integration of programming activities into existing curricula not only supports those curricula but provides relevance and context.

Integration does not happen spontaneously. Considerable expertise in programming, curriculum development and leadership is required if integration is to be successful. Teachers, and particularly student teachers, need considerable assistance in developing skills and techniques in integrating programming into various curricula. In addition they need to be provided with a repertoire of different types of programming activities for children of different ages, abilities and interests. Perhaps the most potent form of assistance is given by exemplary activities within in-service and pre-service training contexts.

4   PEDAGOGICAL TECHNIQUES

The broad question of how much and what type of instruction is best has been hotly debated (Papert, 1980; Pea and Sheingold, 1987). At one extreme, direct instruction is the major teaching mode. At the other, there is almost no direct instruction. However, the literature does identify some key factors within social and classroom organisational contexts, culture, and teaching practices that serve to enable the programming process. These factors are supported by both quantitative and qualitative research. The pedagogical techniques suggested include balance between guidance and discovery, the adoption of an apprenticeship system, and extensive consultation and collaboration.

On the issue of the balance between guidance and discovery Mandinach (1987) reports that explicit instruction generally facilitates skill acquisition, while indirect instruction is more likely to result in transfer. Unfortunately, explicit teaching of the language is both commonly accepted and potentially counterproductive for the transfer effects sought (Johanson, 1988). Nevertheless, Pea and Kurland (1987) note that while explicit instruction and the associated fact learning approach to programming are unlikely to result in complex cognitive changes, so is unsupported spontaneous exploration. The literature also strongly suggests the need for 'significant self-direction' (Johanson, 1988); too much teacher-imposed structure not only makes projects seem arbitrary and uninteresting, but is also less likely to evoke students' 'full attention and involvement' (Kurland, Clement, Mawby and Pea, 1987). Leron (1985) suggests that it is a major educational challenge to find ways by which teachers can help children without sacrificing 'the spirit of meaningful and exploratory learning'. He suggests that making available a study guide helps children learn powerful ideas through partial direction and prompts them to reflect on their results, but acknowledges that his suggestion is a quasi-Piagetian approach to learning. He argues that while there is a resultant trade-off of some of the freedom inherent in a Piagetian approach, there is a deeper understanding of the ideas behind the programming activity (Leron, 1985). Finding the 'right' balance between guidance and discovery is crucial. Johanson (1988), echoing the advice of Papert and others, warns of the danger of directing children into learning the syntax and structure of a programming language and its possible interference with the intended goal of problem solving skill development. Lehrer (1993) emphasises that exemplary instruction should focus on design skills rather than syntax and semantics.

The teachers within our study moved from what could be regarded as an unstructured approach to one that was slightly structured. In essence their approach was to give sufficient direct instruction in the initial stages to enable children to begin individual projects with some success. Using Logo and HyperCard, it was found that children needed very little instruction before they were able to begin to work independently. Then children were encouraged as the need arose, individually or collectively, to draw further on the teacher as a resource. Teacher assistance took the forms of questions to assist children to reflect on their problems; encouragement for them to interact with and seek advice from other children; suggestions to consult reference manuals; and small group explanations or demonstrations. At all times the teachers ensured that their input was just sufficient to bring the children to a level where they could continue unassisted. An important aim was that children continued to have a strong sense of being in control and having ownership of their project.

Another technique that has been suggested is the adoption of an apprenticeship system. Pea and Kurland advocate this as an effective, even the best way of teaching programming (Pea and Kurland, 1984c).

A third approach involves extensive consultation and collaboration. Some researchers suggest that there is a danger that collaboration results in the borrowing of code without the student understanding what the code does, or why. Kurland et al (cited in Pea and Sheingold, 1987) warn that '... an over reliance of other people's code that is beyond the understanding of the borrower is unlikely to lead to a deeper understanding of programming'. However, our research suggests that the use of borrowed code may be a crucial stage in learning to program and one that is enhanced by the collaborative process. Our studies have revealed that the borrowing of code occurs among school pupils and teacher education students alike and that such a practice equates, in the first instance, to the use of a 'tool'. Contrary to the warning that the borrowing of code might not promote deeper understanding of programming, teachers and lecturers in our study believe that the practice of borrowing code may ultimately enhance understanding of programming concepts.

5   OTHER FACTORS

Papert and Pea, perhaps the best known representatives of what are ostensibly polarised views relating to the educational value of programming for young children, have identified several other key pedagogical factors that facilitate the successful integration of programming into elementary schools. These include allocation of time (Papert, 1980; Pea and Kurland, 1984) and access to computers (Papert, 1980).

Johanson (1988) emphasises that depth and duration of exposure are essential to the development of operational thought and that these probably have 'not been achieved in empirical studies to date'. Kurland et al bemoan the fact that: 'Even after two years of study, many students had not learned enough to have any hope of transfer effects to other disciplines or problem areas' (Kurland, Pea, Clement and Mawby, 1986). More specifically, Pea and Kurland (1984b) and Kurland, Mawby and Cahir (1984) comment that 'achievement of expert programmer status takes enormous amounts of time - perhaps 1000 hours'. Pea and Kurland (1984a) also comment that we cannot expect the benefits of programming to emerge in the space of a year. Papert's views on the importance of extensive exposure to computers are well documented. Neophyte programmers need regular, on-going and extensive opportunities to program.

6   CONCLUSION

Traditional in-service and pre-service courses for teachers tend not to teach programming. Where they do there is a tendency to teach through exercises in syntax. Such an approach is counter-productive. What is much more likely to succeed is an approach that embodies knowledge of pedagogical approaches that have worked well in classrooms, a strong emphasis on philosophical and educational underpinnings, significant self direction, a balance between guidance and discovery, and a changed role for the lecturer. A compelling argument for teachers having a knowledge of programming sufficient to integrate it into the curriculum is that programming is one of the few ways in which children can take control of their academic environment and experience a sense of empowerment. As one teacher said "Being able to program is like being in charge of magic".

Discussion of the arguments that have been made for the teaching of programming to young children, including programming's relationship with more general problem solving, possibilities of transfer of learning from programming to other areas of the curriculum, changes in learners' attitudes to errors, the encouragement of learners' reflection and thinking about thinking, and effects on learners' self confidence and feelings of empowerment in learning, are also important components of teacher preparation in this area.

There is a widespread view that programming can bring unique educational benefits to elementary school children. If those benefits are to be manifest in educational outcomes within schools then it is suggested that teacher education courses be informed by the literature on approaches and practices that work well in classrooms and that all elementary school student teachers be exposed to programming activities as an essential part of their training.

7   REFERENCES

Clements, D.H. (1986) Effects of Logo and CAI Environments on Cognition and Creativity. *Journal of Educational Psychology*, **78**, 4, 309-18.

Dalbey, J., and Linn, M.C. (1986) Cognitive Consequences of Programming: Augmentations to Basic Instruction. *Journal of Educational Computing Research*, **2**, 1, 75-93.

Glaser, R. (1986) Education and Thinking: The Role of Knowledge. *American Psychologist*, **39**, 2, 93-104.

Johanson, R.P. (1988) Computers, Cognition and Curriculum: Retrospect and Prospect. *Journal of Educational Computing Research*, **4**, 1, 1-30.

Kurland, D.M., Clement, C., Mawby, R. and Pea, R.D. (1987) Mapping the Cognitive Demands of Learning to Program, in R.D. Pea and K. Sheingold (eds.) *Mirrors Of Minds: Patterns Of Experience in Educational Computing*. Ablex Publishing Corporation, Norwood, N.J.

Kurland, D.M., Mawby, R. and Cahir, N. (1984). *The Development of Programming Expertise in Adults and Children*. Paper presented at the Annual Meeting of the American Educational Research Association, New Orleans.

Kurland, D.M., Pea, R.D., Clement, C. and Mawby, R. (1986) A Study of the Development of Programming Ability and Thinking Skills in High School Students. *Journal of Educational Computing Research*, **2**, 4, 429-58.

Leron, U. (1985) Logo Today: Vision and Reality. *Computing Teacher*, **12**, 5, 26-32.

Mandinach, E.B. (1987) Clarifying the "A" in CAI for Learners of Different Abilities. *Journal of Educational Computing Research*, **3**, 1, 113-128.

Papert, S. (1980) *Mindstorms: Children, Computers and Powerful Ideas*. Harvester Press, Brighton, Sussex.

Papert, S. (1985) *Computer Criticism vs Technocentric Thinking*. Paper presented at Logo 85, Cambridge, MA.

Pea, R.D. (1984) *What Will It Take to Learn Thinking Skills through Computer programming?* Paper presented at the Annual Meeting of the American Educational Research Association, New Orleans.

Pea, R.D. and Kurland, D.M. (1984a) *Logo Programming and the Development of Planning Skills, Technical Report No. 16*. Bank Street College of Education, Chicago.

Pea, R.D. and Kurland, D.M. (1984b) On the Cognitive Effects of Learning Computer Programming: A Critical Look. *New Ideas in Psychology*, **2**, 2, 137-168.

Pea, R.D. and Kurland, D.M. (1984c) *On the cognitive Pre-requisites of Learning Computer Programming, Technical Report No. 18.* Bank Street College of Education. New York.

Pea, R.D. and Kurland, D.M. (1987) On the Cognitive Effects of Learning Computer Programming, in R.D. Pea and K. Sheingold (eds.) *Mirrors of Minds: Patterns of Experience in Educational Computing.* Ablex Publishing Corporation, Norwood, New Jersey.

Pea, R.D., Kurland, D.M. and Hawkins, J. (1987) Logo and the Development of Thinking Skills, in R.D. Pea and K. Sheingold (eds.) *Mirrors of Minds: Patterns of Experience in Educational Computing.* Ablex Publishing Corporation, Norwood, New Jersey.

Pea, R.D. and Sheingold, K. (eds.) (1987) *Mirrors of Minds: Patterns of Experience in Educational Computing.* Ablex Publishing Corp., Norwood, N. J.

Walker, D. and Schaffarzik, J. (1974) Comparing Curricula. *Review of Educational Research,* **44**, 1, 83-111.

8   BIOGRAPHIES

John Oakley is a senior lecturer in the School of Teacher Education at Charles Sturt University. He is a former school principal and has been lecturing since 1974, and in computer education since 1982. He was the foundation editor of 'Australian Educational Computing' and in 1993 was awarded the NSW prize of 'Computer Educator of the Year' and the Australian Council for Computers in Education prize of 'Educator of the Year'. His current research interests relate to the process of technological innovation in schools with particular reference to computerised spatial information systems and children as programmers.

Anne McDougall has worked as a secondary teacher in Australia and then as a computer programmer in the USA. In 1973 she took up a research fellowship in computer education at the University of Melbourne, developing software for use in undergraduate teaching. Her subsequent lecturing and research work has been concerned with computers and learning at secondary and primary school levels. She is now an Associate Professor in Educational Computing at Monash University.

14

A new approach to teaching information technologies: shifting emphasis from technology to information

Peter Hubwieser, Manfred Broy, and Wilfried Brauer
Fakultät für Informatik der Technischen Universität München
D-80290 München, Germany

Abstract

Being aware of the increasing pedagogical challenges posed when using and teaching IT in schools, we have begun a widespread initiative at the Technical University of Munich to improve the practice of teaching IT in secondary schools in Bavaria. We offer a curriculum to students who intend to become secondary school teachers. The goal of the curriculum is to offer students a more general viewpoint, leaving behind the more narrow hard- and software specific approaches that schools have followed most often. Guided by the process of developing software, we propose to concentrate on modelling techniques, especially object-oriented versions. We intend, furthermore, to educate as many teachers at a university level in computer science as possible. To that end we have developed a new, lean curriculum for the education of teachers, which also serves as a basis for an in-service training project. In addition, we plan to improve the access that schools have to modern information technologies. We have built an Internet node for a variety of rural schools in Rosenheim.

Keywords

Secondary education, teacher education, curriculum development, information technology, modelling, software engineering

1 INTRODUCTION

Recognising the steady growth in the importance of modern information processing concepts in everyday life, visible, for instance, in the number of multimedia computers and levels of Internet access in the homes of our students, it can no longer be accepted that there is almost no teaching of modern concepts of information technologies in our schools.

With the intention of improving the practice of teaching IT in secondary schools in Bavaria, the Technical University of Munich has begun a widespread initiative, strongly supported by the Bavarian Ministry of Education, Culture, Science and Art.

1.1 The Bavarian 'Gymnasium' as our main target

Today the majority of children seek to enter higher educational levels. Therefore, we have concentrated our efforts currently at this school level, which means that we are dealing with the so-called 'gymnasium'. This type of school covers 9 years of education, and is placed at the highest of the three educational levels that are offered to students in Bavaria once they have completed primary school at the age of 10 years.

1.2 Current education in IT

At the moment, the only obligatory IT education in Bavarian gymnasiums is a requirement termed "IT Basic Instruction". In this, each student gains about 60 hours of IT lessons, distributed through regular classes in mathematics, economics and German language, mainly dealing with aspects of use within the hard- and software provision of the schools. The teachers responsible for these courses generally lack any educational background in IT. Therefore, this system produces results which are rather varied.

Building on this weak basis, it is possible for students to choose a range of optional IT courses. The variety that is offered depends to a large extent upon the number of teaching hours remaining after the timetabling of obligatory classes.

2   THE INFORMATION-CENTRED APPROACH

First of all, we considered which underpinning philosophy of education in IT should be used. We decided to choose the process of software development as a guide, because it is the ideal paradigm for the task when structuring information. Observing how this process moves forward, starting from a rough real-life situation, passing through the construction of proper models, producing data structures, algorithms, program code, and finally to an implementation on a specific machine, we identify at each step an increasing dependence upon the details of the environment in which the software is implemented. In teaching IT, we firmly believe that the first two steps of this development process are the most beneficial, as they are the most general and the least environment-specific.

2.1 Abstraction of general concepts

In emphasising modelling techniques as the main topic of the suggested IT lessons, we offered general techniques to the students so that they could handle various types of complex information, even if there was no computer or any other hard- or software involved. Starting from a real-life situation example, the students were instructed in the development of proper models without considering any aspects of implementation. The modelling is based on application and on the problem to be solved. This allows us to concentrate on the structure of the information, not on a specific problem solving technique such as an algorithmic, object-oriented, set-based, or rule-based one. Specific techniques should be chosen after the completion of the modelling-phase, and not before.

2.2 Data models

The structural components of the system chosen are described by data models. From a traditional point of view these structures would be static, with the dynamic aspects modelled separately by global functions. This technique might be appropriate when acquainting students with a rough structure of the application problem. We suggest they use a graphical method to represent static data structures, using a special vertex- and edge-marked graph where the vertices represent data types, the edges denote by their particular form the method of composition, and by their titles the name of the components.

When describing the dynamic aspects of the data model, we prefer the object oriented method, which aims at combining static data structures (attributes) and functions (operations) to form classes. This approach offers a 'narrow semantical gap' (Jacobson, 1989), which avoids the separation of data and functions that arises from the von Neumann concept with program and data storages, allowing the modelling to be determined by the hardware structure. Human beings prefer to think in terms of interacting subjects and objects (Anderson, 1985), and this should be respected within modelling techniques. We suggest using an object modelling technique analogous to Rumbaugh (1991), and Booch (1994).

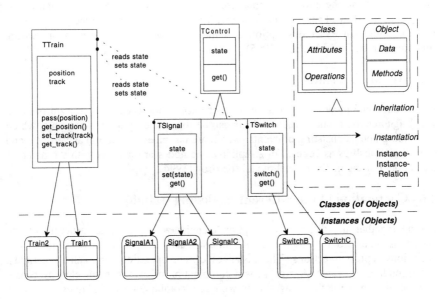

Figure 1 Representation of an object modelling technique

Teachers should be aware that from a mathematical point of view, a data model is based upon a family of carrier sets and a family of functions, as described by Broy (1995) or Goos (1994). The students are instructed to create a graph with nodes representing objects and edges defining relationships between the objects, which could be hierarchical relationships like inheritance and instantiation or other associations like communication relationships.

The object model provides the framework for the other model types which follow.

2.3   The dynamic model

The behaviour of a system or subsystem can be described by a number of well-known state transition diagrams, which can be represented by graphs, the vertices defining states, the edges representing transitions. An extensive description of the mathematics is found in Goos (1994). Each diagram represents a process which transforms information. The edges can be marked with three types of information: in the first instance, the initial (triggering) action must be written, then either the condition for the transition can be specified, or the action that is carried out by the transition, or both.

2.4   The functional model

Not knowing the precise way in which the information is transformed, the functional model (see Figure 2 below), consisting of well-known data flow diagrams, describes only the communication aspects between processes (information transformers), active objects (data sources and consumers), and passive objects (data storage). This type of modelling will not be applicable once processes or objects are created dynamically. As long as the flow of information is static, it illustrates well the interactions between the processes. An exact description of data-flow models using stream processing functions can be found in Broy (1995).

2.5   Action diagrams

In the functional model the transformation of information is carried out by processes, which ignores their inner structure. This can be illustrated by action diagrams, which are again graphs, consisting of events (which are instances of actions) as vertices, and causal relationships as edges. For simplicity, the nodes are marked with the name of the action. For the mathematical model see Broy (1994).

2.6   Correlation of the different modelling techniques

Putting together the different description techniques, the internal structure of the system is separated into objects which interact according to their operations. The operations represent actions. The instances of the operations are called methods, corresponding to events. A process is a combination of events, connected by causal relationships in the action diagram, as well as a combination of methods. The state transition diagrams provide information about the behaviour of processes, transitions representing events, and states describing the content of attributes. The data flow diagrams carry information about the communication and interaction between the single parts of the system.

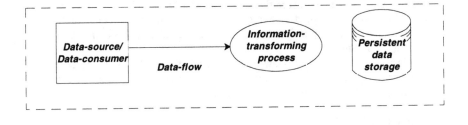

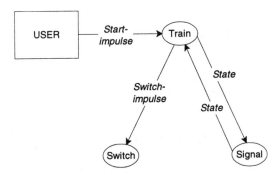

Figure 2 Representation of a functional model

2.7 Method

The IT lessons we propose are based on examples and real-life situations to a great extent, in order to illustrate the abstract concepts as much as possible. Therefore, no standard path through the teaching process can be defined. We indicate outlines of how a lesson could proceed, trying to emphasise the most important aspects.

Often a sequence of lessons will start with the introduction of the problem, presenting the situation in as illustrative a way as possible, and aiming to motivate the students.

The introduction should be followed by a detailed but informal description of the problem, using word processors wherever possible. This ensures that the description can be used again, and makes it possible to combine the work of parallel teams, each dealing with a particular set of the problems.

After discussing the informal description, the central part of the lesson begins: the modelling phase. In most cases it will be sufficient to construct perhaps two of the models described above, depending upon the characteristics of the problem. The students should be supported during this phase by the use of a flow-chart program, which leads to designed representations and avoids frustrations arising when needing to merely repeat the drawing of nearly identical pictures.

The review of the models produced will lead to a method of complementation that is appropriate to the situation. The main goal at this point is to illustrate the modelling results, not to train perfect users of specific programs or sophisticated programmers. Thus we use generic software, such as spreadsheets, and databases, as well as specific software. Using programming languages may sometimes be helpful, but the level of syntax should be kept to a minimum. If this is not possible, the teacher should use preprogrammed routines to ensure this. An interesting option for realisation would be to use CASE (Computer-aided-software-engineering) tools that directly transform the graphic representation of a model into program code. Ideally the output would be a ready-to-run program.

The last step is a critical review of achievements, possible alternatives, possible improvements, associations with those problems already solved, as well as social consequences of IT use in this specific situation.

3   EDUCATING TEACHERS

As indicated above, one of the main reasons for the stagnation of IT education in Bavarian schools during the last decade has been the lack of university-educated teachers. In co-operation with the Bavarian Ministry of Education, Culture, Science and Art we aim to educate at least one teacher per gymnasium, which means some 400 teachers in total in the next decade. These graduated teachers would serve as consultants and promoters for the development and realisation of this new concept of teaching IT.

3.1 Our curriculum for teacher education

Teacher education in IT in Bavaria is suffering currently from the fact that it is only possible to undertake it alongside a regular university education in two other scientific disciplines, such as mathematics and physics.

We expect students to complete the course in 3 years, to accompany their education in the two other main disciplines. We suggest that they attend the full set of 4 introductory lectures which cover the basics of automata, formal and programming - languages, algorithms and data structures, theories of complexity and calculability, machine architecture and operating systems, the building of interpreters and compilers, distributed systems, and communication. Building on these basic lessons, we expect students to attend special classes about database systems, data structures, software development, operating systems, networking, and the teaching of IT.

In order to get an appropriate mathematical background, we suggest that students attend basic lessons in analysis and linear algebra, which is obligatory for all students of engineering or natural sciences.

3.2 The compact course of study

Considering the current economic situation in Bavarian schools, it is not likely that there will be more than about 200 IT teachers entering service in Bavaria during the next decade. So we have offered a form of in-service training to increase the number of university-trained IT teachers in employment. We have developed a specific in-service course of study with all lessons provided on one specific day of the week. The teaching load of the participants is reduced by 6 hours each week. Using the free lesson time between the semesters to run special classes, we were able to reduce their studies to 2 years. At the moment, the first course is running with 20 participants, the next will be launched in September 1996 with about 25 members. The University of Erlangen-Nuernberg will duplicate this concept and start a parallel training course in Autumn 1996.

4 REFERENCES

Anderson, J.R. (1985) *Cognitive Psychology and Its Implications*. Freeman and Co, New York, Oxford.

Booch, G. (1994) *Object-Oriented Analysis and Design*. Benjamin/Cummings, Redwood City, CA.

Broy, M. (1994) *Informatik. Eine grundlegende Einführung, Teil III*. Springer München.

Broy, M. (1995) Mathematics of Software Engineering. Invited Talk at MPC 95, in B. Möller (ed.) *Mathematics of Program Construction*, July 1995, Kloster Irsee, Lecture Notes of Computer Science. Springer, Berlin Heidelberg.

Goos, G. (1995) *Vorlesungen über Informatik, Band 1*. Springer, Berlin Heidelberg.

Jacobson I., Ericsson M. and Jacobsson A. (1995) *The Object Advantage*. ACM Press, New York.

Rumbaugh, J., Blaha, M., Premerlani, W., Eddy, F. and Lorensen, W. (1991) *Object-Oriented Modeling and Design*. Prentice-Hall, Englewood Cliffs, NJ.

5 BIOGRAPHIES

Dr. Peter Hubwieser gave classes in mathematics, physics and computer science for 10 years at Bavarian gymnasiums, until he moved out of the teaching service in 1992 in order to write his dissertation in theoretical physics, completed in 1995. For the last two years he has been seconded to the Technical University of Munich, with the remit to improve the situation with regard to IT use in Bavarian gymnasiums.

Prof. Dr. Manfred Broy is ordinarius for software technology and was recently awarded the "Bundesverdienstkreuz am Bande" for his contribution to improving the quality of commercial software.

Prof. Dr. Wilfried Brauer, ordinarius for theoretical informatics, is well-known for his works concerning IT teaching, especially within the German "Gesellschaft für Informatik" as well as within IFIP, acting as vice chair from 1979 and as chair from 1985. In 1984 he was one of the authors of the UNESCO-IFIP Modular Curriculum in Computer Science and was invited as a lecturer at the IFIP World Congress in 1989. Recently he was elected as a member of the very honourable Bavarian Academy of Sciences.

Section 5: Support agencies and their roles

15

Advisory centre for new technologies - an addition to teacher training

Wolfgang Weber
Landesinstitut für Schule und Weiterbildung
Referat Z2, Paradieser Weg 64, 59494 Soest, Germany

Abstract

With the advent of new media for education we have set ourselves the goal of improving the quality of learning. Because of the dynamic development in this field it is nearly impossible for individual teachers to obtain an overview of what is on offer and to find new media which can support their lessons effectively. This is why an advisory system for new technologies has been built up in North Rhine-Westphalia: this comprises one central advisory centre and five regional ones.

The central advisory centre periodically produces information papers to provide orientation in the field of new information and communication technologies. In particular it compiles information on all new media on the market for teaching and learning and evaluates these media with respect to technical, theoretical and media-related educational aspects. Bibliographic information of these media, evaluation reports and also practice reports are stored in the database SODIS (Software Documentation and Information System). This database is a joint product of the German states and the Republic of Austria. The aim of this work is to find new media from the mass which can improve the quality of learning. Such media are assessed as being *examples of 'good new media' for learning*. Project ideas and exemplary lessons are specially developed, prepared and tested.

The regional advisory centres are places where teachers can obtain all this information and counselling, too. Here teachers can examine and test all the examples of 'good new media' for learning and judge them for themselves. Regional advisory centres are places where contacts can be made and information exchanged. The regional centres can react in a flexible and individual way to teachers' needs. When invited, the regional advisors supervise and advise working groups, evaluate the results and incorporate them into the system. They also go into schools and do on-the-spot counselling. They find out where information is required and react with offers or by passing information on to the teacher training institutions with whom they closely co-operate.

Keywords

Communications, learner centred learning, multimedia, open learning, support services

1   INTRODUCTION

In North Rhine-Westphalia, when we talk about the use of computers in the classroom, we distinguish between 4 areas:
* basic training in information and communication technologies (ages 13 to 15);
* computer science as required in compulsory choice/differentiation courses (ages 15 to 16);
* computer science as an elementary or advanced level course for upper grades of grammar school (ages 17 to 19);
* use of new media in individual subjects or for cross-curricular teaching.

Of these four areas the only one compulsory for all pupils of all types of schools is the basic training in information and communication technology. The objective of this training is for pupils to get to know, by means of three examples, how new technologies can typically be used. They are to examine the basic structures and functions of these new technologies by themselves and to reflect upon and judge the effects of their use. The training is carried out for approximately 60 lessons with topics such as 'Newspaper', 'Department Store', 'Ecosystem Forest', 'Carbon Cycles', 'Industrial Robots' or 'CAD/CAM' within the framework of those subjects which offer suitable points of contact with these topics (Der Kultusminister, 1990).

In subsequent years pupils may deepen the knowledge acquired during the basic training by attending computer science lessons. However, as pupils decide by themselves on their individual school career, they may or may not decide to take up this subject. What is typical for all three areas outside the basic training is the fact that here, the computer itself, with its components, and especially its software, become the objects of study.

For these latter three areas in-service training for teachers has, in some cases, been taking place for more than ten years in North Rhine-Westphalia. Depending on which area the teachers want to qualify for, these in-service training courses last for approximately 20 to 40 days; universities also offer additional courses for those teaching computer science as a subject in the upper grades. In some regions and in certain fields demand for this kind of training is already declining because schools no longer require the training.

2   NEW MEDIA IN THE CLASSROOM

In an increasingly open form of teaching, i.e. where pupils to a much greater extent obtain the information needed for their questions or problems themselves, where they decide more independently and self-responsibly about the tools they want to use for their work, new media play an increasingly important role in improving the quality of learning and teaching (see Figure 1).

Here we are talking about new media which, in addition to the traditional media, support lessons either continuously or at certain times only.

The use of such media rarely requires a special computer room since, in general, not all pupils use these media at the same time. There is, however, a need for individual computers to be accessible when the need for their use arises. Ideally, such computers would be situated in a special media corner within each classroom. Alternatively, it would make sense to have computers available in some central media area (for example, in the library) or to have mobile units which can be taken to wherever they are needed at the time.

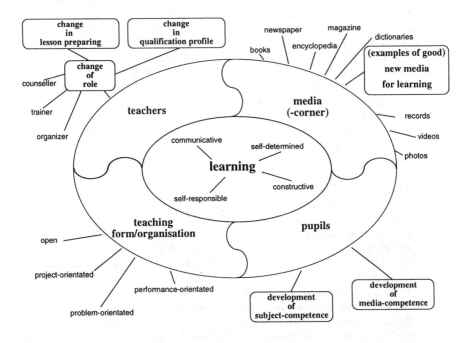

Figure 1   Examples of 'good new media' cause changes in the classroom

2.1   Orientation in the market

Because of the dynamic development in the market of new media, it is nearly impossible for individual teachers to obtain an overview of what is on offer and to find new media which can support their lessons effectively. A great deal of help is provided by the database SODIS (Software Documentation and Information System) which contains information on all new media for education available on the market. This database is a joint product of the German federal states and the Republic of Austria.

By means of this database every teacher can find out with little time and effort which new media are available for his subjects and topics. As there is already quite a wide range on offer, the teacher will usually have the choice between various new media which might be suitable for his lessons so that a mere market overview is not sufficient. Here again, the database provides help: for most new media it offers evaluation reports and, in some cases, practice reports on lessons actually held. Guided by these reports, the teacher is generally in a much better position to judge which of the media are really suited to his/her special purpose.

2.2 Evaluation of new media for education

The evaluation reports are written by experienced teachers who are continuously trained to qualify them for their special task. A special catalogue of criteria, which itself is continuously being updated and adapted to current developments, forms the basis of every evaluation. This catalogue of criteria (Landesinstitut, 1996) is quite extensive. It is sub-divided into technical, theoretical and media-related educational aspects. The following small extract (media-related teaching methods) may give an insight into the kind of questions which the evaluating teachers have to deal with:

- Does the medium itself pose the questions and problems or does it rather evoke a questioning attitude on the part of the user, for example, by questioning things, raising the user's doubts, causing amazement, pointing out discrepancies or provoking the user?
- Does the medium contribute towards an individualisation of learning? In particular, does it, in an appropriate way, take into account:
- different possible approaches to the topic;
- different types of learners;
- different kinds of socialisation?
- To what extent does the medium obstruct, facilitate, evoke or support:
- actively constructive and performance-orientated learning?
- the unaided procurement, evaluation, processing and internalisation of information?
- the user's potential to structure complexities in a self-determined, independent and self-responsible way and to divide them into sub-complexities?
- the user's potential to experiment, to explore, to model - to learn by discovery?
- thinking in terms of correlations and interdependencies, building (complex) mental models? Does it lead towards a more systemic and holistic way of thinking?
- the discovery and uncovering of meta structures - learning by transfer?
- the reflection of the user's own learning process - 'learning how to learn'?
- To what extent does this medium, i.e. this particular way of dealing with factual contents, stimulate more intense communication or co-operation with others - or does it rather obstruct such processes?
- Does the medium itself provide occasion to leave the medial world again (for example, are there suggestions to make use of additional resources for the work or proposals to gather one's own experience) or does the medium 'entrap' the user?
- Does the medium itself or its use convey or reinforce attitudes, sets of values, thinking in roles and such like? Is this made obvious by the medium or does the medium give rise to a critical reflection on this?

The aim of this work is to find new media from the mass which can improve the quality of learning.

2.3 Examples of 'good new media' for learning

Examples of 'good new media' for learning are new media that comply with today's requirements for programming, factual content, subject-related and media-related teaching methods, and which help improve thinking and recognition, i.e. learning.

Among other things this means new media:
- which permit quicker learning or a better illustration of the subject matter or which help achieve a deeper knowledge than could be achieved by means of conventional media;

or

- which allow new methods of exploration to be used in the classroom;

or

- which make such new pedagogically meaningful objectives achievable as could not or could hardly be achieved to date.

In addition to this, these new media for learning must invite actively constructive and performance-orientated learning as well as support a school education which is experience-, science-, and future-orientated.

3   ADVISORY CENTRES FOR NEW TECHNOLOGIES

The need for information and the questions and problems teachers are faced with regarding new media for their lessons vary from person to person. It is hardly possible to meet these needs by means of the traditional in-service teacher training which is determined by what is on offer rather than by the actual need.

In order to deal with these needs in an appropriate and flexible manner, the federal state of North Rhine-Westphalia has set up, over the past few years, an advisory system which comprises one central advisory centre for new technologies and five regional ones. The regional advisory centres are places of call for teachers - places where access is provided to all the information compiled in the advisory system and where advice is given on all questions regarding the use of new technologies in class. Regional advisory centres are places both for exchanging information and for making contact with others.

At the regional advisory centres teachers can:
- get information and advice on all questions about equipping schools with new information and communication technology. A wide range of hardware and software products are available here for examination and testing, in particular, interfaces, sensors, functional models etc. for use in the classroom.
- do on-line searches in the database SODIS with the assistance and advice of the centre's staff. Teachers can, of course, also subscribe to the database SODIS for their school.

- examine and test all exemplary new media for learning since they are all installed on computers here. This way it is possible for them to get their own impression and to judge the media themselves.
- be given individual advice on all questions concerning the use of new media in the classroom - up to and including assistance in the actual planning of lessons.
- find out about new ideas for lessons and suggestions for projects with respect to the exemplary new media. They can discuss them with the centre's staff and can contribute new ideas and examples of their own to the system.

The staff of regional advisory centres:
- establish contacts between teachers who are grappling with identical or similar questions or problems. On request, they also supervise and advise working groups which have been established in this way; they evaluate the results of this work and incorporate them into the advisory system.
- go into schools to give teachers on the spot advice if so required.
- find out where information or advice is required on a general level and react by making appropriate offers themselves or by pointing out the discovered needs to an institution for teacher training.

4   ACCEPTANCE AND PROSPECTS

Initially, teachers reacted rather cautiously to this new way of getting information and advice. Initially, they had been used to in-service teacher training oriented towards what was on offer (rather than towards actual needs). Here, by contrast, the teacher's own active initiative was asked for.

Quite soon, however, all those who had taken up the offer discovered with how little time and effort they could get hold of up-to-date information, how very individually their questions and problems were dealt with, how inexpensively they could try out many things themselves and how much their own work could be enriched by contacts with other teachers beyond their own school boundaries. Today, the advisory centres are much-frequented and it is advisable to make an appointment prior to going there.

In order to deal with teachers' needs and interests even more appropriately and comprehensively, the following ideas are currently being considered:
- A combination of the advisory system for new technologies with a similarly designed system for traditional media. In the future, any competent advisory system on media will have to take into account traditional and new media in combination.
- The possibility of making use of telecommunications. Up-to-date information particularly can be made available to teachers in a way which costs even less time and money than it does so far. The co-operation between teachers over great distances could be supported more effectively.
- Making the offers and possibilities of the existing nets - especially the Internet - accessible in such a way that they can also be used directly for educational purposes by teachers and pupils. This aspect has given rise to additional hope for an improved quality of learning.

5 REFERENCES

Der Kultusminister des Landes Nordrhein-Westfalen (ed.) (1990) *Vorläufige Richtlinien zur Informations - und Kommunikationstechnologischen Grundbildung in der Sekundarstufe I.* Die Schulen in Nordrhein-Westfalen, 5051, Frechen.

Landesinstitut für Schule und Weiterbildung (ed.) (1995) *Orientierungshilfe zur Ausstattung von allgemeinbildenden Schulen mit Hard- und Software.* Verlag für Schule und Weiterbildung, Bönen.

Landesinstitut für Schule und Weiterbildung (ed.) (1996) *Prüfung Neuer Medien für den Unterricht.* Verlag für Schule und Weiterbildung, Bönen.

6 BIOGRAPHY

Wolfgang Weber was born in 1954, and studied mathematics and biology at Bielefeld University between 1973 and 1979. He was a teacher at the Gesamtschule between 1979 and 1990, and made a study of computer science between 1988 and 1991. Since 1990 he has been deputy head of the Advisory Centre for New Technologies at the State Institute for Schools and Further Education of North Rhine-Westphalia, Germany.

16

A knowledge based model of a networked teachers' training centre for in-service training with information and communication technology

David Passig
Bar-Ilan University
Ramat-Gan, Israel

Abstract

This article suggests a philosophical framework for an Israeli model of a computerised Networked Teachers' Training Centre (NTTC). It describes a community model being developed by a local community and the Education Ministry of Israel. The article clarifies the mission statement of the NTTC. It delineates what is being done in training three groups of teachers in three disciplines: science, mathematics and literacy through a rich Information and Communication Technology (ICT) environment. It provides an evaluation of this initial phase and draws the multidisciplinary approach of the centre for a communal curriculum development as its second phase.

Keywords

Teacher education, information technology, knowledge based

1 INTRODUCTION

The committee for scientific technological education recommended in its report (Harari, 1992) to the Israeli Ministry of Education to establish regional support centres for the study of mathematics, science, and information and communication technology (ICT). These centres would be set up by subject areas, and would be equipped with all the necessary means of communication - computer communication and other audio-visual means - in order to assist teachers in their developing needs.

The 'Tomorrow 98' staff, which was set up in the Ministry of Education to realise the Harari Committee recommendations, published a list of principles and goals and called upon local communities to suggest programmes and 'creeds' for regional teachers' centres on the basis of the committee's recommendations. The staff called on them to propose programmes for co-operation between the staff and interested municipal forces.

Following the manifesto of the 'Tomorrow 98' staff the education department of the Ramat Hasharon city initiated an educational program for a networked community teachers' centre. This article describes the goals and mission of the centre as drafted by the steering committee in co-operation with the local authorities and the 'Tomorrow 98' staff. It clarifies the philosophical basis and community 'creed' for the goals defined, and reports on the results of the evaluation of Stage 1 of the project.

2   KNOWLEDGE BASED TEACHERS' CENTRE

It is customary to refer to the present era as 'The Information Age'. However, there are those who claim (Harkins, 1992; Perelman, 1993) that we are entering a different era - the Knowledge Age. It is not sufficient, in the Knowledge Age, just to have skills and training for accessibility to information in order to have an advantage over others. The Knowledge Age argues for the need for skills to achieve a successful application of information in real time. Those who possess skills for gathering information in real time, analysing it, classifying it, and organising it with new meaning are the ones who will acquire social, cultural, and economic advantages.

In previous generations the isolated elite had to handle information that was voluminous and complicated in order to direct the efforts of people to improve their living conditions. These efforts took place in relatively small communities. In the Knowledge Age, on the other hand, information in imaginary amounts can be available to many who will compete globally in its use. In order for human society to succeed in directing its efforts and improving living conditions efficiently it will need a considerable number of students, citizens, and thinkers who will make their contribution such that they will be able to contribute additional human, ethnic, and special cultural value to existing information (Passig, 1995).

In order to train teachers to manage an educational environment which will enable converting information to knowledge, it is only natural to set up a supportive environment that will enable teachers to train themselves and to try out the learning processes which transform information to knowledge. We must do more than just build a supportive environment for teachers which trains them mainly to access and deal with information, as is being done in Europe (Veen 1995; Bruce, 1995) and in the USA (Welch, 1995).

3   THE MISSION OF THE RAMAT HASHARON NTTC

The mission was formulated as follows:

"The networked centre for teachers in Ramat Hasharon will work on developing innovative skills and talents for teaching in computerised work environments in professional and multifarious fields of knowledge.

The centre will train the teachers of the community to integrate the use of information resources in the processes of teaching/learning, to assemble collections of computerised learning materials for colleagues in the community, and to develop community information resources on special subjects.

The networking system that the centre will operate will enable access to materials and discussions between groups of colleagues.

The centre will develop and accompany leading teachers who will serve as agents of change for teaching in computerised environments in the schools of the community. The areas of knowledge in the centre are: sciences, mathematics, literacy, and ICT."

The Networked Teachers' Training Centre was established during the first three months of setting up the project (September-December 1995). The regional networks known as BBS are more suitable to defined professional communities. They are separate from world networks, such as Internet, which are connected to millions of users with access certification all over the world. The regional networks are intended for a more limited number of users for designated purposes. They offer quicker, more economical and more efficient services which can be independently run according to predefined needs. Therefore, they are especially suited for educational needs.

4   TRAINING ARRANGEMENT

Since the Ramat Hasharon support centre aspires to train the educational community for the construction of knowledge and information, and since the accord of teacher colleagues supports the process of knowledge construction, the training of teachers in the centre itself was put into the declaration of goals.

In Stage 1, 41 teachers are taking advanced study courses in frameworks of 240 hours, six instructors in various fields, and a steering committee. The steering committee consists of an academic advisor, the project manager (director of the education department of the Ramat Hasharon Council), a pedagogical co-ordinator, and five subject area heads. All of them, 55 in all, were equipped with colour computer notebooks loaded with various software packages and communication tools. The teachers were encouraged to take the computers home and use them for their personal needs too. The teachers in Stage 1 were chosen from elementary and junior high schools. In Stage 2 (academic year 1996-7) the NTTC will include high school and kindergarten teachers. In Stage 1 the centre is open one day a week. In Stage 2 the centre will extend its operation for additional days in accordance with the number of participant teachers.

Table 1 Stage 1 Participants

Field	Instructors teachers	Elementary teachers	Junior high teachers	Total	Hours
Mathematics	2	8	8	16	240
Literacy	2	9	6	15	240
Sciences	2	6	9	15	240

The teachers participating in Stage 1 were chosen from fields of knowledge which were recommended by the Harari Committee and those being taught in the schools - sciences, mathematics, literacy, and ICT. The training of teachers in new learning methods and materials in each field was turned over to national leaders developing modern teaching materials.

4.1 Mathematics

The advanced study courses in mathematics were taught by the mathematics staff of the Weizmann Institute headed by Dr. Rina Hershkovitz and Dr. Alex Friedlander. The courses focused on a number of topics.

<u>Elementary school teachers</u> - use of calculators and computers on the basis of a deeper understanding of mathematics; another view of mathematics as a profession composed of authentic problems; geometry teaching methods in combination with varied means and graded applied problems.

<u>Junior high school teachers</u> - Learning methods with interactive ICT; organising the learning process in a computer integrated classroom; alternative ways of evaluation in teaching mathematics with ICT.

4.2 Sciences

The advanced study courses in the sciences were conducted by Dr. Sarah Klachko. The courses focused on a number of topics.

<u>New materials</u> - deepening the knowledge of the teachers in two subjects in the sciences - ecology and energy.

<u>Continuity of learning</u> - building a continuity of learning from the elementary to the junior high schools with the two chosen subjects.

<u>Preparation of learning materials</u> - preparation of activities in the chosen subjects and setting them up in the network.

4.3 Literacy

The advanced study courses in literacy were conducted by the literacy staff of the centre for literacy in Levinsky College, headed by Dr. Hanna Ezer. The courses focused on two topics.

<u>Literacy teachers</u> - deepening the knowledge of the teachers in the didactic field of literacy and exposure to computer applications in teaching literacy; special emphasis was placed on the formation of the concept of their function as literacy advisers to teachers in various subjects.

<u>The teachers in general</u> - in the plenary meetings all the teachers studying in Stage 1 were exposed to theoretical and practical problems in literacy and ICT; all the teachers also received training in a variety of computer applications - word processing, information retrieval programs, computer communication, and multimedia tools.

5 EVALUATION

5.1 First questionnaire

A first evaluation procedure was conducted at the first meeting with the teachers before beginning any activity in the centre. Forty-one teachers participated and filled out a two-part questionnaire. In the first part there were 19 closed questions concerning their willingness to accept changes at personal and school levels, their readiness to learn how to use new pedagogical tools, and their positions concerning computers and computer communication. In the second part the teachers were asked to indicate those things which, in their opinion, teachers need today in order to successfully perform their function.

At first we analysed factors in order to put together the questions which examined the same world of content. In this analysis we found four factors which satisfied the criterion Eigen value>1. These factors are:

- The attitude of the teachers towards computers. This factor explained 22.9% of the variation.
- The apprehension of the teacher about teaching with the aid of computers. This factor explained 12.7% of the variation.
- The teacher's readiness for changes. This factor explained 11.5% of the variation.
- The attitude of the teacher towards the need to use new pedagogical tools in their work. This factor explained 9.0% of the variation.

At the second stage we have calculated the internal reliability coefficients (Kronbach alpha) for all four factors. Factor 1 - 0.90, Factor 2 - 0.68, Factor 3 - 0.67, and Factor 4 - 0.54.

Clearly, the internal reliability of the first factor is the highest, that of the second and third factors is reasonable, and that of the fourth factor is low (a partial explanation for this may lie in the small sample number).

The possibility of a linear connection between the four factors was examined. It was found, according to the Pearson correlations which were calculated, that the lower the teacher's apprehension for working with computers the more positive his or her attitude to computerised communication was ($r=-0.27$, $p<0.05$). Also, the more the teacher reported a stronger aptitude towards new pedagogical tools and to adapt to them, the more positive was their attitude towards computers ($r=0.37$, $p<0.01$).

5.2 Second questionnaire

Three months after the beginning of the activity in the centre, the teachers were asked to fill out a second questionnaire. The questions examined various aspects of the project (satisfaction on the part of the various professions, atmosphere during the lessons, motivation, and involvement), and the criteria for success as defined by the steering committee (understanding of the connection between the professional and the interdisciplinary parts, introduction of changes into teaching, mastery of computer applications).

The answers clearly indicate that the teachers attended cheerfully and were motivated to learn (97%), and that the material studied was relevant to the level of their school classes (87%). All the teachers (100%) felt that the instructors were professional, that they were committed to the success of the project, that there was a positive atmosphere, and that there was co-operation in the lessons.

A significant part of the group (85%) indicated that they saw changes in their work as teachers following their participation in the project, and that the training instilled a desire in them to read and study by themselves. There were no significant differences in the responses of the elementary school teachers and the junior high school teachers.

The purpose of this questionnaire was to follow up the effect of the project on the work of the teachers. We expected that the more the project advanced the greater the percentage of teachers who would report on the influence of the materials learned on their work in the classroom. It seems that already at this stage of the training (three months from the outset) at least a third of the teachers participating felt that there was an effect on their work. Particularly salient were the effects on their ways of thinking in preparing lessons (61%), on the technical possibilities that were available to them (61%), on understanding the needs of the students (70%), on the form in which material was transmitted in the lesson (54%), and on the integration of the computer in the work (67%).

6   CORRELATION

After analysing the second questionnaire, we set up Pearson correlations in order to examine whether there was a linear connection between the teachers' answers at this stage and their answers to the first questionnaire (which was given out before the beginning of the training).

The results show that just as the teachers reported in the first questionnaire a more positive attitude towards computers and computer communication, so they reported after three months that they are attending classes cheerfully and are motivated to learn (0.60=R), that they are satisfied with the lessons on the computer (0.50=R), and that they feel involved in the learning process (0.66=R).

Three months after the beginning of the year long training the teachers reported that the training already had an effect on their work by enabling them to communicate better with their students (0.61=R), by enabling them to work with other teachers (0.41=R), and to understand better the subject being studied (0.42=R).

The results showed that just as the teachers revealed in the first questionnaire a greater readiness for change at the personal and school level, so they reported after three months that they saw changes in their work as teachers (0.49=R), that the instructors showed a complete commitment to the success of the project (0.68=R), that the training had already had an effect on their work in their way of thinking when preparing lessons (0.53=R), in relating the material with other materials (0.60=R), and in better understanding the needs of their students (0.45=R).

From these correlations it can be clearly inferred that the teachers after three months had already developed positive attitudes to computers and computer communication and a readiness for changes in their personal and school level. They indicate that the teachers were greatly satisfied with the training set-up on a community model of a teachers' centre and in a technologically rich environment. The correlations also indicate advantages of the community model as a factor which generates a quite rapid effect on the teacher's classroom work.

7   GOALS FOR A SECOND STAGE

National projects of information resources for teachers on the model of "Science Community" (http://www.lamda.org.il) and international projects like Teacher's On-line, which supply daily lesson systems to teachers in various fields of knowledge (http://www.southwind.net) answer principally the need to give teachers access to updated resources of materials in the subjects they are teaching. However, the model of the community teachers' centre, which we are reporting here, set for itself a more developed goal. Since we identified the developing tendency in modern society, characterised by a Knowledge Based Environment, we set a goal to design an environment in which the teachers in the community would be trained to derive knowledge from information. We believe that we are transgressing reality if we should settle for a design of a support environment for teachers that just prepared them mainly to access, to deal with and to extract information.

For this purpose the steering committee of the centre met towards the end of Stage 1 and framed the following goals for Stage 2.

1. Interdisciplinary and multidisciplinary training.
2. Extending the activity to kindergarten and high school teachers, school principals, and students.
3. Expanding the activity - from local community activity to functional regional activity.

8   REFERENCES

Bruce, A. (1995) *SCET Contact: The Development of a National Bulletin Board Service for Schools - Results and Evaluation of a Pilot Project in Scotland Covering 150 Secondary Schools.* A paper presented to The Open Classroom Conference, Oslo (September 95).

Harari, H. (1992) *Report of the Supreme Committee for Education in Technological Sciences.* Ministry of Education and Culture, Israel, August 92.

Harkins, A. (1992) *Knowledge Based Learning: Bridging Industrial Education to the Knowledge Age.* Saturn Institute, St. Paul, Minnesota 55104.

Passig, D. (1995) Teaching Programs in Virtual Environments: Directions and Future Needs. *Computers and Education,* January, **32**.

Perelman, L. (1992) *School's Out: Hyperlearning, the New Technology, and the End of Education.* W. Morrow, New York.

Veen, W. (1995) *Telematic Experiences in European Classrooms: Overview and Evaluation.* A paper presented to The Open Classroom Conference, Oslo (September 95).

Welch, A.S. (1995) *What Stimulated the Rapid Growth of Distance Learning in the USA.* A paper presented to The Open Classroom Conference, Oslo (September 95).

9   BIOGRAPHY

David Passig teaches future technologies at Bar Ilan University, Israel. He develops curricular materials in the areas of multimedia and virtual reality.

17

Educational seminars focusing on use of information technology to enhance learning of curricular topics

Sindre R Øsvik
Municipal School Director in Giske Kommune,
Leader of Norwegian Educational Computer Society,
Øvre Nordstrand, N-6050 Valderoy, Norway

Abstract
This paper presents a concept of educational development based on a series of seminars used by the Norwegian Educational Computer Society, to support educational use of IT. The seminars focus upon the uses of IT when teaching curricular subjects and topics, and aims to produce practical and useful lessons where IT is an integral part of the lesson or a learning-tool.

Keywords
Professional development, classroom practice, collaborative learning, integration, pedagogy, teaching materials

1   INTRODUCTION

During the last 5 years the Norwegian Pedagogical Computer Society (NPD) has organised short seminars on educational uses of Information Technology (IT). This paper will focus on the idea and purposes of these seminars: aims; methods; and results.

NPD was founded in 1986 to enhance the educational uses and usefulness of IT. In contrast to the national computer society which existed prior to this date, NPD focused on the pedagogical uses of IT, rather than the technology itself. It is more correct to consider NPD to be an educational society rather than a computer society, but NPD is an associated member of the national computer society (DND), which is the national member of IFIP.

2   SUPPORTING TEACHERS' EDUCATIONAL USE OF IT

To fulfil the ideas and aims of NPD, different courses and seminars have been organised. From the very beginning in the mid eighties, the introduction of the technology, and the types of software were considered to be important, and met with interest from teachers. But the educational effects were of minimal interest, often close to none at all. Some teachers using IT in their teaching continued to do so, while others spent time away from school on a course but did not change their teaching practice when they returned to the classroom even though it was pedagogical change that had been originally intended.

The practice of any teacher, any professional, can be considered to be based on three different levels of need:

- professional reflection (ideology).
- planning (justification).
- actual classroom practice.

Consistency between the levels is not always found. The NPD seminars aim at presenting IT tools to enhance learning: by linking the levels of practice, from reflection and planning to actual classroom practice. Teachers need to be offered support in such a way that they can be empowered educationally and personally by the technology. They need to know that they can handle the technology in **their** setting, and that they not only can be, but have to be, responsible for the learning situation in the classroom, in the same way as the student is responsible for her/his own learning. Users at all levels need to **own** the technology, so that it is a natural and necessary tool in their teaching and learning situation.

3   WORKING SEMINARS ON EDUCATIONAL USE OF IT

The seminars are designed to provide such help, with the focus on usefulness in an ordinary classroom setting, related to the subsequent weeks of planning, within the given curriculum, using available software and other learning materials. The seminar participants work together to develop their ideas and make it possible to carry out uses in practice. By the end of the seminar the participants have to present their educational plan in writing; with references to the curriculum, stressing educational aims, giving practical details of how to make the plan useful to others (as an idea, or to run in their own classes). These educational sketches are then made available by copying and distributing them to interested teachers on demand.

NPD has run five such seminars since 1991. The first was on the use of spreadsheets in teaching mathematics, followed by two seminars on 'Teaching Norwegian as a Second Language using IT', and a working seminar on multimedia and 'Educational use of the Internet'.

4   AIMS OF THE SEMINARS

The use of IT should be focused to support the students' learning of a given topic, which the teachers themselves choose, and decide how to prepare for teaching in their classes. The teachers, participants of the seminar, prepare a real lesson they will give in their class, and the plan is written down in such a way that other teachers can understand what, why and how to teach the topic in their class.

Every student in primary and secondary education has the right to be taught at her/his own level. This means that teachers do not teach classes, but individual students, that happen to be organised in a class or a group. The use of IT has to reflect this right, and the aim of the chosen topic has to originate from those contained in the national curriculum guidelines. The use of IT has to support learning, and can be used alone or together with other learning materials.

5   METHOD AND ORGANISATION

After registration and the welcome, the seminar programme is presented. Initially the ideas and concept of the seminar are presented, stressing that it is a **working** seminar, where participants are its' success or failure. NPD, the organisers, act as facilitators. We recognise that we are dealing with pedagogical experts.

Leaving the seminar some two days later, the teachers will be prepared to undertake a lesson or more in their classes. In announcing the seminars, the teachers are asked to bring ideas about the topic they wish to prepare for teaching in their classes after the seminar. During the first session, the participants are asked to present themselves and the subject/topic they want to prepare. They are told to note the others' topics, and identify suitable partners for co-operation during the course.

There follows a pedagogical reflection on the use of IT, before some pieces of software are presented. There is time to examine the software, discuss IT uses and form working groups. This takes about half a day, and then it is time to work in groups (with 2-4 teachers in each group) for about another day. The last part of the seminar is used to present and to discuss. Each group delivers a printout of their presentation, and before leaving they get a copy of all of the educational concepts produced and presented at the seminar. After the seminar, NPD has the right to sell the copies.

We present a common framework for producing these concepts:
1. Title of the topic and the name of the group members.
2. Aims for the lesson(s).
3. Intended group/level of students.
4. Why IT is a useful tool in this learning situation/topic.
5. Resources necessary: equipment, software, other learning material, level of knowledge of the student, preparations made by the teacher.
6. Organisation: of classroom, students, equipment (how much, where: classroom/library, etc.)
7. The lesson(s) in detail (the group decides the level of detail needed, and also the time required for the lesson(s)).

The first three tasks described above are decided by the teacher grouping. The major investment of time and effort is in the discussion and production of point 7. We have experienced extremely interesting discussions when teachers are justifying the uses of IT and deciding the organisation of learning situations/lessons.

6   SEMINAR OUTCOMES

The series of seminars have resulted in the production of five master-copy sets of practical teaching lessons, of variable quality. With very few exceptions, the participants have given the seminar high marks when considering its usefulness. They have indicated that they have both learned a lot about IT, and have gained educationally. Some reports indicate that some teachers had previously participated in many IT courses which had no positive outcomes. They soon forgot what they had learnt, and their knowledge was never practised in their own classrooms. What they indicate they learn in these seminars is educational usefulness of IT, combined with a confidence to start using the technology in their own classroom situations.

They carry a proof of their learning from the seminar: the copied booklet, with ideas which can be discussed and shared back in their own school. This form of outcome was rare, and teachers indicated that they wanted more seminars of this kind.

One of the seminars was duplicated and run twice, identically. The first group appeared to consist of people who really wanted to take part in the seminar. The second group turned out to be more mixed in their intentions, because some had been urged by others to join the seminar. While the first group unanimously applauded the seminar, ranking it to be the best seminar they had ever joined, the next group gave a mixed critique. Most reported satisfaction, but some offered many complaints, about computers not being available when they wanted them; about the computers not working; that they did not see that IT could in any significant way improve their teaching; and that the art-reproduction was better in books than it was on computer graphics. What the organisers noted was that some of these participants were not motivated, they did not want to be at the seminar from the very beginning.

The second group was likely to be more representative than the first group of teachers in most schools. For a representative, or **normal**, teacher, the seminar has to focus more upon motivation. Course programmes have to be given at a slower pace and have to be more detailed, not least when it comes to instructions on the use of the technology. Finally, curriculum need, the need for integration, and showing that IT can support learning, must be stressed to a much greater extent.

7   CONCLUDING REMARK

NPD can be considered a self-help interest group, organising a rather small group of enthusiasts, teachers and administrators concerned with matters of pedagogy, technology and educational policy. We have not made a follow-up study to any of our seminars. We therefore cannot indicate the success of the seminars, to see if the enthusiastic teachers leaving the seminars are really using the lessons they have prepared, or if they are used by others buying them. It seems unlikely, in fact, that teachers buying the resources would use them in lessons, as they are written. But it may be possible that a teacher can find a good idea, or get some inspiration in ways to use some of the software and learning materials described, to produce their own concepts of the situations into which IT can be integrated. The concept of these seminars appear to provide a useful opportunity, because of the focus for teachers to real life teaching preparation. In this way, IT can be identified as a really useful means to support teaching and learning.

8   BIOGRAPHY

Sindre Røsvik is currently a municipal director of Giske Kommune Norway, and for 10 years has been the chairman of the Norwegian Educational Computer Society (NPD). His main interests have been concerned with the development and implementation of educational policy with a particular focus on IT and education.

18

In-service teacher education - a way towards integrating information technology into secondary level curricula

Yvonne Buettner
Fachstelle Informatik der Lehrerinnen- und Lehrerfortbildung
Postfach, CH-4133 Pratteln, Switzerland

Abstract
This paper considers the integration of information technology (IT) into secondary 1 level schools (6th to 9th grade, with pupils 12 to 15 years of age), and describes the situation in north-western Switzerland. Our strategies for moving to the integration stage of informatics use are presented. We have a cascade ('snowball') system to introduce IT use with a range of change agents. A main focus is the in-service teacher education. During the past three years we have made regular surveys to identify the situations in the schools and in the class rooms.

Keywords
Teacher education, curriculum development, integration

1   INTRODUCTION

This work is located in north-western Switzerland, where I am responsible for the in-service teacher education. The pre-service education of teaching staff is provided by other institutions. This paper presents the results of our experiences, both the successes and problems!

With reference to the work of the professional group at the WCCE 95 Conference in Birmingham, the final report identified three stages when moving towards integrating IT, which all countries seem to be moving through.

The Techno Ghetto Stage

Specialised teaching staff are concerned about the topic of new information technologies. Students are primarily taught programming, and a dedicated course is created within the curriculum.

The Keyboarding Stage
The rapid distribution of increasingly less expensive personal computers and the associated software development forces policy makers to deal with the information age. The process of integrating informatics into all subjects is initiated.

This stage is dominated by a broad but basic level of handling, manipulating and operating software by teaching staff involved. Computers are increasingly being recognised as tools for class preparation. It is possible to start directly with the implementation of this second stage.

The Integration Stage
Students are using the new information technologies in all subjects for various tasks ranging from keyboard writing to information retrieval. They are applying the computer quite consciously, and they have a clear notion of its impact on today's society.

2   THE PRESENT DEVELOPMENT IN NORTH-WESTERN SWITZERLAND

From 1988 to 1992 the widespread implementation of informatics in secondary level 1 schools was planned and prepared. We were able to profit thereby from the experiences made in other parts of Switzerland; we started directly at the second, the "keyboarding stage". The goal was the integration of informatics into all subjects.

Initially we offered teachers courses in basic handling techniques. Especially interested teachers started to write lessons showing how they would integrate informatics in their subject. At that time we had to begin at square one: there were no textbooks available on the market for integrated informatics teaching.

In our canton we planned for an introductory period spanning 5 years, from 1992 to 1997. At the outset most of us were of the opinion that after these 5 years informatics would be totally integrated into all subjects. Secondly, we felt that no dedicated class rooms should be necessary and, thirdly, that the majority of students would bring with them from home some computer knowledge.

Experience from those pioneering years has given us a number of additional insights:

- We did not anticipate the lasting **resistance** against computers in general **by some teachers.** The causes of such resistance are not explored in this paper particularly. Many teachers have fixed prejudices about informatics at school, prejudices about programming, algorithms, etc. originating in the "techno ghetto stage". Therefore they are not able to recognise the continuing value of information technologies for their own work and for their students' education.
- We underestimated the **time factor.** Five years was not enough for an integration on a broad scale encompassing 60 schools with 10,900 students, 430 teachers, and the support needed for 1200 computers and associated equipment. In Birmingham it was stated that all teachers must go through the "keyboarding stage". They have to feel at ease in using computers before venturing into the teaching of informatics themselves.

- We did not anticipate the following **side factors of the integration**:
  - integration of informatics needs interdisciplinary teaching. This calls for teamwork within the staff which is rarely practised by our teachers.
  - teaching from the front of the class is no longer feasible with only a few computers in the classroom. Even young teachers coming directly from pre-service tend to teach from the front of the class.
  - pedagogues must reconsider what knowledge and how much will be delivered. Schools must teach also how access to knowledge is gained and, how information should be prepared and processed. The teachers have not yet learnt to deal with the specific demands of the information age.

As in every successful pioneering venture we had to adapt the process to address the experiences and obstacles indicated above.

Currently we expect a completion time of 15 to 20 years from the onset to reach the complete integration of information technologies. This may appear on first impressions to be a long time, but we are dealing with a cultural change on a large scale, and such changes demand a longer period of time.

3   STRATEGIES FOR GETTING INTO THE THIRD STAGE, THE "INTEGRATION"

It seems that we have found a successful and valid concept and process for the integration of information technologies despite the restrictions due to the delay arising from the experiences mentioned.

The direction of the necessary energy and drive that has been generated from our advisory centre has now changed: what was a push for informatics has become a pull from the side of teachers, staff and students. This means that nowadays teachers are approaching us for help and support; this is an important key, they want to be able to realise their own ideas and ventures.

3.1 In-service change agents

- The computers were our **first agents**, in the sense of ambassadors! All staff study rooms were equipped with sufficient Macintosh machines. The idea was to give the teaching staff the opportunity to practice and indeed to profit from colleagues' experiences. This proved to be an important factor of success. Many teachers realised the value and time benefit brought from using the computer as a daily tool.
- We set up a **central informatics office** with the name "Fachstelle Informatik der Lehrerinnen und Lehrerfortbildung" where knowledge and understanding is being gathered and then distributed to all schools in a "snowballing" system. The informatics centre performs the following tasks: organisation of the informatics in-service courses; documenting examples and cases studies of lessons; keeping up-to-date with all relevant hardware and software; lending out special equipment such as digital cameras, scanners, etc.; support and consultation to individual teachers; co-operating with similar institutions in Switzerland and abroad.
- The informatics centre, together with a small staff of **informatics trainers**, sets targets and prepares for the content of all in-service courses. The trainers themselves are active teachers and thereby our agents to the schools.

•   Each school has an **informatics representative** who is a teacher in charge of supporting and advising his or her colleagues. The informatics representative is gaining continued IT education from our office from specifically designed courses. They help locally with technical problems and they serve as information carriers to and from the informatics centre.

•   Every teacher may contact the centre and receive information and lesson examples and, eventually, hardware support.

I am convinced that this support service available for everybody and at any time is another key factor to successful integration.

Although this means of realisation required an informatics centre, it cannot be termed centralistic; the schools are completely autonomous in integrating informatics into daily school life. This can be done by incorporating IT use during dedicated weeks, regular scheduling, or integrating informatics topics into all subjects. This autonomy is forcing the teachers to deal personally with information technologies and hence they are initiating their own in-service education.

3.2   Changes in the schools and in the classrooms

During the past three years regular surveys have been undertaken to gather information about the IT teaching in classes. We wanted to identify what was really happening in the classes and to get some facts and figures. Based on this survey, we were able to adapt and improve the in-service informatics courses.

During the introduction, the students' informatics curriculum was structured in six areas: basic handling and operation, daily use, impact on society, general vocational preparation, relationship of man to machine, and technical aspects.

The following figures indicate the teachers' activities related to the frequency of occurrence within their own class. All questionnaires were returned. The three vertical bars represent responses for each of the past 3 school years.

1. Basic handling and operational skills
We recognise that basic handling and operational skills occur very frequently. However, the frequency on the left side is diminishing and that on the right hand side is growing.

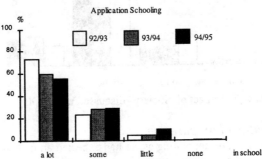

Figure 1 Frequency of basic handling and operational skills in schools

2. Daily use

Here the use of informatics in daily life is being considered, such as computer games, household gadgets, registration scanning, etc.

Teachers seem to be familiar with this part of the curriculum as the majority of responses is towards the left-hand side.

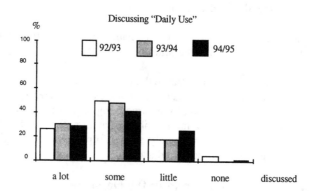

Figure 2 Frequency of "Daily Use" discussed in schools

3. Impact on society

This section includes topics on the protection of data, telecommunications, etc. The majority of results are towards the right-hand side of the table. In our opinion, teachers should consider this field to a greater extent. The slight increase on the far left-hand side is a hopeful indicator.

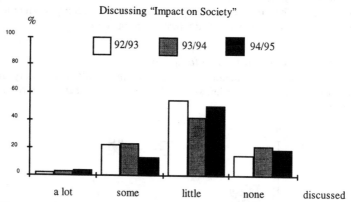

Figure 3 Frequency of "Impact on Society" discussed in schools

4. General vocational preparation

This result is somewhat disappointing as we had expected an increase in responses on the left-hand side of the graph. However, in-service courses have not been offered in this field.

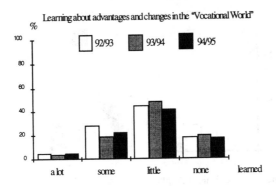

Figure 4 Frequency of "General Vocational Preparation" in schools

5. Relationship of man to machine

This theme is difficult to teach as it deals with the boundaries between man and machine, including artificial intelligence and being able to react responsibly to IT users. In the results there is a slight decrease in responses on the left-hand side of the graph.

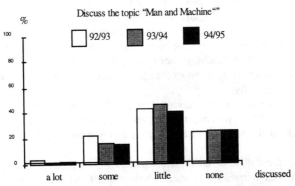

Figure 5 Frequency of "Relationship of Man to Machine" in schools

6. Technical aspects

Robotics, switching, and inputs and outputs are included in this field. Switching, and inputs and outputs are topics that have become less important for school informatics. These topics will be transferred to optional courses.

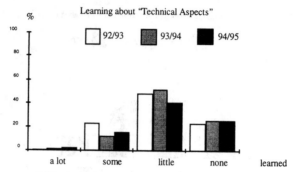

Figure 6 Frequency of "Technical Aspects" in schools

In summary, it appears that we are still working to a large extent within the 'keyboarding stage'. We have to further strive towards integration. Furthermore, it has become clear that the goals of our students' curriculum have been reached to a large extent; we will soon adapt these to improve them.

3.3   The present situation of the teachers

Stimulating teachers has not always been possible, and teachers need to invest both time and interest to achieve significant outcomes. Learning to handle and to become computer literate requires that many hours are spent using the new tool. Integration of informatics into the teaching routine often appears as a far away mountain top to be reached! To gain support, teaching staff have teamed up to jointly prepare lessons and to split the work at hand. Also an exchange of documentation on informatics lessons is taking place regionally.

Beside the influences of the advisory centre, the outside world exerts a certain pressure upon teachers. Students themselves want to become familiar with the new tools and information possibilities and, the computer sneaks into homes and marriages!

Incidentally, about 40% of all female teachers would prefer specially dedicated in-service informatics courses for women. These requests have not been met so far, as it really appears not to further necessarily the issue of integrating ... informatics! Of greater importance would be the opportunity to find more women as trainers.

3.4   In-service education curricula

Informatics trainers
With the rapid development of information technologies, the curricula are now also in continuous change:

Our first trainers' **program in 1988** was strongly biased toward technical aspects and programming. For four weeks discussion concerned switches, systems architecture, machine language, programming in Pascal and Smalltalk, theory on telecommunication, artificial intelligence, CAD and NC.

One week was given to basic operational skills, whereas today this is a prerequisite for participation. Another week was dedicated to writing informatics lesson plans and the final week to methods of adult training.

In the second trainers' **program in 1992** the greatest part of the content had shifted towards adult training and integrative teaching with informatics, with a full week given to technical aspects. Programming had been dropped altogether from the course. As a new element, we introduced a weeks' practice in an industrial or service corporation.

At the time of writing, we are planning the third trainers' **program for 1996**. Technical aspects have been dropped altogether; main issues are methods of adult training and of integrating informatics into lessons. The future trainers will themselves prepare topics like telecommunication, virtual realities, etc., and test those mutually in their own courses. The industrial practice week will be maintained as most teachers have little knowledge of how far information technologies have advanced in the vocational world. We are now able to drop the preparation of lessons as enough developed material already exists. Last, but not least, the duration of the trainers' program has been significantly reduced.

1988 Themes	1992 Themes	1996 Themes
Hardware	Hardware	
Programming		
Telecommunications Artificial Intelligence		
CAD, NC Databases		
Application training		
Informatics lessons	Informatics lessons	
Methods of adult training	Methods of adult training	Methods of adult training
	Industrial practice	Industrial practice
		Individual specialisation
		Test courses

Table 1 Development of the Teacher Trainer Curriculum

Regular supply of in-service courses

In addition to the teacher trainers' courses, we provide other ranges of in-service courses not mentioned within this paper. Our main goal is to help teachers to get to the integration stage. There is no prescribed curriculum in informatics, the objective is stated only as "the teachers themselves are responsible for acquiring the necessary capabilities for teaching their classes with the help of integrated informatics".

We expect this general goal to be a real motivation in their teaching, but with the disadvantage that some teachers will remain at the 'keyboarding stage'.

4   SUMMARY AND CONCLUSIONS

Reaching integration means advancing through the 'keyboarding stage'. This stage may extend beyond that presumed, and the step to integration may prove to be for many teachers greater than expected.

The cascade ('snowballing') concept, using informatics representatives, trainers and the informatics centre, has been successful. Our prime task has shifted from overcoming disinterest or shear resistance of teachers, towards integrating informatics into all subjects. The drive and direction of support from our knowledge and educative informatics centre has changed: a push of informatics has become a pull from the teachers. Problems in the updating of software or hardware can be well handled by today's existing structures; the existing willingness and flexibility of the teaching staff must not be over stressed.

To reach our goal, "integration of informatics into all subjects", we must continue our efforts; of particular importance is an unbroken flow in the supply of relevant courses.

6   BIOGRAPHY

Yvonne Buettner works and lives in Switzerland, where she is a trained teacher, experienced in the pedagogical field of information technologies. She has been a member of the Department for In-Service Teacher Training since 1988. She has worked on the concepts and practice of integrating information technologies into secondary schools in north-western Switzerland. Since 1992 she has been the head of the group with responsibility for in-service training, production of background materials, evaluation and procurement of software and hardware, and for maintaining contacts within Switzerland and with foreign countries.

Section 6: Ways to support teacher education and teacher educator

19

Breaking the cycle of ignorance: information technology and the professional development of teachers

Jean D.M. Underwood
ESRC Centre for Research in Development, Instruction and
Training, School of Education, University of Leicester
21 University Road, Leicester LE1 7RF, UK

Abstract

Despite numerous national and local initiatives there are still many schools within the UK which have yet to take Information Technology (IT) on board in any meaningful way. For the majority, IT flourishes only in pockets of good practice within the school. Lack of resources both in terms of hardware and software and in terms of adequate training are often cited as the prime causes of this failure to advance. The research literature on teacher expertise, however, suggests that there is a more fundamental reason for the lack of progress: the inherent resistance to meaningful change within our profession. What is the nature of this resistance and how may it be overcome? Here evidence drawn from the formal evaluation of Integrated Learning Systems in UK schools will be used to illuminate our understanding of the process of professional development of teachers.

Keywords

Professional development, attitudes, classroom practice

1   INTRODUCTION: THE CYCLE OF IGNORANCE

The starting point of this paper is the discussions held by IFIP Professional Groups 3.1 and 3.5 at the World Conference on Computers and Education (WCCE) held in Birmingham in 1995. The groups noted with concern that despite earlier predictions of a bright electronic future for education, as the end of the century draws nearer, the reality in our classrooms does not match the vision. Although there are pockets of excellence, where IT is playing a significant part in supporting both the learner and the teacher, on the whole we are faced with a bleak landscape of poor or non-existent use of IT. Explanations for this state of affairs generally focus on the lack of resources but the WCCE working group argued that of equal significance is the poverty of knowledge within the teaching profession as a whole. Student teachers characteristically claim that their reluctance to use IT to support their teaching is due to a failure in their formal training which they describe as at best inadequate and at worst non-existent. Sadly, the knowledge base of the majority of practising teachers and of teacher educators is itself fragmentary. It is not surprising therefore that many students are receiving inadequate training. Tutors are not confident in using the technology to support their own instruction and they therefore provide poor role models for the students. As student teachers tend to teach in the way they have been taught - not the way they have been told to teach - they in turn fail to use the technology effectively.

The WCCE working group concluded that there was in effect a *Cycle of Ignorance,* a function largely of the rapidity of the IT innovation cycle, which results in poor classroom practice. They argued that this *Cycle of Ignorance* must be broken and that the most cost effective strategy to achieve this would be to target the IT capabilities of teacher educators. To effect this goal it would be necessary to identify good practice and develop strategies for disseminating that practice across the profession. In brief, the strategy for breaking this *Cycle of Ignorance* consisted of:

• Providing effective role models of good practice for new teachers by raising the IT knowledge of the teacher educators. Although it was acknowledged that providing teacher educators with personal IT skills would not necessarily impact on their pedagogy, it was assumed that it was a necessary prerequisite to pedagogic change.

• However this was seen as only a beginning. The technology is on an exponential growth path and one of the consequences of this is that the tools we now have available are increasingly specialised and subject specific. This subject-specific skills-base needs to be identified.

• For all professions there is a body of skills, knowledge and understandings that are unique to the profession. It was noted that we had yet to specify what the professional practitioner's IT capability would entail, but it was felt that it should include a critical awareness of how specific uses of IT implicitly support or promote specific epistemologies, and the implications of any one approach to IT on the overall process of learning.

• In order to ensure the development of good classroom practice we should identify those factors that will support effective transfer into the classroom.

• This process of self development then needs to be repeated with our students. As teacher educators we need to have both a vision and clearly articulated goals for promoting our students' IT development. The students need to be exposed to many different implementations of IT within the classroom and to have the opportunity to experiment with and evaluate those models. Will this in turn place additional pressure on the teacher educators, or is it enough to provide effective role models for students, and as a profession ensure that a strong, positive signal is transmitted to the student teachers?

• Finally we concluded that there is a critical need for an appropriate and continuing level of professional development for all educators, whether initiate, novice or expert.

The model implicit in these discussions was one of filling the empty vessel through apprenticeship or experiential learning. If we can provide appropriate knowledge and experience first to the teacher educators and then to their students it will be possible to achieve the potential of an electronic classroom. While it was acknowledged that the identification of such appropriate experiences was no trivial matter, and that there were additional barriers such as resource levels that would impede progress, there was a collective feeling that the job was one of scale rather than the identification of more fundamental problems.

Initially depressing though it may seem, I should like to argue that this is not the case and that there are more fundamental issues to be addressed. In order to do this, I would like to draw upon the extensive literature on teacher expertise gathered across a variety of subject domains. As Desforges (1995) points out, we know a lot about novice and expert teachers, but our knowledge is largely descriptive. For example, it is well established that expert teachers have a wealth of subject knowledge, while novices have a more fragmentary and less rich understanding of, for example, the pedagogy of their specific subject area. Further, expert teachers are more flexible in their response to classroom events while novice teachers tend to be more wedded to their lesson plan. Such descriptions have led to a number of stage models of teaching (for example, Berliner, 1988) but these models have done little to illuminate our understanding of the process of how novice teachers reach a level of expertise as opposed to a level of experience.

2 CHANGING PRACTICE

There is a wealth of evidence that teachers, in general, are not given to questioning their professional practice. Teachers at all levels appear to behave in ways that maximise predictability in classrooms (Doyle, 1986) and when their routine operations do not appear to get predictable pupil behaviour, they put in place those actions that will return classroom interaction to the normal status (Brown and McIntyre, 1992). Desforges and Cockburn (1987) argue that teachers have a way of ignoring or absorbing data without recourse to restructuring their conceptions of teaching. They do not seek explanations of the discrepancy. It is not that teachers are insensitive to the 'unusual' in their classrooms, but that their first and most persistent tactic in dealing with discordant or discrepant behaviour is to enforce 'normality'. This resistance to change within our profession crosses age phase and subject boundaries. As Galton (1987) and others have shown, the practice of teachers is remarkably consistent over lengthy periods of time, maintaining the *status quo* is the norm.

How then does change take place? Are there no circumstances under which we can cause a shift in practice? The evidence from the formal evaluation of Integrated Learning Systems (ILSs) in UK schools suggests that change in practice is possible (Underwood, Cavendish and Lawson, 1996). The key purpose of the trial was to evaluate whether ILSs could be used effectively in UK schools, but a subsidiary goal was to observe the impact of the technology on classroom practice. In particular we were interested in the development of teachers' IT skills as they worked with pupils using the system. As the project developed, however, it became apparent that our initial assumptions about the development of IT capability provided a very impoverished view of what was to happen. We identified five areas of impact on teachers working with the ILS. These were impacts on:

- IT skills development,
- classroom practice,
- learning styles,

- reflective practice, and
- levels of collaboration.

Evidence for these effects was available from each of the schools that made a conscious effort to involve their staff fully in this curriculum development. There was, however, a minority of schools that elected to divorce the classroom practitioner from the active use of the ILS. In these schools there was little impact on teacher development in any of the areas we discuss here.

The effects on professional practice documented in this project are of primary interest largely because change is so difficult. Why should working with an ILS, a massive, ability-sensitive but nevertheless drill and practice program, effect change? The first comment to make is that much of the change appeared to be centred on the use of the diagnostic reports produced for individuals and groups of children by the system. Figure 1 shows a section of a typical course report.

Figure 1 Part of a Student's (Sian) Course Report for MATH CONCEPTS

Course Report   Wed Apr 13 1994   08:16   For Student(s) 6-99
MATH CONCEPTS
This line gives information on Sian's current performance
6 SIAN .....Apr 13 1994 IPML:4.71   ATT:29   COR:22 %COR: 76%

These lines give information on Sian's cumulative performance					
SES	**TIME**	**TATT**	......**%COR**	**REVQ**	**AVG**
48	8:15 1500	79	2	5.54	

AD(addition)	DC (decimals)	ME (measurement)
5.65	**5.45**	**5.50**
100%	**92%**	**85%**

Key		
SES	Total number of sessions	TIME Total time in hours and mins.
TCOR	Total number of questions correct	%COR Total percentage correct
IPML	Initial placement level	REVQ Number of strands of work of concern
AVG	Current average level - this *approximates* to grade level	

Desforges (1995) argues that just as scientists will adhere tenaciously to a theory, ignoring conflicting data, unless a new and more encompassing theory evolves, teachers adhere to their current practice, ignoring the research evidence, until or unless that evidence provides a clear practical application into the classroom. The diagnostic reports produced by the ILS had ready application into the classroom. One teacher argued that it helped him as a teacher and that it was now second nature to him to use the diagnostics and produce an appropriate response to a child. For example, he noted that the spelling reports identify individual words and groups of words with which a child has been having difficulty. For this relatively inexperienced teacher, who was acknowledged as weak, the diagnostic support from the system had allowed him to operate at a competent level. Moreover, the senior management in his school commented that the insights he was achieving from using the system were now showing benefits in other areas of his teaching.

Chinn and Brewer (1993), working in a constructionist framework, identified four factors that influence the restructuring of current pedagogic knowledge and practice. They are:

- the effect of 'old' knowledge.
- the quality of anomalous data/experience.
- the depth of processing.
- the availability of alternative cognitive structures.

Here I would like to focus on two of those factors - the teachers' responses to anomalous data, and their depth of processing or level of reflection about those data. Interviews with teachers in the ILS project revealed that teachers viewed the data contained within the diagnostic reports as both reliable and revealing. The following quote is typical of those from many experienced teachers *'the detailed diagnostics are very useful, they often confirm my intuitions but do occasionally highlight problems or successes that I have not noted.'* This acceptance of the quality of output from the system (the quality of anomalous data/experience) is an essential prerequisite to any change in practice.

In addition, our observational data and teachers' own perceptions of their practice showed that teachers were operating as reflective practitioners. The restructuring of knowledge is dependent on not only the acceptance of anomalous data by the teacher but also on the depth of processing of that data. For a few teachers the ILS raised profound questions about what it is to be a teacher and what was actually happening in their individual classrooms. The following example shows the level of that reflective thought. The teacher, commenting on her pupils' progress when using the ILS, stated that *'All the children are successful but the most able also benefit the most'* and she went on to ask herself *'Is that happening in my classroom as well?'* She had also noted that after two years on the system the children were still motivated, that they liked competing against themselves and that they were also happy to tackle new things because they were in a non-threatening non-judgmental environment. Although she perceived that the system corrected, even punished, errors it was *'not personally offensive as it often is in the classroom.'* She understood her power as a teacher and knew that one mis-placed word from her was far more meaningful and could be far more damaging than anything the system said to the children. This teacher felt that working alongside the ILS was in a very real sense a refresher course for herself as a teacher. Chinn and Brewer argue that such deep processing or restructuring of knowledge is most likely to occur when there is strong personal involvement with the matter to hand, as is clearly shown by this teacher.

3   CONCLUSIONS

The research evidence shows that teachers are more likely to close down rather than open up to experience, that is their practice becomes more stable and resistant to change over time (Desforges, 1995). If change is to be brought about through experience then that experience must not only be provocative, but it must be meaningful in both a personal and practical way to the teacher. Throughout the ILS study it has become apparent that the reporting system of the ILS was perceived by teachers as providing not only reliable but valid data on their children. These data had personal meaning for the teachers and were readily applied to the classroom. As one teacher commented *'I would be very reluctant to allow the system to be taken away. BUT it does matter how you use it. It's not a delivery system but a partner with children and teacher in the learning process. You must think of a partnership to get the full benefits out of the system.'* However, interacting with the system has proved to be a stimulus to teachers' professional development. At one level teachers have seen the ILS as a support tool helping them to identify weaknesses in their children's understanding. That is the ILS had provided practical solutions to real classroom problems. In addition, for a few teachers it had led to a rethinking of what it is to teach. The implications of the ILS effect for classroom practice have a significance beyond our understanding of the value of the software *per se*, in that they support current process models of professional development and provide us with some suggestions of how IT can be introduced successfully to a conservative profession.

4   REFERENCES

Berliner, D.C. (1988) Implications on studies of expertise in pedagogy for teacher education and evaluation, in *New Directions for Teacher Assessment.* Educational Testing Service, 39-68, Princeton, N.J..

Brown, S. and McIntyre, D. (1992) *Making Sense of Teaching.* Routledge, London.

Chinn, C.A. and Brewer, W.F. (1993) The role of anomalous data in knowledge acquisition: a theoretical framework for science instruction. *Review of Educational Research,* **63**, 1-49.

Desforges, C. (1995) Experience and knowledge for teaching. *Learning and Instruction,* **5**, 385-400.

Desforges, C. and Cockburn, A. (1987) *Understanding the Maths Teacher.* Falmer Press, Lewis.

Doyle, W. (1986) Classroom organisation and management, in M.C. Wittock (ed.) *Handbook of Research on Teaching.* MacMillan, New York.

Galton, M. (1987) Change and continuity in the primary school: the research evidence. *Oxford Review of Education,* **13**, 81-93.

Underwood, J., Cavendish, S. and Lawson, T. (1996) Technology as a tool for the professional development of teachers, in B. Robin, J.D. Price, J. Willis and D.A. Willis (eds.) *Technology and Teacher Education Annual, 1996.* AACE, Charlottesville.

5 BIOGRAPHY

Jean Underwood is Co-ordinator for Information Technology in the School of Education, Leicester University and chair person of the Association for Information Technology in Teacher Education. She is currently a member of three inter-university research groups investigating the role of IT across all age phases.

20

From personal use to classroom use - implications for teacher education in France

Georges-Louis Baron, Eric Bruillard and Alain Chaptal
INRP -TECNE   *IUFM de Créteil*   *CNDP -DIE*
91 rue Gabriel Péri   *Route de Brévannes*   *91 rue Gabriel Péri*
92120 Montrouge   *94 861 Bonneuil cedex*   *92120 Montrouge*

Abstract
If Information Technology is widely spread in society at large, all studies show that its integration in schools occurs slowly and poses many problems related to school organisation, the contents of curricula, teachers' opinions, etc. We will consider in this paper the possibility of the transfer between a teacher's personal and professional practice and discuss the implications for teacher education.

Keywords
Teacher education; information technology; integration; attitudes; social issues

1   INTRODUCTION

If Information Technology (IT) is widely spread in society at large, all studies show that its integration in schools occurs slowly and poses many problems related to school organisation, the contents of curricula, teachers' opinions, etc. The problem is known to be very complex, and it would be nearly as surprising to identify a single factor influencing classroom integration than to find a magic wand ensuring it. However, teacher education is certainly a key issue, since teachers are in charge of organising and facilitating students' learning.

We will consider in this paper the possibility of the transfer between a teacher's personal and professional practice and discuss the implications for teacher education. In effect, it is our opinion that, in order to develop student-centred activities, it is necessary to develop in the first place teacher-centred activities in the field of computer assisted presentation tools.

2   TWO VIEWS ABOUT IT INTEGRATION INTO CLASSROOM ACTIVITIES

2.1 The issue at stake

There is little doubt that the traditional model (a teacher who speaks, students who listen and write) is still dominant in the French educational system. However, the idea of using resources to teach (mainly to improve the transmission of knowledge) is gaining popularity. But this process is slow. The idea that each teacher knows better than anyone else (including his/her own colleagues) how to produce these tools or resources is still very strong and results in a noticeable lack of a culture of use with resources or documents.

Furthermore, the idea that subject expertise leads to teaching expertise without pedagogical preparation has been for years a rather classical act of faith in France, that is now losing credibility. In the realm of IT, there have been recurrent opinions maintaining that teachers acquainted with technology can afterwards easily invent creative ways to use them in the classroom. As time has passed, however, it has become clear that things are more intricate than was initially believed. Hardly anyone, nowadays, would seriously think that it is sufficient to provide untrained teachers with powerful hardware and software to ensure that they will use them efficiently.

Integrating IT into teacher classroom practice poses problems of inter-teacher transfer (how can "success stories" which have occurred in particular contexts be adapted to other situations?) and problems of "intra" personal transfer (how can abilities in personal computer usage be used in professional practice?). An issue much debated in France, that has consequences for teacher education, is as follows: is it sufficient to train teachers in the use of "bureautic software" (generic software), that is to say word processors, spreadsheets, presentational tools and other related software? The answer is certainly not straightforward and various opinions are expressed by a range of commentators currently.

2.2 Examples

Optimists claim that one can see good reasons why transfers should exist: teachers live in a world of information technology and get more and more proficient in the use of IT related devices. It would be rather surprising that they should be unable to operate transfers towards their professional life or, at least, that such links could not exist. This concept may be supported by the use of software to produce documents, for example. Because the software acts as a tool to improve efficiency and productivity, it helps teachers in tasks that do not interfere with their traditional expertise. It seems reasonable to assume that their use will spread, as it has done previously with photocopiers or spirit duplicator devices.

At the same time some indicators suggest that the rate of personal computer ownership of future teachers is becoming quite significant, but with differences in level according to subjects taught: the highest rates of ownership being with teachers of technological fields, followed by scientific ones and, some way behind, literary subjects (Baron and Bruillard, 1996).

If a banal usage of IT in education is far from being widely spread, it does seem to be increasing. A recent French survey of second degree teachers' classroom use of audio-visual aids (n=622) showed that, among teachers who consider themselves to be well equipped with IT, 46% claimed to be frequent users of audio-visual aids in their classrooms. However, this was the case with only 13% of those who had little home equipment (Chaptal, 1995). Conversely, among frequent users, the level of school equipment seemed less important.

2.3 Counter-examples

On the other hand, however, counter-examples may be given: technologies like tape recorders, radio, photographic equipment, are commonplace, but do not have an important impact on school practice. Pocket calculators are widespread devices, but their uses are not fully developed. Recent studies show that teachers think that children should not use calculators as they may not master the techniques of mathematical operations with integers (Bruillard, 1995). How can one hope to integrate a technology against teacher will?

An important issue is that pocket calculators are instruments liable to interfere with curricula and that they can easily be used outside teachers' control. This certainly contributes in a major way to the fact that they are not spontaneously integrated. More generally, all innovative interactive instruments pose specific problems: how is it possible to control their uses, how sure is it that the investment in time will be beneficial? (Bruillard and Baron, 1996; Baron and Bruillard, 1996). The same is true, in the French context concerning the technology of education. Due to pedagogical traditions, many teachers are neither enthusiastic nor prepared to use it, inasmuch as it could interfere with the control they exert on the classroom situation.

An example may be drawn from the Minitel example. Minitel is very commonplace in France as there are more than 6.5 million of these very simple, freely distributed, network terminals in households and offices (this is roughly twice the number of customers of the most important American on-line service providers). Many experiments have been launched, that showed that Minitel has a real potential as a communication tool between classrooms, notably when it was used by convinced elementary teachers (Guihot, 1993). Nevertheless, the overall use of telematics in schools remains limited compared to its levels of social use.

When Centre Nationale de Documentation Pédagogiques (CNDP) launched its Educâble Service (a near video-on-demand service, which consists of a bank of 850 pedagogical films connected to a Minitel service, from which subscribers to a cable site can select the films they need when they wish to use them in their classes), it was discovered that without specific training sessions there was only very limited use of the interactive part of the service (Briantais, 1994; Debats, 1994; Filippi, 1994). This is remarkable, when you recognise that one of the most popular Minitel telebooking services is specifically targeted for teachers. That is to say, the same teachers who frequently ordered goods through a Minitel at home, and found it user-friendly, do not want, or do not dare to use it in the classroom without training. This is not surprising, since using tools in a classroom context is a public performance that requires much more competence than domestic uses that tolerate failures.

On the other hand, one must not forget that user-friendliness is probably not the final word for technology integration. Let us remember the important use of a spirit duplicator or mimeograph (which certainly was not very friendly) by teachers before photocopiers became affordable for schools. These tools spared time and efforts for teachers in their everyday tasks. They were very simple but efficient and we can assume that this was the reason for their success.

3   AN ANALYSIS OF SOME TRANSFER CONDITIONS

As Larry Cuban remarked (1986), teachers adopt those technologies which are affordable more easily, which provide ways to solve *their* problems, and which allow them to reinforce their control on educational processes. According to Bridget Somekh (1995), educators must be convinced of the educational value of technological innovation to incorporate it in their curriculum planning. She argues that the approach of teachers concerning the role of the computer should not be limited to that as tutor or as a neutral tool, but that it should become a cognitive tool, which requires specific kinds of competencies.

Considering the issue of transfer between personal and professional practice, we fully agree with those authors, but would like to add some further remarks. Firstly, instruments which are designed to solve subject specific problems, since they can replace and potentially interfere with human skills, occupy a very specific place. Their mastery is undoubtedly necessary but certainly this is not enough, since effective transfers will depend upon curricular issues that do not have individual but have social solutions. Possible solutions are constantly being built and tested, with the help of the community leading research in the field, but it will certainly take time for some of them to be established.

Regarding other technologies, the studies we are leading on the issue of IT integration into education suggest that there are no systematic transfers from teacher's personal expertise towards classroom practice, which implies that something else is needed, to which pedagogical engineering ("ingénierie éducative") might contribute significantly (Chaptal, 1994).

Trying to understand why some uses might "succeed" led us to look for pertinent factors. This exercise is difficult, since there are so many intertwined variables which intervene. Integration should be thought of in a multi-faceted way: in one respect, within the ordinary framework of classroom teaching and, in another respect, within the school, but in activities occurring outside the scheduled courses; we will focus here on the analysis of factors playing a part in the integration of information technology, except for the case of software instruments. First, we will list variables that seem important to us, considering them according to three levels: a macro level (in the society at large); a meso level (relative to schools) and a micro level (relative to classroom practice). Then, we will discuss critical issues about presentation tools.

3.1 Important context variables

Macro level	Meso level (school organisation)	Micro-level
Social diffusion (social access) Cost (investment and recurrent use) Range of use Typical use (limited to school, cultural, professional, technical, familial, entertainement…)	Integration in the curriculum Compatibility with the school organization Existence and type of institutional support Forms of approach prescribed Teachers' culture of using documents	Extent of teacher control (on contents / on the production, on the interaction with students) Types of usage Position regarding pedagogy This latter issue appears manifold: collective presentation tool; teacher's usage, inside or outside classroom; individual student use, spontaneous or prescribed by the teacher

Table 1 Context variables playing a part in the integration of IT in schools

Table 1 gives an overview of the different variables to be considered when analysing possible integration of educational technology devices in schools. Considering a specific technological device, it is possible to attribute values to all these variables and to obtain a global analysis for its possible integration. Actually, every technology is not characterised by the same "signature". The variables we have so far presented may serve to define critical issues, which might be predictors of the possible level of integration: ease of use, versatility, ease of production, extent of control by the teacher. We cannot discuss here in any detailed way the different types of "signature" referring to different technologies and will only focus on the case of presentational tools.

3.2 The case of presentational tools

The concept of presentation software is generally thought of as being relatively wide, since it spans simple overhead acetate generation to computer assisted experimentation and interactive schema presentation. Many uses are possible, from the occasional presentation of documentary evidence to structured interactive demonstrations in geography, mathematics, natural sciences, etc. The characteristic point is that the initiative comes from the teacher, who uses the tool like a kind of electronic blackboard. It is plausible that, without revolutionising teaching, those presentational tools could offer an increasingly useful place in teacher practice, along with classical audio-visual means.

The same tools can, in effect, be used in the production and presentation process, and hence reinforce teacher control. This production process is rapid, and can be controlled by teachers. Access becomes commonplace, ease of use and ease of production become more and more real.

Social pressure is increasing and will have an impact on the teacher's business, which may lead to new ways of organising schools. This new process is seen merely, at first sight, as an improvement of the traditional way of teaching.

We believe that forms of transfer from personal uses by teachers *towards some classroom uses* will exist, corresponding to the use of software presentational tools. This is the key hypothesis of a co-operation project developed between France and

Québec, which was initiated a year ago and is currently operating under the name "École Informatisée clé en mains" (on-going results are presented in Puimatto and Bibeau, to be published). In any case, teachers have to be prepared for possible changes which will in some ways affect their job.

4   IMPLICATIONS FOR TEACHER TRAINING

Teacher training remains a critical issue (see for example Baron and Bruillard, 1994; OTA, 1995; Davis et al, 1995). But which forms of teacher education? What is going to be valuable in helping students to pass certification is likely to be more used in colleges of education. What is very new or that which implies significant changes in traditional ways of teaching is likely to have only a marginal place, which may mean that it is used just-in-case it is needed. Can trainees be helped to gain confidence when using IT? How is it possible to prepare them to be creative teachers afterwards?

The answer is not easy. Even if novice teachers master new technological tools, they often have no real ideas about how to integrate them into their teaching practices. After a couple of years of practice, they have acquired some confidence in their competencies in teaching, but their technological mastery has often decreased. Many experienced teachers are not interested in technology, do not volunteer to attend training sessions about technology, and cannot therefore integrate technology into their practice. How can a process of change be initiated?

We suggest that a possible solution might be to train pre-service teachers to use presentational tools, distinguishing three successive steps, corresponding to three thresholds:

- First step: being able to produce paper documents using a word processor.
- Second step: integrating different forms of resources from a variety of places for producing documents.
- Third step: producing computer presentations.

This initial training, of course, will not be entirely sufficient, and further in-service actions will have to be developed. One important obstacle, however, is the fact that many mentors are not trained. Specific training is needed for these advanced teachers as well as a service aiming at providing teachers with adequate support both in the field of technology itself (which must not be underestimated), and in the field of flexible resources. This is one of the goals of the "ingénierie éducative" approach, which is both a service activity and a publishing one. With the development of solution providers, such as the "ingénierie éducative" approach, the time may soon come for information technology to be an actual answer to teachers' needs and no longer be a playground for technologists misunderstanding their business.

5 REFERENCES

Baron, G.-L. and Bruillard, E. (1994) Information technology, informatics and preservice teacher training. *Journal of Computer Assisted Learning*, **10**, 2-13.

Baron, G.-L. and Bruillard, E. (1994) Towards the integration of information technology in compulsory education? Potentialities and constraints, in J. Wright and D. Benzie (eds.) *Exploring a New Partnership : Children, Teachers and Technology.* North Holland, IFIP, Amsterdam.

Baron, G.-L. and Bruillard, E. (1996) Information Technology in French Education: Implications for Teacher Education, in B. Robin, J. Price, J. Willis and D.A. Willis (eds.) *Technology and Teacher Education Annual 1996,* Proceedings SITE 96, AACE, pp. 59-62.

Briantais, E. (1994) Educâble - the Educational Cable Televideo Library - a Service of Pedagogical Films on Demand. *EMI,* **31**, 2, 71-76.

Bruillard, E. (1995) *Usage des calculatrices à l'école élémentaire et au début du collège. Etude de cas dans le Val de Marne.* Rapport interne 95/01, IUFM de Créteil, 97p. + 76p. (annexes).

Bruillard, E. and Baron, G.-L. (1996) Interests of Mathematical Interactive Instruments in teacher training, in B. Robin, J. Price, J. Willis and D.A. Willis (eds.) *Technology and Teacher Education Annual 1996,* Proceedings SITE 96, AACE, pp. 177-180.

Chaptal, A. (1994) A policy for change : Instructionnal Technology Project Management, in J. Wright and D. Benzie (eds.) *Exploring a New Partnership : Children, Teachers and Technology.* North Holland, IFIP, Amsterdam.

Chaptal, A. (1995) Vous apprendrez demain. *Education and Management,* 16, CRDP Créteil, pp. 38-41.

Cuban, L. (1986) *Teachers and Machines: The Classroom use of Technology since 1920.* Teachers College Press, New York.

Davis, N., Willis, J., Fulton, K. and Austin, L. (1995) The Current Status of Technology Teacher Education: An International Comparison. *Technology and Teacher Education Annual 1995.* AACE, Charlottesville, USA, pp. 801-804.

Debats, P. (1994) The Practical Use of the Educational Cable (Educâble) Service. *EMI,* **31**, 2, 77-80.

Filippi, A. (1994) Teaching by Cable in the Nord/Pas de Calais Region. *EMI,* **31**, 2, 81-85.

Guihot, P. (1993) An experiment of computer mediated communication in French schools. Proceedings of the IFIP Conference, *Informatics and Changes in Learning,* pp. 227-250. Gmunden, Austria.

OTA (Office of Technology Assessment) (1995) *Teachers and Technology: Making the Connection.* OTA-EHR-616, Washington D.C.

Puimatto, G. and Bibeau, R. (eds.) (to be published) Technologies de l'information à l'école: stratégies d'intégration. *Actes du séminaire Ecole Informatisée Clé en mains.* Presses du Québec, CNDP, Montréal, Paris.

Somekh, B. (1995) The Implications of Requiring Preservice Teachers to "Evaluate the Ways in Which the Use of Information Technology Changes the Nature of Teaching and Learning". *Journal of Technology and Teacher Education,* **3**, 2/3.

6   BIOGRAPHIES

Georges-Louis Baron, professor of education, is head of the TECNE Department of the French Institute for Educational Research. Having worked for many years in the field of informatics in education, he is currently interested in the social and cultural issues related to the integration of information technology within the educational system.

Eric Bruillard is a senior lecturer in computer science at the University Institute for Teacher Training of Creteil. A specialist in hypertext and educational applications of artificial intelligence, he has a long experience of primary teacher training and a strong interest in the social issues of information technology.

Born in 1949, **Alain Chaptal** is an engineer, who graduate from 'Ecole Nationale Supérieure des Télécommunications' (1972). He was first involved in experimental video projects for schools and resource centres. He joined CNDP (Centre National de Documentation Pédagogique) in 1981 to implement new technologies (for example, electronic mail, and video facilities). Since 1991, he has been 'Directeur de l'ingénierie éducative' (head of the instructional design department) at the CNDP, responsible for introducing new technologies and expertise, and the use of new audio-visual technologies, computer science and telecommunications in the field of education. He is also in charge of the educational service proposed for French cable TV 'Educâble', and the production of educational software and multimedia programs.

21

The integration of information technology into teachers' decision-making

Steve E. Kennewell
University of Wales Swansea
Department of Education, Hendrefoelan, Swansea SA2 7NB, UK

Abstract
The teacher-thinking framework has rarely been applied to research concerning the integration of IT into teaching and learning. This paper explores two main aspects of teachers' decision-making where the integration of thinking about IT can have a major impact on their classroom effectiveness: the planning of teaching and learning activities, and the monitoring of student progress during a lesson. Shulman's framework based on different forms of teachers' knowledge is used to examine the current barriers to teachers' integration of IT into their planning. In particular, the consistent finding that experienced teachers merely assimilate IT into existing approaches to teaching topics is considered to result from teachers' reliance on curriculum knowledge and content knowledge of IT, together with a general pedagogical knowledge which does not allow them to exploit IT fully. Further illumination of classroom issues is provided by McIntyre's concepts of 'normal desirable state of student activity' and of 'student progress'. This theoretical analysis leads to practical conclusions concerning future research and the design of in-service and initial teacher education programmes.

Keywords
Secondary education, professional development, teacher education, classroom practice, information technology, teaching methods

1 INTRODUCTION

The evidence for the learning benefits of IT in the curriculum steadily mounts, but the failure of most teachers to make significant usage of the computer in the classroom at secondary education level is also well documented. This is not a paradoxical situation, since the studies which provide the evidence for learning gains have mainly been carried out in laboratory-style environments, or in the classrooms of teachers who have either been nominated as being particularly effective, or who have willingly come forward to participate in action research, technology innovation or curriculum development projects. Even in the naturalistic studies like those of Olson (1988), the teachers "volunteered to 'adopt' the computer". In the absence of extra support from an expert advisor or project team, it seems that relatively few teachers make significant use of the computer in the natural course of teaching and learning.

In any case, there is no reason to believe that mere usage of computers will result in improvements in learning, nor that studies of usage will divulge any useful evidence about how the promised learning benefits can be achieved. The ImpacT project (Watson, 1993) looked at a number of classrooms with 'high' IT usage and a number with 'low' IT usage. The overall findings were inconclusive, and the greatest illumination was provided by a small number of detailed case studies. These indicated "the importance of the interaction between hardware/software availability and use, and the role of classroom organisation and management and teaching styles". Cornu (1993) calls for an "integrated pedagogy" which "uses new technologies as a fundamental component. Evidence concerning integrated pedagogy is rare, however, and we need frameworks within which to identify and analyse qualitatively the factors involved in the effective integration of IT into teaching and learning.

2   FRAMEWORKS FOR STUDYING IT INTEGRATION

There are many studies concerning the factors influencing teachers' take up of IT (see Gruneberg and Summers (1992) for a review of these), and it is possible to identify frameworks for the study of IT in education which are quite well developed, such as those concerning the 'impact of technology on learning' and the 'institutional support for change'. There has been relatively little attention paid to the 'teacher thinking' framework, however.

Veen (1993) has identified the importance of teaching styles and of teachers' beliefs about their subject and about teaching in general. He highlights the extent to which teachers assimilate IT into existing styles of teaching, and change beliefs only slowly. Carey and Sale (1993) investigated teachers' change to a more 'facilitative posture' when teaching with IT, but found no significant difference. Although Sherwood (1993) found that many teachers who had integrated IT had changed styles in response to the computer, these teachers seemed to have beliefs which pre-disposed them to change and made them highly motivated. Offir and Katz (1995) further highlighted the significance for IT integration of teachers' general motivation to innovate and change practice.

Whilst there is consistent evidence that most teachers are now favourably disposed to the idea that IT can improve learning in their subject, teachers also give consistent responses concerning the barriers to use of IT in their classrooms which they perceive. The list of obstacles almost always includes difficulty of access to computers, software unsuited to the curriculum, and lack of time to prepare lessons with computers (see, for example, Pelgrum and Plomp (1991)). Yet it does not appear that merely providing hardware, suitable software or time to develop skills and plan lessons will enable teachers to fully exploit the undoubted potential of the technology to enhance teaching and to give learners more opportunity to satisfy their individual and group learning needs. Research into in-service teacher education consistently finds that teachers request that more attention is given to classroom implementation.

I shall explore the issues of IT integration within teacher thinking constructs under two main headings: planning lessons and monitoring student progress.

3   EFFECTS OF IT ON TEACHER PLANNING

It is now normal for IT to be integrated into the **planned** curriculum, particularly in England, Wales and Northern Ireland where the learning of IT is part of the statutory requirements and the national curriculum organisations have encouraged an integrated approach. In most cases, these curriculum plans result in IT being part of the curriculum which students receive. But the quality and quantity of students' experience is very varied (OFSTED, 1995), and if the effectiveness of learning with IT is to be improved, teachers must develop the knowledge which enables them to integrate IT into their everyday planning and decision-making.

Shulman (1986) identifies three types of subject knowledge relevant to teaching: subject content knowledge (the facts, concepts and structures of the subject concerned), curricular knowledge (understanding of programmes and materials designed for the teaching of particular topics at particular levels), and pedagogical content knowledge. This last form includes "the most powerful analogies, illustrations, examples, explanations, and demonstrations ... the ways of representing and formulating the subject which makes it comprehensible to others ... an understanding of what makes the learning of specific topics easy or difficult ... the preconceptions that students of different ages and backgrounds bring with them to the learning". Wilson, Shulman and Richert (1987) extend the list of forms of teachers' knowledge to include knowledge of other content, knowledge of educational aims and knowledge of learners. Although all these suggested forms of knowledge are relevant to the issues of IT in education, the subject knowledge types, together with general pedagogical knowledge, appear to have the most significant implications for the issue of integration. I will examine each of these knowledge types in turn.

Curricular knowledge of IT involves knowledge of software, resource packs, and ideas for activities. This knowledge is relatively easy to develop, and enables the teacher to incorporate IT activities into lessons. But unless the teacher can evaluate the activities and relate them to the pupils' developing concepts, they may neither illustrate, explain, demonstrate - or make comprehensible - the topic being taught. Consider, for instance, the science teacher who has obtained a spreadsheet template which models the energy flow for a room. He may be content to implement a straightforward activity where pupils insert data into the model and read off the results obtained. This would miss the opportunity for the 'What if ...' questions which will be needed for the students to gain a real understanding of the relationships amongst the variables.

So, perhaps *content knowledge about IT* itself is a more promising matter. Certainly, an increasing number of teachers are gaining subject knowledge of IT, through initial teacher education, in-service education and training (INSET) and personal use for professional and leisure purposes. However, although this may give teachers the confidence to use IT in the classroom, they may not be able to transform their knowledge for pedagogical purposes in the way that Shulman (1987) describes. Furthermore, few teachers are developing conceptual knowledge of informatics as a discipline, and it is debatable whether the sort of limited experience and training that is available to most teachers will enable them to construct representations of IT concepts which are adequate to support pedagogical reasoning and action. Consider the history teacher who has learned informally to retrieve bibliographic information from the library using IT, and has received training on the setting up of a file of census records from the 19th Century. She still has some way to go in order to be able to plan an appropriate sequence of instruction and activities for pupils which enable them to pose suitable hypotheses and provide evidence for or against them using this new source of primary data in addition to the more familiar media of text and images.

The integration of IT into *subject content knowledge* is more difficult to achieve, since IT must become part of the way the teacher knows his own subject. For instance, Carey and Sale (1993) quote Becker's (1990) finding concerning teachers of English in US schools that "most lessons related to composing and expressing ideas in writing do not involve the use of computers" and that lessons involving IT "focus on teaching students how to use word processing programs", rather than on the effective or creative use of language. And, whereas, traditionally, mathematicians have come to know about graphical representations of functions through laborious plotting of points and drawing of curves, students can now come to know this topic through typing the relevant formula into a graph plotting program. This difference may well make a fundamental difference to their thinking about whole areas of mathematics. There is a vicious circle operating here; IT can only be part of the way one knows a subject if one has learnt through the use of IT oneself. The more recent entrants to the teaching profession may be in this position, of course, and we must hope that the current impetus for higher education (HE) to integrate IT into teaching and learning will help break this cycle of IT deprivation. Currently, however, there is little sign of even young student teachers thinking about aspects of their subject through IT-based representations.

The role of IT in *general pedagogical knowledge* is covered well by Somekh and Davies (1991), as they set out the changes in pedagogy which may be necessary in an IT learning environment. Together with further points identified by Kennewell (1995), they correspond well with the sort of pedagogical practice which has been found to be most effective generally in bringing about long term learning. As an illustration, Hoyles and Sutherland's work (1989) on learning mathematics in a Logo environment highlights the general knowledge the teacher needs about managing the learning environment so as to give students ownership of their tasks and to support them in their particular approaches.

However, Hoyles and Sutherland's work also shows that merely adopting this general approach is not sufficient without the application of specific *pedagogical content knowledge* to the design of tasks and to intervention during students' work on them, in order to challenge the students' intuitive thinking and stimulate the development of formal concepts. It is this understanding of how the teacher should combine with the IT resources to help the student make progress towards specific learning objectives and enable the level of attainment to be raised.

4   EFFECTS OF IT ON TEACHERS' MONITORING OF LESSON PROGRESS

The analysis in terms of teachers' knowledge types gives us some insight into the relation between teacher thinking and IT learning environments. But there is another level of analysis which also needs to be addressed. Brown and McIntyre (1993) identify two types of concept that teachers use to determine their actions during the course of a lesson: the *normal desirable state of classroom activity (NDS)* and *student progress*. The NDS is the set of conditions of certain behavioural variables which the teacher considers the most appropriate. This is a well-developed concept for experienced teachers, and they will be able to vary the conditions desired, without any apparent mental effort, according to the class, the activity, and the stage of the lesson. Any departure from the NDS will stimulate a brief decision-making process concerning action to be taken, and in most cases will result in an intervention procedure which may be either a routine response or a more considered interaction with a student or students. The 'progress' concept is a dynamic one which allows them to monitor changes in the state of task completion or, more rarely, cognitive change in students. This concept supplements NDS in decision-making, and may cause the teacher to intervene if student progress, individually or as a class, is perceived to be unsatisfactory.

We can see here how a teacher's thinking must change significantly if IT is to be integrated into a lesson, since the IT environment changes the NDS conditions from those which she has developed and refined over the years. Furthermore, the usual signs which indicate student progress (or lack of it) may also be missing, particularly if there are no marks of paper to show for a period of activity. It has been noted (Watson, 1993; Kennewell, 1995) that pupils generally measure their progress only in terms of producing the perceived outcome of the task set, rather than in terms of their actual learning. In an IT environment, teachers often share this product-only view of progress and do not take the opportunities offered for improved monitoring of their students' development of understanding. The teacher must learn to recognise new conditions as desirable and recognise new signs of progress - possibly conditions and signs that would have been contra-indicators in traditional classroom situations, such as movement around the room and animated conversation between students. Although such conditions are not unique to computer-based activity, there may be changes to the way a teacher should react in an IT environment, since the computer is helping to manage the learning and behaviour of the students. In return for this help in management, the teacher can help the computer to aid student progress by intervening with probing questions and challenging tasks.

5   IMPLICATIONS FOR RESEARCH AND FOR TEACHER EDUCATION PROGRAMMES

There are many issues still to be explored concerning the link between teachers' knowledge and their use of IT. It is not clear, for instance, how the adoption of different types of educational IT application - specific CAL packages, flexible teacher tools, and generic software tools - depends on teachers' own capability with IT. We need a greater number of qualitative studies which explore the place and development of IT in teacher thinking through techniques such as concept mapping, interviews about instances, and stimulated recall.

The above analysis in terms of teacher thinking helps to explain why in-service teacher education centred on the technology or on the curriculum has been found to be inadequate in bringing about the integration of IT into lessons, and work in different countries over recent years suggests that a whole-school approach (Ridgway and Passey, 1991) and a teacher-centred approach (Owen, 1992) should be adopted more widely. Furthermore, it suggests that we should look beneath the surface of the cliché excuses for failure to use technology and give due consideration to teachers' thinking about IT in their day-to-day planning of lessons and monitoring of learners' progress. The next major steps in the widespread integration of IT should be supported by the use of the teacher thinking framework in the design of teacher education programmes. Such programmes should help teachers to develop their general pedagogical knowledge by evaluating curriculum knowledge, planning how new IT subject knowledge may be applied, and seeking feedback from the interactive classroom environment. Indeed, explicit discussion by participating teachers of their concepts of pedagogical content knowledge, normal desirable state and student progress should help them to generalise and transfer what they learn from isolated IT activities in the classroom.

We can also draw conclusions regarding initial teacher education. Veen (1993) suggests that "initial teacher training programs should be playing a more aggressive role in changing the situation", but he concludes that initial teacher education "should not aim at the 'know-how' of ... the actual use of IT in schools", and that instead, later teacher development initiatives should pursue this aim. It would, indeed, be wrong to focus entirely on **technical** know-how in initial teacher education programmes. But all the evidence discussed here indicates how difficult it is to change established practices and that experienced teachers tend merely to assimilate IT into their existing approaches. It is therefore vital that IT should gain a foothold in student teachers' nascent **pedagogical** know-how.

There is no predetermined body of pedagogical knowledge which we can just <u>issue</u> to student teachers, of course. Indeed, they will start to construct their own knowledge before their course of teacher preparation, and will continue developing it (we hope) long afterwards. Their general and subject-specific pedagogical knowledge will interact and grow together. This growth will be very rapid during the early stages of their careers, and so it is vital that IT must start to permeate their planning and decision making during the initial period of teacher education.

6   REFERENCES

Becker, H. (1990) *How computers are used in US schools: basic data from the 1989 IEA Computers in Education survey.* Centre for Social Organization of Schools, Johns Hopkins University, Baltimore.

Brown, S. and McIntyre, D. (1993) *Making Sense of Teaching.* Open University Press, Buckingham.

Carey, D. and Sale, P. (1993) A comparison of high school teachers' instructional postures in regular classrooms and computing environments. *Journal of Information Technology in Teacher Education,* **2,** 181-192.

Cornu, B. (1993) New technologies: integration into education, in D. Watson and J.D. Tinsley (eds.) *Integrating Information Technology into* Education. Chapman and Hall, London.

Gruneberg, J. and Summers, M. (1992) Computer innovation in schools: a review of selected research literature. *Journal of Information Technology in Teacher Education,* **2**, 255-276.

Hoyles, C. and Sutherland, R. (1989) *Logo Mathematics in the Classroom.* Routledge, London.

Kennewell, S. (1995) Education for IT capability: progress and barriers in South Wales schools. *Welsh Journal of Education,* **4**, 81-94.

Offir, B. and Katz, Y. (1995) The teacher as initiator of change: fact or fiction? *Curriculum and Teaching,* **10**, 63-66.

OFSTED (1995) *Information Technology: a review of inspection findings 1993-4.* HMSO, London.

Olson, J. (1988) *Schoolworlds, Microworlds.* Pergamon, Oxford.

Owen, M. (1992) A teacher-centred model of development in the educational use of computers. *Journal of Information Technology in Teacher Education,* **1**, 127-138.

Pelgrum, W. and Plomp, T. (1991) *The Use of Computers Worldwide.* Pergamon, Oxford.

Ridgway, J. and Passey, D. (1991) *Effective in-service education for teachers in Information Technology.* NCET, Coventry.

Sherwood, C. (1993) Australian experiences with the effective classroom integration of information technology: implications for teacher education. *Journal of Information Technology in Teacher Education,* **2**, 167-180.

Shulman, L. (1986) Those who understand: knowledge growth in teaching. *Educational Researcher,* **15**, 4-14.

Shulman, L. (1987) Knowledge and teaching: foundations of the new reforms. *Harvard Educational Review,* **57**, 1-22.

Somekh, B. and Davies, R. (1991) A pedagogy for information technology. *The Curriculum Journal,* **2**, 153-170.

Veen, W. (1993) The role of beliefs in the use of information technology: implications for teacher education, or teaching the right thing at the right time. *Journal of Information Technology in Teacher Education,* **2**, 139-154.

Watson, D. (ed.) (1993) *The ImpacT Report.* Department for Education and Kings College, London.

Wilson, S., Shulman, L. and Richert, A. (1987) '150 different ways of knowing': representations of knowledge in teaching, in J. Calderhead (ed.) *Exploring Teachers' Thinking.* Cassell, London.

7   BIOGRAPHY

Steve Kennewell taught mathematics and computing in secondary schools in England prior to a period as a specialist computing teacher and then IT Advisory Teacher for the City of Birmingham. He now lectures in IT and mathematics education in South Wales, and has particular research interests in teacher education, mathematics education, the development of IT capability, and computer modelling across the curriculum. He is joint editor of the journal Computer Education.

22

An adventure in integrating educational computing within teacher education

Phil Nanlohy
Faculty of Education, University of Western Sydney, Macarthur
P.O. Box 555, Campbelltown, NSW 2560

Abstract

As the study of Information Technology (IT) in initial teacher education courses has developed, more emphasis has been placed on educational computing within curriculum areas and on the use of computer-based resources in children's learning. Teacher education institutions have provided instruction through discrete educational computing subjects, through the permeation of these studies into curriculum subjects and through mixes of these two approaches. Use has also been made of telecommunications, practicum and school based subjects. This case study describes the use of CD-ROM adventure software to permeate IT into initial teacher education, the prior classroom trials of the learning strategies being taught and the students' responses to this experiment.

Keywords

Elementary education, teacher education, classroom practice, literacy, multimedia, pedagogy

1   INTRODUCTION

The historical development of Information Technology in Teacher Education (ITTE) began with discrete computer literacy subjects, then discrete educational computing subjects and moved on to the permeation of these studies into other curriculum subjects and into practicum and school based subjects (Robinson, 1996; Oliver, 1994; Heppell, 1993; Wright, 1993; Pratt, 1993). Discrete subjects are close to the traditional university model of subject specialist teaching but Information Technology (IT) studies have the benefit of linking these understandings to the student teachers' future work role. Wright (1993) discussed the case for separate Information Technology subjects to develop the computer literacy of student teachers. He believes the "challenge is to educate for a future in a technology-centred information age - the opportunity is to apply technology to revolutionise the process of education".

An alternate approach has been termed an integrated or permeated approach. Here educational computing is taught within curriculum-focused subjects. Pratt (1993) cautioned that "Permeation cannot succeed without staff expertise but staff will not gain expertise unless they are required to teach IT as part of their course". Oliver (1994) argues that, like school teachers, teacher education lecturers and teacher education students need to experience models of IT use in their own learning before such technologies will be adopted for use with the children the student teachers will teach. Robertson (1996) supports Oliver's view that permeated IT should be designed in such a way as to provide more than a token integration of IT into a few subjects. He suggests that "coherence and progression pose greater challenges for the permeated approach".

Downes (1993) surveyed a cohort of final year student teachers from Western Sydney about their experiences with IT during a block practicum. They reported minimal use of IT in the classrooms in which they had been working. Half the group had experienced a discrete "computers in education" subject prior to the practicum and half the group would complete this course after their school experience. There was no significant difference in IT usage between these two groups. Where IT use had been reported it was the teaching practice of the class teacher that was the main determinant.

These findings suggest that it is classroom teachers using computers who are best placed to provide examples of good practice for student teachers and teacher education lecturers. Sherwood (1993, pp. 172-176) reported the views of Australian teachers who were experienced in using IT in their working lives. Almost 76% replied that the use of computers in their classroom had made a difference to teaching methods. These teachers reported that "the most significant change .. has been the move from teacher-centred to student-centred classrooms". The problems identified by Sherwood were in part: inadequate training both at preservice and in-service phases: lack of teacher educators with direct experience of educational computing; limited resources and finances.

2   PERMEATION OF ITTE AT THE UNIVERSITY OF WESTERN SYDNEY

Following a course review in 1991 the primary teacher education program at the University of Western Sydney (UWS) in Macarthur underwent major changes. This review recast the structure of the undergraduate degree into a more integrated model. As a result there was no longer a discrete compulsory educational computing subject in the core program. A decision was made to integrate educational computing into other appropriate curriculum subjects. Specialist educational computing lecturers within the faculty volunteered to be part of the teaching teams of these subjects. In this way they were able to assist in the design of integrated tutorial activities and assignment tasks. By 1995 the degree programme had evolved to a stage where there were four subjects from a total of eighteen designed to include educational computing.

The permeation model being trialled at UWS, Macarthur Faculty of Education involves the integration of educational computing as a methodology in curriculum areas through provision of computer based tutorials in appropriate subject units within the degree course.

"We are trying to:

- improve quality of teacher training to improve educational outcomes for the children our students will teach,
- reflect good practice in schools,
- broaden lecturers' skills and understandings,
- reflect the philosophy of Bachelor of Teaching" (Nanlohy, 1994).

3   SCHOOL TRIALS OF ITTE STRATEGIES

It has been the practice of the specialist IT lecturers at UWS to conduct research and trials of IT-based learning strategies in classrooms. In this way they learn from school teachers and their students in order to teach their students about being effective users of IT. In the present case study this has been achieved by cultivating opportunities for trialling of exemplary software in senior primary classes. The exchange of skills and information benefits both the school and the university. The school has the services of the lecturer to assist with its staff development. The university benefits because one of its staff can obtain recent and relevant experience within their field of expertise. The nature of the relationships in this arrangement are different from the usual relationships in teaching practice. The student teacher does not meet the school teacher or the students. The lecturer is not placed in the role of supervisor or adviser but rather is a learner first and a teacher second. Heppell (1993, p. 233) believes that the "current generation of children are literally the first children of the information age". This type of school based trial provides opportunities for teacher education lecturers to learn about classroom and home use of IT from children whose experience of literature and of communication technologies is different from those of adults. The lecturer is able to experiment with appropriate IT classroom software and strategies as shown in Figure 1.

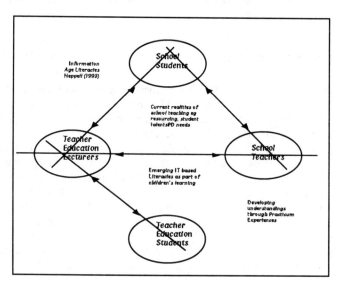

Figure 1 Relationships between teacher education stakeholders

Heppell (1993) suggests that teachers and teacher educators need to understand the emerging capabilities of the 'information generation'. Teacher educators should "become more immersed in the entertainment and edutainment media that are increasingly common currency in young children's day-to-day language and lives". Negroponte (1995) suggests that the model for learning in the future might be seen in the way children learn to use "simulation tools (like the popular SimCity) and more information rich games".

4   TRIALLING THE ADVENTURE WITH PRIMARY STUDENTS

In the trial that led to changes in the UWS teacher education course, the CD-ROM adventure game "Mist" was used to stimulate purposeful writing with two groups of senior primary students. "Mist" is a prominent example of CD-ROM adventure software. Clicking the mouse in a given direction allows the user to appear to "walk" through a world depicted with finely rendered graphics. Movement is smooth and the point of view is that of "first person participant."

Why use the "Mist" CD-ROM adventure?
This adventure program is a popular game that is an example of an emerging class of mass media text. This program melds mathematics and literacy in an investigation that unfolds a hidden mythical realm. It is useful in a classroom setting because the program provides significant cognitive challenge, has clear links to aspects of state curriculums and provides an experiential learning environment.

The "Mist" adventure has a relatively non-violent scenario. There is emotional violence inherent in the struggle between the male protagonists, Atrus and his sons Sirrus and Achenar. The main female character, Catherine, the mother of this warring family, is cast in a passive role. However "Mist" is most successfully completed by students in pairs or small groups who solve its puzzles through discussion and collaboration. This may be why this adventure is attractive for girls who in the main have stayed away from the "drop dead" variety of computer games. Dale Spender suggests that girls who reject the violent games that feature death and competition are showing good sense. She points out that girls "are interested in personal relationships, in the ongoing story of existence" (1995, p.187).

Teaching plan for the first classroom trial
The first trial took place in an inner-urban Sydney school. The teacher was keen to offer her academically gifted students the opportunity to create personal narratives of the mystery text form. She suggested ten groups of three, with a girl and two boys in each group. The author visited initially the class one afternoon each week to lead whole class activities, and later to conduct writing conferences with each group. The groups had one hour each week to use the "Mist" program.

In weeks 1 to 3 "Mist" was introduced to the class through demonstrations and discussions, and by the end of this period they had reached the stage of individual writing. During the following 4 weeks writing conferences were held in the withdrawal room off the classroom where the computer was housed. Observation notes were kept of the conferences and the group game play. In order to help the students develop their story, questions were asked by the author on the plot and structure of their narrative, how they were to plan the next stage and how they were arranging to work together.

The two most common observations made of the children during this trial described a high level of competition between groups and the disharmony within groups. The gender balance of the adventuring groups (all had two boys and one girl) and the behaviour of the boys meant that these otherwise intelligent, confident and articulate girls were marginalised during their time on the computer, often physically. Efforts to encourage sharing were only partially successful in that only "old solutions" were exchanged in the class discussions. The girls were often left to complete writing tasks after the weekly writing conference. With the exception of two groups, the children's writing was generally at or below their usual standard. The two groups that did write in a co-operative way completed sophisticated texts of a standard well above their previous competent standard.

To get the students' views on the trial, they were asked to complete two feedback sheets. In discussions about the roles played within the groups, the dominant boys explained that they ignored the roles and took control of the game because of their impatience with the other team members. Quick success with the problems of the program was seen as justification for behaviour they acknowledged as inappropriate. The same group expressed a disappointment in the non-lethal nature of the adventure.

Second trial in a country school

Some of the issues addressed in the design of the second classroom trial (which was carried out in a rural central school in a farming area in NSW, where the class had a high level of access to technology) were:

- a stronger focus on "Mist" as a text to shape the content of the student's writing and on the writing and drawing processes used by the program's authors,
- role definitions with clear responsibilities to other group members described and practised as the adventure was introduced to small groups,
- early encouragement of a co-operative environment with regular sharing sessions and creation of "clue cards" as cryptic hints for their peers,
- writing tasks both at the adventure and back at desks described and monitored,
- the "Mist" Story 1 and 2 sheets were retained to provide a first draft structure for the children's narrative and recount texts and to provide feedback on the students' experiences with the program.

This trial had a much more positive set of outcomes. While the younger members of the cross grade classroom lost interest in the adventure, the more senior members were eager to continue. In interviews recorded two months after their trial finished, the children were able to recall in detail the events of their adventure. They had definite opinions on the positive value of the experience for the writing tasks that were involved, but were less impressed with a rigid implementation of the group roles and recording of the events of their adventuring. They reported that the rotation of duties would sometimes be abandoned after the group members had settled into preferred roles. When the girls in the interview group were asked about the lack of active female characters in the adventure scenario they responded that this did not matter so much because they "liked the way the game was played". When questioned on this point they said that they liked the collaborative nature of the decision making required to play the game and the detail and depth of the stories embedded in the adventure.

5   THE UNIVERSITY TRIAL

For the first semester intake of teacher education students in 1995, initial contact with educational computing was part of a compulsory subject called "Foundations of Literacy and Maths". This subject was delivered during tutorials lasting a total of four hours each week for 13 weeks. The tutorials were divided into two hours of 'Introduction to Children's Literacy' and two hours of 'Introduction to Elementary Mathematics'. Educational computing activities were used in these tutorials to illustrate the principles and classroom strategies being discussed. An assessment task worth 20% of the subject grade was designed to draw on what the students had learnt during both aspects of the subject. In addition the subject was intended to satisfy the university-wide compulsory "computing competencies" (UWS, Macarthur, 1995, Calendar p. 137). The assignment was intended to demonstrate good teaching practice suitable for using this type of software as a part of literacy learning in an elementary classroom.

Aided by lecturers and written support material, the students were asked to spend at least ten hours outside tutorial time exploring the same program used with the trial schools. They were asked to use this experience to create a variety of written products that reflected their experiences within the program. Of the 154 students who completed the assignment, work samples were collected from 135 (88%) who were divided into 66 groups.

The university students found that they were initially frustrated by the ambiguity of the adventure but given time and some success became enthusiastic about the inspiration it provided for their writing. A high proportion of the cohort (45 out of 66 groups who returned the survey) specifically mentioned variations of the word "frustrated" in describing their experience with the adventure. The cohort also reported that as they became more comfortable with the adventuring they began to enjoy the experience and got a heightened level of reward perhaps because of the difficulties at the outset:

"Frustrated, Relieved, Distressed, Excited, Sense of achievement, Enjoyable" (Group 33)
"Honestly it was very frustrating, however very enjoyable and extremely challenging" (Group 25)

They were impressed by the graphics technology of the adventure and the inclusiveness of the interface. The students found the small group structure to be very supportive, a way of sharing the workload, and of being more successful in the adventure. This was a useful insight into the nature of group tasks in a university setting.

"Working in pairs was more rewarding, one played one wrote. If one missed information the other might pick it up" (Group 39)

There was a contrast between the university students' and the school students' approach to these experiences. The school students plunged enthusiastically into the game and engaged deeply in the adventure to solve its puzzles. The university students came reluctantly to the technology and many played only as much of the game as was needed to complete the assignments. There was a small group of teacher education students who organised a "Mist Game Day" after the assignments were done because they wanted to be free to play the game without the compulsion of assessment tasks. Where the school students found the writing tasks a chore, that got in the way of their enjoyment of the "game", the teacher education students found delight in writing the journals and the stories because these were familiar tasks and they were well prepared by their experiences in the adventure.

6   FUTURE PERMEATION OF ITTE AT THE UNIVERSITY OF WESTERN SYDNEY

There are some lessons from this use of school trialled IT strategies for the design of university level teaching and learning in the permeated model. They may be summarised with the following points.

- The trial at UWS, Macarthur pointed to the reluctance of teacher education students to 'engage" with computer programs beyond utilitarian purposes like word processing. If permeation is to happen it has to be at the level of integration with curriculum and not as a clip-on application like "word process this assignment".
- The provision of detailed support did not work. A better way might be to provide the lecturers in the teaching team with "in class coaching" as a professional development strategy. In the terms of Joyce, Weil and Showers (1992) this would help "build communities of professional educators" (p. 381). The primary students did not need IT support.

The lessons from the primary students' trials are:
- allow for the fun.
- do not be too prescriptive in the processes you expect the small group to use.
- expect that the school students will be your teacher and be open to their suggestions for improving the use of IT in their classrooms.
- Within a teacher education faculty the implementation of a permeation strategy must be lead by an evangelist who has the support of the leadership of the faculty and who is skilled in supporting adult learners. Such an evangelist has a key role to play in the design of courses, subjects, lectures and tutorials.

Concluding comment

It has become a truism that human society is moving into an information age. The implications of the development of information processing technologies for society are manifold (Spender 1995; Negorponte 1995; Ong, 1982). Spender posits the demise of print as the main medium for information transfer and suggests that the nature of learning and the current support structures for learning will change. She suggests that the "concept of a (university) degree will become rapidly and increasingly inappropriate". She believes that the qualifications offered by degrees is "based on the premise that you could be trained once and that was it. These days, there is widespread recognition that learning is an ongoing process". Teacher educators are in a privileged position to respond to these imperatives. They are able to offer experiences to their students that will help them in turn prepare their students for the changing world.

7   REFERENCES

Downes, T. (1993) Student Teachers' experiences in using computers during teaching practice. *Journal of Computer Assisted Learning*, **9**, 17–33.

Heppell, S. (1993) Teacher Education, Learning and the Information Generation: the progression and evolution of educational computing against a background of change. *Journal of Information Technology for Teacher Education*, **2**, 2, 229–237.

Joyce, B., Weil, M. and Showers, B. (1992) *Models of Teaching*. Allyn and Bacon, Boston.

Nanlohy, P. (1994) *Integration of Computer Based Learning into Preservice Teacher Education*. Paper presented at the Teaching and Learning with Information Technology Conference, Sydney, April 1994.

Negorponte, N. (1995) *Being Digital*. Hodder Headline, Sydney.

Oliver, R. (1994) Information Technology Courses in Teacher education: the need for integration. *Journal of Information Technology for Teacher Education*, **3**, 3, 135–146.

Ong, W. (1982) *Orality and Literacy - The Technologizing of the Word*. Routledge, London.

Pratt, D. (1993) Effective strategies for Information Technology in Teacher Education: the use of an evolving permeation model. *Journal of Information Technology for Teacher Education*, **2**, 1, 53–61.

Robertson, J. (1996) Promoting IT competencies with student Primary teachers. *Journal of Computer Assisted Learning*, **12**, 2–9

Spender, D. (1995) *Nattering on the Net Women, Power and Cyberspace*. Spinifex, Melbourne.

UWS, Macarthur (1995) UWS Macarthur Competencies Policy. *University of Western Sydney Calendar*, p. 137.

Wright, P. (1993) Teaching Teachers about Computers. *Journal of Information Technology for Teacher Education*, **2**, 1, 37–51.

8   BIOGRAPHY

Phil Nanlohy is a lecturer in Educational Computing at the Faculty of Education, University of Western Sydney, Macarthur. His main research interest is investigating successful implementations of teaching and learning with Information Technology at both student and whole school level.

23

Training teacher educators: a case study of integrating information technology into teacher education

Qi Chen
Department of Psychology
Beijing Normal University, Beijing 100875, China

Abstract

The use of IT has had, over the last decade, a growing influence on our educational systems and this is particularly prevalent as we approach the next century, with promises that the Information Technologies will revolutionise education. This paper reports on the findings of a survey of Information Technology and Teacher Education in four secondary schools in China. The investigation shows the current situation of computer use in those secondary schools, the teacher educators' understanding and their attitudes to the integration of the new technology into the curriculum. In conclusion, suggestions for training have been made based on the above investigation and these will be implemented in the spring of 1997.

Keywords

Attitudes, collaborative learning, computer assisted instruction (CAI), information technology, integration, research

1   INTRODUCTION

The use of IT has had, over the last decade, a growing influence on our educational systems, and this is particularly prevalent as we approach the next century, with promises that the Information Technologies will revolutionise education. However, starting to utilise the IT tools that are available to schools requires a deep understanding of the structure of our institutions. In fact, most of these tools do not fit into the method of conventional classroom instruction, and it is only our teachers who can transform the classrooms. The teacher is considered to be the most critical factor in the effectiveness of CAI, and his or her attitude to and competence of using computers and integrating computers into classrooms will directly influence the effectiveness of CAI (Chen, 1994; Watson, 1993). Today it is "teacher training", which includes pre-service training and in-service training that has to come onto the agenda to promote the integration of IT into education.

The training of pre-service teachers has gained wide concern. Many researchers, such as Jongejan et al (1990) all urged that the pre-service teacher should be trained to the level of being comfortable with the use of the computer and develop their abilities and self-efficacy to integrate technology as an instructional tool. Special curriculum subjects such as educational technology should be offered to pre-service teachers. In addition, IT should be integrated into the pre-service training itself, so that the pre-service teachers could learn about computers and their use in learning and teaching, at the same time as they are being personally educated in the learning process in an IT environment. This important means to train pre-service teachers has been strongly stressed by some researchers (Gooler, 1989). A survey of new teachers conducted by Handler (1992) and Pigott (1995) revealed for example, that using and observing computers during pre-service training programmes contributes greatly to later practice when integrating IT into instruction - that is, "they teach as they were taught".

In China, normal schools (which are senior high school level, with pupils approximately 15 to 18 years of age) are responsible for the training of pre-service teachers for elementary schools. The application of IT in normal schools will not only increase the quality and efficiency of these schools themselves, but will also advance the integration of IT in schools generally through the influence of their graduates. However, as some researchers reported (Criswell, 1989; Handler and Pigott, 1995), the application of IT in teacher education in the developed countries is still insufficient to meet the needs of education development. It may be worse in China's system of teacher education. Accordingly, it is an urgent need to promote the integration of IT into teacher education, while the training for teacher educators is one of the major prerequisites. For this reason, we selected the training of teacher educators for our research issues, and conducted this survey to find out the situation in terms of their competences in and attitudes towards IT, together with its integration into instruction, which is considered to be the basis of training.

2   METHOD

Instruments
The questionnaire was developed in the form of a 5-point Likert-type scale, in reference to the research literature concerned. The first part is designed to collect the demographic characteristics of the sample, including ages, genders, subjects taught, and educational backgrounds. The second part concerns the teachers' experience of familiarising themselves with computers and CAI. The purpose of the third part is to find out the sample's competence in computer usage and its integration into instruction, including knowledge about and skills in the use of hardware, software, programming, CAI and instructional software development. The fourth part of the questionnaire reflects the sample's concerns about various kinds of competence to be trained. Finally the teacher educators' attitudes towards the computer and its use in instruction, are demonstrated in the last part.

The sample
197 teacher educators from 4 secondary schools in Beijing were selected by means of stratified random sampling, and 185 valid questionnaires entered the final analysis.

Procedure

The investigators explained the purpose of the questionnaire initially, then the teacher educators answered it independently without signing their names.

Data management and analysis

The responses were recoded and converted to scores, according to the structure of the questionnaire. The data was managed with database software and analysed using Spss/pc+.

3   RESULTS

3.1   General information about the sample

Background information

The age distribution of the sample is listed in table 1.

Table 1 Age distribution of the sample

Age	Frequency	Percent
-25	16	8.6
25-35	68	36.8
35-45	36	19.5
45-	65	35.1
Total	185	100.0

The groups of "younger than 35" and "older than 45" make up most of the sample. The sampled teacher educators, 61% of which are female, included all the subjects taught in secondary schools. 79.1% of them had gained a university Bachelor's degree and the others were almost all graduates from polytechnic schools.

Experience of using computers

67.9% of the sample reported having used computers themselves. 19.7% of them had some experience of applying computers in instruction, while only 2 out of 185 educators had used computers for more than 5 lessons. 60.8% of them had some knowledge of CAI, whilst only 9.2% reported having been taught systematically. (In addition, only 10% of them had ever written any instructional software, and only 6.2% of them had experience of programming instructional software, most of whom majored in maths or sciences).

3.2   Competence on the computer and its integration into instruction

Five kinds of competence

As shown in the table 2, all competence levels listed were considerably low.

Table 2 Educators' competence on the computer and its integration in instruction

Competence	Mean	SD	Minimum	Maximum
Hardware	2.03	.97	1.00	4.50
Software	1.65	.94	1.00	4.89
Programming Language	1.56	.83	1.00	4.67
CAI	1.80	.95	1.00	4.67
Courseware development	1.38	.66	1.00	4.67

Note: The numbers in the columns of mean, minimum and maximum are scores on a 5-point scale.

Whilst it can be assumed that the ability for programming language and instructional software development is not really necessary for teacher educators, the knowledge and skills to integrate IT into instruction are mandatory, and the levels indicated accordingly are far more worrying. MANOVA illustrated significant difference among these three kinds of competence - on hardware, software and CAI (P=.0000), among which the competence level in CAI was found to be the most insufficient.

Since no significant difference in the levels of competence was found between the two groups "younger than 25" and "25 to 35", they were aggregated into one group, and thus only 3 age groups exist. One way ANOVA among these three groups demonstrates significant differences in the five kinds of competence (P<.001). The order is "younger than 35" > "35 to 45" > "older than 45".

There is no significant gender difference in any of the five kinds of competence except that female educators are found to be more capable of CAI (T=2.40, df=155, P=.018).

3.3 Value on the competence to be trained and attitudes towards IT and its integration into education

The survey examined the values that educators placed on knowledge about and skills of using hardware, programming, application software, CAI and instructional software development, as training contents for teacher educators or student teachers, and their attitudes towards IT and its integration into education.

Competence, attitudes and value on the competence to be trained

As shown in table 3, there was no significant correlation between the knowledge level and attitudes. Since most of the sample had no experience of CAI, we reconsidered the relationship using only those who had used CAI, and found that the competence in CAI use was highly correlated with the perceived value of training in software knowledge for student teachers (P<.05), that is, the more they knew about CAI, the more strongly they stressed training about software knowledge for student teachers.

Table 3 Analysis of correlation (* P<0.05, ** P<0.01)

| | Attitudes of total sample | | Attitudes of CAI conductors | |
	Over Computer	Over CAI	Over Computer	Over CAI
Knowledge of CAI			0.5949**	0.3999
Hardware ET	0.1355	0.3839**	0.2646	0.2164
Programming ET	0.2573*	0.4897**	0.3998	0.4905*
Software ET	0.3846**	0.5549**	0.6665**	0.5313*
Integration ET	0.2038	0.7523**	0.1982	0.6010**
Development ET	0.1725	0.5410**	-0.0271	0.2117
Hardware ST	0.0616	0.2705*	0.2210	0.2048
Programming ST	0.1622	0.3965**	0.3540	0.4637*
Software ST	0.1359	0.5051**	0.4332*	0.5460*
Integration ST	0.2038	0.7523**	0.1982	0.6010**
Development ST	-0.0054	0.3379**	0.0296	0.2276

Note: ET stands for training for teacher educators while ST stands for training for students.

The relationship among educators' competence with and attitudes towards the computer and its application in education, and values placed on the competence to be trained was analysed. As far as the sample was concerned, there was no significant correlation between the competence and attitudes, and the relationship between the value and attitudes was complicated. In detail, the attitudes towards CAI were significantly correlated with the perceived value of training (P<.01) and the perceived value of training in hardware knowledge for student teachers (P<.05). The attitudes towards computers were only linked with values placed on training teachers' programming language and the uses of application software with significant correlation coefficients. However, as far as the teachers with CAI experience are concerned, significant correlation was found between the level of CAI knowledge and attitudes towards the computer (P<.01), between views about training for application software use and attitudes towards the computer (P<.05). Furthermore, attitudes towards CAI were significantly correlated with three kinds of training skills of teacher educators and student teachers, whose correlation coefficients decline as follow: integrating IT into instruction, using application software, and programming.

The effects of teacher educators' characteristics on their view of training
Statistical analysis shows that there are no differences between genders on their perceived values of training contents. An ANOVA using age (x3) and education (x3) as independent variables was performed on the values placed on training content. Although not detailed here, the analysis reveals some significant effect or interaction effect on the teacher educators' view of integrating IT into the curriculum and instructional software development. Young teacher educators pay nearly the same attention to integrating IT into the curriculum, regardless of their educational backgrounds, while for older teacher educators, educational background has a significant effect, in that those from Higher Education pay more attention to the integration of IT within the curriculum. For training teacher educators' in developing

instructional software, we found that teacher educators from Higher Education tend to regard this more highly. This difference is also more significant in the older group rather than the younger group.

Moreover, teacher educators' experiences with computers and CAI has an impact on their views towards training. Results of T-tests indicate that teacher educators with CAI experience pay more attention to the training teacher educators' ability to integrate IT into the curriculum, and training students' ability in this respect. Teacher educators with some CAI knowledge think it more critical to train an ability for programming, and the uses of application software. Teacher educators who have written CAI script regard more highly the training for the integration of IT into the curriculum, training the ability of developing instructional software, and training students' ability to integrate IT into the curriculum.

Effects of subject variables on attitudes
Finally we found that the teacher educators' age, gender and educational background have no significant effect on attitudes. However, past experiences of using CAI do influence attitudes to some degree. In particular, teacher educators with some knowledge of CAI show a more positive attitude towards the computer than do those who have written CAI script.

4 DISCUSSION AND PROPOSAL

Teacher educators' attitudes towards IT and its integration into instruction: exciting or worrying?
Teacher educators in this survey were all highly positive and active in IT use and its application in instruction in spite of their differences. Exciting as it seems, we are concerned that there was no significant correlation between competence and attitudes. Only when those with experiences of integrating IT into classrooms were analysed separately, could high correlation between knowledge and attitudes be found (P<.05). Educators may have expectations for computer use which are too high and do not consider restricting factors sufficiently, such as the ability level of students, the objectives to be achieved, and the content to be taught, or they may just invest blindly in purchasing facilities and hardware which are fashionable. This is often found to be so when computers are introduced into schools (Hodgson, 1986; cf. Hodgson, 1994).

In general, there are three stages which seem to occur during the implementation of IT into teacher education. In the early stage (which we term Stage 1), most of the policy makers, administrators, teacher educators and teachers do not recognise the wide ranging importance and implications of computer technology in education, and so they do not know WHY to change. Therefore, only computer teachers and technicians are involved in the use of Information Technology. There is still a large percentage of secondary schools in China which are at this stage. In the second stage, Stage 2, the policy makers and educational administrators, teacher educators and teachers are forced by the rapid development of new technology to think about how to meet the needs of the information age. They start to invest money to purchase facilities, hardware and software, and to train teachers. Some of them even reward those subject teachers who are willing to use computers in their teaching. They have realised the importance of IT and have good intentions, but do not know HOW to use it in schools or WHAT changes should be encouraged. Finally, the ideal stage, Stage 3, is when the administrators and teacher educators understand the role of IT in education and have changed in respect of both their professional practice and research. They must develop mature experiences in integrating IT into teacher education for initial teacher education and in-service teacher training.

Training teacher educators to integrate IT into instruction: an urgent and difficult task

Research results indicate that although Beijing is advanced with respect to education development among cities in China, teacher educators' abilities in instruction with IT is rather poor. The average competencies recorded are too low to meet the demands of carrying out instruction in an information-rich environment as well as teacher training. It is an urgent need to improve teacher educators' skills in order to ensure and enhance the effect of teacher training. We must also face up to this rather poor situation and endeavour to train teacher educators first.

As reported, teacher educators' educational theories are out of date particularly in the area of CAI. What they need most are both the theory and practice of integrating IT into instruction. Many of them have little chance of accessing computers or using technology in education because of the low level of economic and technical conditions, which creates an unimaginably difficult situation for training. Many teacher educators have no intention of developing instructional software because of their lack of ability. Certainly, it is not necessary for everyone to design and develop software, and the experience from computer industries indicates that there is no need for teacher educators to repeat the work of others. In this collaborative society, teachers should know how to choose and take advantage of information and spend more of their time in preparing for their students.

Training should consider prior cognitive structure, and focus on the young teacher educators, especially the active ones

Some research (Cornu, 1992; Watson, 1993; cf. Hodgson, 1994) show that the training model that relies on a core of highly motivated teachers, expecting to pass their knowledge and pedagogical agenda on to their colleagues through a "cascade" effect has limitations, and in many cases the anticipated effect has not worked. However, this plausible view is not necessarily strong evidence against establishing a core of experts. In China, our teacher educators' competence in IT is so low, and the variances among individuals so great, that it will take a long time to improve them all. Thus, we must take advantage of a core and help them become the experts. Though their change can never be directly passed on to other teachers, the collaborative team learning will be helped by these pioneers acting as experts to organise new co-operative teams. We propose co-operative learning therefore, to activate and maintain the "cascade" effect, and our research is on-going.

Content and organisational model of training

To date our training has only focused on technology itself, which is of little help to our teacher educators in obtaining competence in the integration of IT into instruction. However our research is in accord with that of Collis (1994) and Taylor and Stuhlman (1995). In addition, Oliver's study (1995) showed that in pre-service training of teachers using IT, those who emphasise pedagogy tend to more frequently use computers in instruction than those who only devote themselves to the technology itself. We intend to train those active teachers in the secondary schools with:

- basic computing skills;
- up-to-date theories of learning and instruction;
- the wide ranging effective applications of IT in education;
- the trends of IT uses in education, and those aspects which are misleading computer uses in education;
- how to select and evaluate software, and how to integrate new technology into classrooms, etc.

Some recent literature (Hunsaker and Johnston, 1992; Hollings and Worth, 1992) indicated that co-operative team learning will help teachers to absorb the researchers' thoughts, through discussing and negotiating instructional design and study. Gradually, such instruction will lead them to become expert teachers. Perhaps through this training model, we shall see teacher educators improve their ability to integrate IT into the classroom.

5   REFERENCES

Chen, Q. (1994) Some thoughts on CAI. *Journal of Beijing Normal University*, **5**, 92-98.

Criswell, J.R. (1989) Rethinking microcomputer instruction as a part of teacher education reform. *Educational Technology*, **29**, 11, 40-43.

Collis, B. (1994) A reflection on the relationship between technology and teacher education: synergy or separate entities? *Journal of Information Technology for Teacher Education*, **3**, 1, 7-25.

Gooler, D. (1989) Preparing teachers to use technologies: Can universities meet the challenge? *Educational Technology*, **29**, 3, 18-21.

Handler, M. (1992) Successful strategies of increasing technology in preservice programs, in *Technology and Teacher Education Annual 1992*, AACE, Charlottesville, Virginia, USA, 326-328.

Handler, M.G. and Pigott, T. (1995) Technology preparation for preservice teachers: do they feel prepared for 21st century classrooms? in J.D. Tinsley and T.J. van Weert (eds.) *World Conference on Computers in Education VI*, 1045-1055.

Hodgson, B. (1994) The roles an the needs of the teacher, in J.D. Tinsley and D. Watson (eds.) *IFIP WG 3.1 Working Conference: Integrating Information Technology into Education*. Spain: Generalitat de Catalunya, Departament d'Ensenyament, 25-34.

Hollingsworth, S. (1992) Learning to teach through collaborative conversation: A feminist approach. *American Educational Research Journal*, **29**, 2, 373-404.

Hunsaker, L. and Johnston, M. (1992) Teacher under construction: A collaborative case study of teacher change. *American Educational Research Journal*, **29**, 2, 350-372.

Jongejan, T. (1990) Teacher training for technology education in schools of education. *Journal of Computing in Teacher Education*, **7**, 1, 3-11.

Taylor, H.G. and Stuhlmann, J.M. (1995) Project KITES: Kids Interactive with Technology and Education Students, in D. Harris (ed.) *NECC '95 Proceedings*, NECA, 201-206.

Watson, D.M. (ed.) (1993) *The ImpacT Report: An Evaluation of the Impact of Information Technology on Children's Achievements in primary and secondary schools.* Centre for Educational Studies, King's College, London.

6   BIOGRAPHY

Qi Chen is a professor of educational psychology in the department of psychology at Beijing Normal University. She has been involved in research in computers in education since the 1980s. She has investigated the variables affecting the outcomes of computer use in classrooms, and has published papers on this theme. More recently, she has focused particularly on teachers' training in IT at different levels of education, especially upon the training of teacher educators.

Section 7: Case studies of teacher and school development when using information and communication technologies

24

Networking educational change: meeting the challenge of systemic school reform

Bruce Rigby
Directorate of School Education,
525 Collins Street, Melbourne, Victoria 3084, Australia

Abstract

Teachers and schools face unprecedented calls for change which have resulted in a demand for improved teacher education and professional development that cannot be met using established methods. School level interpretation of, and response to, policies and driving factors has produced important answers to the challenge. Computer assisted networking provides a mechanism by which teachers can learn directly from each other and provide peer support in an environment which is enhanced by, but not dependent upon, the participation of teacher trainers and administrators.

Keywords

Professional development, teacher education, innovation, Internet, networks, open learning

1   INTRODUCTION

Calls for educational change are nothing new, but there has probably never been a time when the demands on teachers have come from so many directions or indicated such radical change in content, style and the medium of delivery. Today's educators must not only deal with the call to replace traditional teaching styles with progressive or innovative approaches for pedagogical reasons, but must also address issues such as the fundamental change in the nature of enterprise and employment, declining interest in academic specialities, an increasingly market driven system of education and research, and the pervasive cultural impact of technology and the mass media.

Meeting these challenges will require improved teacher education, both pre- and in-service, an expectation that teachers will accept the responsibility for ongoing professional development and collegial sharing, and that systems will develop a growing sense of professionalism amongst teachers. Based on past experience, it is unlikely that these challenges will be met using traditional approaches alone. Acting in isolation, faculty boards, curriculum committees and government planners are likely to produce partial solutions at best - policies and plans which rely on the goodwill of teachers and the education community generally for adoption and success. Acting alone, training institutions are generally able to contribute solutions only in specialised areas, which lack a mandate or the capacity to bring about systemic change.

The challenge of systematically educating teachers in any particular field is exacerbated by the length of time taken for the results of research and pilot programs to impact on teacher training and professional development programs. This is particularly the case when the topic is the effective classroom and professional use of technology, a field in which the message and even the medium is changing from year to year.

This paper examines the process of networked educational change in the state of Victoria, Australia, where the government has introduced a new outcomes based Curriculum and Standards Framework (CSF), and where a target has been set to provide professional development for 6,000 teachers per year over four years in the effective classroom and professional use of information technology and telecommunications (IT&T).

2   THE DYNAMICS OF A TEACHING CAREER

A typical teaching career is formed by a series of events, processes and drivers which help teachers to acquire and refine skills and strategies within the prevailing policy environment and the social context of school and surrounding community. The events include pre-service teacher education and in-service professional development, typically involving a training institution. Training institutions typically are also involved with research, the results of which hopefully inform teacher education (see Figure 1).

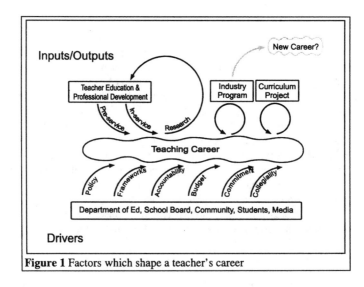

Figure 1 Factors which shape a teacher's career

Many teachers also become involved in curriculum development projects or industry experience programs. Such programs are vital because they not only allow for personal professional growth but also provide an infusion of ideas into the profession generally. Unfortunately for the profession, talented teachers sometimes choose not to return to school after experience in industry, a reminder that school teaching needs to be made as rewarding as alternative professions if the best teachers are to be retained.

The drivers which affect the direction and shape of a teacher's career include factors dictated by the system (policy, curriculum frameworks, accountability and budget) and human factors such as personal commitment and collegiality.

3   SYSTEM WIDE PROFESSIONAL DEVELOPMENT

Is it possible to provide appropriate professional development and support to 40,000 teachers as they implement changes to teaching practice in accordance with a new curriculum and standards framework while simultaneously assisting 6,000 teachers per year to make effective educational use of information technology?

3.1   Limitations of existing models of teacher education

Established models of professional development centre on the development of courses and related materials, and the provision of face-to-face meetings of teachers. The meetings typically take place outside the school setting, requiring replacement of teachers (Figure 2).

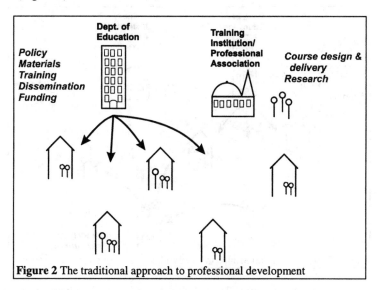

Figure 2 The traditional approach to professional development

Owing to the high level of commitment in schools, it is doubtful that Victoria's professional development targets could be met by conventional face-to-face techniques alone, even if courses and funding were available. Limitations to the traditional model of professional development for the delivery of rapid systemic professional change are as follows:

- additional workload is always required.
- course content is often peripheral/unrelated to own teaching.
- face-to-face courses are likely to create bottlenecks in delivery under high demand.
- subservience may lead to lack of control.
- it fails to reward teacher initiative.
- it is slow to respond to research and teacher/school innovation.

3.2 A networked model

It is proposed that many component solutions to the training and development dilemma lie in the hands of talented educational practitioners who independently embark on missions aligned with broadscale change agendas. Solutions include examples of best practice from the classrooms which are finding their way onto the Internet through self publishing, or the collection of best practice case studies which are now seen as a valuable aid to professional development and school planning. Another component solution is the improved capacity for teachers and mentors to meet and share views within a busy schedule.

By working with teacher networks and taking advantage of computer mediated communication and information sharing techniques, it should be possible to provide teachers with a suite of tools appropriate to the contemporary educational challenges more quickly and with a greater sense of professional ownership and control than would be possible using traditional approaches.

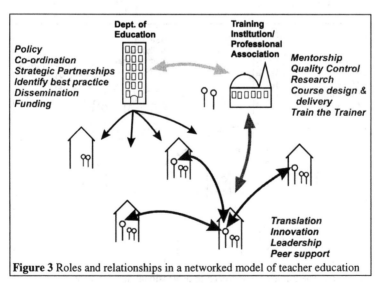

Figure 3 Roles and relationships in a networked model of teacher education

The networked model (Figure 3) includes the players involved in traditional professional development but identifies new roles and the widespread harnessing of school based innovation and expertise which are possible for the first time through the Internet. Using the World Wide Web and the Internet it is possible to draw together in one virtual space resources including those created by course leaders, related information from other sources, and asynchronous (and possibly synchronous) discussions and activities. Furthermore, these resources are equally accessible from classrooms, offices, homes, professional meetings or any place where computer facilities are available.

Peer supported professional development can take place concurrently with collaborative networked classroom activities in which technology and student focused learning can operate as catalysts for teacher change.

Characteristics of networked professional development are as follows. They:
- harness distributed innovation and leadership.
- emulate best/leading practice in schools.
- can be formal or informal.
- reward teachers for innovation and leadership.
- emphasise practical rather than theoretical solutions.
- remove bottlenecks using open learning/flexible delivery.
- increase ownership and professionalism.
- use open learning techniques to complement face-to-face delivery.
- aggregate diverse support elements.
- link research to best practice.
- create new roles for teachers, teacher educators and education authorities.

A key factor in the development of networked professional development is the support of existing initiatives and human networks. Experience from a range of situations has shown that a functional electronic network does not result from a good idea. There must be an imperative which justifies the time commitment to involvement in that virtual group. Virtual communities work well, on the other hand, when participants have an agreed mission and need for working together. Digital technology is useful in so far as it increases the opportunities for working together or increases the productivity of the group.

3.3 The role of open learning

There is considerable scope for the use of open learning techniques in meeting systemic professional development needs. It may, for example, be cost effective for teachers to undertake specialist courses operated by remote institutions or involving on-line mentors.

In another application, structured materials can be made available via the Internet as well as forming the basis of a face-to-face professional development program. In this case "the course" is available to all on demand and participation in the face-to-face component becomes a social experience in which participants form a self supporting cohort. This model is used in Victoria in a program which helps teachers explore classroom applications of the Internet (*Learning with the Internet* materials accessible through SOFWeb URL: http://www.dse.vic.gov.au). The course is delivered face-to-face by trained teacher tutors in schools around the state. The materials are freely available via the World Wide Web and are updated in response to feedback from tutors and participants. Discussion groups associated with each module of the course provide for peer support and problem solving amongst participants and students.

4   NEW ROLES FOR TEACHERS AND TEACHER EDUCATORS

The model identifies important new roles for each of the established stakeholders:

- Students become learners and leaders in the global classroom.
- Outstanding classroom teachers become teacher-mentors and teacher-researchers.
- Teacher trainers and educational researchers provide quality control for innovative work in schools and stimulate discussion amongst the practitioners. Research is increasingly focused on the operational classroom.
- Professional associations become a resource organisation for all teachers rather than members only.
- Administrators and planners assist in the development of a shared vision, identify compatible policies, projects and initiatives and promote the development of collaborative links.

All of these elements are currently coming together under the 'Classrooms of the Future Program' operated by the Directorate of School Education in Victoria. National and state curriculum agendas are being interpreted and implemented by professional associations and district networks of teachers. The teachers are creating virtual resource centres and meeting places on the World Wide Web. The Directorate is providing limited funding and facilitating linkages between associations, other teacher networks and teacher education institutions.

The Directorate has established also a World Wide Web server known as SOFWeb (Schools of the Future Web URL: http://www.dse.vic.gov) which serves as a directory to exemplary resources and professional development for teachers. SOFWeb is being used to share the results of these efforts and also to support students and teachers in the pursuit of collaborative learning activities. In 1996, at least 500 of the state's 1,740 state funded but self managing schools will be involved in Global Classroom Projects involving the International Education and Resource Network (I*EARN) and a host of other government and non-government organisations in networked student and teacher activities. Every government school is expected to be connected to the Internet by a dial-up modem connection or better by the end of 1996.

Universities in Victoria are becoming increasingly involved with school based curriculum and professional development, either through government funded programs (for example, the National Professional Development Project). It is hoped that through providing mentorship for school based innovation new research interests and opportunities will arise.

4.1   Credit for school based innovation

A key element of the networked professional development model is the possibility for teachers to gain recognition and credit for school based innovation and leadership. This is necessary to validate the additional effort contributed by practising teachers to the professional lives of their colleagues. An important way to reward effort is by the award of University certification or course credits for work done under the specified guidelines. The guidelines may require completion of assignments or mentorship and reporting writing. The quality of work by teacher innovators is likely to be improved by the involvement of a university based mentor. Mentors may also require the teachers to report and present the work being done, further disseminating the work and raising the professional standing of the teacher. A growing number of certification and mentorship schemes are available through universities in Victoria.

5   CONCLUSIONS

Traditional methods of professional development will not adequately meet the needs of teachers. "Top down" policy development and implementation may even confound and delay broadscale solutions by disenfranchising the people most needed to bring about change in schools, the dedicated teachers who are willing and able to act productively on their own initiative.

The network model does not replace traditional approaches to professional development. The same teacher training institutions will be involved and in most cases will continue to offer established pre- and in-service teacher education courses. It is hoped however, that the content of courses will be more readily updated as a result of close contact with school level innovation and that open and flexible learning techniques will be employed to minimise training bottlenecks.

There are other possible models available for increasing access to professional development, for example the use of self-paced multimedia materials, with and without in-built certification. The networked model uniquely maps onto and strengthens established professional and social structures and processes. This should be the ultimate goal of any professional development program.

6   BIOGRAPHY

Bruce Rigby manages a range of projects for the Victorian Department of Education aimed at improving learning opportunities and outcomes for students through the use of information technology and telecommunication. His experience as a teacher, scientist, technology consultant, curriculum developer and professional developer have enabled him to build links between the different players in the field of teacher education and professional support.

25

The PIT-project: A teacher networking approach for broad-scale use of ICT

Pieter Hogenbirk
PRINT/VO
Plotterweg 30, 3821 BB Amersfoort, The Netherlands

Abstract

The PIT-project is an initiative of PRINT in the Netherlands. The main objective is to stimulate and increase effective integration of ICT in eight disciplines in lower secondary education. The PIT-project started in 1993 and has worked with more than 50% of all schools, over 2,000 teachers and over 30 curriculum specialists. The Project uses the strategy of teacher networking to bring teachers together to train them, to develop materials for their own situation and above all to share and learn from each other's experiences. Alongside the physical aspects of the networking, attempts are made to elaborate on telematic support for the teachers involved in the networks.

An extensive external evaluation has been carried out throughout the first two years (round one and two of the project with 196 schools). The most important conclusions of this evaluation are:

1. The implementation of computer use in the classroom increases significantly during the PIT-Project.
2. The teachers state that the networking is very supportive for their professional development.
3. A multiplier-effect seems to develop in the schools involved in the Project.

So the PIT-strategy appears to be a very effective alternative to more traditional in-service training.

The announcement of a third round in September 1995 in which the participating schools have to invest their own funds to join the project, resulted in a subscription of another 230 schools. Another 40 new networks have been formed consisting of 20 to 30 teachers. From November 1995 until November 1996 they will be participating within the new set-up and will be called 'PIT-teachers' at 'PIT-schools'. In the Netherlands this term has become accepted as a commendation.

Keywords

Secondary education, attitudes, evaluation/summative, national policies, networks, support services

1   INTRODUCTION

In a period of 8 years of national projects (1985-1992) which focused on introducing information technology in secondary education in the Netherlands, an infrastructure was set up, hardware and software became available in the schools and many good examples of how to use IT were implemented in schools. All of this was part of a national strategy (Hogenbirk and Diepeveen, 1993). Yet at the end of this period the incidental use of IT as a tool in the daily practice of education was limited to some teachers in some subjects in a minority of schools (Pelgrum, 1993). The Dutch government decided to assign the management of PRINT (the PRoject on the Implementation of New Technologies) to set up a project focusing on the use of information technology (IT) within lower secondary education between 1993 and 1996. Later, the scope was broadened to involve communication technology (ICT). The project addresses the new curriculum for all pupils from 12 to 15 years old, called 'Basic Education', introduced in 1993.

2   THE DESIGN OF THE PROJECT

PRINT launched the PIT Project (Veen, Hogenbirk and Jansen, 1994) by supporting a maximum of 200 schools with 'Projects on Information Technology' (so called PIT-schools). This can be translated into English as 'Schools with Spirit' or 'Schools with Projects in Information Technology'. PRINT invited three rounds of involvement (March 1993, March 1994 and September 1995) where every school for secondary education could subscribe to projects in, preferably, three out of eight school subjects: Dutch (mothertongue), German, French, English, mathematics, physics and chemistry, biology, and technical skills. In each discipline there was a choice of one from four or five themes, such as information retrieval, learning strategies, remedial teaching, reteaching, differentiation in time or content, strategies on how to study, assessment and experiments in laboratory sessions, all of them in combination with ICT.

The PIT-schools have an educational advantage when they participate (free counselling and help). In rounds 1 and 2 they received 24,000 guilders (about 12,000 dollars) each year, to spend on hard- and software, but also to pay for extra time for the teachers involved. For round 3, the money supplied by the government was limited to the organisation of the project and the support of the networks. Schools participating in this round have to fund all other expenses themselves.

3   THE ORGANISATION

For the first and second rounds more than 500 schools responded. 125 schools were selected for the first round starting in 1993 and 71 for the second round in 1994. For the third round another 230 schools subscribed and they were all able to participate.

In total, for the three rounds, 77 social and physical networks (or Theme Groups) were formed, each consisting of one or two subject teachers from approximately 15 schools. Each network tackles one of the themes defined for their discipline. The networks meet face-to-face six times in a school year. The participating teachers are instructed and coached by Theme Group Leaders from the three national Educational

Advisory Centres, exchange information and professional insights, work on their personal and professional development, and develop, comment on and evaluate new materials. Each PIT-school is encouraged to participate in at least three networks in three different subjects in order to get a critical mass of users of computers in every school. Each participating school appoints a so-called 'PIT-co-ordinator' for managing the project at the school, giving support, and assisting in the making and implementation of school policy on IT.

Finally the administration of the school is committed, setting up a contract in which the duties of both parties are stated. The PIT-co-ordinators and a member of the administration of each PIT-school attend special sessions about implementation support and policy-making.

4   ON-GOING EVALUATION

In order to monitor the project, but also to evaluate the process going on in the schools and among the teachers, an on-going evaluation was defined. With the wide range of activities going on in the PIT-project, three different sources of information were used: the PIT-co-ordinators, the PIT-teachers and the Theme Group Leaders. The evaluation for the first two rounds was carried out by the Faculty of Educational Science and Technology, Department of Instrumentation Technology (ISM), of the University of Twente in the Netherlands (Collis and Moonen, 1995). In this paper only the major conclusions of this evaluation study are given.

Level of the CBAM Model	Type of concern	Action toward the innovation
1. Minimal Awareness Level	1. "Should I know something about this?"	1. Casual interest in getting information about the innovation
2. Some Knowledge	2. "How does this work?" "Can I figure it out and handle it?	2. Interest in browsing and exploring
3. Some Use of One or Two Types	3. "Is there a manageable way I can use these in practice?"	3. Tries some things in practice
4. Regular Use	4. "How can I make this part of my day-to-day practice?"	4. Makes some uses of IT routine in his/her instructional setting
5. Regular Use and Leadership Role	5. "How might I stimulate my colleagues to see the educational potential of this?"	5. Makes regular use of IT in instructional practice and also works in various ways to stimulate his/her colleagues to also make use of IT

Table 1 Adapted by Collis and De Vries (1993) from the CBAM Model (1977)

The framework of the CBAM Model was chosen (Hall, Loucke and Rutherford, 1977)

to study the degree to which:
- the PIT teachers move to higher levels of involvement in using IT in instruction during their participation in the PIT-project;
- a multiplier effect occurs in the PIT-schools, so that other teachers not directly participating in the PIT-project also move to higher levels of the CBAM Model.

Based on other research about teachers' reactions to computer-related innovations in schools (Collis and De Vries, 1993), the CBAM Model was simplified as shown in Table 1 above.

The increased use of IT in instructional practise by the PIT-teachers was a major positive outcome of the evaluation, which was tracked by a variety of indicators:
- a significant increase was self-reported in CBAM level by the teachers, from 2.57 at the start of the project (October 1993) to 3.73 at the conclusion (May, 1995). (See Figure 1 below.)
- the observation by the PIT-co-ordinators that all or nearly all of the PIT-teachers in their schools were 'trying new things' with IT in their instructional practice.
- a synthesis of the case studies, showing that in eight of the nine PIT schools studied in depth, a major conclusion was that more use of IT was occurring, and occurring because of PIT.
- an analysis of Theme Group Leaders' reports on the teacher discussions and the teachers' increased sharing of 'success stories' during the course of the project.

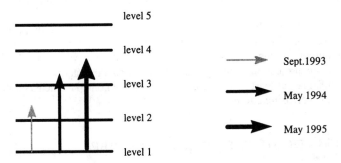

Figure 1 The increase of the CBAM-level of PIT-teachers in the first round

The PIT-co-ordinators were asked to indicate their levels of satisfaction with the PIT-teachers on the project. The results of this question are represented in Figure 2 below.

The majority of the teachers indicated that they were (mostly) satisfied with the project, and only a small percentage indicated 'mostly negative' results. It is clear that, in a setting in which so many teachers have rather different backgrounds, different starting points in experience in instruction with IT, and different expectations on the personal outcome of the project, that these results are strongly positive. In order to obtain qualitative feedback from the participants, the opportunity was provided to add positive as well as negative remarks. Some typical remarks added by teachers and co-ordinators were:

"Please continue in the other disciplines and in higher secondary education."

"Our self-made material was printed in your booklet!"

"Fund the development of new software."

"There should be more material for lower vocational education."
"You should bind the schools to facilitate the participating PIT-teachers."
"We have problems with obtaining money for a system-operator, for replacement and renewal of the hardware."
"We want more information about new multimedia and the Internet."
"Educational publishers should invest more money in making good software."
"Compared to other projects on stimulating the use of computers, PIT is a number one HIT."

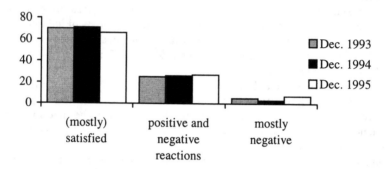

Figure 2 Satisfaction of PIT-teachers, as observed by the PIT-co-ordinators

There were two sets of indicators to evaluate the multiplier effect of the project in the participating schools. The PIT-teachers observed a significant change in the level of use of computers by their non-PIT colleagues: from CBAM level 1.96 at the beginning of the project to 2.74 by May 1995. Also the majority of the PIT-co-ordinators (70%) felt at least some increase in IT use by non-PIT teachers and another 18% felt it was increasing strongly.

5   TELEMATIC SUPPORT IN ROUND THREE

As the project met its goal in supporting a maximum of 200 schools, the Government did not want to continue this expensive means of support. So, a third round of PIT was set up to which schools could subscribe, but without receiving additional money. In order to make it as efficient and effective as possible only 8 themes were defined for using ICT in instruction, in the 8 subjects mentioned above. All the experiences, physically produced in booklets, about new or updated software, gathered in the first two rounds, were trialled in six face-to-face meetings for each network. In order to make it even more attractive to participate in this new round, the aim was to form regional networks in order to reduce travelling time for the teachers. Furthermore, a system of telematic support was also designed. This support consisted of three major elements:

- a training course on using the Internet (one afternoon session for the Theme Group).
- stimulating the use of e-mail by the teachers in the Theme Group to communicate with each other, to exchange remarks, questions and provisional

products.

- maintaining a site within the PRINT-site for every subject to give and raise information that could be relevant for the teachers.

These latest features were also available for other teachers and people who were interested. All of these sites were moderated by the Theme Group Leaders themselves, or by experts who are familiar with the networks.

The idea emerging from this telematic support is that people who know each other professionally, who have met and still meet each other on a regular basis, are supported more effectively by the Internet than by other means of communication.

As the third round of the project started in November 1995, there are no results yet available which indicate the outcomes of the project or the validation of this hypothesis. In May 1996 a questionnaire for this group of participants will be used to gather evidence.

6   CONCLUSIVE REMARKS

Using human networks of groups of teachers, exploring a certain theme within their own professional subject appears to be a powerful strategy for changing the attitude towards new types of educational behaviour.

Important elements in the setting up of such a network strategy are to:

- gather teachers who do not differ a great deal across a scale of involvement.
- put emphasis on the teacher's own professional development and on the exchange of experiences.
- facilitate teachers directly or even better by the commitment of the school administration.
- realise a balanced mix of easy to use materials and more time consuming ways of improving teaching methods, of training and exchanging experiences, of face-to-face meetings and other means of communication.
- give members of the network the opportunity to call on help and support during the project but also afterwards.

7   REFERENCES

Collis, B. and De Vries, P. (1993) *The Emerging Trans-European Network for Education and Training: Guidelines for Decision Makers*. Commission of the European Community, Task Force Human Resources, Education, Training and Youth, Brussels.

Collis, B. and Moonen, B. (1995) *The PIT Project: Final Evaluation Report*. Faculty of Educational Science and Technology, University of Twente, Enschede, The Netherlands.

Collis, B. (1995) Teacher Networking: a nation-wide approach to supporting instructional use of computers in the Netherlands. *Australian Educational Computing*, September 1995.

Hall, G., Loucke, H. and Rutherford, W. (1977) *Measuring Stages of Concern about an Innovation*. University of Texas Research and Development Centre for Teacher Education, Austin, Texas.

Hogenbirk, P. and Diepeveen, T (1993) Towards an information society: the policy of changing education in the Netherlands, in A. Knierzinger and T. Moser (eds.) *Informatics and Changes in Learning.* IST, IFIP, Gmunden.

Hogenbirk, P., Collis, B. and van Pelt, E.J. (1995) *The Dutch PIT-Project.* Paper presented at the World Conference on Computers and Education (WCCE '95), Birmingham, UK.

Pelgrum, W.J., Janssen Reinen, I.A.M. and Plomp, T. (1993) *Schools, Teachers, Students and Computers: a Cross-National perspective.* IEA, The Hague.

Norris, C. (1993) Assessing and evaluating teacher concerns. *The Computing Teacher,* **20**, 5, 27-29.

Veen, W., Hogenbirk, P. and Jansen, F. (1994) The Implementation of Communication and Information Technologies in Teacher Education in the Netherlands, in *Workshop Teacher Education and Communication and Information Technologies: Issues and Experiences for Countries in Transition.* University Twente, Enschede, The Netherlands.

8   BIOGRAPHY

Pieter Hogenbirk has been a teacher in secondary education. He was involved in the development of innovative educational materials at the universities of Utrecht and Amsterdam. In 1987 he became project manager within the NIVO-project, with a follow-up in the PRINT-project from 1989. He has been in charge of managing projects on development of the curriculum, courseware and in-service teacher training, and the implementation of materials and training for informatics and Computer Aided Learning. From 1993 he has been head of the PRINT-management for secondary education. PRINT is carrying out more than 100 projects for development and implementation of the use of ICT in secondary education.

26

A case study - a New Zealand model for teacher development in information technology

Kay J. Rye
A. R. P. Ltd
P. O. Box 10, Okato, Taranaki 4652, New Zealand

Abstract

As a part of implementing the New Zealand Curriculum Framework, the Ministry of Education has provided funding for a three year nation-wide teacher development programme in Information Technology across the Curriculum (Information and Communication Skills are one of the Essential Skills in the New Zealand Curriculum Framework).

Contractors delivering the 1995 teacher development programmes had to address: the teacher's own knowledge of information technologies, including communication technologies; use of information technology across the curriculum including using information (written, graphic and aural forms), handling information (textual and numeric data), investigations (problem solving activities, interactive fiction, simulations); and development of a school policy for information technology.

My contract targeted 90 primary and 20 secondary teachers in two North Island rural provinces. School sizes ranged from a sole charge primary school with a roll of 19 students to a large (900+) single-sex high school.

To create a sense of centre for teachers coming from a wide area geographically, I asked for schools to become Focus Schools. These schools provided a venue for all workshops as well as two staff members as Focus Teachers. The role of the Focus Teacher was to assist at all workshops as well as to provide ongoing support for their workshop teachers. An added bonus was that after the contract was completed these teachers could continue to be resource people in their immediate teaching community.

Keywords

Elementary education, secondary education, professional development, information technology

1   THE PROGRAMME

Over a ten month period, each teacher attended three full day workshops and received a minimum of three in-school visits. Each workshop focused upon one computer application as well as other Information Technology tools. A week before each workshop all Focus Teachers attended a training day to familiarise themselves with the content and activities to be offered.

Workshop 1 focused upon the use of a word processor. The participating teachers were asked to rate themselves as either a beginner or expert user.

The beginners were drawn together into a discussion about keyboarding techniques and basic classroom management when faced with 30 students and just one computer. I believe that just as students need daily practise to develop reading skills so too do they need daily practise to develop word processing skills. To assist teachers to develop a classroom programme which allows this development to occur, we provided a booklet of starter activities. The beginner teachers were then sent off to trial some of the activities for themselves.

Those teachers who had decided they were advanced users were set tasks which used other Information Technology tools alongside the word processor. Some took a 35 mm. camera and created a photo essay about the New Zealand native trees in the school grounds. Others experimented with making popcorn and then recorded an audio taped recipe. The script and cassette cover were both generated on the word processor.

At the end of the day each teacher shared their work with the whole workshop group so that everyone could see the end result of each activity.

Workshop 2 (mid year) focused upon the use of a database. The other tools used were fax machine, audio conferencing telephone and a video camera. The teachers were divided into two groups for the day. Each group began the day with teachers sharing samples of student work.

I have always found the classroom use of databases limiting as it takes so long for students to gather and correctly enter enough data to have a large number of records to manipulate. A set of 30 records is just as easy to manipulate physically (each student takes one record) and the sorting and searching can be done with the paper records. Thus sample databases and questions were supplied on disk for each of the three platforms in commonly used applications (Microsoft Works for Windows, Clarisworks and Advantage) so that they could access the activities back in school.

Following a 1 hour session of working with the activities they began to create a database. We wanted the subject of the database to be something which every student had had experience with, hence we chose a 'Sweet Idea' database (the subject of the database was lollies - also called confectionery or sweets). Teachers of various school levels decided on the six field names which would be appropriate for their students. So the field names junior teachers chose were: name, cost, colour, shape, sugar coated, flavour; while the middle school teachers chose field names like: name, cost, colour, shape, size, flavour; the senior primary went for field names like: name, cost, colour, taste, texture, flavour; and secondary teachers selected field names such as: name, colour, calorific value, density, cost, taste. Using real samples, the teachers built and tested their database. They then designed some questions to accompany it.

Meanwhile the other group was coming to grips with the video camera as a means of presentation (English Curriculum Viewing strand). In groups of six to eight, they were allocated characters from well known scenarios. Their task was to produce a short video promoting their scenario. Each character was to appear in front of the camera and speak for 30 seconds. It was a surprise to find that so many participants were reluctant to appear in front of the camera despite expecting their students to do so. The resulting video was exchanged with the other group's video and viewed. Group members then prepared questions to put to the characters. A copy of the questions was faxed to each video group so they could prepare their responses. Each group then used a hand-free phone to participate in an audio conference, taking turns to ask questions and to answer questions.

Workshop 3 featured spreadsheets, together with sessions on 'Policy and Implementation Plans', CD-ROM selection and 'Techno Lusting', and 'Creating your own Graphics'. The focus of the day was more on teacher utilisation than classroom usage. The spreadsheet session followed the format of the database sessions in that they first explored some sample spreadsheets and activities before creating a spreadsheet. Again the samples and questions were provided on disk to take back to the classroom. The examples were for a mark register, a cash flow for allocated budgets, a sector survey of a pine plantation, and a costing exercise for a DIY fence.

CD-ROM selection and 'Techno Lusting' sessions compared the topic information available on three commonly used CDs - Encarta, Comptons and Explorapedia. The teachers were asked to consider the topic information they sourced from each CD in terms of reading age, relevance to the New Zealand curriculum and appropriateness of the information for their students.

The 'Policy and Implementation' sessions dealt with issues arising in developing a school vision of Information Technology, developing a three year plan to implement this vision, budgeting and teacher development.

2   BETWEEN WORKSHOPS

To ensure some follow up activity, teachers were asked to plan a class activity which used the Information Technology tools modelled in each workshop. The activity had to fit into their existing classroom programme. Between workshops, I visited each teacher. Each visit was initially time tabled for 45 minutes to an hour in duration. This was later changed to a half day per two teachers. During a visit the teacher and facilitator were to discuss the progress towards achieving the goals set at the workshop. Advice and suggestions could be made at this stage. In actuality more teachers used the visit time for forward planning and discussing ways of implementing the tools across the curriculum. Later the time was spent in a variety of ways: demonstrating and teaching students and teachers how to use new software packages; working alongside students as they used the tools; discussing and advising on long term plans and strategies with principals; and giving technical support (especially for remote rural schools).

Data from the final evaluation forms indicated 85% of teachers on the contract found the in-school visits useful. They commented that:
"visits clarified issues";

"visits forced me not to procrastinate";
"visits useful for discussion and enthusiasm";
"visits gave practise, answers to questions and refreshed my ideas";
"visits were another way of checking that what we were doing was correct if a problem arose".

3   EVALUATION RESULTS

Ongoing evaluation was conducted throughout the course of the contract. Each workshop was evaluated in terms of the activities offered. Each teacher's use of Information Technology tools in their classroom programmes was tracked at the midpoint and end of the contract.

A final overall contract evaluation was carried out after the final workshop (110 teachers were surveyed, and some 85 teachers responded). This evaluation looked at four areas - the teacher's personal development, the contract content and delivery, student learning and teaching gains, and teacher's use of information tools in the classroom.

The teacher's personal development was gauged on a 0 to 5 scale: 0 indicating no skills or knowledge; and 5 indicating very skilled and knowledgeable. If 2.5 is taken as being a confident user, in the area of:

WORD PROCESSING: more than half of the teachers who responded were less than confident users at the beginning of the contract. Only 3 indicated they had made little progress, all others ranked themselves higher than 3 by the end of the contract.
DATABASES: slightly less than a half had no skills or knowledge at the beginning of the contract. More than half had reached 2.5 by the end of the contract. Many Acorn users did not always have access to a software package away from the workshop.
SPREADSHEET: again slightly less than a half had no skills or knowledge at the beginning of the contract. Acorn users did not always have access to a software package away from the workshop.
GRAPHICS: despite every platform having a graphics package of some description, the teachers were not wide users of these packages. Many found the process of inserting Clipart to be involved, and not something they could do once and then leave for some weeks.
CD-ROM: the skills and experience in this area directly reflected the number of CD-ROM machines in schools.
35 mm. CAMERAS and VIDEO CAMERAS: whilst most teachers owned a camera and many also had access to a video camera, only a few enthusiasts used them in class. Developing costs and the initial capital cost of the equipment were two factors influencing student usage.
FAX MACHINES: there was, surprisingly, a high proportion of teachers who had never sent a fax, but all quickly became confident users. Recent New Zealand research indicates all secondary and almost all primary schools own a fax machine, so we have to ask where is the fax sited and who is allowed access?
AUDIO CONFERENCING: whilst the concept of audio conferencing was well received, teachers made limited use of this tool. Only two of the schools on this contract had telephone lines installed into classrooms.

INTERNET: again teachers were limited in developing skills with this tool for similar reasons - access to telephone lines, access to a provider at a reasonable cost, provision of basic equipment.
CONFIDENCE: it was a pleasure to see that nearly all respondents felt confident enough to pass skills on to their students and to try to work problems out for themselves by the end of the contract. It is to their credit that more than half felt sufficiently confident to teach another adult too.

3.1 Teacher use of IT tools in the classroom

Sixty five out of 70 questionnaires handed out were returned. Here is a summary of the responses (not all questions were answered):

Eleven out of 65 teachers used less than 6 IT activities in their classroom programmes.

Thirty seven out of 65 teachers indicated they used lots (> 15) IT activities in their classroom programmes.

Twenty out of 65 used activities in all main learning areas, a further 14 indicated language as the main learning area and a further 4 indicated social studies.

Twenty five out of 65 identified equipment as their greatest problem - equipment which was inaccessible, old, insufficient for the number of students.

Twenty five identified time as a problem. For most teachers there is a problem in finding time to become confident and competent users. Secondary teachers have the constraints of a school timetable in terms of accessing equipment which over-rode any problems they may face in terms of student / equipment ratios.

Many teachers identified the necessity for:
a)   small groups or pairs of students to use the tools.
b)   clear guidelines/routines/rules.
c)   support of student tutors, student peers, parents, office staff, aides, when students are using tools away from the classroom.
d)   usefulness of timetables or rosters for equipment use.
e)   being flexible within their teaching time.

Others identified the need to have good classroom organisation to address:
a)   teacher time required with junior students.
b)   time frames required by different students.
c)   low ratio of equipment to students.

I thought that two teachers were well on their way to effectively using IT tools in the classroom when they responded:
"It helps if children are accustomed to a co-operative learning model, although initially the teacher needs to be available"; "One becomes more of a 'gofer' rather than an instructor".

Responses to a question about student attitude were overwhelmingly positive:
"Children who don't usually like language are writing a lot for their friends at other schools";
"Comfortable using IT tools which are available and used all day";
"Keen to use a variety of media";
"Excellent support and follow up from interested parents";
"Those who aren't successful the first time are willing to have another go".

The teachers' perceptions of information technology before the contract were varied:
"a blur, hadn't heard of it";
"mainly concerned with computers";
"did not appreciate that there was more";
"information technology is the use of technology rather than conventional methods".

Following the contract the perceptions had changed to statements such as:
"as a vital part of the learning process";
"skills to access information and to develop learning";
"using IT devices to discover, collect, organise, present and convey information".

3.2   Student learning outcomes

IT tools: All students used computers, most students also used photocopiers and telephone technology, many students were using fax, video and still cameras.
First hands-on experience: For most children using a fax and/or photocopier was a first. Several also used fax, video, CD-ROM, video camera, hand-free telephone and e-mail for the first time.
Organisation models used: Paired or small groups of students was used most often.
Frequency of task types: Most students used the tools within skill-based activities and topic (unit) activities. Least frequently used tasks were tutorials.
Student gains/achievements using IT tools: 61 respondents reported a huge list of gains, many noting increased confidence in using the tools, especially computers, other responses commonly noted were gains in - information processing skills, personal organisation skills, problem solving skills, interaction with others, application usage (word processing, spreadsheet, database), wider knowledge of tools available and used in and out of school, professionally published written language, audio-conferencing skills particularly for reaching remote sources, willingness to be a risk taker, fun while learning!

3.3   So what happened in classrooms?

A class of Year 0 to 1 students studying the weather (in science) arranged for four schools across the North Island to fax them a series of weather reports taken throughout a nominated day. The data was turned into a series of graphs for the class to analyse and interpret. A class report was compiled and together with all the graphs was faxed back to the schools who had provided the initial data.
  A class of Year 3 and 4 students were learning about New Zealand cities and towns. They faxed, phoned or wrote to Information Centres as well as using books and local knowledge (people). The information was then reorganised into a brochure targeting

tourists. A copy of the brochure was faxed or mailed to one of the featured places of interest for comment. Many places responded positively.

A class of Year 5 and 6 students were exploring healthy eating. The items available in their school canteen were individually placed on the food pyramid. Groups then faxed a random selection of neighbouring schools requesting copies of their canteen items. This information was displayed in the same way and the schools were ranked according to the perceived food value offered in their canteen. Copies of the class report were faxed to the contributing schools.

A class of Year 7 and 8 students used 35 mm. colour photographs and word processed text to compile a school profile. Working in pairs, they were required to photograph and interview all adults who were involved in the school, from the principal to the cleaner. Each interview had to be written up in an appropriate genre. The profile was published in a clear file folder and, after being taken home by a different student each night to share with their parents, was located in the school foyer for visitors to enjoy.

Secondary teachers and their students experienced significantly more problems in completing IT classroom activities for reasons mentioned above, but a Year 11 class successfully recorded photographic images of all seven of their town's World War memorials and published these with brief captions. After sharing their work with their parents they planned to give the booklet to the local Servicemen's Association.

Three other Year 11 classes successfully used audio conferencing within their social science programmes to speak to local and national personalities on the topics of 'Leadership Roles' and 'The New Zealand System of Government'.

I gratefully acknowledge and thank the New Zealand Ministry of Education for their financial support in funding this Teacher Development Contract and the Telecom Education Foundation for their support in providing equipment and advice for this contract.

4   BIOGRAPHY

Kay Rye is a trained primary school teacher who has used computers and other IT tools in her classroom. She has taught in urban and rural schools at both primary and secondary level, worked for the University of Waikato Teacher Support Services and two years ago set up a private company to deliver professional development programmes.

Currently Kay is delivering an Information Technology Teacher Development Contract for part of the week, teaching computer studies, overseeing an audiographics and satellite live television second language initiative, as well as working with two remote rural school clusters to implement innovative curriculum delivery projects through Information Technology.

27

Communication - learning - information technology applied examples

Lisbeth Appelberg
Department of Child and Youth Education, Special Education and Guidance
Umeå University, S-901 87, Umeå, Sweden

Abstract

The projects named "The Children of the Future I and II" are research and development projects concerning children and information technology. The first project began in the autumn of 1990 in the University College of Falun/Borlänge. Tommy Isaksson, now at Umeå University, is the project leader and Björn Flising, at the University of Gothenburg is responsible for the evaluation. The first project included members from thirteen municipalities throughout Sweden and today twenty schools, pre-schools and after-school care centres participate. Since 1993 our department has been closely connected with the project through one class and one after-school care centre, both part of a lower primary school near Umeå in northern Sweden. Apart from Lisbeth Appelberg and Göran Nilsson, students in some undergraduate programmes at our department are also involved in the project when on practice for a period of weeks in the school. Based on the experiences of the project we have created a distance-learning course concerning information technology and learning in which the participants are, among others, teachers, pre-school teachers and recreation leaders involved in the project.

Keywords

Communications, database, distance learning, information technology, software, technical innovation

1 "THE CHILDREN OF THE FUTURE"

1.1 Background

"The Children of the Future" is a research and development project concerning children and information technology. The project began in the autumn of 1990 and is an expansion of earlier projects which started in 1985 at Falun/Borlänge College (Isaksson, 1991). This work culminated in the starting of the project "The Children of the Future I" which lasted from the autumn of 1990 until the summer of 1993 (Flising, 1995). The cost for participating is ISEC 20,000 per year. In addition to this, there is the cost for the staff participating in seminars twice a year and for the children and the staff to join the annual festivals. "The Children of the Future II" includes children aged 6 to 12 years and educators from 20 municipalities in Sweden. Both children and educators have access to advanced communication equipment such as computers, printers, modems and computer programs. Some examples of the software used are graphics and communication programs, word processors with and without spellcheckers, databases, desktop publishing programs of various types, electronic mail programs, communication programs, programs for scanning in pictures and graphics, etc.

1.2 The goal of "The Children of the Future" and the children's tasks

The goal of "The Children of the Future" is to increase the children's social competence so that they will be able to develop the knowledge and skills necessary for them to grow up successfully into today's and tomorrow's information technology society. This includes the use of information technology both in a constructive manner and as an aid to understanding today's society. It is the understanding and not the technology that is paramount. In the policy documents for both schools and after-school care centres, the importance of equal opportunity for all children is stressed. For the project this means that equal opportunities issues concerning girls and children from lower socio-economic groups are greatly emphasised.

The goal for the teachers, the recreation leaders and pre-school teachers and other people who participate in the project is to increase their knowledge and competence in today's technological society, and in how they can work with new technologies in order to provide children with the prerequisites for growing up today. In addition it is important to develop knowledge of modern childhood and to allow educators to develop their own methods for planning, carrying out and evaluating their work.

The children design electronic newspapers, history books, communicate with other children through a database network, develop databases, qualify for "computer driving licenses" and write relay stories, to name but a few of the activities. They have also held exhibitions and led computer courses for their parents. Once a year the children from the different groups meet at a "Children of the Future" festival.

1.3 Documentation and evaluation

All the work is documented and evaluated. Every group in the project keeps diaries and logbooks as well as turning in written and oral evaluation reports. Regular planning and evaluation seminars are held and the children are interviewed and answer written questionnaires. A preliminary report (Flising, 1995), with an overview for the years 1994-1995, shows that in autumn 1994 there were 47 educators participating in the project, 36 women, 11 men and 477 children (237 girls and 240 boys). Most of the children were in grades one and four (as the intention was to follow them during the whole project period). There were between 20 and 26 children in 13 of the participating groups. In 4 groups there were 16 to 20 children and in one group only 12. The number of children in two combined classes with children aged 10 to 12 years were 39 and 51. There will be a final report on the project in 1997. One of the most important things in this preliminary report is that the girls seem to participate in the work with IT to the same extent as the boys, in some groups even more. Only when it comes to using the computers for games is there a higher representation of boys.

2   "THE CHILDREN OF THE FUTURE" AT LINBLOMMAN

2.1   Staff and children at Linblomman attend "The Children of the Future"

Since the autumn of 1993 our department has been involved in the project in co-operation with the staff and children in one section at Linblomman, a lower primary school near Umeå.

Linblomman has mixed age classes. Children of different ages work together in the primary grades 1 to 3 and in the upper primary grades 4 to 6. Sometimes the two age groups even work together. The children sit together in mixed age groups which allows them to share experiences, and they strengthen their sense of self-value by changing roles within the group. For example, a pupil in the second grade who had a difficult time in the first grade can help a new pupil in the first grade and thereby gain a sense of accomplishment.

In November 1993 an agreement was made between the Department of Child and Youth Education, Special Education and Guidance, Umeå University and a section at Linblomman concerning the project "The Children of the Future". In our department we had started to develop knowledge about how to use IT as a tool in working with children and we felt we needed to co-operate with a school in one section of Linblomman over a period of four years to support their participation in the project. This support covers the annual fees and the journeys and hotel costs for four members of the staff at Linblomman allowing them to join the two seminars each year. As they did not have the necessary IT equipment, we have stationed a computer with a modem, a scanner and a camera at the school. We meet with the staff once a month and between times, we communicate with the aid of computers. I have followed the work at Linblomman some days each semester and documented the work with a video camera (Appelberg, 1994; 1995).

Autumn 1993. The guidelines for the work with "The Children of the Future II" were drawn up at a conference in Falun in November 1993. Four of the staff from Linblomman participated in the meeting. Three themes were formulated for the coming work.

A. The Children's Network - The following activities should be covered during Spring 1994: the children should be introduced to the computer; all children should take a computer licence; the children should write articles about their neighbourhood and the articles should be sent to those involved in the project in other schools and after-school centres by electronic mail; the children should make a newspaper from a selection of some of the incoming articles from all over the country; the children should be introduced to the writing and sending of electronic mail to pen friends.

B. The Network for Education - The staff of the schools and after-school centres should build up an educational network through which they could share experiences and help each other with questions which have arisen. The staff members should learn: about different software, for example Claris Works; how to download/send letters; how to download/send files; how to send pictures.

C. Contact with other countries - The members of the project should establish international contacts to make it possible for the children to communicate by electronic mail with children in other countries.

2.2 Progress with IT at Linblomman

Spring 1994. January: The children were introduced to the computer. The order in which the children were introduced was decided by lot. The children were trained in the following steps: turn on the computer, open the disk drive, start Claris Works, write some text, save the text, close the programme, open the programme again, open the file you saved, write more text, save, close the programme again, close the disk drive and choose "Special" on the menu, and close. This work took about 30 minutes for each child. There were some differences depending on whether the children had any earlier experience. Some parents have had doubts about their children working with computers because of the risk of radiation, but the staff mostly received positive feedback on their work with the children and computers.

February: To obtain their licences the children had to prove that they could successfully cope with the computer and perform the thirteen steps. The children also had to promise three things: they would take good care of the equipment; they would help each other while working on the computer, and they would not touch each other's document on the computer. To achieve this, it took around 30 minutes per child. By the end of February all twenty-three children had obtained their licences. Photos of the children were taken with a camera connected to the computer. Many children started to use the graphics programme, as they could print out the pictures in colour.

Spring 1995. During the spring every child in the group wrote a page about themselves on the computer, a task that took quite a long time. All the pages were sent to the other groups and at the same time the children got information about the other children in the project. All the children in grade three had the responsibility to read all the incoming messages every Monday afternoon. The children communicated quite a lot with two other groups by "chatting". They appreciated getting answers immediately. In the after-school time, the children composed lots of pictures with the help of the computer.

Autumn 1995. The work continued as in earlier semesters. The newcomers had to take their driving licences and this work has been running smoothly as many of the children in grades two and three know how to handle the computer. During this period the children have been "chatting" a lot. One can follow their chatting on the computer ,but also the printed documents where one can see the patterns of discussion on various matters.

<u>Spring 1996</u>. A report from Linblomman in February 1996 follows: The work with the children continues. Just now a lot of effort is being put into finding sponsorship for the journey to "The Children of the Future" Festival 21-23 May in Höllviken (in the southern part of Sweden, about 1,300 km from Umeå). There are many things which are not yet settled. We have now divided the class into four groups with one responsible leader in each group. These groups have established contact with some other groups in the country who are also going to the festival in May. We now work 40 minutes per week with our groups leading them forward, increasing their knowledge about computers. In addition the children work on the computers approximately one hour per day doing different school subjects. At the moment we have two computers with printers and some special equipment in the classroom for children with special needs. We have one "Children of the Future-Mac", a colour printer and a scanner in a small room. In a big room outside the classroom there are two more computers. We also have one laptop. The children have started to work with pictures and the scanner in research projects. The children are using the software Kid Pix quite a lot, making mathematical fairy-tales and when they are designing pictures in their after-school time. Every Thursday the children from the pre-school visit the class/after-school centre and the children from the second grade work with the Kid Pix programme and function as "tutors" for the pre-school children. The children in grade four now have their own computer identity and are able to communicate with some special friends in Sweden. We are also planning for the children in grade six to make a homepage for our school.

3   DISTANCE LEARNING COURSE

Our Department runs distance learning courses in 'Computers and Learning'. Many of the teachers, pre-school teachers and recreation leaders involved in the project "The Children of the Future" participate in these courses which extend over a period of two years. The course is given at a slower pace. The course carries 20 credits, which corresponds to twenty weeks of work, but is spread over a period of two years. The aim for the students is to increase their knowledge of and competence in today's information technology society. They need to know how they can work with new technologies in order to provide children with the prerequisite skills for successful living in today's society.

We have not yet been able to make a final evaluation of our first course but it has been possible for me as a teacher to follow my students very carefully. I have come to know them well, better in fact than if I had met them in large groups in classes. At the beginning of every course we take pictures of the students and the teachers, and install these pictures in the computer system, which helps us to remember individuals. Even though the students can get on-line support, there have been quite a lot of difficulties and problems arising from the technology.

4   SUMMARY

Although the "Children of the Future" and the co-operation work with Linblomman has not been completed and evaluated, we have seen that members, both staff and children, have learned a great deal about IT and how to use it in different ways. The videos I have taken at Linblomman also show that in meeting the stated goals, the staff communicate to support: equality of opportunity, listening, shared feelings of solidarity within groups, children with special needs, creative activity, planning, children-parents-staff contact, and the development of links with other children in Sweden and with children in other countries. We also know that most of the students are satisfied with the distance learning courses.

5   REFERENCES

Working reports

Isaksson, T. (1991) *KBI-projektet Ny informationsteknologi på fritidshem, Lägesrapport 1986-1988, arbetsrapport 2, Rapport 1991:2.* Högskolan i Falun/Borlänge.

Flising, B. (1995) *Framtidsbarn II, preliminär rapport 1995.* Pedagogiska instiutionen, Göteborgs universitet.

Posters and presentations

Appelberg, L. (1994) Poster and video presentation of The Children of the Future/Enfants du Futur, IEDPE (Institut Europeén pour developpement des potentialites de tous les enfants) Conference in Paris, 7-9 November.

Appelberg, L. (1995) Poster and presentation of The children of the Future at the IFIP Conference, Computers in Education VI WCCE´95, Birmingham, 23-28 June.

6   BIOGRAPHY

Lisbeth Appelberg holds a BA degree, and was a pre-school teacher for twenty-five years. From 1977 she has been a senior lecturer at Umeå University, from 1992 in the Department of Child and Youth Education, Special Education and Counselling.

28

Teacher professional development in a technology immersion school

Anne McDougall
Faculty of Education
Monash University, Clayton, Victoria 3168, Australia

Jennifer Betts
John Paul College
John Paul Drive, Daisy Hill, Queensland 4127, Australia

Abstract
This paper describes a model of teacher professional development in place, in a school with a very high concentration of computers and related technologies, being used in the delivery of its curriculum. The model emphasises on-site resourcing for ongoing professional development experiences for teachers, concurrent and integrated with their classroom teaching.

The school's policy involves integration of the technology with all appropriate aspects of the curriculum throughout all year levels of the school. This has, of course, had major implications for teacher professional development, and the paper outlines strategies used to respond to this challenge.

Keywords
Professional development, infrastructure, portable computers

1   INTRODUCTION

This paper describes a model of teacher professional development in place, in a school with use of a very high concentration of computers and related technologies integrated across the curriculum. The model emphasises on-site resourcing for ongoing professional development experiences for teachers, concurrent and integrated with their classroom teaching.

John Paul College, a large independent co-educational P to 12 college in the suburbs south of Brisbane, Australia, has had an ambitious curriculum technology program under development since the early 1990s. The principal, believing that the educational product being offered to the young of our nation was irrelevant to students who would live out their lives in the 21st century, implemented a deliberate decision to integrate modern technology across the curriculum and to immerse students in the technology for their learning.

The progressive curriculum in place at the college specifically encourages students to increase their abilities to learn about and apply computing technologies as tools across all curriculum areas; computing as a discipline area in itself is not studied. This extensive integration of computer technology has been motivated by two fundamental assumptions:

- If a person is to participate fully in, contribute to, and influence the future of his or her world, he or she must have the capacity to develop and communicate ideas through the media of his or her time.
- Computing technology enables the facilitation of learning experiences which could not be provided in any other way.

Present facilities at the school include personal notebook computers for all students from Years 5 to 10, desktop computers, printers, scanners and network ports in all classrooms, more networked desktop computers, printers and scanners in a library/resource centre, banks of CD-ROMs available to all the computers via a network throughout the school, and access to the Internet through a nearby university.

The college's policy of integration of the technology with all appropriate aspects of the curriculum throughout all year levels of the school has, of course, had major implications for teacher professional development, and what follows summarises strategies used to respond to this challenge.

2   FORMAL PROFESSIONAL DEVELOPMENT PROGRAM

The school acknowledges that teachers themselves have not grown up or been educated in the digital era. Teachers need help to employ the resources of computing comfortably, using the same professional expertise and criteria as they do in using other educational resources. The principal's ongoing active sponsorship of the initiative was crucial to the professional development programs that have been established.

Two key areas of need were identified. The first was the development of technical skills such as the navigation of the operating system or the construction of a database. The second was the application of computing to achieve an educational outcome such as constructing a database and applying a query to compare and contrast.

The principal formed a steering committee to oversee the introduction of new technologies across the curriculum. Executive membership of this team includes the Director of Curriculum Technology, the Head of Information Services, and the Computer Systems Manager. The group is effective because of the alliance between the curriculum, information and technical sectors, and the understanding that the introduction and integration of new technologies into the mainstream curriculum is driven by educational imperatives. The committee is known as CONTACT, Co-ordination Of New Technologies Across the Curriculum Team.

This team is responsible for directing and managing the technology within the college, including the identification of core skills that would need to be introduced to the staff systematically, in the context of the discipline areas where possible. To assist staff in recognising specific areas where they need to develop and maintain competence, a table, cross referencing teaching areas with planned applications is provided.

During the college's formal school-based professional development, CONTACT administers a significant proportion of the technology related material. The view is that a professional development program should treat teachers as expert learners and should model itself on the type of teaching it promotes. Workshops are often held in response to staff requests; they are hands-on and activity based, provide choice of content, cater for a variety of learning styles, and include a reflective component. A typical evening program might open with a keynote speaker, followed by a range of workshops from which individual teachers select which to attend, dinner, a "sharing session" for viewing successful computing applications from various faculties or areas of the school, and a final workshop session.

Staff at the school are required to undertake four days of in-service education per year. Teachers maintain a personal profile recording their participation in the school-based professional development program, community education, and any other professional development activities they might undertake, such as attendance at a conference. This record can be used at times of staff appraisal.

3   COMPUTING CO-ORDINATORS

Key teachers with qualifications and experience in educational computing have been employed by the college and allocated to various levels within the school. The tasks of these computing co-ordinators include curriculum planning and development of curriculum materials with the classroom teachers, working with individual teachers on curriculum technology problems and innovations, and regular classroom visits to support introduction of new ideas and activities by the classroom teachers.

The computing co-ordinators do not have regular classroom teaching responsibilities, enabling them to offer "on-the-job" training for the rest of the staff. Through sharing of skills and ideas the co-ordinators provide a considerable amount of professional development experience for teachers, informally, on-site, and integrated with their regular teaching activities.

The co-ordinators follow a timetable which provides regular visits to classrooms in their allocated sections of the school. These classroom visits are carried out for several purposes. One is co-operative planning; a computing co-ordinator can advise and assist staff with the development of units of work integrating computer technology in a meaningful way within the overall curriculum. Another is class consultation; the co-ordinator and the classroom teacher are able to work co-operatively in implementing new ideas in the class. Assistance may be in the form of a demonstration lesson given by the co-ordinator, or the use of team teaching of a new activity or unit of work.

Ongoing curriculum development is another responsibility of the co-ordinators. They meet regularly with the school's curriculum personnel to discuss, and amend as appropriate, the college's 'Progressive Curriculum Document'. The co-ordinators are concerned with all aspects of its implementation, the integration of computing related learning outcomes and the co-ordination of computing across the curriculum.

An important role of the co-ordinators is to develop the skills of both the students and the classroom teachers. Individual teachers seek advice and assistance with development of their personal computing skills as well as on curriculum-related issues, and secondary school level co-ordinators provide tutorial assistance for groups of students who require help.

The computing co-ordinators also assist in the planning and development of the technology component of the formal professional development program described in the previous section.

4   COMMUNITY EDUCATION

During the evening and weekends, John Paul College Community Education provides a range of courses which cater for the needs of the community. Many of these courses are associated with computer applications; they are free of charge to all staff members, and teachers are encouraged to attend. Generally these short courses teach users about specific application packages; typical examples are use of a word processor or spreadsheet, or of the Internet.

5   INFORMATION TECHNOLOGY

Staff members in the Library/Resource Centre are closely involved with the ongoing professional development program. Their duty statement includes the assertion that the role of the teacher librarian is to work with classroom teachers to maintain students' abilities in areas of analysing, synthesising, applying and creating information with and through electronic media.

Teachers can seek further curriculum resource information and support from these staff members, who have been allocated time for this purpose. Help here might include information about and strategies for finding and assessing useful Internet sites and CD-ROM software to supplement print and other information resources when teachers plan their presentation of particular topics.

These staff are also present when teachers are planning and developing units of work. The teacher librarians search the Internet for relevant pointers and select or design appropriate resources to support curriculum and educational outcomes. The teacher librarians also work closely with teachers to restructure the research processes used by students.

6   FINANCIAL SUPPORT

Financial assistance is offered by the school for all teachers to purchase their own notebook computers, for looking at and marking students' work, much of which is submitted on disk, and for their own record keeping, administration and planning.

Occasional financial assistance is also available for teachers to attend conferences and other outside professional development activities.

7   TECHNICAL SUPPORT

Technical information and support is provided for teachers by a group called the CAVE (Computer and Audio Visual Engineers), a support and development centre for technology within the school. Many teachers and administrators will have experienced times when technology and the problems it causes seem to make its use a waste of time; with an on-site support centre a telephone call away, teachers have these experiences reduced to a minimum. CAVE personnel support teachers' work with the technology in a number of ways. Probably the most used facility is the Help Desk. A solution to a problem can be found by making a telephone call. Often problems can be solved using the telephone consultation technique; if not, personal assistance is usually provided. If further help is needed, an appointment can be made for a personal tutorial.

The CAVE group maintains the notebook computers at the school, including an "over the counter" service for repairs to, or temporary replacement of, computers for both staff and students. Maintenance of support hardware is another of the CAVE's functions.

The college has over 200 desktop computers plus peripheral devices (fileservers, modems, printers, scanners, CD-ROMs and an Internet connection via a permanent ISDN line), all of which are kept in operation by the CAVE technicians.

Research and development is an important part of the support work of the CAVE personnel. They attend conferences, subscribe to many journals, and belong to local user and support groups for their own professional development.

8   CONCLUSION

Professional development for all staff has been a vital component in the integration of educational computing across the curriculum at the John Paul College. Key aims have been to provide a level of competence whereby all staff are confident in using the new technologies, and to provide a frame of reference that enables the exploitation of the technological resources across the curriculum.

The professional development model used at the college, emphasising on-site resourcing for ongoing professional development experiences for teachers, concurrent and integrated with their classroom teaching, is proving an effective approach. It treats teachers as expert learners, and encourages them to see themselves as learners and facilitators of their students' learning.

Helping teachers to break away from the conventions of traditional practice which have in the past so limited the way new technologies have been applied to education is a challenging task. The strategies described in this paper are proving effective in this endeavour.

9   BIOGRAPHIES

Anne McDougall has worked as a secondary teacher in Australia and then as a computer programmer in the USA. In 1973 she took up a research fellowship in computer education at the University of Melbourne, developing software for use in undergraduate teaching. Her subsequent lecturing and research work has been concerned with computers and learning at secondary and primary levels. She is now an Associate Professor in Educational Computing at Monash University.

Jennifer Betts has worked as a primary teacher in Australian schools. In 1990 she became involved in an innovative computing project in a state primary school in Queensland, and since then she has worked in several schools introducing intensive curriculum technology projects. Currently on leave from her position as a computing co-ordinator at John Paul College, she is working on a collaborative research project between the College and Monash University, and is completing a PhD in educational computing.

Section 8: Considering the integration of information and communication technologies within subject teaching and within teaching methodologies

29

Using videotaped lessons to analyse changes in teachers' teaching practices of mathematics

Menucha Weiss
The University of Chicago School Mathematics Project
The Technion Technical Institute for Israel, 41/18 Hasayfan Street, Ramat Hasharon 47248, Israel

Abstract
The paper describes the use of videotaped lessons to analyse the changes that occurred in the teaching of mathematics of sixteen elementary school teachers who participated in a local program to become specialists for teaching mathematics in grades 4 to 6. The analysis focuses on the ways in which the data was obtained, coded, and analysed. Changes were observed in the overall structure of the lessons, the inclusion of manipulatives and problem solving into the curriculum, and the development of thinking skills. The analysis of the videotapes provides an important tool to monitor changes in teachers' practices, raise their awareness about these practices, and reflect on the conditions needed to consolidate the change.

Keywords
Teacher education, case studies, classroom practice, evaluation/formative, evaluation/summative

1   INTRODUCTION

Since 1986, the Teacher Development Component of UCSMP has been exploring the idea of mathematics specialist teachers in elementary schools. The belief is that from fourth grade onwards, it is unrealistic to expect the average generalist teacher to have the necessary content and pedagogical knowledge to teach five or six different subjects well. An alternative is to retrain generalist teachers to serve as content specialists and as resource consultants to their colleagues in the primary grades.

UCSMP's initial work with mathematics specialists in elementary schools began with a two year project in six Chicago public schools between 1986 and 1988. The positive results of case studies (The Mathematics Specialist Project: A Report of Three Schools, UCSMP, 1990) conducted in three of the schools, resulted in a grant from Ford Motor Company which led to the expansion of the experiment to sixteen other school districts in the USA through the UCSMP Institute of Mathematics Specialisation.

2   RESEARCH METHODS

For a closer look at the impact of the programme and the changes in mathematics teaching, four of the districts were looked at in greater detail. The end of year reports sent to UCSMP by the staff developers, the teachers and the principals were analysed. In addition, the lessons of sixteen teachers from these districts were videotaped twice, one year apart, at the beginning of the programme and towards its end.

We do not maintain that the lessons are representative of the ways in which the teachers taught. It is assumed that the teachers attempted to conduct one of their "better lessons", and to reveal their ideas about how mathematics should be taught. Reflective discussions about the videotaped lessons taken at different periods during the in-service sessions can help analyse the teachers' changed beliefs and practices, and the mechanisms needed to consolidate them.

3   VIDEOTAPING PROCEDURES

Videotaping was done with two VHS cameras with directional microphones and fluid-head tripods, one to film the teacher, and the other to film the students. Cameras were usually set up a few minutes before the beginning of the lesson, to familiarise the students and the teachers with the set-up.

The teacher's camera followed the teacher closely during the course of the lesson, and zoomed in for a close-up shot when the teacher explained an important issue in the lesson.

The students' camera filmed general shots of the classroom, as well as close up shots of specific children engaged in the lesson's activities.

The teachers and the students were not given any specific directions before the taping. They were asked to act as they would in any other lesson, and ignore the cameras as much as possible. Teachers and students were assured that the videotapes would be used for research only. Copies of the teachers' videotapes were given to the teachers.

4   THE CODING PROCEDURE

The coding system used to compare the sets of two lessons per teacher followed some of the criteria described in the paper "Traditions of School Mathematics in Japanese and American Elementary School Classrooms," by James W. Stigler, Clea Fernandez and Makoto Yoshida. presented at ICME, Quebec City, Canada, August, 1992.

The outlines of the lessons were drawn. A clear indication of the amount of time dedicated to each activity in the lesson enabled a comparison of the allocation of time to the different activities conducted in the lessons, and the qualitative analysis of the teaching procedures. Accurate transcription of the public discourse during each of the lessons allowed exact quotations of teachers' and students' words, the coding of the questions into six different categories (name/identify questions; calculate questions; count questions; explain how or why questions; higher thinking skills questions; check status questions), and the analysis of the type of thinking skills developed by the teachers.

5   THE CHANGED PRACTICE OF TEACHING MATHEMATICS

The use of manipulatives
Using manipulatives to explain the mathematical concepts was often mentioned by the teachers as one of the main impacts of the in-service programme. The base ten blocks were the most frequently used manipulatives to help students understand subtraction and addition in whole numbers and in decimal fractions. We looked at the ways the base ten blocks were used in the classrooms to determine whether teachers shifted from the algorithm approach to solving computation.

Most teachers insisted on preserving the paper and pencil routines for solving the algorithms with the use of the blocks. Students were told that the objectives of using the blocks was to "make connections in the mind between the paper and pencil method of recording and the blocks." But the teachers did not believe that through the manipulations of the quantities represented by the blocks, equivalence and regrouping would become obvious. Teachers frequently warned students to avoid making mistakes that resulted from incorrect alignment of the numbers, and corrected the mistakes by using the technical explanation of the algorithm. They did not allow students to manipulate the quantities represented by the blocks to find the nature of the mistake.

Only one fifth grade teacher used the base ten blocks to explain the nature of the problem of the day presented to the class. Her lesson dealt with addition and regrouping of decimal fractions, and she showed how the fare of a taxi drive can be calculated if it is broken into tenths to which different prices are assigned.

The inclusion of problem solving activity
The importance of incorporating problem solving activities into the lessons and teaching students how to solve them, was constantly reiterated during the in-service sessions. The videotapes reveal that most teachers complied with the recommendation and allocated time during their lessons to solving at least one problem.

The types of problems introduced
The types of problems that were solved in the classrooms varied with the teachers and with the grade level of the classrooms. For every teacher, very little change can be observed in the types of problems that were introduced. Most problems dealt mainly with factual knowledge and the comprehension of terms, and the solution demanded an application of a simple one-step mathematical operation to the situation described. Only one teacher, who taught gifted students, posed open-ended problems which had more than one solution and which demanded an involvement over an extended period of time. For only one teacher did the problem of the day present a different representation of the mathematical concept to that studied.

Teaching problem solving skills

Most teachers taught problem solving in a similar manner. They read out the problem aloud, allowed students some time to solve it, moved between the tables and offered occasional help. Manipulatives and calculators were usually on the desks, and their use was encouraged.

For most teachers getting the correct answer was of utmost importance, and their questions were usually very concise and focused. Mistakes were usually detected by the teacher and the proof for the correctness of the answer was not checked. Students were asked to pay attention, and show, by hand, their agreement with the suggested answer. In case of a disagreement, teachers did not attempt to create a cognitive conflict, but reviewed the procedures, to detect the wrong step.

Only one teacher stressed the ways in which problem solving skills can be acquired. She had her fourth grade students assemble all the problems in a special book, and reiterated the necessary steps to understand the problem: look for the necessary information, make a sketch to illustrate the problem, calculate the answer, and write it.

A major change in developing problem solving skills can be seen in the ways a fourth grade teacher taught the same concept of number of different combinations in the two lessons. In her first lesson almost half of the time was devoted to calculations of the values assigned to the cells of a 10 x 10 grid which represented the number combination of bats and gloves (different prices) that could be bought for less than $100. Very little time was allocated to sharing solutions and explanations of answers.

Her second lesson was devoid of calculations. It was divided into four short sections, and time was devoted to the exploration of the differences in the results incurred by slight changes in the numbers. To arrive at the answers, her students manipulated tangible objects to test out the different arrangements. In the discussions that followed, students' seat work (where pupils are seated and work individually on drill and practice activities) with the manipulatives, alternative solutions were suggested and patterns were explored. At the end of the lesson the teacher also asked her students to describe, in writing, how they solved the problems.

Time allocated for thinking

To determine whether in the second lesson teachers allocated more time for thinking, we defined total thinking time as the sum of minutes allocated during the lessons to the following activities:

- Time between the assignment of the problem and the beginning of the public discourse.
- Time for sharing answers and different solutions.
- Time for exploring mistakes.
- Time for writing about concepts studied in class.

Since the lessons differed in length, the duration of thinking time was calculated as a percentage of the total class time.

The findings show that during their second lesson most of the teachers allocated more time to activities that involved thinking. Increase is not apparent in lessons where the objectives of the lessons were to familiarise students with manipulatives, or specific skills.

It was also anticipated that as a result of the programme, less time would be devoted during class to seat work which involved the practice of algorithms and procedures taught earlier. This occurred for eight teachers. The change was especially prominent in the second lesson of a teacher who gave exactly the same lesson both times. In her second lesson there was a decrease of 34% in time for seat work. In the first lesson she explained the objective of the lesson (to measure angles), handed out protractors and worksheets, instructed her students to solve the problems, collected the work, summarised the lesson, and assigned homework.

In the second lesson, she asked her students to sort out cards according to the geometric figure illustrated on them, and infer the objectives of the lesson from the activity. Her students then measured angles with a protractor, and compared the different triangles. The lesson ended with a summary by the teacher and homework assignment.

The types of thinking skills developed

Transcription of the public discourse enabled the types of thinking skills teachers tried to develop to be determined. All the questions teachers asked were listed and coded. For almost all the teachers, the total number of questions asked by teachers during the second lesson was lower than the number asked in the first lesson. This seems to suggest that, for most of the teachers, the pace in the second lesson was slower, and teachers were more willing to release some control over the process of learning in the classroom, to have their students work in groups or explore the concepts on their own.

Following Stigler, Fernandez and Yoshida (1992) only the teachers' questions which elicited responses from the students were included. Teachers' rhetorical questions, or questions that students were unable to respond to, were not included in this coding. Six types of questions were found and are described below.

- Name/identify questions elicit a name or a quantity of an object, and include questions like: "How much was the fare?", "A triangle is named by what?", "What's the first thing I have to do?", "Guesstimate how many balls are in the bottle".
- Calculate questions elicit a number, and include questions like: "five minus six", "three times nothing", "is nine closer to zero or to ten", and rounding numbers.
- Count questions engage students in reciting numbers in succession, and include statements like: "Do I have 18 in here? Let's see, one, two, three" etc., "How many obtuse angles do each of these polygons have", or "the first multiple of 7 is seven, and the next are...".
- Explain how or why questions encourage students to describe a thinking process that took place. Questions like: "How do you know?", "How did you figure this out?", "Why do you have to regroup?", "Tell me how you solved this", "What is the pattern?", "What will happen on the nth day?" etc. fall into this category. This category also includes questions which require students to check or compare their answer against the information in the problems to validate their solution.
- Higher thinking skills questions require students to apply a certain concept to another situation, or generalise a concept. Although these questions vary in complexity, they are considered together in one category because the thinking skills involved are higher than the ones listed above, and because their rarity in the lessons does not justify categorising them into separate groups.
- Check status questions are used to check the position of the silent majority of the students in the class with regards to the suggested technique or solution. Questions

like: "Who agrees?", "How many found this?", "Is anyone confused?", "Thumbs up, thumbs down" fall into this category.

Our discussion will focus on the first five categories alone. In the first three categories students need to retrieve from their memory a name or a well known procedure, or repeat known steps formerly suggested in class. The fourth and the fifth category develop students' understanding and insight.

The most frequently asked question by all teachers was of the name/identify type. Changes in the number of questions in each category asked by teachers in the second lesson are shown in the following table:

Table 1 Changes in the types of questions asked by teachers in the second lesson

Type of Question	Number of Teachers	Direction of Change
Name/identify	8	-
Calculation	3	-
Count	4	-
Explain	6	+
Higher thinking skills	5	+

The most dramatic change is seen in one teacher whose first lesson resembled the typical mathematics lesson taught by a language arts teacher. She first read from the textbook the definition of geometric shapes: circle, diameter, radius, chord, arc and semicircle, reviewed the terms, instructed her students to create a body circle, and name the geometric terms of the lines created by the students. This entire activity, and the seat work that followed it with the textbook, revolved around the memorisation of the terms.

In her second lesson, most of the time was devoted to rounding numbers, sorting them, cutting and pasting small triangles to create a big triangle from the small pieces in which the numbers appeared. The public discourse did not reveal an increase in the number of questions that involve higher thinking skills because the students worked quietly in their groups, but the actual activities performed in the lessons demonstrate a shift in this teacher's concept of what constitutes a good lesson of mathematics. In our conversations with the teacher after the lesson she indicated that before the programme, she would never think of devoting a whole regular lesson to such activities. She would only assign them in enrichment classes.

6   SUMMARY AND CONCLUSIONS

Teachers do not usually welcome the intrusion of the cameras into their classrooms. However, our experience shows that they can be persuaded to be videotaped if an attitude of mutual trust and commitment to learning is created in the group.

Videotaping teachers in the classrooms is a powerful tool which can be used to demonstrate changes in teachers' teaching styles. Its utility can be enhanced if the videotaped lessons are used for reflective discussions to understand the underlying processes revealed in the teaching segments, as well as teachers' routine ways of operations.

The videotaped lessons provide real life examples of the actual behaviour of all the constituents in the process of learning. Teachers, colleagues and staff developers can use the videotaped lessons to understand and improve their teaching skills, monitor actual occurrences in the classrooms and reflect upon their consequences. Evaluators can use videotaped lessons to sample lessons and determine the outcomes of the programme.

This article explains the methods used to analyse videotaped lessons of teachers who participated in four in-service programmes to develop specialised teachers for mathematics in the elementary schools. The comparison of the overall structure of the lesson, the analysis and of its specific sections, and the coding of the types of questions asked during public discourse, offer a measuring stick to determine and analyse qualitatively changes that occurred in the teachers' practice. These methods enabled us to demonstrate changes in the following areas that were suggested by all the programmes:

- Use of manipulatives.
- Inclusion of problem solving activities in every lesson of mathematics.
- Types of problems that were chosen.
- Teaching problem solving skills.
- Time allocated for thinking.
- Types of thinking skills developed.

Teachers followed the messages and suggestions of the staff developers and changed some of their teaching strategies. The close analysis of the lessons reveal that help is still needed to complete and consolidate the cycle of change.

7   REFERENCES

Stigler, J.W., Fernandez, C. and Yoshida, M. (1996) Traditions of school mathematics in Japanese and American elementary classrooms, in P. Nesher, L.P. Steff, P. Cobb, G. Goldin and B. Greer (eds.) *Theories of mathematical learning.* Lawrence Erlbaum Associates, Hillsdale, NJ.

8   BIOGRAPHY

Menucha Weiss has been involved in designing educational IT materials to be used in schools. She wrote the two evaluation reports for the Teacher Development Component of the University of Chicago School Mathematics Project. Since 1994 she has conducted the formative evaluation of the mathematics programme in "Tomorrow 98" in Israel.

30

Computer integration in the mathematics study of pre-service teacher education - experiences with Project CIMS

Herbert M. Loethe
University of Education Ludwigsburg
Postfach, D-71602 Ludwigsburg, Germany

Abstract

A compulsory course for beginners in 'Introduction to Mathematics' integrates constructive and algorithmic aspects of the concepts involved by using the functional-applicative language Scheme with subject specific and notational extensions (Scheme-L). This course is a basis for further courses in mathematics and computer science.

Keywords

Elementary education, secondary education, teacher education, algorithms, mathematics, teaching materials

1   INTRODUCTION

There are currently two areas of computer innovation in German schools: the use of computers as an activity in different subjects (mainly with standard software, called 'basic education in information technology') and computer science as a separate subject (called 'informatics') or as units of school mathematics. In most of the German states the basic education in information technology is a compulsory part of the instruction at a secondary school level. The teaching of informatics is mostly optional. Teachers of mathematics play an important role in teaching both aspects and in organising and managing the hard- and software installations in schools.

Three observations emerging after more than 20 years of innovative work in this field led us to the starting theses of our project CIMS. Firstly, in-service training is in general limited and unable to create fundamental knowledge and habits. Consequently, in-service trained teachers in general do not change their practice and are slow in picking up innovations in the field of computer use and computer science. Basic education in the use of computers should be a part of pre-service teacher education.

Secondly, even the use of computers with standard software in school requires teachers to have a fundamental knowledge about computers and the basic concepts of computer science. It is not sufficient for effective teaching that teachers are only one step ahead of their students in managing the software. They are undertaking major changes in their subject without any background knowledge and without being able to aim at certain objectives. The teacher has to make sure that such activities in school contribute to the education of the students and are not just a training in software use.

Thirdly, teachers of mathematics are the ones who have to be educated to establish some kind of computer literacy in school which is not restricted to the mere use of standard software. Unfortunately, 'computer literacy' has been redefined every five years in the past. Our thesis is that the fundamental concepts of computer science should be taught, closely related to school mathematics, since the didactics of mathematics (as a science) has the methods and experience to deal with the goals of general education.

2   MATHEMATICS AND INFORMATICS IN PROJECT CIMS

If we consider computer science or informatics more as a scientific and less of an engineering discipline we can see that it is similar to mathematics in content, thinking style and working habit; informatics deals with the 'dynamic' aspects of the abstract representation of knowledge, while mathematics stresses the 'static' ones. In addition to that, some concepts and contents of computer science are so important and fundamental that they must enrich future school mathematics. The research discipline of mathematics cannot any longer be the only reference for defining the school subject.

It is our strong feeling that traditional school mathematics has to change. On the one hand, the applications of mathematical methods are mostly applied in the reality of science, industry, and commerce when using computers. On the other, larger parts of the school mathematics curriculum should be rethought and redesigned because of the impact of Computer Algebra Systems (CAS) which trivialise larger parts of the subject.

We can compare the new role of informatics in relation to school mathematics to geometry. Geometry has grown out of geodesy (the engineering aspect) and the application of mathematical methods has not been driven from the subject (like theoretical physics). There was always an intensive interaction between abstract mathematics and geometry, as illustrative application. Mathematical structures, thinking styles, representations, etc. were induced by geometry. In a comparable way, some sub-disciplines of informatics should be incorporated into school mathematics as constructive applications. A concrete algorithmic style of thinking should be a training in school and used to work out specific aspects and facets of mathematics. In our present judgement the functional-applicative style of thinking and writing algorithms is an adequate one for school and teacher education.

As a consequence of our perspective of the situation and future development, we started the project CIMS (Computer Integration in the Mathematics Study) for reorganising the mathematics study of teachers at our university. Since 1991 every student teacher for secondary level mathematics (and, since 1993, in addition, for elementary level mathematics) has to work through an introductory course

'Introduction to Mathematics' (logic, set theory, combinations, concepts of numbers, theory of numbers, mathematical structures). The important point is that after years of optional courses in computer science for student teachers the department came to the opinion that all students of mathematics have to do computer work at this level of abstraction at the outset of their study (using a local network and text processing systems goes without saying). As a conceptual bridge between mathematics and computer science we referred to the concept of 'function' and the applicative paradigm of programming.

Traditionally the course 'Introduction to Mathematics' was taught in lectures with smaller practise groups doing related paper and pencil work. We enrich the course in several ways. The lecture is done in the traditional style, but it integrates mathematics with dynamic concepts of informatics. It is now based on an elaborated textbook. The left hand pages contain just text in a rather concentrated form: definitions, theorems, proofs, concepts of computer representations, algorithms, etc. This part is not presented for reading in advance or for self-study. The lecturer will teach the subject matter and the students do not need to make notes. During the teaching process the lecturer will sketch illustrations, calculate examples, perform algorithms, assign small exercises and so on. All these activities are prepared on the right hand pages of the textbook and can be completed by the students. After certain sections, traditional paper-and-pencil exercises are assigned as material for tutored group work. In the same way, the practical work with computers is included in the textbook. But not only are assignments given, there are also explanations of language elements and programming techniques, etc. Students usually work through this material in tutored computer sessions in the computer laboratory, but the material is written in a way that they can also work at any other time, and elsewhere, using our network or their home PC. The intended working style of students in the computer sessions can be characterised as a learning by interaction with the dialogue system: experimenting and exploring, learning by debugging, self-demonstration of concepts, and so on. In the context of CAI, this style of computer use for learning was often called the problem solving mode, and it is part of the LOGO philosophy (for example, Papert, 1980). Like Papert, we feel that giving a lecture about mathematics is not sufficient, students have to be put in a situation for actively undertaking mathematics.

3   THE INTERACTION BETWEEN LECTURE AND COMPUTER WORK

On the basis of PC Scheme (TI, 1990) we have programmed extensions which are closely related to the subject matter of the course. There are just translations of keywords into German (since German wording is often more precise than English); the use of infix-notation for algebraic operators and others, many special procedures and functions for mathematics, etc. For instance, suitable co-ordinate graphics, turtle and space turtle graphics packages (Loethe, 1992) are implemented. Some of this work is comparable with Simply Scheme of Harvey-Wright (1994), but our packages are specifically designed for use in the context of mathematics.

The students are introduced to the Scheme-L System by means of turtle graphics. After this, they use the system as a calculator for factorial and binomial coefficients, while in the lecture the theory of combinations are taught. In addition, they use the system as a medium for self-demonstrating the different combinations by using pre-defined functions. This mode of self-demonstration is considered an important way of working with the mathematical concepts concretely, trying out conjectures, experimenting, getting a feeling, for example, for the increasing number of combinations, and so on. In the context of the theory of combinations the mathematical concept of 'set' and the informatical concept of 'list' are introduced as complementary techniques of data abstraction. Lists are used throughout the course as the fundamental data structure in Scheme.

The conceptual interaction between mathematics and informatics should be made clear by the discussion of the concept 'function' to some extent, which is fundamental for mathematics and functional-applicative languages like Scheme. Every kind of mathematical object can be transformed by a function; there are no restrictions in mathematics. This fact excludes imperative computer languages (with the von-Neumann bottle neck) to be considered as reasonable tools for computer use in mathematics. The concept of a pure function is exactly the same in Scheme and in mathematics (besides the fact that in mathematics infinite domains are allowed also). In Scheme-L we can use the arrow notation as an infix-notation which is closer to mathematics than the prefix lambda-notation of standard Scheme. The following is the functional object 'squaring':

```
((x) -> (x * x))
```

The naming of a functional object is done by one of the following expressions:

```
(square:=((x)->(x*x)))
(def square((x)->(x*x)))
```

An alternative way of defining a function is to use the calling pattern:

```
(def (square x) (x * x))
```

```
[1](square 3)
9
```

This flexibility in notation is an important aspect of the methodological design of the course. The system has to be accommodated by the learner and the learner should not be stressed in having to deal with strange notations if this is not necessary. Another case is the use of parentheses. Since the standard mathematical notations are so ambiguous, the Lisp notation is unavoidable.

The variable x in these expressions is a so-called bound variable. The concept of bound versus free variables is important for both mathematics and computer science:

```
(def (parabola x) (a * x * x))
```

Traditional mathematics does not make this concept very clear, and refers to a more psychological than logical way of thinking about them, such as: free variables are called 'parameters' or a variable which varies 'slower' than a bound variable; or a free variable is something which has a value in a certain working context. Computer languages have a specific technique (called scoping) for looking for the value of the free variable in certain environments.

Another aspect of the concept of function is that functions can have side effects on the environment, the screen or other devices. Traditional mathematics does not deal well with this aspect (except for the concept of automata). Here we have a possible enrichment of the traditional mathematical concept of 'function'. In our course functions can have side effects on the environment (database or memory). By incorporating this typical technique of imperative programming into the concept of function we can establish a link to imperative programming without stressing it. In general we avoid the imperative thinking style about algorithms and prefer the recursive one.

Recursively formulated algorithms are thought to be abstract and difficult to understand. In the context of our course, we do not have these difficulties since the problems are rather small and mostly last-line recursive. In order to give an example, consider the divisor list after a test number t of an integer n:

```
(def (divisor-list-after t n)
  (cond ((t > n) ())
        ((t divides n)
         (cons t (divisor-list-after (t + 1) n)))
        (else  (divisor-list-after (t + 1) n))))
```

('divides' is a pre-defined infix-operator for number theory.) The students need only to understand the function which is presented and explained in the lecture, to change it to a more efficient version, and to write functions with an analogue structure.

To learn a mathematical theorem means, in our opinion, it is necessary not only to understand its content, the domain of applicability and the idea of its proof, but also to know its constructive use, for example, as an algorithm. For instance, the theorem of Euclid states that there are infinitely many prime numbers. This is closely related to the function 'the next prime number after a given number':

```
(def (next-prime-after n)
  (if (prime? (n + 1))
      (n+1)
      (next-prime-after (n + 1))))
```

(prime? is a predicate which was developed previously in the lecture and tested in the practical computer work by the students.) The constructive meaning of the Euclid theorem is that his function always stops since the 'next' prime number always exists. The proof cannot be given by arguments related to the finite algorithm, but the mathematical proof of the theorem is strongly motivated by this constructive aspect.

It is by no means the goal of this course to give an introduction to programming with Scheme. The examples used are rather simple, and closely related to mathematical problems. We are more concerned with the concepts and their constructive aspects. The example divisor-list-after offered describes the upper limit of complexity of a Scheme function in this introductory course.

4   EXPERIENCES

The course is still an innovation in process. Evaluations in the past by questionnaire or tutor comments were used to redesign the concept and rewrite the material over a one year cycle. Some of the results of our last questionnaire gathered after the winter semester course 1995/96, indicated that, in general, the students very much liked the elaborated manuscript, especially the structuring of the theory (left pages) and activities (right pages): 73% indicated that it was helpful, 21% neutral, 3% not necessary, and the rest were at the extreme ends. The statement "The right pages encourage me to work actively and struggle with the subject matter" was commented upon: 4.5% indicated that it was not true, 23.9% neutral, 64.2% true, and 7.5% that it was strongly true. The statements about the interaction between mathematics and computer work with Scheme are the most important for our project. We report them in more detail. The students were asked to comment on the statements using a 5 point scale:

>   not at all true --- not true --- neutral --- true --- strongly true.

We give the percentage of their answers (n=67 in most cases) in parentheses: "Mathematics education should be done without computers, since undertaking both together is too difficult" (9.0%, 35.8%, 22.4%, 25.4%, 6.0%); "I got a better understanding of mathematical concepts and methods by undertaking mathematical and computer work in an integrated way" (9.0%, 22.4%, 28.4%, 26.9%, 11.9%).

While these comments are rather positive, the concrete work with Scheme was reported more negatively: "The work and challenge in using Scheme supports my mathematical understanding" (20.9%, 31.3%, 32.8%, 10.4%, 4.5%); "The work with Scheme demands a high level of abstraction" (1.5%, 6.0%, 20.9%, 55.2%, 14.9%); "The work with Scheme demonstrates mathematical concepts to me" (10.4%, 22.4%, 40.3%, 25.5%, 1.5%). However, some responses do not seem to be very serious: "Dealing with Scheme disguises the mathematical content" (9.0%, 32.8%, 31.3%, 20.9%, 6.0%); "I do not understand recursive programs" (20.9%, 31.3%, 26.9%, 10.4%, 6.0%). The reaction to the statement: "The parentheses in Scheme are extremely troublesome" (7.5%, 11.9%, 11.4%, 20.9%, 40.3%) is considered to be emotionally derived due to the difficulty the beginners had in computer sessions. Later on in their study, students realised the merits of parentheses and complained in other courses with computer activities about the lack of transparent syntax in Logo or Maple.

The questionnaire was given at the end of the course. All students who did not complete the course are not represented. Unfortunately, we have at the moment no control over the number of these students, or over their motivation and plans. They can change the subject of their study or postpone the course. The results given seem to be rather too positive in comparison to our other observations (but in any case are very encouraging for the project). One important general observation of lecturers and tutors is that the whole student group becomes polarised by the practical computer work. There are students who are attracted to the computer work and get a lot of positive feedback on their work in mathematics. On the other hand there are students who try to avoid computer work completely. An extensive study on the individual working style of students in the whole learning environment is presently under way. The most encouraging result is the unbiased and natural way that students use computers later in other courses of their study. So, we are able to observe a process of habituation to this integrated work in the whole student population.

I would like to thank Rose Vogel for her intensive work in the project and all other colleagues of the department for their contributions and encouragement.

5   REFERENCES

Harvey, B. and Wright, M. *Simply Scheme: Introducing Computer Science.* The MIT Press, Cambridge Massachusetts, London, England.
Loethe, H. (1992) Conceptually Defined Turtles, in C. Hoyles and R. Noss (eds.) *Learning Mathematics and Logo,* pp. 55-95. The MIT Press, Cambridge Massachusetts, London, England.
Papert, S. (1980) *Mindstorms: Children, computers, and powerful ideas.* Basic Books, New York.
TI (1990) *PC Scheme: User's Guide and Language Reference Manual.* The MIT Press, Cambridge, Massachusetts, London, England.

6   BIOGRAPHY

Herbert Loethe is a professor of mathematics and computer science at the University of Education Ludwigsburg, Germany. He has done extensive work on Computer Assisted Instruction and Computer Sciences in schools since the early 1970s. More recently he has worked on the introduction of Logo languages in schools and teacher training, and its relationship to mathematics.

31

Learning to bridge classroom and computer laboratory activities in mathematics education

Vincenzo Auricchio, Giuliana Dettori, Simonetta Greco and Enrica Lemut
I. M. A., C.N.R.
Via De Marini 6, 16149 Genova, Italy

Abstract

When introducing computer laboratory activities in mathematics education, some training for in-service teachers appears essential, to help them revise school programmes and to address issues related to teaching habits, didactical planning and computer laboratory organisation. In order to make computers an effective support to mathematics teaching, we think that class and computer laboratory uses should be given equal cognitive importance. Training courses should be hands-on, provide models rather than recipes, and include the formation of working groups connected to the research world.

Keywords

Teacher education, classroom practice, curriculum development, innovation, mathematics, software

1 INTRODUCTION

Computer laboratory activities in secondary schools are more and more diffused across subjects in many countries, and in the past few years most schools have been equipped with personal computers and software packages. Though experiences with different topics are mentioned in the literature (Plomp and Pelgrum, 1991; Veen, 1993), computer laboratories are mostly used in connection with mathematics, due to its natural conceptual relationship to informatics. The introduction of computer laboratory activities in mathematics curricula has been proposed for different purposes in the official programmes of different countries. One approach consists of focusing mainly on raising computer abilities; mathematics is only a privileged application field (Selwood and Jenkinson, 1995). The opposite position considers the use of computer laboratories as a means to improve teaching and learning of mathematics, hence shifting the focus from informatics to mathematics.

In Italy, a National Informatics Plan (PNI, 1991) was proposed at the end of the last decade with the aim of introducing concepts, languages and methods of computer science in non-specialised secondary schools; a secondary aim was to apply them in mathematics teaching. This plan included a training phase for mathematics teachers, which did not result in really effective outcomes, basically for two reasons: the courses tried to fulfil both the above mentioned aims and did not sufficiently deepen either of them; the interaction between teachers and trainers was limited to the training period and no further assistance was provided during actual school work.

Some training for teachers appears essential (Burke, 1994) not only because some of them are still not familiar with computers, but also because it is necessary to modify mathematics programmes in some ways. This task is difficult because there is no previous teaching tradition to rely upon. A suitable revision program entails deciding whether to focus the activities on informatics introduction, or upon mathematics support. We think that the basic computer introduction should not be the responsibility solely of the mathematics teachers, but should instead use computer laboratory hours available to improve teaching of their discipline.

This paper is focused on mathematics rather than informatics, and on how to retrain mathematics teachers (which we will mention as teachers from now on) to fruitfully make use of computer laboratories. We argue that a suitable integration of class and computer laboratory activities is necessary to make it a valid support in mathematics education. This requires that teachers not only revise school programmes and teaching habits but also extend to the computer laboratory the didactic contract established in the class.

In this paper, we start from an analysis of computer laboratory characterisation; then we analyse problems faced by teachers when introducing computers in mathematics education; next we consider different relationships between class and computer laboratory; finally we discuss training of in-service teachers.

2   COMPUTER LABORATORY CHARACTERISATION

Computer laboratory activities in mathematics education can exploit, either for introducing or for deepening concepts, the characteristics of software of different kinds, such as educational software, commercial software or programming languages. For instance, in the case of algebra, spreadsheets can be used for introducing basic concepts such as variables and functions, symbolic computation systems can help in defining and applying algebraic manipulation rules, and graphical representation systems can provide an easy graphical resolution of equations. Using computers affects the learning environment, since it raises in students new mental images that teachers need to take into account (Noss and Hoyles, 1992), and provides consistent feedback (Tall, 1991), hence changing the traditional "pedagogical triangle" (Rosvik, 1994) of the relations between students, teachers and knowledge into a "pedagogical tetrahedron". However, computers cannot substitute for teachers, whose leading role remains essential.

There are different opinions about the role actually played by computers: on the one hand, some teachers consider it simply as a tool, like a text book or a compass, hence failing to exploit its full potential; on the other hand, others consider it like a real subject of interaction, without emphasising its limits from a cognitive point of view, hence not stressing what it can be expected to perform and what must always be done by the user. Computers should be considered rather as very particular tools with characteristics different from any other tool used in school: its potentialities stem from its capabilities of interaction, its limits from the fact that its interaction can follow only fixed schemes depending on the running program, without any personal possibility of changing the thread of discussion.

Using a computer requires abilities firstly of how to learn to interact with an operating system and with the syntax and the logic of different programs. Hence, every time a new software program is used, it is necessary to spend some time getting used to it. This delay, however, has the advantage of forcing the user to pay more attention to the mathematical elements that are being learned; for instance, using a symbolic computation system can help students to become aware of the difference between semantic and syntactic rules.

Computers allow fast computations, visualisations of two- and three-dimensional objects, simulations of casual events, and this offers several advantages. It is possible to:

- discuss the same mathematical concept from different points of view, which usually leads to a deeper understanding and a better mastery of concepts (Duval, 1994; Schwarz and Dreyfus, 1995); for instance, geometrical transformations can be completely described by means of equations, but also using a graphical representation clarifies the concept better;
- change the presentational order of some concepts, based on their relative degree of difficulty (Tall, 1991); for instance, the resolution of equations can be introduced graphically before completing the study of algebraic manipulation rules;
- focus on resolution strategies rather than on performing calculations, which can improve problem solving activities (Fey, 1989);
- emphasise the meaning of mathematics concepts (Rothery, 1995) before being able to formally handle them; for instance, derivatives computed by some software can be used to find minima and maxima of a function, based on their meaning, before learning to compute them.

Computers lead students to a more active role, not only because they are required "to do things by themselves", but also because they feel motivated to ask more questions, as is witnessed also in the literature (Offir et al, 1994). This deeper involvement can also give the occasion for some cognitive considerations:

- exploring conjectures can lead to distinguishing conjectures from demonstrations.
- solving problems by trial-and-error can emphasise the power of formal methods.
- discovering rules by analysing the output of some software can make it easier to remember them and to understand their meaning.

3   PROBLEMS TEACHERS FACE IN THE COMPUTER LABORATORY

When including a computer laboratory activity in a mathematical course, teachers face problems of several kinds during preparation, development, and delivery. Problems faced are made more difficult by the fact that a teaching tradition in this field is not yet available. Before starting this activity for the first time, some *preliminary problems* need to be solved. In particular, teachers should:

- face possible personal idiosyncrasies against using computers.
- face the concern of seeing their role weakened (Chaptal, 1994).
- overcome the fear of using a tool which is possibly newer to them than to their students (Sendova, 1994).
- accept that they will need to change their teaching habits (Marshall, 1994).
- understand that using computers aims at a more effective teaching, not to make their work less tiring.
- reach a sufficient knowledge of the hardware and some software that will be used.
- learn that computer arithmetic is somehow different from the traditional form, since numbers that can be represented by a computer are a discrete and limited set, unlike real numbers; this does not result in some applications, but is evident in others.

Concerning the organisation of courses, *didactical planning problems* arise that should be analysed by the teacher before starting a course, or in the class preparation phase during the school year. They include:

- establishing whether and how their didactic "contract" should be modified;
- considering which concepts can be better mastered by the students if introduced by using computers;
- evaluating which software is most suitable for topics to be taught; since more than one software program related to the same topic can exist, and there may be no didactical guides or experience reports to rely on, so performing this choice can be puzzling;
- understanding when students are able to use a given tool so that they can really take advantage of it.

Teaching problems arise during the course of computer laboratory sessions themselves; they can be tackled a priori only in a general way; how exactly these problems will show up cannot be completely predicted, since they arise from the interaction with the students:

- time should be more accurately controlled than in traditional teaching (Jones, 1995), because computer laboratories are usually accessed for a limited number of hours, which need to be used to their best effect, and because it is easier for students to work at different paces in computer laboratories than it is in traditional teaching;
- often there are fewer computers than students in the computer laboratory, hence it is necessary to organise working groups; this entails deciding how many students can fruitfully work together, and if groups should be formed always by the same members and, if not, how often and how they should be changed, if and how individual work should alternate with group work;
- it is more difficult to control the work of all students, because of possible different technical problems at the same time;
- helping students to learn is more complex, since the teacher needs to understand not only obstacles related to mathematics, but also those related to the logic operation of computers;

- evaluating student's work is more difficult (Passey and Ridgway, 1994), because most software currently in use does not keep track of all performed steps, while in traditional tests the students themselves can be required to record the steps of their work and reasoning.

4 POSSIBLE RELATIONSHIPS BETWEEN CLASS AND COMPUTER LABORATORY

How to give an answer to the above issues is strictly dependent on the mutual relationship between class and computer laboratory organisation, which can take different forms.

In some cases, class and computer laboratory are conceived by the teacher as separate modules; in both of them students are taught mathematics, but activities performed are not explicitly connected. Though both environments can be fruitful, some opportunities of cognitive growth are missed. For instance, if equations are solved in the class by formal methods, and in the computer laboratory graphical software is used to study function intersections (but the teacher does not call the student's attention to the fact that an equation can be interpreted as an intersection of two functions so that a graphical approach can be used to solve equations), then a possibility of gaining a general view and a better mastery of the involved concepts is missed.

Sometimes the teacher tries to connect class and computer laboratory activities, but gives greater emphasis to one of the two environments. If the computer laboratory is used only to support conjectures or to apply theorems already demonstrated in the class, then this activity is conceived as a service to class work; though meaningful exercises can be carried out, students get the impression that new concepts and theorems can be introduced only by a theoretical approach. Vice versa, if new concepts and theorems are introduced always by heuristic work in the computer laboratory, and only later is it completed from a theoretical point of view, students can get the message that all mathematical knowledge is obtained by generalising particular cases, and they can be led to underestimate the importance and the need of a theoretical approach to mathematics concepts.

The advantages of both approaches can be achieved by considering class and computer laboratory as environments with equal importance, which is possible, since their potentialities are not in conflict. In both of them teachers can carry out directive activities aiming to build a shared knowledge, students can solve problems autonomously, and ideas can be compared by common discussions. Thus, the teacher should integrate class and computer laboratory activities from a cognitive and a cultural point of view, by considering each as a starting point for the other one, according to the current need, hence producing a continuous and balanced learning experience.

5 TRAINING IN-SERVICE TEACHERS

Training experiences have been carried out in many countries, but often teachers have not been satisfied with the outcomes achieved (Handler, 1993). In particular, they complain that at the end of the training period there are no support personnel to contact in case of need, and that it is difficult to apply what they have learned in everyday teaching. This last issue seems to arise, at least in Italy, because of the structure of courses offered, which lasted a short period and concerned technical aspects of computers and programming languages, and marginally application software, without any self-contained and well organised didactical material. Some mathematical topics were treated as examples of software use, rather than as the subject of the teaching and learning process. Based on this experience and on the teaching problems mentioned in Section 3, we can identify issues related to training in-service teachers.

The three groups of problems are equally important, since each of them, if not suitably addressed, can lead teachers to take decisions not to use computer laboratories or to use them ineffectively. The preliminary issues, except for the acquisition of technical knowledge that must be covered during the training courses, are essentially psychological or cultural, and can be overcome by addressing the remaining groups of problems during the training, provided that the teachers become aware of their existence. Indeed, understanding potentialities and limits of the tools that they are going to use, and getting aware of possible teaching issues and suitable approaches to them, can raise the self confidence that is essential to positively accept this new experience.

Concerning the other two groups of problems, it is important to give models, rather than recipes, in order to make explicit the philosophy underpinning a proposal, not only because teaching problems can arise in different forms, but also because the technology available changes very rapidly so that teachers need to be able to take autonomous decisions on various issues. Hence, training courses should offer criteria, to analyse the potentialities and the applicability of packages rather than be limited in showing their use. Moreover, since comparison and discussion are fundamental for taking balanced decisions, teacher training, after an initial intensive period, should be organised in the form of working groups, strongly linked to research in mathematics education, in order that experiences, problems and suggested solutions can be shared, in particular that concerning their actual work in school. Both intensive courses and working groups should be hands-on, that is, they should give teachers direct experience of using a computer laboratory on the topic they are going to treat.

Though it is not possible to exhaustively address the above-mentioned problems in this paper, we want to outline solutions that seem reasonable, arising from our experiences.

The choice of topics to tackle in the computer laboratory depends both on an analysis of difficulties, usually met by students, and on the software available for that purpose. When more than one software program on a given topic is available, simplicity, robustness and richness should be guiding criteria to make a choice. Simplicity is important, since software which is too sophisticated would require that both teachers and students use long periods of time to learn to use it, and probably also distract the user from concentrating on the proposed mathematical concepts. Simplicity of use includes a user-friendly interface, but does not mean that a software program should solve problems without requiring cognitive effort or much work from the students.

Robustness means that an error in the input data will not cause the student to input all data again or even to restart the program; this feature is important since students are usually not very skilled when typing data.

Richness of features does not mean choosing the package with more functions, but looking at which functions are useful for teaching, since many complex operations are not required in school. In this respect, it is not necessary to periodically get the most recent version of the applied software, but rather to evaluate whether the newly added features are really an improvement from a didactical point of view. Moreover, sometimes it seems convenient to use different software for different purposes, even within the same topic, so as not to limit the choice to didactical software. For instance, in the case of algebra, Derive is a package which can be used effectively, but a more suitable introduction to equations can be made by using a spreadsheet (Dettori et al, 1995; Auricchio and Greco, 1995), while using some software that allows the integration of text and formulas in the same working sheet helps students to comment on the work done, hence reflecting on it more than they usually would. Another reason for using more than one software program is that one can be more suitable for making conjectures, another for developing applications. However, the number of different packages should be as limited as possible, in order to avoid wasting effort with technical rather than mathematical notions.

The choice of a suitable software program depends on didactical aims, which are related to a student's current abilities and knowledge. Using a software program to do faster what is already mastered allows them to focus on concepts that are to be learned. For instance, if a teacher wants his students to learn graphical representations of function, he should not use a program that draws graphs automatically, but one that requires all parameters involved to be chosen. Later, for introducing the graphical method to solve equations, a graphical software program is adequate, because students need to focus on the solution method.

If a student needs individual support, it is appropriate not to force him to use a different software program, but rather the same software in a different way; for instance, the teacher can ask him to verbalise his reasoning before translating it into software commands, or not to use some commands that automatically produce operations he does not yet master. Hence, the didactical contract established in the class should be confirmed also in the computer laboratory, extending it to meet the characteristics of this learning environment.

Let us now consider problems arising during the course of computer laboratory sessions. The first problem to solve is its physical organisation, that is, how to match students and computers, especially if there are more people than machines. Working in groups has the advantage of compelling students to share and compare their thoughts, provided that groups are small enough to give space to everyone; in general, groups of two seem the most productive. On the other hand, individual work leads each student to face problems by himself, and this gives a measure of individual abilities and limits. Working together influences the level of attention: it can help students to concentrate more on their work, but it can also be an occasion for distraction. Moreover, working with a class mate is not always immediately engaging, but it is a skill that needs to be acquired and refined. From the point of view of teaching, it may be easier to control group work than individual work, since the number of resulting strategies to be analysed is smaller, but it can happen that interesting approaches or means will not emerge. We believe that it would be advisable to alternate individual and group work, both in the class and in the computer laboratory, possibly with students taking turns to work individually, if the number of computers is not sufficient; this alternation can also increase the student's self confidence. Exploring conjectures and solving very complex problems seems to be performed better in groups, while verifying concept acquisition and solving standard problems seems more appropriate for individual work. The initial group setting can be decided by the teacher or by the students; what matters is that the teacher checks that all groups work effectively, possibly changing the composition of some of them according to need, but not so often as to prevent the group members developing an understanding of each other.

Group work can make the evaluation of the performances of every student more difficult, which in the computer laboratory is difficult as well for individual work, since most software does not keep track of single steps performed. Evaluation can be improved by asking the students to mark on paper the performed operations, as well as recording the obtained results. Individual evaluation can be supported by personal observation and by experiences of individual work. While class and computer laboratory are equally important from an educational point of view, they require different cognitive abilities. A global evaluation of the students should give the right balance to skills developed in each environment.

Since occasions for discussing collateral problems are more frequent in the computer laboratory than in the class, and it is easier to loose the thread of the lesson, we suggest that teachers prepare a detailed scheme of the content to be developed in every lesson, which refers also to maintaining the student's work at a similar pace. Only questions asked by few students, or groups of students, should be discussed individually, while issues shared by most students should be the objects of common discussion, in order both to save time and to contribute to the building of a shared base of knowledge.

6   REFERENCES

Auricchio, V. and Greco, S. (1995) *Un itinerario didattico per l'introduzione all'algebra supportato da software commerciali*. Tech. Rep. n.16/95, IMA CNR, Genova, Italy.

Burke, W. (1994) The search for a coherent approach to the development of Information Technology in the school curriculum, in J. Wright and D. Benzie (eds.) *Exploring a New Partnership: Children, Teachers and Technology, IFIP Transactions* **A-58**, 49-56. North-Holland, Amsterdam.

Chaptal, A. (1994) Policy for change, in J. Wright and D. Benzie (eds.) *Exploring a New Partnership: Children, Teachers and Technology, IFIP Transactions* **A-58**, 49-56. North-Holland, Amsterdam.

Dettori, G., Garuti, R. and Lemut, E. (1995) From arithmetic to algebraic thinking by using a spreadsheet, in R. Sutherland (ed.) *Algebraic processes and structures*. Kluwer.

Duval, R. (1994) Représentation sémiotique et coordination des registres. Paper presented at the *46th Congress of the CIEAEM*, Toulouse.

Fey, J.T. (1989) School algebra for the year 2000, in *Research issues in the learning and teaching of algebra, Vol. 4, NCTM*. L. Erlbaum.

Handler, M.G. (1993) Preparing new teachers to use computer technology: perceptions and suggestions for teacher educators. *Computers and Education*, **20**, 2, 147-156.

Jones, D. (1995) The introduction of an Information Technology project: personal computing in the classroom, in J.D. Tinsley and T.J. van Weert (eds.) *Proceedings of the WCCE 95*, pp. 327-336.

Marshall, G. (1994) Cautionary verses: prospects and problems in achieving the aims of the computer revolution, in J. Wright and D. Benzie (eds.) *Exploring a New Partnership: Children, Teachers and Technology, IFIP Transactions* **A-58**, 49-56. North-Holland, Amsterdam.

Noss, R. and Hoyles, C. (1992) Looking back and looking forward, in C. Hoyles and R. Noss (eds.) *Learning math with Logo*. MIT Press.

Offir, B., Katz, Y.J. and Passig, D. (1994) The utilisation of "open" courseware for developing an enquiry approach in the study of non-scientific subjects, in J. Wright and D. Benzie (eds.) *Exploring a New Partnership: Children, Teachers and Technology, IFIP Transactions* **A-58**, 49-56. North-Holland, Amsterdam.

Passey, D. and Ridgway, J. (1994) The development of informatics capability in elementary schools: what to do, and how to make it work, in J. Wright and D. Benzie (eds.) *Exploring a New Partnership: Children, Teachers and Technology, IFIP Transactions* **A-58**, 49-56. North-Holland, Amsterdam.

Plomp, T. and Pelgrum, W.J. (1991) Introduction of computers in education: state of the art in eight countries. *Computers and Education*, **17**, 3, 249-258.

PNI (1991) La verifica del Piano Nazionale per l'Informatica nelle scuole secondarie superiori. *Annali della Pubblica Istruzione*.

Rosvik, S. (1994) A look back at the conference, in J. Wright and D. Benzie (eds.) *Exploring a New Partnership: Children, Teachers and Technology, IFIP Transactions* **A-58**, 49-56. North-Holland, Amsterdam.

Rothery, A. (1995) Computer algebra and the structure of the mathematics curriculum, in L. Burton and B. Jaworski (eds.) *Technology in mathematics teaching*, 329-343.

Schwarz, B. and Dreyfus, T. (1995) New actions upon old objects: a new ontological perspective on functions. *Educational Studies in Mathematics*, **29**, 259-291.

Selwood, I. and Jenkinson, D. (1995) The delivery of Information Technology capability in secondary schools in England and Wales, in J.D. Tinsley and T.J. van Weert (eds.) *Proceedings of the WCCE 95*, pp. 565-575.

Sendova, E. (1994) A computer in the classroom: a catalyst for a creative partnership, in J. Wright and D. Benzie (eds.) *Exploring a New Partnership: Children, Teachers and Technology, IFIP Transactions* **A-58**, 49-56. North-Holland, Amsterdam.

Tall, D. and Thomas, M. (1991) Encouraging versatile thinking in algebra using the computer. *Educational Studies in Mathematics*, **22**, 2, 125-147.

Veen, W. (1993) How teachers use computers in instructional practice: four case studies in a Dutch secondary school. *Computers and Education*, **21**, 1/2, 1-8.

7   BIOGRAPHY

Giuliana Dettori and **Enrica Lemut** are mathematicians, working as researchers at the Institute for Applied Mathematics of the National Research Council of Italy. Their main research interest is in mathematics and technology education.

Vincenzo Auricchio and **Simonetta Greco** are mathematicians, collaborators of the Institute for Applied Mathematics of the National Research Council of Italy. They are interested in mathematics and technology education.

32

Integrating graphing technology into teacher education: a case study of an algebra program for prospective secondary school mathematics teachers

Beverly J. Ferrucci
Keene State College
Keene, NH, USA 03435-2001

Jack A. Carter
California State University
Hayward, CA, USA 94542-3092

Abstract

The use of technology to facilitate algebraic learning has recently flourished. Using graphing technology, researchers have found that it becomes very natural to add visualisation to the standard algebraic techniques used in the mathematics curriculum. In particular, students utilising computer graphing have been found to solve more complex equations, even equations that do not admit an algebraic solution. The research literature also supports the enhancement of algebraic thinking in students through open-ended and exploratory activities that focus on applications, alternative representations of functions, and the use of graphing technology. This case study investigated a pre-service education course for prospective secondary school mathematics teachers which utilised activities, such as those described above, that were especially well facilitated through the use of graphing technology.

Keywords

Secondary education, teacher education, case studies, mathematics

1 INTRODUCTION

Studies of content and methods of teaching algebra have tended to emphasise the value of problem solving approaches, open-ended inquiry, and the allowance of ample time for the development of concepts, generalisations, and skills (Rachlin, 1987).

Alternative approaches for teaching algebraic functions, for example, those that focus on the relationships between tabular and graphical representations, have also received favourable reviews in the literature (Kaput, 1988; Ruthven, 1990). Other studies have concentrated on the development of the fundamental algebraic concepts of function and variable through explorations of problems while much of the graphing work is relegated to computing tools. These technologically enhanced approaches intend to place mathematical decision making in students' hands while engaging them in analysis of realistic problems (Kieran, 1992; Heid, 1990). In a teaching experiment Yerushalmy and Schwartz (1993) applied a corrective approach that enacted simultaneous, linked representations of functions to build understanding of algebraic entities. The researchers concluded that effective instruction should restructure the curricular emphasis in algebra and provide environments in which students can explore their understandings and test generalisations from these understandings.

Overall, research on instruction in algebra has focused on didactic approaches that minimise the amount of symbolic manipulation and introduce algebraic situations in less abstract environments. A basis of these approaches consists of using hand-held and other graphic technology as an aid in learning algebraic representations, while another component often involves the recording of case studies of instruction in algebra that show the effective use of these technologies.

2   THE CASE STUDY

A series of case studies to investigate teacher preparation programmes for secondary school mathematics teachers from selected institutions in the USA was a basis of the current report. In particular, this report was based on one case study that explored an instructor's efforts to integrate graphing technology into students' pre-service teacher education programme in mathematics. The instructor in this case study was a professor at a four-year state university in which there is a programme that graduates approximately 15 secondary school mathematics teachers per year. The instructor's students in this case study were enrolled in a course in methods of teaching secondary school mathematics, and the instructor permitted two researchers to observe each of the class sessions during the entire term. The instructor was particularly concerned with instructional techniques in algebra since each student was student teaching in one or more algebra classes at local secondary schools. As a result, the instructor devoted considerable class time to alternative approaches for enhancing algebraic thinking and many of these approaches incorporated the use of graphing technology.

After observing and taking notes during the instructor's classes, the researchers independently completed rating scales. At the conclusion of the course, those classes that received the highest ratings were analysed with respect to content and pedagogical approach. This report outlines the most highly rated algebraic activities among those observed. Subsequent analysis of the instructor's classroom activities showed that seven types of activities dealing with algebraic thinking were especially well facilitated through the use of graphing technology.

2.1 Identifying equations with their graphs

In this activity the instructor displayed a co-ordinate grid showing parts of the graphs of three quadratic functions. Students were asked the following questions: (1) How many parabolas are displayed in the graph? (2) Which of the equations do not correspond to points in the graph? (3) What range of values for the graph would clearly show all four parabolas? The observers noted that new and unfamiliar aspects of algebra were apparent in the types of questions the instructor asked. Moreover, the students needed to use ingenuity and graphing technology skills to answer these questions. In a concluding summary of the lesson, the instructor noted that similar types of activities were helpful in reinforcing students' understanding of other types of algebraic graphs: rational expressions, piecewise functions, and transformations. The instructor's application of previously acquired knowledge to new and unfamiliar situations appeared to the observers to accentuate many essential components of algebraic thinking and problem solving.

2.2 Fitting data to lines: the mile record

In this activity the instructor presented a chart showing selected men's mile world records from 1865-1993. The chart indicated that the world record had dropped steadily. Using graphing technology students were asked to work in teams to graph the data (year and record time), find the equation of the line of best fit and graph this equation. Once equations of the line of best fit had been determined, the instructor asked the teams to use these equations in order to respond to the following: (1) Cole set a world record in 1981. Estimate this record time. (2) Bannister was the first to run the mile in under four minutes (3 minutes 59.4 seconds). Estimate the year of this record time. and (3) Assuming a linear trend continues, when might a 3:30 record be set? The instructor emphasised that there were several subtleties involved in algebraic solutions to these kinds of problems. Specifically, these related to the empirical nature of the discernible relationship, the assumption of steadily decreasing records, and physiological limits for such records. In viewing this activity the observers were impressed by the instructor's ability to make students aware of the preceding types of subtleties. Such awareness appeared to enable students to gain a better understanding of the algebraic modelling of practical problems.

2.3 Fitting data to curves: Challenger failure data

In a next class session, the instructor provided students with data from the Challenger space shuttle. These data, the instructor explained, provided an opportunity to model the gasket failures that led to the explosive destruction of the shuttle just after its launch. Particularly, the data indicated the temperature at launch and the number of damaged gaskets in each of the preceding launches. The instructor asked the students to predict the expected number of gasket failures for a specific temperature at the time of launch. By using data in which there was (and was not) evidence of gasket damage, students were able to find that the restricted data set was best modelled by a linear function, and the entire data set was best modelled by a logarithmic function. With both data sets, students had the opportunity to observe the appropriateness of the fit and to predict the failure rates of the gaskets that evidently caused the disaster.

2.4 Solving traditional algebraic equations

These activities ranged from the solution of polynomial equations to solving non-linear equations simultaneously. In each instance the graphical solution provided an alternative and exploratory counterpart to traditional approaches. Linear equations were solved by inputting the left and right sides of the equations as separate functions, graphing these functions, and finding the value for which the two expressions were equal. Solutions of this kind appeared to help these students better understand which transforms preserve the equivalence of the equations and why. Approximate solutions of higher order and systems of equations provided another example of how graphing technology could provide an alternative solution as well as a check on an algebraic solution. These approximations frequently involved applications of the zoom and trace options in the graphing technology. By using the graphing technology and then describing their estimation techniques, students appeared to be developing an improved understanding and articulation of algebraic thinking.

2.5 Solving non-traditional algebraic equations

In this activity the instructor offered the class a single example: Solve the equation $2^x = x^{10}$. Working in groups the students found that traditional algebraic methods produced no headway. Consequently, graphical or numerical procedures were the only recourse. By defining the left and the right sides of the equation as separate functions, many of the students were able to use the zoom-and-trace feature of a grapher to find two intersection points. But, some students were also able to locate a third root by means of graphing the difference function.

2.6 Modelling with linear programming

Two entire class sessions were devoted to this topic by the instructor. The sessions emphasised the fact that function graphers provided an excellent vehicle for graphing systems of linear inequalities, locating corner points, and evaluating objective functions at the corner points to find the optimum value. In one project students were able to model the production of graphing calculators by a company intending to maximise profits. These modelling activities provided examples of applications that appeared to stimulate and develop higher level thinking without sacrificing mastery of conventional algebraic skills.

2.7 Verifying identities

The class session devoted to verifying identities included the verification of a variety of algebraic and trigonometric identities. These activities appeared to motivate as well as enhance existing algebraic thinking among the prospective teachers. For example, students were readily able to verify the difference of cubes factoring formula by entering the left and right sides as separate functions, graphing these functions, and visually checking that the graphs coincide. Similarly, students were able to confirm various identities involving the sine, cosine, tangent and other basic functions. The observers noted that in attempting these confirmations students had an opportunity to refresh their knowledge of basic identities and verify these identities without the use of lengthy algebraic proofs. The experience gained in these types of verifications appeared to sharpen thinking skills and provide a visual reinforcement of algebraic thought processes.

3   IMPLICATIONS

The preceding activities were those rated most highly in enhancing algebraic thinking during the course of the case study. Based on the accompanying review of the literature, there are several educational implications that can be drawn.

This report described how one secondary teacher educator addressed algebraic misconceptions with prospective teachers and used graphing technology as a means of alleviating these misconceptions. Consequently, a potential benefit of using graphing technology is to offer classroom teachers a tool that will aid in making sense of their students' algebraic thinking and thereby help in better understanding the varied responses that are effective among different learners.

This case study was derived from the work of an instructor whose views were consistent with those expressed in current reform initiatives. Research (for example, Kieran, 1992) suggests that many prospective secondary school mathematics teachers do not have a well developed concept of algebraic processes, particularly as these processes relate to technology. This is in spite of these students having memorised numerous formulae and algebraic manipulation techniques. The lack of conceptual development observed in these prospective secondary school teachers is apt to reflect a more widespread problem. The understanding of algebraic processes is a complex issue, and this study has identified some of the key instructional components of such understanding within the context of a teacher education course that has been enhanced through the use of technology.

4   REFERENCES

Heid, M.K. (1990) Uses of technology in prealgebra and beginning algebra. *Mathematics Teacher*, **83**, 194-198.

Kaput, J.J. (1988) *Translations from numerical and graphical to algebraic representations of elementary functions*. Paper presented at the annual meeting of the American Educational Research Association, New Orleans, LA.

Kieran, C. (1992) The learning and teaching of school algebra, in D.A. Grouws (ed.) *Handbook of Research on Mathematics Teaching and Learning*. Macmillan, New York.

Rachlin, S.L. (1987) Using research to design a problem-solving approach for teaching algebra, in *Proceedings of the Fourth Southwest Asian Conference on Mathematics Education*. Singapore Institute of Education, Singapore.

Ruthven, K. (1990) The influence of the graphic calculator on the transition from graphic to symbolic forms. *Educational Studies in Mathematics*, **21**, 431-450.

Yerushalmy, M. and Schwartz, J.L. (1993) Seizing the opportunity to make algebra mathematically and pedagogically interesting, in T.A. Romberg, E. Fennema and T.P. Carpenter (eds.) *Integrating Research on the Graphical Representation of Functions*. Lawrence Erlbaum, Hillsdale, NJ.

5   BIOGRAPHIES

Beverly J. Ferrucci is a Professor of Mathematics and the chair of the Mathematics Department at Keene State College in Keene, NH. She received a doctorate in mathematics from Boston University as well as a doctorate in psychometrics from Boston College. She is a member of the Research Advisory Committee of the National Council of Teachers of Mathematics (NCTM) and a documenter for the Recognizing and Recording Reform in Mathematics Education Project of NCTM. Her research interests include the pre-service and in-service education of teachers in mathematics and technology and cross-cultural studies of prospective mathematics teachers.

Jack A. Carter received graduate and undergraduate degrees from the California State University System and a doctorate in mathematics education from the University of Texas at Austin. Since 1981 he has taught in the Departments of Mathematics and Computer Science and Teacher Education at California State University, Hayward. His research interests include the teaching and learning of mathematics, comparisons of national systems of mathematics education, and the use of technology in mathematics instruction.

33

Software evaluation as a focus for teacher education

David Squires
School of Education
King's College, Waterloo Road, London SE1 8WA, UK

Abstract

In this paper the use of educational software evaluation as an organising theme for IT related teacher education is considered. Effective educational software evaluation involves a high degree of knowledge and understanding of teaching, learning and curriculum design. Developing software evaluation skills can provide rich opportunities for teachers to acquire knowledge and understanding in these areas. The relationship between software evaluation and teacher education is discussed in terms of a novel software evaluation paradigm, the 'Perspectives Interactions Paradigm', which adopts a situated view of teaching and learning. This discussion provides a basis for proposing a strategy for a software evaluation based school-focused approach to teacher education in the use of IT.

Keywords

Secondary education, professional development, teacher education, evaluation/summative, research, software

1   INTRODUCTION

Teachers in all disciplines are now commonly expected to use information technology (IT) to support teaching and learning. For example, in delivering the National Curriculum for England and Wales, teachers are expected to provide pupils with 'opportunities, where appropriate, to develop and apply their IT capability in their study of National Curriculum subjects' (Department for Education and Welsh Office, 1995, p. 1). To do this effectively teachers need to develop skills and awareness relevant to the use of IT in their disciplines. Effective educational software evaluation involves a high degree of knowledge and understanding of IT related teaching, learning and curriculum issues. Developing software evaluation skills can provide rich opportunities for teachers to acquire this knowledge and understanding and in this paper software evaluation as a focus for teacher education in the educational use of IT is discussed.

2   APPROACHES TO TEACHER EDUCATION

The course-based approach is a common model for in-service education. Morant (1981) describes it as a 'top-up' approach. It assumes teachers can be educated by correcting deficits in their knowledge. Most courses are short term with no plan for individual development and Millar (1990) points out that this approach is compatible with the deficit model of teacher education (Eraut, 1987). This model assumes that teachers are deficient in skills due to limited initial training, or lack knowledge because they have failed to keep up to date.

   School-based teacher education programmes can be described as being initiated, planned, and executed by school staff for teachers actually serving in the school (Millar, 1990). The rationale of this approach is that it is easier to identify relevant needs (Henderson, 1979; Morant, 1981). This approach links to two further paradigms for teacher education identified by Eraut (1987); the change paradigm and the problem solving paradigm. The change paradigm requires teachers to accommodate to local and nationally imposed changes, for example, the introduction of a statutory national curriculum in England and Wales. The problem solving paradigm is geared towards dealing with issues and developments in teachers' schools.

   Millar (1990) cites Howey (1986) as describing the priority of a school focused agenda as 'the improvement of those conditions and processes which most directly affect the quality of education of students within a given school' (p. 24). This approach typically involves contributions from staff within the school and external consultants, and course attendance. School-focused education attempts to realise the advantages of the school-based approach and minimise the disadvantages of courses. This approach clearly relates to the problem solving paradigm. It also relates to a fourth paradigm identified by Eraut (1990); the growth paradigm in which teacher education is seen in terms of personal development and career needs.

3   EDUCATIONAL SOFTWARE EVALUATION

It is now commonly advocated that cognition and learning are situated in specific learning contexts (for example, Brown, 1989; Pea, 1993; Clancey, 1994). Brown refers to learning being 'idexicalised' to the context in which learning occurs, meaning that learning is inherently associated with the context in which it takes place. This implies that it is not possible to evaluate an educational artefact, such as a software package, as an educational device in its own right; it is only possible to evaluate the actual or perceived use of a software package in an intended or existing educational setting. Thus a situated approach to software evaluation should be adopted.

3.1 Predictive and interpretative evaluation

Attention to context is straightforward when the actual use of software is being evaluated as the evaluation is an interpretation of observed use. Such evaluation can be called 'interpretative evaluation'. In contrast, 'predictive evaluation' is concerned with the prior evaluation of a software package before it is used with students. The use of a package is imagined in intended learning situations, i.e. the evaluator mentally simulates the use of the package so that an attempt can be made to evaluate the package in context.

3.2 Common approaches to educational software evaluation

Checklists and frameworks are the conventional software evaluation tools, but, as discussed below, they do not allow a situated perspective to be adopted.

Checklists for software evaluation

In a critical examination of the checklist approach to predictive evaluation McDougall and Squires (1995a) identify a number of problems. These problems are symptomatic of a failure to adopt a situated perspective. Some stem from a focus on the software application as an object of evaluation in its own right rather than the evaluation of its use in context. Others indicate that the diversity and complexity of the classroom, and the teacher's role in managing this, do not feature in the design of checklists. Also, evaluation in different subject areas requires different criteria to be used (Komoski, 1987).

Frameworks for software evaluation

Many writers have advocated the use of frameworks to describe the use of educational software. For example, classification by category (Pelgrum, 1991), description of the roles that it is intended to fulfil (Taylor, 1980) and links to commonly accepted educational rationales (Kemmis, 1977).

The focus in classifying by application type is on the software package itself, without consideration of its use in particular educational settings. Classification by educational role emphasises the way software is intended to perform rather than the roles of the teacher and the learner. The use of educational software is conceived primarily from the designer's perspective, which does not encourage a situated approach to evaluation with the designer's decisions interpreted in the context of the use of a package. Links to educational rationales encourages a view of software as belonging exclusively to one paradigm, hindering its evaluation in a variety of contexts. Classification by software environment promotes a superficial distinction between software in terms of attributes rather than context.

3.3 The 'Perspectives Interactions' paradigm

Squires and McDougall (1994) have proposed a situated paradigm for evaluating educational software which is based on the mutual 'interactions' between the principal 'actors' involved in the classroom use of software. Three actors contribute to the learning situation of a package; two live actors (teacher and student) and one passive actor (designer). The situation in which the package is used is defined by the interactions between these perspectives.

The student-teacher perspectives interaction

The interaction between the perspectives of the student and the teacher explicitly relates to the situation in which learning takes place. It implies a consideration of how the introduction of computers into the classroom may change the distribution between the teacher and student(s) of responsibilities for teaching and learning.

There are many reports of software use acting as a catalyst for a wide variety of off-computer activities. In these situations teachers assume the role of manager and resource provider. Collaboration between peers, particularly in small groups, is very important when IT is used (Hoyles, Healy and Pozzi, 1994), notably in terms of enhanced peer discussion (Chatterton, 1985). When IT is used in the classroom teachers can be regarded as managers and supporters, as opposed to directors, of student-focused activities.

The student-designer perspectives interaction

The interaction between the student's and designer's perspectives relates to how the use of the software can aid learning. A tenet of a situated view of learning is that it takes place in a constructivist fashion. An essential aspect of an evaluation of the use of a software package is the extent to which it can support a constructivist approach.

Honebein, Duffy and Fishman (1993) have argued that authenticity and stimulus or concept complexity are crucial in constructivist learning environments. They identify three conditions for authenticity: a sense of ownership of learning, engagement in global activities which go beyond mastery of local skills, and use of multiple perspectives in problem solving.

The teacher-designer perspectives interaction

The teacher-designer perspectives interaction relates to the designer's notion of the curriculum relevance of the intended use of the package. Teachers need to appreciate this and assess how valid it is in personal terms. Evaluation with respect to this interaction is a question of how the designer's and evaluator's perceptions of the curriculum match.

Curriculum issues may be explicit, implicit, or even absent, in the design of educational software. Explicit curriculum issues are evident in packages that have been designed for a defined course or curriculum. Implicit curriculum issues stem from cultural assumptions made by designers, for example, the American bias of many CD-ROMs. Absence of curriculum issues arises when software not originally intended for use in education is used in schools, for example, wordprocessors. Assessing software with explicit curriculum aims simply requires a comparison of these aims with a syllabus. Evaluating software which initially has no curriculum aims requires some imagination as to whether and how the software might be used in an educational context. In this case it is not a question of mapping the teacher's intentions onto the designer's; rather it is a matter of assessing how teachers can impose their perceptions on the use of software.

4 SCHOOL-FOCUSED 'PERSPECTIVES INTERACTIONS'

The 'Perspectives Interactions' paradigm has been used successfully as part of a teacher education course (McDougall, 1995b). The situated nature of the paradigm also makes its use with a school-focused approach appropriate. Both predictive and interpretative software evaluation can feature in this approach. Predictive evaluation brings a realism to courses by relating software to classroom use. Interpretative evaluation can assist reflection on practice.

4.1   The student-teacher 'perspectives interaction'

The student-teacher perspectives interaction relates to classroom practice. As such there is a natural link to interpretative evaluation of the use of software in classroom settings. School-based work which involves teachers evaluating practice in their own schools will provide the most authentic environment for them to appraise their own practice or work by colleagues.

4.2   The student-designer 'perspectives interaction'

The student-designer perspectives interaction implies that teachers should be able to appreciate the significance of theories of learning in software design. Courses provide the best forum for presenting a wide range of learning theories. Teachers can attend presentations by experts and use a broad range of software that they would not typically have access to in their schools. Work located in schools could augment course-based work. For example, evaluation groups, perhaps chaired by an 'expert' from the course, could meet to appraise the learning theories implicit in software used in the school. There is scope for linked interpretative evaluation, using the idea of observing the use of software as a 'window on the mind' (Weir, 1985).

4.3   The teacher-designer 'perspectives interaction'

In the teacher-designer perspectives interaction the relative emphasis on school-based and course-based approaches will depend on the extent to which the school follows a prescribed curriculum. When there is a national curriculum, as in England and Wales, there may be more emphasis on a course-based approach. However, there is always a need for some school-based work. For example, the appropriate environment for developing evaluation skills for the assessment of implicit curriculum issues is the school itself in ethnically mixed schools.

5   SOFTWARE EVALUATION FOCUSED TEACHER EDUCATION

The analysis in Section 4 indicates that considering the 'Perspectives Interactions' paradigm gives a comprehensive framework for coherent school-focused programmes consisting of:

- School-based interpretative evaluation of classroom practice of the use of software.
- Courses on learning theories, perhaps linked to school-based evaluations.
- A mix of school and course-based work to develop curriculum evaluation skills.

A programme incorporating all of these elements would provide coverage of the three main issues in teaching practice - pedagogy, curriculum and learning in authentic contexts.

6 REFERENCES

Brown, J.S., Collins, A. and Duguid, P. (1989) Situated Cognition and the Culture of Learning. *Educational Researcher*, **18**, 32-42.

Chatterton, J. L. (1985) Evaluating CAL in the Classroom, in I. Reid and J. Rushton (eds.) *Teachers, Computers and the Classroom*. Manchester University Press, Manchester.

Clancey, W.J. (1994) Situated cognition: how representations are created and given meaning, in R. Lewis and P. Mendelsohn (eds.) *Lessons From Learning*. North-Holland, Amsterdam.

Department for Education and The Welsh Office (1995) *Information Technology in the National Curriculum*. HMSO Publications Centre, London.

Eraut, M. (1987) In-service Teacher Education, in M. Dunkin (ed.) *The International Encyclopaedia of Teaching and Teacher Education*. Oxford University Press, Oxford.

Henderson, E. (1979) The concept of school-focused in-service education and training. *British Journal of Teacher Education*, **5**, 1, 17-25.

Honebein, P.C., Duffy, T.M. and Fishman, B.J. (1993) Constructivism and the Design of Authentic Learning Environments: Context and Authentic Activities for Learning, in T.M. Duffy, J. Lowyck and D.H. Jonassen (eds.) *Designing Environments for Constructive Learning*. Springer-Verlag, Berlin.

Hoyles, C., Healy, L. and Pozzi, S.(1994) Groupwork with computers: an overview of findings. *Journal of Computer Assisted Learning*, **10**, 4, 202-215.

Howey, K. (1986) School Focused In-service: Synthesis Report, in D. Hopkins (ed.) *In-service Training and Curriculum Development: An International Survey*. Cambridge Croome Helm: London.

Komoski, P.K. (1987) Educational Microcomputer Software Evaluation, in J. Moonen and T. Plomp (eds.) *Eurit86: Developments in Educational Software and Courseware*. Pergamon Press, Oxford.

McDougall, A. and Squires, D. (1995a) A critical examination of the checklist approach in software selection. *Journal of Educational Computing Research*, **12**, 3, 263-274.

McDougall, A. and Squires, D. (1995b) An empirical study of a new paradigm for choosing educational software. *Computers and Education*, **25**, 3, 93-103.

Millar, L.C. (1990) *In-service Education and Information Technology*. MA dissertation, King's College London.

Morant, R. (1981) *In-service education within the school*. George Allen and Unwin, London.

Pea, R. (1993) Practices of Distributed Intelligence and Designs for Education, in G. Salomon (ed.) *Distributed Cognitions: Psychological and Educational Considerations*. Cambridge University Press, Cambridge.

Pelgrum, J. and Plomp, T. (1991) *The Use of Computers Worldwide*. Pergamon, Oxford.

Squires, D. and McDougall, A. (1994) *Choosing and Using Educational Software: a Teachers' Guide*. Falmer Press, London.

Taylor, R. P. (ed.) (1980) *The Computer in the School: Tutor, Tool, Tutee*. Teachers College Press, New York.

Weir, S. (1985) *Cultivating Minds: A Logo Casebook*. Harper and Row, New York.

7   BIOGRAPHY

David Squires is a Senior Lecturer in Educational Computing in the School of Education, King's College London. He has extensive experience of design, development and use of software in schools and universities. He is a past co-director of the Computers in the Curriculum Project, a UK national curriculum development project featuring the use of educational software in the sciences and humanities. He currently directs a British Library research project about use of IT-assisted information systems in academic research.

Section 9: Cognition and the integration of information and communication technology uses for the pupil

34

Towards effective learning with new technology resources: the role of teacher education in reconceptualising the relationship between task setting and student learning in technology-rich classrooms

Bridget Somekh
Depute Director, Scottish Council for Research in Education
15 St John Street, Edinburgh, Scotland EH26 OLQ, UK

Abstract

The purpose of this paper is twofold: first, to explore the reasons why it is inherently difficult to use resources - including new technology resources - to generate and support learning in classrooms; and second, to put forward suggestions for an approach to teacher education which might enable new technology resources to be used to much better effect. The paper begins with an analysis of the reasons why it is difficult to make good use of resources such as books in the classroom context, and relates this to difficulties for teachers in setting learning tasks for students. It goes on to argue that although these problems can be overcome by adopting an approach to teaching as reflective practice, these benefits are often lost because the focus of teachers' reflection is upon classroom organisation rather than student learning. The paper ends by suggesting that new technology resources provide an opportunity for teacher educators to redirect the focus of reflective practice towards the teacher's role in setting effective learning tasks.

Keywords

Teacher education, classroom practice, cognition, learning models, pedagogy, resources

1 INTRODUCTION

New technologies, like books, are a tool and a resource for a wide range of human endeavours, including teaching and learning in a range of contexts. In this paper the focus is on only one of these contexts - the classroom. There is evidence that it is not easy to make good use of books in classrooms, so it would not be surprising to find that the same is true of new technologies. Until now the assumption in teacher education has been that new technologies present special challenges and opportunities, and that teachers need extensive support to give them the competence and confidence to use these new resources effectively. While there is no doubt that this is true insofar as managing the technology itself is concerned, we have perhaps neglected the more fundamental problem that all resources are difficult to use effectively in classrooms. In this paper I want to look specifically at the inter-relationship between classroom context, resources, the teachers' role in task-setting and students' learning. This may give some clues to ways in which new technology resources might begin to live up to their promise of generating new opportunities for learning.

2   TRADITIONAL RESOURCES AND THE CLASSROOM CONTEXT

Let us look first at the use made of books as a resource. The Bullock Report (1975) showed that in classrooms in England and Wales students spent very little time reading and, by contrast, an inordinate amount of their time writing. This curious imbalance can better be understood in the light of Tabberer's research into students' use of learning resources (1987) which showed that schools do not appear to require students to develop the wide range of skills necessary to become proactive learners. He describes how the classroom is isolated and lacks relevance to the wider world: 'School frequently appears to ... rely on the habitual exercise of a different combination of skills from those expected elsewhere.' He comments: 'There is .. something unacceptable about education's ability to .. create such dependent learners' (p. 194) and adds, significantly, '(There is) a problem of over-teaching .. a tendency for some teachers to overcome pupil difficulties by failing to set them.' These are highly disturbing findings, describing an outcome of teaching practice so profoundly anti-educational that it is of the greatest importance to understand the contextual factors which bring it about.

3   WHAT ARE THE FACTORS, THEN, WHICH SHAPE THE WAY IN WHICH RESOURCES SUCH AS BOOKS OR NEW TECHNOLOGY ARE USED IN CLASSROOMS?

First, the classroom is a confined space in which a group of around thirty people need to be organised to work in a purposeful way. It is very often a site of struggle for power, between the legitimate authority of the teacher who carries ultimate responsibility for well-ordered teaching and learning, and the multitude of informal trade-offs for status which operate on a micro-political level between student and student. The latter nearly always include challenges to the teacher's authority as a means of demonstrating inter-peer status. A prime aim of the teacher, therefore, must always be to remain in control and ensure the orderly behaviour of all the students (Davis et al, 1992). Jackson (1968) in his classic work on classrooms found that teachers are likely to be engaged in 'as many as 1000 interpersonal interchanges each day', and that in classrooms students learn above all else how to cope with denial, interruption, distraction and frustration.

Second, there is always variation (often very considerable variation) between the prior knowledge and understanding of the students. This makes it very difficult to meet the learning needs of individuals. Teachers normally cope with this by setting tasks to be undertaken by groups - either the whole class group, or smaller groups. Alternatively, tasks may be set individually, often with the aid of resources. Once the tasks are set the teacher has the job of interacting with the students to scaffold the learning process, but the large number of students makes this difficult in practice, particularly as their learning needs are so diverse.

Third, the classroom is normally pervaded by an ethos of assessment, and, to a greater or lesser extent, competition. Those with less formal power - the students - are assessed by the one with more formal power - the teacher. What is assessed is intended to be students' learning, but learning takes place in the head and it is difficult to find evidence for it. So what is assessed in reality is usually each student's performance at a given task. Assessment, however, always takes place within the context of the struggle for power outlined above - so that, depending upon the values of peer culture, individual students may not necessarily wish to be seen by their peers to succeed.

4   THE TEACHER'S ROLE IN SETTING CLASSROOM TASKS

Given the complexity of the classroom context, it may be over-simplistic to assume that the teacher's first concern is to enable learning to take place. When student teachers complain that their training at the university has been of little relevance to their needs when they first stand in front of a class of students, they are probably referring to this mismatch of assumptions and experienced reality. Control, the maintenance of good order and personal survival often become the new teacher's paramount concerns. In practice, the complex and difficult business of teaching and learning has to be undertaken within the constraints of these basic needs imposed on the new teacher by the classroom context. Moreover, behaviours established in these early days soon begin to develop into habits and patterns of practice which can remain unquestioned throughout the whole of a teaching career (Somekh, 1993).

The everyday business of teaching consists first in planning how to achieve the learning goals of the curriculum within this classroom context, and then in attempting to carry out the plans in practice and monitor their outcomes. (It is worth noting in passing that much of the stress teachers experience results from the inevitable mismatch between these plans and their enactment.)

Planning students' learning requires teachers to transform learning goals into practical activities for the students to engage in. The organisational demands of the classroom require that students are busily occupied in activity; the learning goals demand that their minds are concentrated on the curriculum content or matter. If learning is assumed to be - as it is not! - an unproblematic business of transferring factual information from the teacher to the pupil, both sets of demands can be addressed by traditional tasks, such as copying out notes which the teacher first writes on the blackboard. This is why this task is such a perennial favourite. When the learning process is more fully understood, the nature of the teaching problem still remains the same. Learners need to conceptualise what they are learning and the teacher's role is to set a task which will frame and enable this conceptualisation. There are two reasons why it will probably not be enough to say, 'Open your book, read the chapter on X and think about it': first because this is unlikely to motivate the students, and second because it will be impossible to monitor whether they remain on task. Teachers are faced with the problem of designing classroom tasks which make it possible to infer what is going on inside students' heads. In the classroom context, because of the need to maintain order and control, this task needs both to motivate the students and also to organise them into an activity which can be monitored and assessed.

Learning is an invisible process inside the learner's head and it is important to be able to infer that it has taken place. Tasks which can be monitored and assessed, provide some evidence at least. However, Doyle (1979) has shown that in classrooms this integration of assessment with task-setting can seriously undermine the quality of students' learning. At worst it may mean that scarcely any learning occurs at all. In a detailed analysis of classroom tasks Doyle showed that only when tasks place students in some degree of what he calls 'ambiguity' and 'risk' do they make the kind of cognitive demands that result in learning. Ambiguity exists when the student has to take decisions and solve problems: risk occurs when the student is not sure at the outset of being able to complete the task successfully. This kind of cognitive dissonance and exploration is essential for learning to take place. Doyle's research shows that there are many other tasks in classrooms which keep students busily occupied without them actually learning anything. Frequently they occur when the teacher has clarified and/or structured the task to the point where the student has little or no thinking to do. Desforges and Cockburn (1987) note that many tasks in mathematics classrooms involve no more than practise - either in something which the student knows well or, more seriously, where the student simply 'practises' mistakes. Doyle goes further and tracks the process whereby students regularly negotiate classroom tasks with their teachers in order to reduce any elements of ambiguity or risk. Through a process of 'exchanging performance for grades' Doyle's work suggests that students and teachers regularly collude in reducing the quality and range of learning in classrooms. This explains very well Tabberer's perception that 'some teachers overcome pupil difficulties by failing to set them.' However, it seems likely that students are the more devious of the two and regularly persuade teachers that they are less capable than they actually are. Hence, in an early piece of research of my own a thirteen year old girl told me that she was pleased when she had negotiated to carry out a simple copying task rather than the original more challenging task suggested by the teacher: 'because it didn't need any brains' (Somekh, 1980).

5   THE CONCEPT AND ENACTMENT OF REFLECTIVE PRACTICE IN TEACHER EDUCATION

If teaching is to be effective, it is essential that teachers understand the complex relationship between students' learning and their own role as teachers in setting classroom tasks. In response to this need, teacher education in the UK over the past decade has placed considerable emphasis upon approaches which develop the capacity for reflective practice in beginning (and experienced) teachers. However, I suggest that this important work has not made as much impact as it might have done upon the quality of students' learning. I believe that this is because too much emphasis has been placed upon classroom organisation and teacher-student interaction and too little upon the inter-relationship between the teacher's role in task-setting, the use made of resources and students' learning; and that this has been the inevitable result of pressures upon teachers (emanating from school culture and peer expectations) to demonstrate their effectiveness primarily in terms of their skills in classroom organisation.

Many researchers have provided evidence that reflexivity is an essential element of effective professional practice. Elliott (1976) developed the concept of the 'self-monitoring teacher' who adopted a researcher's stance to his or her own practice in order to make it increasingly effective. Dreyfus (1981) developed a model of professional development from novice to expert through a series of stages, and identified 'situational understanding' as the key component of expert performance - i.e. 'situational understanding' is the capacity to analyse and respond to all the complexities of a social situation, holistically, with in-depth understanding (acting apparently instinctively but in reality on the basis of understanding gained through prior experience). Schön (1983) gives a detailed account of 'reflective practice' as the professional's capacity to act effectively in a context of ambiguity and uncertainty, through a process of reflection-in-action which he describes as 'responding to the situation's talk-back.' Elliott (1993) builds upon the work of all these writers in his concept of the good teacher's 'practical wisdom' which develops from reflexive self-monitoring in the light of both overt and tacit professional knowledge, and integrates situational understanding with practical action.

When these ideas are translated into the planning and implementation of teacher training programmes, we run into the same problem as before: i.e. the need to transform learning goals into practical activities that students can engage in. As in schools, so in teacher education, a process of negotiation takes place between the teacher's and the students' perception of students' needs. Hence, learning tasks are developed which will motivate students (in this case beginning or experienced teachers) and ensure that they are willingly and usefully employed on worthwhile activities. Assessment methods are designed to monitor the effectiveness of the activities, but ultimately, the problem of whether or not learning has occurred is simplified by inferring that successful performance on the task set by the teacher (and negotiated by the students) equates to learning.

The nub of the problem is that beginning teachers (through a perceived urgent need), and experienced teachers (through established habits of custom and practice), are more concerned with matters of classroom management and the organisation of learning than they are with learning itself. Thus, when teachers engage in research into their own practice they almost invariably identify research questions which focus upon the complex processes of social interaction in the classroom. This has led, in initial teacher education, to the major focus of tasks designed by teacher educators to engender the capacity for reflective practice in new teachers being upon teacher-student and student-student interaction, and not upon students' learning. Even if the tasks are not framed in this way by the teacher educator they are very frequently renegotiated by beginning teachers to enable them to focus more directly upon their perceived need for classroom organisational skills. There have been some exceptions in funded projects which involved teachers working with the project team to research students' learning (for example, the TIQL project, see Ebbutt and Elliott, 1985; and the PALM project, see Somekh 1991; 1994) but even in these projects considerable effort has been needed to maintain the focus upon learning. This was particularly difficult in the PALM project when teachers faced the added demands of learning how to integrate new technology tools into classroom tasks. Initially, most teachers had insufficient understanding of the learning process and tended to make generalised assumptions about students' learning which often proved untrue when they were challenged as part of the research (for example, that students whose behaviour in groups was passive rather than active were not engaged in learning).

6   USING NEW TECHNOLOGY RESOURCES EFFECTIVELY: A NEW FOCUS UPON STUDENT LEARNING

In recent years a considerable amount of research has contributed to developing a cognitive model which explains the learning process in a helpful way and makes it possible to design more effective learning tasks. In a previous paper I explored ways in which it might be possible to take these theories and use them to develop software which enables and supports learning more effectively (Somekh, 1994). Here, I want to suggest how these theories might be used to refocus the reflective practice approach in teacher education on student learning rather than classroom organisation. I start with the assumption that software resources (and other resources such as books) need to be understood by teachers as an integral part of a three-way process of task-setting. At best, the development of classroom tasks should be shared between teachers and students who should take joint responsibility for students' learning - rather than engaging in the traditional process of exchanging performance for grades. And, at best, when resources offer a significant input to the setting of classroom tasks (for example, interactive software which either sets tasks of itself or provides a tool for creative teachers to set new kinds of tasks) they should be used as an integral part of this task-setting.

Since students' learning should be the central concern of teaching, I am suggesting that teacher education courses should focus on presenting a cognitive model of learning capable of being investigated in the classroom context; and that reflective practice should be presented to both beginning and experienced teachers as a tool for continuously investigating their role in enabling learning through task-setting.

The process of task-setting - i.e. transforming learning objectives into practical activities - should make integral use of new technology resources and traditional resources, such as books. The teacher's role in task-setting is always of crucial importance. Even if software sets tasks for students (devised by software designers), teachers need to integrate these with other classroom activities by setting 'framing tasks' (Somekh and Davies, 1991).

There is space here to give only the briefest outline of the cognitive model of learning which would underpin teachers' continuing investigation of the effectiveness of their practice in setting tasks. The model includes the following elements, each of which has implications for the possible contribution of new technology resources:

- The Vygotskian theory of supporting learners to enable them to move into their zone of proximal development (Vygotsky, 1986).

Interactive software can greatly supplement and extend the teacher's ability to scaffold students' learning, and the greater the number of students the greater the significance of this contribution.

- The theory that learning is a process of developing an ever-increasing set of mental schema to make sense of experience (Bruner, 1966).
  Learning needs to be individualised to enable students to develop new schema which integrate meaningfully with their existing schema. New technology resources can be used by teachers to provide more individualised tasks.

- The central role of discussion in the development of mental schema (Prawat, 1991).
  New technology resources can often be used as a stimulus for a wide range of discussion away from the computer.

- The importance of learning being 'situated' in 'authentic' contexts (Brown et al, 1989).
  Software and multi-media resources can provide 'virtual' experiences which are 'situated' in the sense that they simulate authentic situations; and they can give access to resources used in the authentic social contexts of work and society.

- One key problem in learning is the need to transform ideas and concepts from one symbol system, such as language, to another such as number (Bruner, 1966; Kozma, 1991).
  A range of software now exists which models transformations from one symbol system to another dynamically (for example, talking books which support the teaching of reading).

- The importance of 'proceduralisation' in the learning of complex concepts (Kozma, 1991).
  A range of software and programming languages, such as LOGO, models the process of proceduralising problem solving.

- The importance of metacognition (De Corte, 1990) in developing cognitive engagement of the learners (Kozma, 1991) - what Salaman (1992) calls 'mindfulness' or AIME ('amount of invested mental effort').
  New technology which provides interactive feedback to the learner can be used to develop metacognitive skills which, in turn, develop the capacity for mindfulness/cognitive engagement.

7 REFERENCES

Brown, J.S., Collins, A. and Duguid, P. (1989) Situated Cognition and the Culture of Learning. *Educational Researcher*, **18**, 1, 32-42.

Bruner, J.S. (1966). *Toward a Theory of Instruction*. Harvard University Press, Cambridge.

Bullock (1975) *A Language for Life*. HMSO, London.

Davis, N., Desforges, C., Jessel, J., Somekh, B., Taylor, C. and Vaughan, G. (1992) Quality Teaching and Learning with Information Technology. *Developing Information Technology in Teacher Education*, no. 5, May 1992.

De Corte, E. (1990) Learning with new information technologies in schools: perspectives from the psychology of learning and instruction. *Journal of Computer Assisted Learning*, **6**, 69-87.

Desforges, C. and Cockburn, A. (1987) *Understanding the Mathematics Teacher: a Study of Practice in First School.* Falmer Press, London, New York and Philadelphia.

Doyle, W. (1979) Classroom tasks and student abilities, in P.L. Peterson and H.J. Walberg (eds.) *Research on Teaching: concepts, findings and implications,* National Society for the Study of Education. McCutchan, Berkeley, CA.

Dreyfus, S.E. (1981) Formal models vs human situational understanding: inherent limitations on the modelling of business enterprise, *mimeo,* International Institute for Applied Systems Analysis. Schloss Laxenburg, Austria.

Ebbutt, D. and Elliott, J. (eds.) (1985) *Issues in Teaching for Understanding.* Longman for the SCDC, London.

Elliott, J. (1976) *Developing Hypotheses About Classrooms from Teachers Practical Constructs.* North Dakota Study Group on Evaluation, University of N.D., Grand Forks ND 58202.

Elliott, J. (1993) *Reconstructing Teacher Education.* Falmer Press, London and Washington.

Jackson, P.W. (1968) *Life in Classrooms.* Holt, Rinehart and Winston, New York.

Prawat, R.S. (1991) The Value of Ideas: The Immersion Approach to the Development of Thinking. *Educational Researcher,* **20**, 2, 3-10.

Salamon, G. (1992) *Computer's First Decade: Golem, Camelot, or the Promised Land?* Invited Address to Division C, AERA Conference, San-Francisco, April 1992.

Schön, D.A. (1983) *The Reflective Practitioner.* Basic Books, New York.

Somekh, B. (1980) An Examination of Pupils' Use of Reading Material in a Classroom Situation, in J. Elliott and D. Whitehead (eds.) *The Theory and Practice of Educational Action Research.* Classroom Action Research Network, Cambridge Institute of Education.

Somekh, B. (1991) Pupil Autonomy in Learning with Microcomputers: rhetoric or reality? An Action Research Study. *Cambridge Journal of Education,* **21**, 1, 47-64.

Somekh, B. (1993) Quality in Education Research - the contribution of classroom teachers, in J. Edge and K. Richards (eds.) *Teachers Develop Teachers Research.* Heinemann, London.

Somekh, B. (1994) *Designing Software to Maximise Learning: what can we learn from the literature?* Paper presented at the conference of the Association for Learning Technologies at the University of Hull, September 1994.

Somekh, B. (1994) Inhabiting Each Other's Castles: towards knowledge and mutual growth through collaboration. *Educational Action Research,* **2**, 3, 357-382.

Somekh, B. and Davies, R. (1991) Towards a Pedagogy for Information Technology. *The Curriculum Journal,* **2**, 2, 153-170.

Tabberer, R. (1987) *Study and Information Skills in Schools.* NFER-Nelson, London.

Vygotsky, L.S. (1986) *Thought and Language.* The MIT Press, Cambridge, Cambridge MA.

8   BIOGRAPHY

After a period as Curriculum Development Officer for an educational software group, **Bridget Somekh** worked for seven years at the University of East Anglia, and moved to her current post as Depute Director of the Scottish Council for Research in Education in 1995. Her research projects include Pupil Autonomy in Learning with Microcomputers (PALM, 1988-90) and Initial Teacher Education and New Technology (INTENT, 1990-92) sponsored by the National Council for Educational Technology. She is currently evaluating two projects within the UK Superhighways Initiative, the Scottish follow-up evaluation of Integrated Learning Systems in schools, and the establishment of an Apple Classroom of Tomorrow Teacher Development Centre in Scotland.

35

The electronic spreadsheet and cognitive skills in inquiry oriented biology

Amos Dreyfus, Benjamin Feinstein and Janet Talmon
The Hebrew University of Jerusalem
Faculty of Agriculture, P.O.B. 12, Rehovot, 76100 Israel

Abstract

From a cognitive point of view, a spreadsheet is essentially a tool which enables learners to express intentions by means of formal instructions to a machine, and to assess the consequences of their instructions. While the objectives of "computer-integrated" science teaching remain essentially the same as those of today's traditional science teaching, the integration of the computer into the science teaching-learning processes requires, and provides opportunities to enhance, cognitive skills related to what could be called aspects of the scientific language and culture. These cognitive skills refer to both declarative and procedural knowledge.

Keywords

Secondary education, instruction (CAI), computer literacy, spreadsheet, teaching methods

1   INTRODUCTION

Students learn biology in various situations. The most common one is the more or less frontal lesson in the classroom, where the students may interact with a teacher. Such an interaction gives the students opportunities to benefit from the unique potential of the teachers' main tool, their brain. The adaptive flexibility of the human brain enables the teachers to understand the students' questions, ideas, intentions or motivations even when the students are unable to express them explicitly and clearly, and also to adapt their responses to the needs of the individual students. Teachers *understand,* but their teaching activity is severely hampered by their limitations: as human beings, they act slowly, the number of mental or physical operations which they, or their students, can perform in a limited amount of time is very limited. Consequently, they find it difficult to take care efficiently of every student in the class and to cope with certain objectives which are central to science education. This is why they must look for new partners in their teaching activity, thus creating different learning situations. Such a new partner is the electronic spreadsheet. The spreadsheet is radically different from the human teacher: it works very quickly. It can process with great speed a tremendous amount of data, draw nearly instant graphs, etc. However, its versatility is very limited, since it does not understand half-formulated intentions or ill-expressed instructions. Furthermore, as an open tool, it does not guide the user, but reacts to its instructions. When interacting with a spreadsheet, *all* the students must therefore know very clearly *what* they wish the computer to do for them, and *why*. It is also imperative that they know *how* to express their intentions in the form of very formal and precise instructions, in order to be "understood" by the computer. Because of all these characteristics, the spreadsheet, when used within the framework of carefully designed teaching-learning strategies, can become one of the biology teachers' most powerful partners: it provides opportunities to enhance the development of cognitive skills which are related to the language and culture of scientific inquiry, i.e., to one of the main objectives of modern biological education. Working definitions of a few terms must now be briefly stated, to clarify the educational approach which underlies this paper.

Carefully designed teaching-learning strategies
Although there is no necessary isomorphism between learning *of* inquiry and learning *by* inquiry, strategies of guided inquiry are potentially powerful because they are consistent with strategies of conceptual development or change. Concerning conceptual change, the essential characteristics of the spreadsheet, as an open tool, are: a) the above mentioned requirement that the learners formulate their ideas very clearly, that they make "their implicit reasoning explicit"; and b) the fact that, owing to its "What .. If ..." capacities, and to its efficiency in the computation, organisation and presentation of data, it gives the learners real opportunities to assess "the consequences of their reasoning" (Driver and Scanlon, 1989).

Objectives of modern biological education
Biology is an experimental science, which obtains knowledge mainly by means of hypothetico-deductive methods of scientific inquiry. It is also essentially a quantitative-statistical science, based on samples of populations, and variance is a built-in characteristic of such populations. The verification of hypotheses in biology, on the basis of empirically gathered data, must therefore account not only for central values, such as means, but also for variance. The development of some basic cognitive skills necessary to any empirical-quantitative-statistical "inquiry into life", is considered to be a necessary condition for any meaningful understanding of biology, and has become one of the main objectives of biology education. Such cognitive skills are also essential to the learning of the technologies which confer to biology its socio-human context, such as medicine, agriculture and modern bio-technologies.

Cognitive skills
In the context of the spreadsheet-assisted development of inquiry skills, Royer, Cisero and Carlo's (1993) working definition of cognitive skills, as consisting of "a mixture of specific facts and procedures to use those facts. ... made up of both declarative and procedural knowledge ... acquired through training and /or experience", is especially appropriate. According to this approach, cognitive skills, through the stages of their acquisition, are transformed "from an activity that is slow and highly taxing on the cognitive system to an automated set of activities that may place virtually no load on

the system". Intellectual skills are *tools* which involve conceptual, or principled knowledge, *and* its utilisation, and in Brown, Collins and Duguid's (1989) terms, people who use them actively may "build an increasingly rich implicit understanding" not only of the tools themselves, but also of "the world in which they use the tools". Because of its swiftness in the performance of a wide variety of operations, the spreadsheet provides the students with opportunities to personally and intensively experience various methods and techniques of manipulation of data, so that they may gain the amount of experience and involvement necessary to the development of intuitions and "rich implicit understanding" about cognitive inquiry skills. In other words, they may develop a true, first-hand knowledge of intellectual skills which are part and parcel of the language and the culture of the scientific community.

2   COGNITIVE SKILLS IN SPREADSHEET-INTEGRATED LEARNING SITUATIONS

In order to make an open tool as the spreadsheet "work' for them, the learners must give it instructions. These instructions, which are conveyed to the computer by means of the keyboard and/or the mouse, are the concepts of the language used in the *dialogue* which takes place between the tool and its user (Dreyfus, Feinstein and Mazouz, 1993). Knowing how to give an instruction to the computer (which keys to push and in which order) without understanding the meaning of the instruction is not equivalent to "speaking" to the computer. Pushing a key is akin to emitting a word; giving *intentionally* a meaningful instruction to the computer by pushing a key, is equivalent to conveying specific meanings by means of words. It follows that the technical use of the keyboards should be taught as a language (putting words on meanings) within the context of activities which confer meanings to the words. In this context, a cognitive skill may be regarded to have been acquired when the learner *understands* the concept behind instructions to the computer, and is able to use this concept *purposefully* and *meaningfully*, on *relevant* occasions. The successful use of a cognitive skill to perform a task consists of the following steps:

a)   understanding the task;

b)   selecting, out of a pool of potentially relevant and well understood instructions, the correct one/s or the most suitable one/s (knowing why instruction X, and also why not Y, or why X rather than Y);

c)   using the instruction correctly (in the sense of applying correctly a principle);

d)   using the right "words", i.e., the right keys, to convey the instruction (the technical aspect of the use of the keyboard);

e)   reading and interpreting correctly the computer's response;

f)   deciding if the computer's activity corresponds to the intentions of the learner/user (did the computer do what I intended it to do?), and if the instruction was the right one, or the best one.

It can be seen that the purely technical aspect of the use of a spreadsheet (step d) represents only a small part of the activity of the learners. Actually, it is also the only part about which good advice is routinely given to learners, provided that they know what to look for, in the "help" programs and in manuals. It can also be seen that steps a) to c) refer to the *intentions* of the learner, step d) is the *translation* of those intentions into the language of the spreadsheet, and in steps e) and f), the learner is involved in the *interpretation* and the assessment of outcomes. It is worth noting that in this respect, the situation of the learners who use a spreadsheet is quite different from that of the paper and pencil (without computer) learners. On one hand, when working without a computer, the learners have to perform personally *all* the often very tedious steps of the task, but on the other hand, they remain all the time in full control of the events. When using a spreadsheet, the students do not actually carry out personally any practical part of the task. They do not compute and do not *draw* graphs: they do define the attributes of the graph, and give appropriate instructions to the computer, but after pushing the "enter" key, they *loose control*. *The computer works now for them*, extremely quickly, without giving them any opportunity or any possibility to follow or control the phases of the construction of the output. There are however various reasons why the instructions may have been both inaccurate and intelligible to the computer: the learners may have been unaware of the fact that the instruction they gave was not the one they believed they were giving (misunderstanding of the nature of the instruction), or they may have given the right instruction, but made an error (wrong definition of a range, a field, a variable, etc.). In such cases, the students, who had not been warned by the computer, may have remained unaware of the fact that what they obtained was what they had actually *asked for*, and *only* what they had asked for, but not what they had *intended* to ask for. Steps e) and f) are therefore indispensable, and often very intellectually demanding. The requirement that the learners assess the congruence between their intentions and the outcomes of their work is quite specific to learning situations which involve open tools such as spreadsheets, and is invaluable in the context of strategies of conceptual development, which put a high priority on the learners' clarification of their own ideas and intentions. Indeed students who are able to realise that something is wrong in the type of results obtained, display a good conception of the nature of the task they are involved in, and vice versa.

The spreadsheet learning situation imposes other specific cognitive demands on the learners, or, in other words, gives them other opportunities to develop intellectual skills. The learners must organise the data in such a way as to enable the spreadsheet to "work" with maximal efficiency. They must learn to "think computer", or in this case, more specifically, "think spreadsheet", i.e., to adapt their reasoning to the opportunities offered by the spreadsheet and to its limitations. "Thinking spreadsheet" when organising the data means being able to *predict* the consequences of the organisation on the way instructions will be carried out, a skill which requires a sound understanding of the nature of the operations performed. To exemplify, let us consider a simple and classical experiment.

Bits of potatoes are immersed in distilled water for 20 minutes, then weighed and transferred to sugar solutions of various concentrations. After an hour, they are weighed again. Because of osmotic pressures, the tissues will lose water, and thus weight. The students compute the weight loss as percentages of the original weight, then compute averages and produce graphs which show the relation between the concentration of the solution and the weight loss. Ten groups of students perform the experiment on ten concentrations, i.e., the data will include 100 original weights, 100 weights at the end of the experiment, and the results must show 100 percentages. If the data are efficiently arranged, the 100 percentages may be computed by means of *one* computation (one formula) and *one* "Copy" instruction. Students who have found the most efficient pattern of organisation must have been able firstly to *conceive* it, then to *select* it out of a number of possibilities, i.e., to foresee the consequences of "copying" a mathematical formula to the whole range of data. They must have had a very good idea of the nature of both the required mathematical operation and the "copy" instruction. Since there are other, less elegant and less efficient ways to obtain successfully the correct results, the students may have tried several possibilities, using the "What ... If ..." facilities of the spreadsheet, but even those trials required the skills necessary to ascertain which of the possibilities did best perform the task in congruence with their intentions. Obviously, misunderstandings about the nature of the "copy" instruction in such a case, or about the source and target ranges, or technical mistakes in the typing of the instructions (for example, a5 instead of a6), may have brought about, without any warning, *intelligible but inaccurate* instructions, with their consequences. Actually, many students who appear to have mastered the skills necessary for the use of a spreadsheet, possess only the technical skills needed to happily make the spreadsheet work, but have not achieved the intellectual skills necessary to assess the appropriateness and consequences of their instructions.

A second look at the experiment will show the main characteristics of biological research, as can be demonstrated in the school laboratory: the results are obtained empirically, and the mathematical formula is used to find relations between variables, not to predict them. Each group obtains different results, so that the findings will be based on the values of both means and variance. The spreadsheet gives the students opportunities to develop insights into the nature of these values, because it enables them to cope with true samples in a reasonable amount of time. The spreadsheet is used as used by scientists, which means that it does not *"teach"* the students, but *provides them with opportunities to learn.*

To sum up: inquiry oriented activities in which a spreadsheet is incorporated include the following phases, in sequences and at frequencies which vary:

Phase 1: <u>Understanding the problem and predicting</u>. This phase starts with the presentation of the problem and continues until the students have proposed tentative solutions to the problem, i.e., hypotheses. This is the phase at which students clarify their knowledge and ideas and make them explicit.

Phase 2: <u>Planning.</u> In this phase, the students suggest experimental designs to verify their hypotheses.

Phase 3: <u>Declaration of intentions</u>. The students make explicit the ways in which they intend to process data and results with the spreadsheet.

After phase 3, they perform the experiment or are given empirical data and results, as obtained by scientists.

Phase 4. <u>Processing of the data.</u> This phase includes all the mathematical, logical and organisational operations which are performed on the data, by means of the spreadsheet.

Phase 5. <u>Assessing the congruence between the actual processing of the data and the intentions.</u> This phase may involve modifications in the processing and partial reorganisation of the data.

Phase 6. <u>Analysis of results; comparison between expected and obtained results.</u> This is the phase at which new knowledge is inferred from the results and conceptual change is expected to occur. (In the above mentioned potato experiment, the students are very seldom able to predict at phase 1 the actual pattern of results.)

The integration of the spreadsheet has made the inquiry activity different in several respects from the same activity when implemented without a spreadsheet: inserted into the strategy of inquiry learning, phases 3 and 5, which are new, and phase 4, which is different, account for the treatment of the various types of spreadsheet-related intellectual skills.

3   TYPES OF COGNITIVE SKILLS

The potential of the spreadsheet concerning cognitive skills, especially the most obvious ones, such as graphing skills, has been abundantly inventoried. We will only give a few examples of skills which demonstrate a specific, and somewhat neglected, contribution of the spreadsheet.

As a *computing machine*, the spreadsheet may contribute to the development of an intuitive grasping of the meaning and use of mathematical or statistical concepts, crucial to biological inquiry (for example, means, variance, distribution, significant differences, regression, correlation, plotting, best line, etc.). This can be done at a relatively early age (Dreyfus and Levy, 1996), about notions such as mean and distribution (for instance, the intuitive understanding that the sum of the deviations from the mean is always 0, developed when students try without success to make this sum change).

When used as a tool to switch from one *representation* of data to another one (from table to graph, for instance), the spreadsheet gives opportunities to develop the skills necessary to: a) grasp the nature of various representations (for example, a graph is not a drawing); and b) convey the same global message by means of different methods of representation (students often do not realise that the story told by their table is not exactly similar to that told by their graph, in spite of their intentions).

When used as a tool to *organise* data the spreadsheet is related to important skills of processing of data and of communication, i.e., of transmission of messages (efficient presentation of data, results, relations, etc.).

When the spreadsheet is used mainly as a *database*, the formulation of queries and the sorting of data to verify hypotheses is related to crucial inquiry skills: the "If .. Then .." and the "And ...Or" ways of thinking. More specifically, students learn to try to refute an hypothesis. For example: out of a database on birds, they try to refute the hypotheses "if they have wings, they are birds", "if they are birds, they have wings" and "only if they are birds, they have wings", or quantitative hypotheses of the type "If it is an X, then it is bigger than Y".

4   CONCLUSIONS

From a cognitive point of view, a spreadsheet is essentially a tool which enables learners to express intentions by means of formal instructions to a machine, and to assess the consequences of their instructions. Because of the opportunities with which it provides the teachers and the students along the enquiring sequence "prediction, intentions, processing, assessing, comparing, concluding", the electronic spreadsheet may be an invaluable tool in the development of inquiry related cognitive skills. It should however be clear that the cognitive skills required for, and developed by means of, the use of the spreadsheet are not equivalent to the technical skills which make its use possible. Whereas *technical* skills may be developed by the frequent use of a spreadsheet, the development of cognitive skills *depends* on educational strategies which involve the learner in an interactive dialogue with the machine.

5   REFERENCES

Brown, J.S., Collins, A. and Duguid, P. (1989) Situated cognition and the culture of learning. *Educational Researcher,* **18**, 32-42.

Dreyfus, A., Feinstein, B. and Mazouz, Y. (1993) Keyboard instructions as concepts of the language of quantitative biology in spreadsheet-assisted activities. *Journal of Biological Education,* **27**, 39-46.

Dreyfus, A. and Levy, O. (1996) Are the notion of mean and related concepts too difficult for 5th and 6th grade biology students? *European Journal of Teacher Education,* in press.

Driver, R. and Scanlon, E. (1989) Conceptual change in science. *Journal of Computer Assisted Learning,* **5**, 25-36.

Royer, J.M., Cisero, C.A. and Carlo, M.S. (1993) Techniques and procedures for assessing cognitive skills. *Review of Educational Research,* **63**, 201-243.

6   BIOGRAPHY

Professor Amos Dreyfus holds an M.Sc. degree in Agriculture, and a Ph.D. degree in Science Teaching from the Hebrew University of Jerusalem. He currently heads the department of Agricultural Education and Extension Studies, Hebrew University of Jerusalem.

Mr. Benjamin Feinstein holds an M.Sc. degree from the Faculty of Agriculture. He has been for several years head of the department of Computer-Assisted Learning at the Ministry of Education.

Dr. Janet Talmon holds an M.Sc. and a Ph.D. degree from the Weizman Institute of Science, and she co-operates with the other authors in the development of spreadsheet-integrated secondary school science activities.

36

Computer science education based on fundamental ideas

Andreas Schwill
Informatik V - Universitaet Potsdam
D-14415 Potsdam, Germany

Abstract

We sketch a pedagogical 'theory' based on Bruner's educational psychology that might set computer science education for students and teachers on a well-founded basis and integrate different approaches to teach it, stress its long-lasting fundamentals and give a feeling of its essence. For it we (1) define the notion of fundamental ideas more precisely by several criteria, (2) present a collection of fundamental ideas of computer science, and (3) show how to develop a curriculum that centres around these ideas.

Keywords

Secondary education, teacher education, curriculum development, informatics as a study topic, philosophy, teaching methods

1   INTRODUCTION

Although computer science has been a regular subject in school for a long time, there is still more and more discussion on how and what to teach: should computer science education be oriented more towards its applications, or more towards its fundamentals, or more towards its social effects? How can we improve computer science education with teachers who have not passed a full university education in that field? How can we cope with the rapid developments of computer science, both with respect to curriculum development and continuing education?

On the one hand, people seem to accept that the rapid progress cannot be reflected quickly in school education because of delays in change of curricula, pedagogical reflection, teacher education, etc. On the other hand, since each student will probably face several paradigm changes in future life - with much of the respective knowledge becoming obsolete each time - the skills acquired earlier must be robust enough to meet the challenges of the latest fashion, and also cope with future changes.

The same argument holds with respect to teacher education. Teachers also have to be (re-) trained in a way that enables them, with mild support by continuing education programmes, to integrate new results into their knowledge structure and to reflect and assess recent developments with respect to future relevance, school adequacy and other pedagogical issues.

2   FUNDAMENTAL IDEAS AS AN EDUCATIONAL PRINCIPLE

Whitehead (1929) proposed to deal in school with "few general ideas of far-reaching importance", since the students are "bewildered by a multiplicity of detail, without apparent relevance either to great ideas or to ordinary thoughts". The same situation we often have - as are the author's experiences - if teachers have passed a quick in-service education program in different "modern" subjects of computer science that enables them neither to establish a stable cognitive structure integrating all these subjects nor to teach computer science to their students in a suitable manner.

Bruner (1960) formulated the teaching principle that lessons should be based on the **structure** of science which is defined by so-called **fundamental ideas**. He justified his approach as follows: Learning is mainly for preparing us to master our future life more successfully. In order to cope with changes occurring later in private life, in terms of economy and society, students must be able to **transfer** knowledge acquired earlier to new situations. Of particular interest here is the **non-specific transfer** which relates to long-term (often life-long) effects: We should teach on a meta-level fundamental notions, principles and ways of thinking (so-called **fundamental ideas**) and may hope that students are able to use these abstract solution schemas in modified ("transferred") form for any (even absolutely new) problems that they may face in their later lives.

Non-specific transfer should dominate the entire educational process of schools providing general education: Permanent creation, extension and consolidation of knowledge in the form of fundamental ideas. Therefore - and now we return to Bruner's request - all curricula and teaching methods in computer science classes as well as in-service or pre-service education programs for teachers should stress the fundamental ideas of each topic. Teachers should be enabled to analyse each new subject to be included into computer science lessons in terms of what ideas it is based on and to present it according to the idea-oriented approach proposed in the rest of the paper.

Unfortunately, Bruner as well as subsequent researchers do not provide an explicit definition of fundamental ideas. Instead, they give some examples from several subjects and leave it to the reader to develop an intuitive idea of what the term might mean in general. As applied to computer science we define the notion as follows:

A **fundamental idea** of computer science is a schema for thinking, acting, describing or explaining which satisfies four criteria:

The Horizontal Criterion. A fundamental idea is applicable or observable in multiple ways and in different areas of computer science and organises and integrates a wealth of phenomena.

We call this property the Horizontal Criterion, since the idea may be considered as a horizontal line intersecting a large number of fields where it applies.

The Vertical Criterion. A fundamental idea may be taught on every intellectual level.

Bruner (1960) said that "any subject can be taught effectively in some intellectually honest form to any child at any stage of development". This suggests that a fundamental idea organises the topics of a field also in a vertical dimension: An idea can be taught at the primary school level as well as at the university level. Presentations differ only by level of detail and formalisation. Thus, an idea can serve as a guideline for lessons on every level of the entire educational process and ideas can be revisited periodically in greater depth and complexity (the so-called **spiral principle**, see also below).

The Criterion of Time. A fundamental idea can be clearly observed in the historical development of computer science and will be relevant in the long run.

This aspect is important for two reasons. First, it gives a clue as to how to find fundamental ideas: Scientific notions, concepts or structures of computer science that have a definite historical background are more likely to be fundamental ideas than are recent developments. Second, lessons based on fundamental ideas will not become antiquated as quickly as conventional lessons - a major advantage in teaching computer science given its dynamic evolution.

The Criterion of Sense. A fundamental idea also has meaning in everyday life and is related to ordinary language and thinking - its context being pre-theoretical and unscientific.

Only a precise definition turns an idea "with sense" into an exact notion "without sense". For example, consider "reversibility" as an idea "with sense" and "inverse function" as a purely mathematical formalisation of it "without sense". While we can see examples of reversibility in many everyday situations - do vs. undo - the term "inverse function" has no everyday meaning. From the pedagogical point of view this criterion is closely linked to the Vertical Criterion. Whenever we have to teach a fundamental idea on a low intellectual level, i.e. we have to give students a first vague impression of the idea, we may begin with those situations in everyday life where a fundamental idea becomes apparent. For a more specific explanation see Section 4 below.

3   FUNDAMENTAL IDEAS OF COMPUTER SCIENCE

Currently fundamental ideas have been proposed mainly for mathematics (for example, Halmos, 1981) and some of its branches (for example, Heitele, 1975), but there are very few comments on how these ideas have been worked out. We have tried to determine fundamental ideas by abstracting from the contents of computer science to its ideas in three steps: (1) Analysis of the concrete activities of computer science and their relationships and analogies - after all the central purpose of computer science is to investigate the software development process; (2) Revision and improvement of the results obtained in step 1 by checking whether each idea satisfies the four criteria for fundamental ideas; (3) Structuring the collection of ideas according to their relevance in computer science.

Due to space limitations we only present the final results. There are three fundamental ideas that dominate all stages of software development as well as all activities in computer science:

Algorithmisation

By algorithmisation we denote the entire process of designing, implementing and running an algorithm. The strong relevance of algorithmisation within computer science, as required by the Horizontal Criterion, seems obvious.

A careful analysis of the activities when developing algorithms gives a wealth of other fundamental ideas which may be assigned to four large domains - design, programming, execution, evaluation: during design of an algorithm one often uses powerful paradigms such as *divide and conquer, backtracking* etc. Afterwards this design is carried over into a program using several basic ideas to describe data and control structures, for example, *concatenation, repetition, recursion* of commands and data. The finished program is executed on one or more processors. A fundamental idea here is the notion of *process*, i.e. the separation of description and execution of an algorithm. The last group of ideas deals with assessing the quality of algorithms. The two main criteria are *correctness* and *complexity* each related to several corresponding ideas.

Structured dissection

Dissection covers the process of subdividing an object into several parts in a structured way. That includes a detailed description of the parts, their relations to the whole as well as interactions between the parts. Typical 'objects' in computer science which are dissected in this manner are problems (into sub-problems), algorithms (into procedures or modules), modules (into smaller modules, called hierarchical modularisation), the software life cycle (into different phases), languages and machines (into different complexity classes), etc.

We can distinguish two aspects of dissection, a vertical aspect called *hierarchisation*, i.e. the construction of certain levels of abstraction often distinguished by different language levels, and a horizontal aspect called *modularisation* where an object is subdivided into different parts all of the *same* level of abstraction. The well-known *hierarchical modularisation* is obtained by merging these two aspects. The idea of hierarchisation can be observed in many different contexts, ·for example, level-oriented models of computer architecture, language hierarchies (a main example is the Chomsky hierarchy), machine models, complexity and computability classes, virtual machines, ISO-OSI reference model. With both hierarchisation and modularisation many other "small" fundamental ideas are connected.

Language

Language plays an important role, not only for programming (programming languages), for specification (specification languages), for verification (logic calculi), in databases (query languages), in operating systems (command languages), but there seems to be a general trend in computer science to formulate any facts by a language. This approach has the advantage that it simplifies the view of facts and allows manipulation.

We conclude these brief considerations by presenting part of the catalogue of fundamental ideas of computer science (Figure 1). The complete catalogue will appear elsewhere. Note that names written in italics have been added for systematisation only and denote groups of ideas but are not ideas themselves.

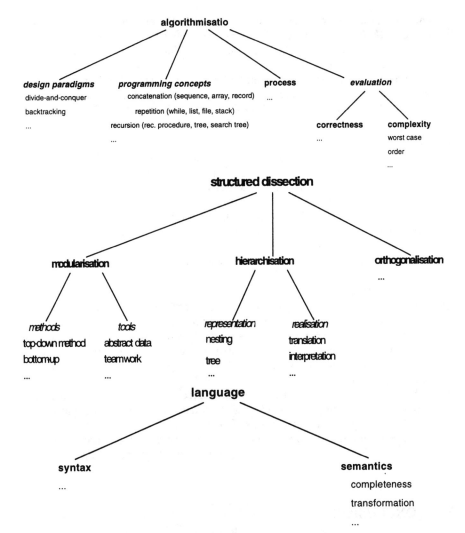

Figure 1 Fundamental ideas of computer science

4 COMPUTER SCIENCE EDUCATION WITH FUNDAMENTAL IDEAS

Bruner (1990) said that lessons oriented towards fundamental ideas have to be organised according to the **spiral principle** which he describes as "The early teaching of science, mathematics, social studies, and literature should be designed to teach these subjects with scrupulous intellectual honesty, but with an emphasis upon the intuitive grasp of ideas and upon the use of these basic ideas. A curriculum as it develops should revisit these basic ideas repeatedly, building upon them until the student has grasped the full formal apparatus that goes with them".

Bruner (1966) also recommended three representations of concepts to be learned: before the *symbolic* demonstration of notions or concepts (by formulas etc.) and their structural analysis students should obtain an intuitive idea of the notions by pictures (*iconic*) and actions (*enactive*).

The following examples illustrate the spiral principle and also demonstrate the Vertical Criterion for two fundamental ideas by sketching subjects for lessons in primary school (P), in grades 5 to 9 (S1) and in grades 10 and above (S2).

Worst case analysis

(P)   Worst case considerations can start with questions like: How long does it take to get to school in the worst case, if the bus is late, if all traffic lights are red, if the roads are icy? Or: How many questions are necessary in order to guess a number using binary search?

(S1) A more formal approach may follow at this level, for example, by relating the runtime to the length of the input and determining the worst case for each input length.

(S2) Formal definition of worst case runtime and proof of lower bounds.

Abstract data type

(P)   The blocks world may be defined as an abstract data type: On a table there are a number of cubic blocks that may be piled up. The only two operations are (1) putting one block onto another one and (2) testing whether a block lies on another one or whether it lies immediately on the table. Is it possible to establish any situation in the blocks world by these two operations (also related are the ideas of completeness and orthogonalisation)?

(S1) The example in (P) may be made more precise here. Problems concerning consistency and completeness of an abstract data type may follow. Which laws hold for the operations in the blocks world?

(S2) On this level a formal notation for abstract data types may be introduced using more complex examples (stack, queue, file). Considerations of implementation may follow.

5   CONCLUSIONS

We have applied J.S. Bruner's principle of orienting lessons towards fundamental ideas to computer science education of students and teachers. So far this approach seems to have the following advantages:

* A subject is more comprehensible if students and teachers grasp its fundamental principles.
* Fundamental ideas condense information by organising incoherent details into a linking structure which will be kept in mind for a longer time. Details can be reconstructed from this structure more easily.
* Fundamental ideas enable teachers (1) to evaluate all the current buzz-words and modern themes of computer science according to school relevance, (2) to find the "beef", if any, in these subjects, and (3) to teach these subjects to their students in pedagogically sound ways.

- Fundamental ideas reduce the lag between current research findings and what is taught in schools (Vertical Criterion). This expresses the conviction of Bruner (1960) that "intellectual activity is the same anywhere, whether the person is a third grader or a research scientist".
- While fundamental ideas remain modern even in the long term (Criterion of Time), details become antiquated very early. So, computer science education based on fundamental ideas can free itself from the innovative pressure of science without the content getting out of date.

At the present time, computer science has no "philosophy of computer science" while established sciences have evolved such philosophies. A collection of fundamental ideas may serve as a first approach in this direction, may help to determine the essence of computer science and to dissociate it from other sciences, and may provide a useful way for thinking about teaching computer science in the classroom.

6   REFERENCES

Bruner, J.S. (1960) *The process of education.* Harvard University Press, Cambridge MA.

Bruner, J.S. (1966) *Toward a theory of instruction.* Harvard University Press, Cambridge MA.

Halmos, P.R. (1981) Does mathematics have elements? *The Mathematical Intelligencer*, **3**, 147-153.

Heitele, D. (1975) An epistemological view on fundamental stochastic ideas. *Educational Studies in Mathematics*, **6**, 187-205.

Whitehead, A.N. (1929) *The Aims of Education.* Macmillan.

7   BIOGRAPHY

Dr. Andreas Schwill graduated in computer science from the University of Dortmund in 1983. Since then he has held research assistantships at the University of Dortmund and at the University of Oldenburg. In 1990 he was awarded a doctoral degree from the University of Oldenburg. Between 1991 and 1996 he was guest professor at the University of Paderborn. Recently he has moved to the University of Potsdam to take up a professorship in didactics of computer science.

Section 10: The increasing need for focus upon cultural and social factors

37

Understanding our instrument of representation

Mícheál Ó Dúill
*Hon Chairman, **Logos** the Logo User Group*
37 Bright Street, Skipton, North Yorkshire, BD23 1QQ, UK

Abstract
The prerequisites of making the computer intellectually transparent to teachers and pupils are addressed in this paper. The nature of computer representation is discussed and the conclusion that we mislead ourselves into perceiving it as a mathematical entity is drawn. A view of the computer as a development of the technology of writing, from passive nominal to active verbal representation, is developed. The computer represents a fundamental advance in our representational capability. Certain consequences for teacher education are outlined.

Keywords
Culture, curriculum policies, implications, information technology, Logo, pedagogy

1   INTRODUCTION

The UK strategy for information technology (IT) in education for the past decade has been to focus upon teaching teachers and pupils to use ever-developing informatic equipment. Consequently, many teachers and pupils are capable IT users. Capability in IT is now deemed a basic skill (Dearing, 1993). Yet, there is concern that education is not making effective use of the new technology, which it appears to be assimilating to extant curricula and social agendas. Papert (1994) suggests, as a factor, the lack of that intellectual 'transparency' we associate with products of the machine age, for example, the steam engine, sewing machine, and motor car. Of the three roles, tutor, tutee, tool, that the computer plays in school, typified by: Integrated Learning Systems (ILS); children 'teaching' computers through Logo programming (Papert, 1980); and using computers 'as appropriate' across the curriculum; none presupposes any discontinuity in the curriculum consequent upon the computer. Current computer use is premised upon the assumption that the curriculum itself need not change (Papert, 1994; SCAA, 1995).

2   INSTRUMENT OF REPRESENTATION

In appearance a computer is a television with a typewriter keyboard; does this truly mirror the nature of the instrument? The words we use to talk about the computer have their etymology in the vocabulary of mathematics; might they mislead us into perceiving it as a mathematical, or 'mathetic' Papert (1994), entity when, perhaps, it is otherwise? What, from an educational viewpoint, is a computer? To begin to answer this question we need to separate out two aspects of the technology: representation and operation.

2.1   The land of OZ

At the computer's lowest level just two symbols, bits, are employed to represent both the data to process and the instructions to process that data. Conventionally, we represent these symbols by the binary digits 0 and 1. The etymological trail for 'bit' leads back but 50 years to a 1946 citation from *Electronic Engineering* (OED, 1972):
The internal working of the machine will be entirely in the binary system, in which number is represented by a series of 1's and 0's the 1's being pulses and the 0's the spaces between.
Two symbols suffice because (Encyclopaedia Britannica):
No smaller number system can be used to represent information since there must be at least two symbols to distinguish meaning.
These sources lead to the perception that the computer is both discontinuous with previous systems of representation and somehow mathematical. The question we now address is whether this 'numerical' linguistic etymology is appropriate for education.

Number or not
The binary system goes back much further that 1946, at least to Gottfreid Leibniz (1646-1716); for whom 1 stood for God and 0 the void. And, in 1846, it appeared in a rather different form as Samuel Finlay Breese Morse's electric telegraph code:
'... a system in which each letter of the alphabet is represented by a sequence of dots and dashes' (Macmillan Compact Encyclopaedia, 1990).
Both Morse code and bit represent information with the absolute minimum of symbols, but are bits number? Let binary numbers be the representation system of the computer. It follows that only positive integers may be represented. This is absurd. But if computer representation is not numerical, what is the precise nature of the symbolic system used? To answer this question we need to reflect upon the development of symbols in general.

Writing
We will start in prehistory within a cave such as that at Lascaux. There, in the devices on its walls, we see our capacity to use both pictorial and abstract representation. Here are the precursors of writing. In the development of writing, for most cultures, there is a progression from pictogram through ideogram to phonetic representation (Hooker et al, 1990). The focus of representation shifts from the thing to the words used to speak of the thing, a change from direct to indirect language based representation.
The alphabetic system took this process further. The symbols came to represent not specific words but the meaning carrying units of the spoken language, a shift from

morpheme to phoneme. The alphabet is a very economical system. Some twenty symbols are sufficient to encode meaning, though not pronunciation, for most languages. The symbols of an alphabet are entirely without intrinsic meaning. Those of the binary system are similarly innocent of intrinsic meaning, while they encode meaning with maximum economy. Therefore, we may best consider binary representation to be neoalphabetic.

Binabet

The position taken here is that the computer binary system is best perceived as linguistic in nature and alphabetic in principle. This computer 'binabet' might better be represented using symbols other than the digits 0 and 1. The symbols O and Z are commended, if only for the literary allusion to the Wonderful Wizard of OZ (Baum, 1900).

2.2 Run selected

When you switch off a computer it stops operating. Electrons cease traversing gates to perform the operation ~(A+B) (Penrose, 1990), an operation we represent in the algebra of George Boole, a contemporary of Morse and Scholes, and work is no longer done.

An important conclusion flows from this: the computer is a thermodynamic engine, cf. a steam engine. It converts energy into information (Stonier, 1992) instead of physical work. The principles of physics apply, as do the engineering considerations of power, precision and entropy. Computing is unidirectional, flowing with the arrow of time.

A new capability

The representation of a computer instruction is isomorphic with the representation of data, both are binabetic. Hence, on a computer, there are two types of word: words that represent things and words that represent actions. In natural language these are noun and verb. The computer provides us with a capacity actively to represent verbs. This is an entirely new capability and extends language beyond the bounds of speech and writing.

We may think of the computer as an alphabetic writing instrument with electronic ink. To the making a mark that writing gave us we have added the capability to change marks with a mark. The LogoWriter expression 'run selected', which activates a highlighted word on the screen provided that that word is a 'verb', encapsulates this new capability.

Medium for communication

We may now evaluate anew the nature of the computer. For instance, we will need to recast our view of multimedia; for all its elements are represented binabetically. Hence, all media reduce to a monomedium: to writing. That all media may be represented, using suitable conventions, within a binary written medium, enables us to communicate more effectively. That a message is written in a verbally active medium enables us to manage its transmission. It may route and check itself as it searches out data on our behalf.

- Computer language, of which Logo is the prime educational exemplar, most clearly embodies the new capabilities of the medium: commands and operations to carry out verbal actions, with nominal inputs for the data.
- The Internet functions because of the new verbal capability of computers and not just because of binary representation - this latter was available with Morse code.
- Natural language variety becomes less of a communication barrier as software enables us actively to represent processes used in translation and language recognition.

The route to understanding Informatics is through language, computer language, Logo.

3   MATHMYTH

It is necessary now, formally, to return to the question of computers and mathematics education. We might equally examine Integrated Learning Systems or Papert's (1980, 1994) mathetic notion. The latter, particularly in turtle geometry, is the more interesting.

Turtle circle

Papert (1994) asserts:

'... the commands FORWARD and RIGHT are a universal set in the sense that they can be combined to produce any possible path or shape'.

This assertion is very problematic. The words FORWARD and RIGHT are computer commands. Representation on a computer is constrained by thermodynamics. Hence, considerations of time and precision make it impossible to represent a circle using these commands. Consider the general polygon procedure used to draw 'circles' on a screen:

```
to polygon :sides
repeat :sides [forward 1 right 360 / :sides]
end
```

Physics or maths

Mathematically, as the number of sides increases so the polygon tends to a circle. Computationally, as the number of sides increases so the limits of speed and precision of the computer are exceeded. MicroWorlds Logo is particularly interesting because once a numerical string exceeds a certain length it ceases to be treated as a number. Type in 1 and the message 'I don't; know what to do with 1' is printed. Type in 10000000000, a figure less than the population of the world, and the response is: 'I don't know how to 10000000000'. The figures have ceased to be a number and have become a word. Though we may include the symbol ∞ in our font collection, the computer cannot, of its nature, represent this concept. The machine is finite and may only represent finitely.

Active verbs

Mathematicians have mistaken the computer's capability actively to represent verbs, operations in mathematics, for a capability to represent mathematics. The converse is the case. Mathematical thinking involves concepts such as infinity, incommensurability, irrationality, and the imaginary. No such concepts are capable of representation on a computer. The computer can, because of its active representational nature, represent, within limits, certain previously unrepresentable mathematical operations. For example, we may now represent actively the operation of addition. Yet mathematics teaching is still premised upon the necessity of teaching a mental capability to add. Mathematicians would employ the computer to assist in this process. This is to deny the fundamental nature of the advance in representational capability we have developed for ourselves. That mathematics education is in crisis is not in doubt, but the crisis is not one of pupils' incapacity to do sums, it is in the failure of mathematics educators to reform their curriculum to make it congruent with a new capability to represent the doing of sums.

Etymological seduction
The problem is that mathematicians are seduced by the etymology of the language we use to talk about the computer. In reality the reason for the development of the computer by mathematicians is isomorphic with that of the Scholes' successful development of the typewriter: the number domain is simpler to work in than the natural language domain. Mathematicians do not appear to have noticed that they are actually using a typewriter.

4   THREE THINGS TO TEACH TEACHERS

Teachers are in an unique position in society. They are removed from productive work and charged with transmitting extant knowledge and culture, whilst at the same time preparing youngsters to progress the culture further. The present time is uniquely difficult for teachers because it coincides with the development of a new instrument of representation, one which entails a discontinuity in our capability to represent the world.

The origins of the species
The first thing teachers need to be taught is the prehistorically long evolutionary process that led to the computer. Teaching teachers about this will entail the weaving together of several separate strands. Teachers will need to learn that the computer:

- did not emerge de novo in 1946, whatever the etymology of the vocabulary;
- is an alphabetic engine, any apparent mathicity being an artefact of its development;
- is an end point in millennia of language development, and not the electronic offspring of C19 manual mechanical marvels such as Babbage's difference engine; and
- extends our representational capability in a discontinuous manner: into the verbal.

The nature of the discontinuity
At the end of the medieval period Western schooling shifted from oral methods, in the ecclesiastical chantry school, to book based learning in the grammar schools. In England the grammar school is held high as a beacon of excellence, but the computer

has made it obsolescent, as did printing the chantry school. To understand this teachers will need to understand the nature of the representational discontinuity the computer embodies.

Both speech and writing represent action (verbs) metaphorically. To communicate an action we need to go beyond what may be said or written down. We demonstrate by mime or gesture, i.e. accompany language with actions. When we employ electrons as ink we put energy into our writing. By this we extend our representational capability beyond language. The computer adds the capability to represent actions actively within a written medium. This is a novel representational capability. It implies upheaval within continuity for the school curriculum. The basis of our learning, the 'letteracy' which Papert (1994) disdains, continues with the added capability actively to represent verbs. In mathematics this is a capability to represent the mental operation of addition within the medium of representation. Without a full understanding of the nature of this change the computer will continue to be assimilated to an extant, nominal, pre-verbal curriculum.

A little Logo

To teach teachers about the nature of our new writing instrument we need to introduce them to language that is of that instrument, to computer language. Logo, designed for education, where commands, verbs, come first, is ideal for the purpose. We need real Logo implementations: Silverman's LogoWriter, where a word highlighted on screen may be 'run' to perform its action; Sendov's Geomland, where Euclidean geometry becomes active; and Kalas' Comenius Logo, where graphics may be treated as words; not the degenerate so called Logo of turtle graphics packages (Ó Dúill, 1996). Suitably developed, Logo offers a route to understanding our new instrument of representation.

Finally

Teachers are working in a time of curricular instability. The nominal curriculum of book based teaching is being rendered obsolescent by a radically new active instrument of representation. Its intellectual transparency to teachers and thence to pupils is essential.

5   REFERENCES

Baum, L. (1900) *The Wonderful Wizard of OZ* (1995 edition). Penguin Books, London.

Dearing, R. (1995) *The National Curriculum and its Assessment: Final Report.* HMSO, London.

Hooker, J. (1990) Reading the Past: *Ancient Writing from Cuneiform to the Alphabet.* British Museum Press, London.

Ó Dúill, M. (ed.) (1996) *Proceedings of EUROLOGO'95*, Skipton.

Papert, S. (1980) *Mindstorms: Children, Computers and Powerful Ideas.* Harvester Press, Brighton.

Papert, S. (1994) *The Children's Machine: Rethinking School in the Age of the Computer.* Harvester Wheatsheaf, London.

Penrose, R. (1990) *The Emperor's New Mind: Concerning Computers, Minds and The Laws of Physics.* Vintage, London.
SCAA (1995) *National Curriculum Orders for England and Wales.* HMSO, London.
Stonier, T. (1990) *Information and the Internal Structure of the Universe: An Exploration into Information Physics.* Springer-Verlag, London.

6   BIOGRAPHY

Mícheál Ó Dúill is the Irish for Mike Doyle. Mike has been involved in computers in education since 1980. A psychology graduate, he has a masters degree in computers in education. For a living he teaches children with severe learning difficulties. As a hobby Mícheál Ó Dúill is Honorary Chairman of **Logos** the (very small) UK Logo user group and Chairman of the Scientific Committee of EuroLogo. He ran the EUROLOGO'95 conference. Mike Doyle is a Liberal Democrat politician, a member of Craven District Council in North Yorkshire and prospective parliamentary candidate for Keighley.

38

Training for information technology use in traditional and futuristic schools

Alnaaz Kassam
Department of Curriculum
OISE, 252 Bloor St. W., Toronto, Ontario M5S 1V6, Canada

Ronald G. Ragsdale
Northwestern State University, TEC Building, B-105, Natchitoches, LA 71497, USA

Abstract

This paper explores the role of technology in changing society and in changing our schools. It proposes that recent educational changes have been implemented as a response to technology, not as a response to our interpretation of what we believe is important to human beings. The paper carries out a critical analysis of schools in the past and in the present.

Keywords

Culture, curriculum policies, implications, information technology, social issues

In 1849, Dickens wrote a book called "Hard Times". In it he describes the following classroom situation between teacher and student:

"Give me your definition of a horse."

(Sissy Jupe thrown into the greatest alarm by this demand.)

"Girl number twenty unable to define a horse!" said Mr. Gradgrind, for the general behoof of all the little pitchers. "Girl number twenty possessed of no facts, in reference to one of the commonest of animals! Some boy's definition of a horse. Bitter, yours."

"Quadruped. Graminivorous. Forty teeth, namely twenty-four grinders, four eye-teeth, and twelve incisive. Sheds coat in the spring; in marshy countries, sheds hoofs, too. Hoofs hard but requiring to be shod with iron. Age known by marks in mouth."
"Now girl number twenty," said Mr. Gradgrind. "You know what a horse is."

She curtseyed again, and would have blushed deeper, if she could have blushed deeper than she had blushed all this time.

Here we see that in the extremely traditional classroom, there is only one right answer to a question. The teacher controls the environment, plays one child against another - humiliating the girl. Later in the same lesson, he humiliates the girl because she says she fancies flowers. The teacher retorts that she must never fancy.

"Fact, fact, fact! ... You are to be in all things regulated and governed by fact. We hope to have, before long, a board of fact, composed of commissioners of fact, who will force the people to be a people of fact, and of nothing but fact. You must discard the word Fancy altogether. You have nothing to do with it" (Dickens, 1965).

The above classroom is an extreme and in fact a satirical portrayal of education in the 19th century. What then is our usual image of the traditional classroom? In a teaching model for traditional education, Frase (1972) describes traditional education as having rigid classroom organisation, knowledge transmitted through passive memorisation, the teacher a disciplinarian and dispenser of knowledge, while the student becomes a passive consumer of knowledge. Evaluation is important and is carried out by the teacher through objective tests.

The following paragraph will describe River Oaks school, a technologically advanced school in Ontario:

By Grade 6, students with keyboarding skills were writing 3,000 word stories and were impressive in their ability to organise these very long tales. Finally, their ability to access information through the Internet or on CD-ROMs - atlases, encyclopaedias, image banks, "conversations" with peers in Japan - allowed them to create richer works. "Interestingly," Ownston says, "while the quality goes up, so do the students' expectations" (Report of the Royal Commission on Learning, 1994).

It is the basic thesis of this paper that deep technological changes in society are in turn affecting schools and their ability to adapt to society's needs.

According to Hargreaves:

The collapse of singular political ideologies, the diminishing credibility of traditional knowledge bases, and the declining certainty attached to scientific expertise have far-reaching ramifications for the changing world of education and the place of teachers' work within it (Hargreaves, 1994).

As is clear, knowledge is no longer a static body of information, which one can acquire through a formal teacher training process. Nor is access to knowledge any longer the domain of teachers alone. The youngest of children in our society have access to programs like Sesame Street that introduce the world of literature, history and geography to toddlers playing on the floor in their living rooms.

Furthermore, with cultures of the world coming together traditional cultural, religious and ethical social structures are increasingly called into question. Further, because of the increasing pace of technology, and the very huge demands of the workplace on the family and the community at large, traditional societies no longer exist.

As the Report on the Learning Commission (1994) states:

The old communities - family, village, parish, and so on - have all but disappeared in the knowledge society. ....But who, then, does the community tasks? Two hundred years ago whatever social tasks were being done were done in all societies by a local community. Very few if any of these tasks are being done today by the old communities anymore. Nor would they be capable of doing them, considering that they no longer have control of their members or even a firm hold over them. People no longer stay where they were born either in terms of geography or in terms of official position and status. By definition, a knowledge society is a society of mobility.

Thus we see that technology has taken over our society and that it has deeply affected our schools. While in Dickens' schools, students were relatively homogenous in terms of ethnic, linguistic and cultural background, they would also be grouped according to socio-economic background with almost no movement upward. If the teacher was king/queen over his/her classroom, his/her domain was made possible only by the fact that it was possible through teacher training to acquire and retain a large proportion of the knowledge available at the time. Changes in knowledge were relatively rare and were slow over time. The teacher could afford to be a strict disciplinarian because the society outside the school was rigid and hierarchical. Students were used to being disciplined by their parents - and their parents were used to being regimented in the hierarchy of the society in which they lived.

In today's school, the teacher is no longer `expert' but facilitator, the student is no longer an empty vessel but an active participant, the skills the student has to learn are no longer memorisation but "learning to learn". The society around the student has changed so much that the student is no longer assured of his/her place in it through a pre-arranged hierarchy.

Students must participate in their government through democratic responsibility. Whereas in Dickens' day one followed the current of the river of life in one's day to day living, today one has to exercise choice in everything one does - choice of dress, choice of place to live, to work, to marry or not, to have children, etc.

The authors of this paper agree that the content of the curriculum must change to reflect changes in the social make-up of its citizens, changes in our knowledge base and changes in our approach to learning. However when it is proposed by educationalists that we no longer need content, that we no longer need courses of study - that choice of content, curriculum and courses of study are subjective and need to be left to individual teachers, then we part company with expert opinion.

We believe that embedded in traditional content, embedded in traditional subject areas are thousands of years of human knowledge, skills and a discipline that we would be foolish to throw out for new forms of knowledge that we will continue to change as fashion demands.

This is not to state that the authors do not believe that students cannot be critical thinkers, independent inquirers and able to search out knowledge on their own, but rather that those abilities are embedded within traditional subjects.

The authors also argue that while technology is changing society, the skills we need to acquire are not just the skills of technology. We need also to have a deep and clear understanding of what it means to be human beings both in an historical but also a futuristic sense.

Technology is very much part of our lives and we cannot afford to ignore it. But the point that this paper wants to make is that while technology is part of the air we breathe, it may not be the solution to our problems in society. In the next section, we shall give a description of how most Western democracies have approached educational change in the past few years, and we shall demonstrate that these changes have all stemmed from technology - either technology as a problem or technology as a solution.

This paper will show that learning goes beyond technology, that the traditions of learning have existed with us for thousands of years, and in ignoring these traditions we may well be throwing out very valuable tools.

In an article on the Common Curriculum, the newly implemented integrated and outcomes-based curriculum in Ontario, Jean Hewitt states that in many countries around the world new curricula are emerging which have a number of common features. They are: broad "essential" cross-curricular learning, specific learning expectations as targets or developmental markings to be arrived at by pre-determined grades, abandonment of the subject or topic focus found in traditional curriculum documents in favour of measurable and observable statements of achievement which includes more generic knowledge, skills and values and a number of new "basics" such as technological literacy and the ability to work collaboratively while both restating and broadening the traditional basics of literacy and numeracy (Hewitt, 1995).

In the above description we see that subjects and topics are abandoned in favour of cross-curricular, generic knowledge and skills. Literacy and numeracy are expanded with new basics such as technology and working collaboratively.

We would like to start off by critiquing the notion that technology and working collaboratively are the same "literacies" as literacy and numeracy. Both literacy and numeracy were traditionally very content-based - with, in the case of literacy, students having to acquire knowledge of a huge canon of cultural knowledge. One can argue that this canon was elitist and did not reflect all members of the society which it pretended to represent - but one cannot react to this by abandoning all specified content which this curriculum is proposing to do.

In terms of numeracy, there is specific content that has taken humanity thousands of years to achieve. It is true that with the arrival of the computer much of the mundane arithmetic that took up our time has been relieved - nevertheless the process of acquiring these skills through specific content gives students a discipline and an appreciation for hard work that we believe is vital to their success in any field.

However, to be fair, that in the case of numeracy or mathematics, equating skills with content will not do the field of mathematics as much harm as in the case of literature, history and geography, - subjects that have actually been abandoned in the new curriculum. The study of literature is given a paragraph and is placed alongside the study of media texts which are defined as printed, visual or oral materials transmitted through a variety of mass communication media (for example, newspapers, films, radio and television programs, CD-ROMs).

Here we see an explicit example of the form of the technology taking over the content - as any adult who had undergone a traditional form of education will realise, the skills associated with becoming knowledgeable and analytical in each of these areas are quite different - one from the other. There is a different discipline, a different skill - a different analytical stance that one must adopt when critically evaluating literature, hypermedia or even a movie.

For example, it is our belief that through acquiring a deep knowledge of literature - through understanding what theme, plot and character development are, we may transfer this understanding to any part of our lives including our reaction to movies.

However, pursuing literature on the World Wide Web may require different skills - students will have to understand the nature of the logic or illogic of hypertext - the web-like nature of making connections - and these have little to do with the genre of the novel, which in and of itself represented a view of society and the novel at the time that it was first conceived.

We believe that underlying all content in the traditional subject areas, there were keys to understanding world views, to understanding and analysing social and cultural heritages - heritages and disciplines which we stand to lose if we simply allow teachers from year to year to make their own decisions about content.

As Emberley and Newell state:

Many classical allegories for liberal education - for example, the voyages of Odysseus or Telemachus - represent a journey of the soul from one's particular time, place, and attachments to the universal and back again to one's own. The same cycle of transcendence and return is sketched by Plato in his Image of the Cave. In our experience as teachers, we find that young people are still naturally inclined to fall in love with this journey to the stars and back.... This journey to the great ideas liberates us from the unthinking conventions and orthodoxies of the day, but only so that we can return to our own way of life better able to appreciate both its defects and its virtues (1994, p. 11).

In fact in the first author's thesis work, she studied two teachers - both teaching side by side, at the same grade level in the same school - but with vastly varying results in the performance of students (Kassam, 1993). In this case, one class was very content based and the other emphasised student creativity and student-centred learning with very little teacher direction.

In observations in these two classes, it was also discovered that those students that came from privileged backgrounds did far better in situations that were child-centred than did students who came from problem family situations. In these cases, students benefited much more from structured environments with specified outcomes and pre-specified content. One can argue that the Common Curriculum comes with outcomes and is not as free as child-centred education to which it came as a reaction - but it is our belief that outcomes and skills are simply not generic - they must be embedded in content to be truly appreciated by students.

As Wallach states:

What needs to be learned is close to the textures of particular fields of work, not removed from them in some abstract realm...Disciplines like the learning of a musical instrument, the craft of poetry writing, or the command over one's body involved in dance all primarily seem to involve matters that are field specific. There are huge conquests of technique that must take place in any of these domains, together with the cultivation of knowledge about styles and forms that lets a person come to understand and hear the difference between a more and a less sensitive rendering of say, a Mozart piano sonata.

Thus we see that in acquiring the cultural knowledge of our society, we need more than just generic outcomes - we need to be placed closely to the content of each of these cultural disciplines. This content can be changed as our knowledge base changes - and with the access to the Internet, this becomes infinitely easier than the publication of textbooks every 10 years. According to Bailin :

(The nature and structure of disciplines) do not consist in static, fixed bodies of information and techniques. Rather, they are traditions of knowledge and inquiry which are alive and open ended. They consist not merely in information but also in questions and in procedures for investigating these questions. And even the bodies of facts are not fixed but in flux, as are some aspects of the inquiry procedures.

And as classroom observations show, teachers when faced with no content react in different ways. Some teachers plan a program and a course of study - others simply arrive with different materials each day, attempting to teach skills defined in the curriculum guideline in an ad hoc fashion. It is our belief that a student who has undergone a traditional education with a strong content base - regardless of whether the content is up-to-date or not - acquires a much stronger analytical, critical and independent work discipline than one presented with varying materials and media from one day to another, one year to another.

However, the authors of this paper do not disagree with all changes proposed in recent years. The reforms of the Common Curriculum, where the student becomes the centre of learning, where knowledge is adapted to suit all student needs and interests, where the student is taught to be independent and critical of resources, are all positive as compared to the days of Dickens, where the horse had only one definition and that was the teacher's.

We have tried to show however, that while technology has placed much more content in the hands of students and teachers, the skills of the discipline - no matter which subject area - are slowly being eroded. We have argued that this has been both a cause and a reaction to technology - technology has provided human beings with infinitely more resources of content, but we have reacted by using the technology to analyse, relate to and deal with these resources. We have argued that analytical discourse and world view come independent of technology and we do not require technology to teach these disciplines to our students.

We have argued in this paper that while the traditional classroom is clearly not the education we need today, the classroom of the future would do well not to discard all content. The inclusion of the content provided by liberal education, albeit with acknowledgement of the cultural diversity of today's democracies and a judicious use of technology is a better alternative than providing generic skills with no clear guidelines for content.

In planning teacher training for technology, let us make of our pre-service students, intelligent but critical users of technology not its blind followers mesmerised by its potential. We shall end with a quotation:

The showy and faddish gestures of educational radicals towards global competitiveness and redressing inequity are, we argue, no substitute for the freedom of the mind and the balanced political judgement aimed at in a liberal education. This is an education which is without ostentation, an education which through gradual and sequential formation of habits and talents produces a critical and impartial mind.

Liberal education, as Leo Strauss once remarked, seeks the light and shuns the limelight (Emberley and Newell, 1994).

1   REFERENCES

Bailin, S. (1988) *Achieving Extraordinary Ends: An Essay in Creativity.* Kluwer Academic Publishers, Boston.

Begin, M. and Caplan, G. (1994) *For the love of Learning: Report of the Royal Commission on Learning.* Queen's Printer for Ontario, Toronto.

Dickens, C. (1965) *Hard Times.* Harper and Row, New York.

Emberley, P. and Newell, R.W. (1994) *Bankrupt Education: The Decline of liberal education in Canada.* University of Toronto Press, Toronto.

Frase, L. and Talbert, G. (1972*) Individualized Instruction: A Book of Readings.* Merrill, Columbus.

Hargreaves, A. (1994) *Changing Teachers, changing times.* Cassell, London.

Hewitt, J. (1995) Giving Voice to the Practising Professional: How Students Learn. *Orbit*, **26**, 1.

Kassam, A. (1993) *Teaching for Creativity in the Age of Computers: An Ethnographic Study.*

Ontario Ministry of Education and Training (1995) *The Common Curriculum: Policies and Outcomes Grades 1-9.* Queens's Printer for Ontario, Toronto.

2   BIOGRAPHY

Dr. Alnaaz Kassam is a Senior Research Officer at the Ontario Institute for Studies in Education, University of Toronto. For the past 10 years she has worked in researching the use of technology in Ontario classrooms. In the last two years, she has headed a project which used the Internet to promote intercultural understanding in Canadian schools. She is particularly interested in the preservation of world cultures in the face of new technologies. At present she is working on a book entitled: The Other Story: the Internet and Intercultural Understanding in Canada.

Dr. Ron Ragsdale is Professor of Educational Technology at Northwestern State University, Louisiana, where he has been teaching for the past year. Prior to this posting, Dr. Ragsdale was Professor in the Department of Measurement, Evaluation and Computer Applications at the Ontario Institute for Studies in Education, University of Toronto. His primary interests are evaluating the impact of computers on the educational process, with a particular focus on the contrast between expectations and outcomes. He has authored two books published by OISE Press, Computer in the Schools: A Guide for Planning, and Evaluation of Microcomputer Courseware. His most recent book, published by Praeger, is Permissible Computing in Education: Values, Assumptions and Needs.

39

The computer as a toy and tool in the home - implications for teacher education

Toni Downes
University of Western Sydney, Macarthur
P.O. Box 555, Campbelltown, NSW 2560, Australia

Abstract

The paper will present the findings of some recent research into children's access to and use of computers in their homes and discuss the implications of these results for pre-service teacher education. The study involved over four hundred children who had computers in their homes. The children were aged between five and twelve years and came from a variety of social, economic and cultural backgrounds in urban Sydney. All children regularly used a computer in their home or some one else's home.

Significant themes that emerged from the discussion were that children move easily between the notion of the computer as a toy and a tool, and that they bring the language of 'play' with them when they use the computer as a tool. Children learn to use the computer using a variety of strategies including "watching" and "sharing". Some direct teaching from other family members occur, and when it does it is in the mode of "just in time" coaching. In many families, the children themselves are the expert, and have learnt what they know through 'fiddling' and 'exploring'. Also, when children were comparing their experiences at home and at school, mention of issues such as lack of access and control at school were common.

Keywords

Elementary education, teacher education, parents, social issues

1 INTRODUCTION

There are a number of children in today's elementary classrooms who are confident, competent and regular users of computers in their homes. The purpose of this study was to discuss with these children the computer experiences they have within their homes and their schools. In these discussions the children described the physical and social environments within which they used their home computers. The findings raised a number of issues that need to be considered by practising and pre-service teachers.

2   THE DESIGN OF THE STUDY

The study involved over four hundred children who had computers in their homes. The children were aged between five and twelve years and came from a variety of social, economic and cultural backgrounds in urban Sydney.

The first stage of the study involved 190 children from years K to 6 in three schools in south west Sydney. Children in each of these schools who regularly used a computer in their home or someone else's home took part in discussion groups. Regular users were defined as children who used a computer at least two or three times a week for games and/or other purposes.

The second stage of the study involved about 250 children from eleven primary schools in urban Sydney. The schools were chosen, as their communities represented a wide range of social, economic, cultural and language backgrounds. In each school, 4 boys and 4 girls from each of years 3 to 6 were interviewed using a structured interview schedule. As in Stage One of the study, children were selected on the basis that the parent(s) reported that their child was a regular user of the home computer.

This stage was designed to seek clarification of the issues raised in the first stage of the research. In particular, an attempt was made to determine what similarities and differences existed across children who regularly used computers at home, and across their families and communities. The following characteristics were identified as key factors that might be associated with differences: gender and age of the children; the number of computers in the home; the computing experiences of the parents; the socio-economic and cultural background of the families; and the children's school experiences.

Discussions were videotaped and interviews audiotaped as well as recorded in the interview schedule. After transcription, responses were analysed using both qualitative and quantitative methodologies.

3   SOME KEY FINDINGS OF THE STUDY

Some of the key issues which have implications for classroom practice are access, use, the way children learn to use the computer, and their perceptions about the differences between school and home computing. Each of these will be discussed below.

Access

The processes involved in selecting the children for the two stages of the study clearly indicated that in all schools there were children who had no access to a home computer, children who had access to basic equipment (a computer and a printer) and a significant number of children who had access to a wide range of the latest technologies. These included two or more computers, coloured printers, CD-ROM drives and in a very small number of cases modems. As expected, the percentage of children in each of these three categories was proportional to the wealth of the school communities and the related characteristic of parental use of computers in their place of work.

A range of factors influenced children's access to home computers. These included location of the computer, ownership (who 'owns' it and who uses it most), and rules about its use. In general children had reasonable control over their access to and use of the home computer equipment, even when the computer was located in a private space such as a bedroom or a parent's study. Younger children had more rules about supervision, older children about maximum duration of use. There were rules about when, how often and for how long children could use the computer. Some children also described rules that differentiated the types of uses such as only being allowed to use it for school work and not being allowed to play games. This notion of priority uses also applied to users, with parents and older siblings doing work having clear priority.

Use of home computers

The children used computers for a variety of purposes and were comfortable moving between playing games and doing work on the computer. While game-playing remained a common activity, many of these children regularly engaged in writing and drawing activities and used information-based programs for leisure as well as school-related work.

Boys and girls reported the same frequency of game-playing on the computer, but boys were more likely to own and operate a dedicated video-game machine in the home as well as the computer. Girls were more likely to report that they wrote stories (narratives) for leisure on the computer, while younger boys and children without printers were more likely not to write stories. Overall the gender differences, in terms of types of use reported, were minor. This is in contrast to Wheelock (1992) who found a common gender-segregated pattern of usage among the children in the homes in the late 1980s. At that time the home computer was still very much an innovation and those families could be considered early adopters. In the current study, the few families who had a modem in the home could be considered early adopters. In these homes the children who used the modem themselves to connect to the Internet or other telecommunications activities were invariably male.

Another feature of children's use relates to the interaction of playing and working environments. Many children, particularly the younger ones, used the language of play and games to describe their use of common tool software: *"I can play PAINTBRUSH and print my favourite pictures"; "I play books* (when referring to reading electronic texts)*"* and *"my favourite games is KID PIX"*. A number of older children also used similar language or described how they 'played' with information in a serendipitous way: *"Well we got this atlas. And I like going into that and you pick your countries. And you bring it up and they show you the flag and you can play the anthem."*

Learning to use the computer

According to most children (75%) they learn to use the computer by having another person show or teach them what to do. The tutor is usually a family member. Fathers and brothers were named as the tutor twice as often as mothers and sisters. An additional 12% of students said that they learned by watching someone else use the computer, which is an indirect and more passive way of learning. The remainder of learners were taught by school teachers and extended family members such as uncles, aunts and cousins. Only 10% said that they taught themselves or read the computer manual.

Following the initial teaching period the responsibility for learning is gradually handed over to the child. Children were asked if they could fix problems themselves. 41% of the children said "no", 28% said "sometimes, depends or mostly" and 28% said "yes". There were noticeable differences in these responses. Children who had one or more parents using a computer at their work were almost twice as likely to have a positive response to the question. As well, older children were slightly more likely to have a positive response. Interestingly gender had no relationship to the children's responses. Children were also asked whose assistance they sought when they encountered difficulties with something on the computer. In general, fathers were the first person to be called for help.

Differences in home and school use

Seventy per cent of the children preferred to use a computer in the home environment rather than the school environment. The type of computer hardware and software available in the home and school environments was the main reason given by children for their preference.

Preferences for home computing varied between the schools from 50% to 93% in more affluent communities and where children had more computers in their homes. In community housing neighbourhoods computing activities at school were appreciated by higher percentages of students (up to 27%). Other reasons that children preferred to use the computer at home were the quieter environment, their familiarity with the computer, less restricted access, control over and ownership of the computer.

Frequency of computing varied in the home and school environments. Seventy three per cent of the children in this survey used their home computer two or more times each week. Only 20% of children said that they used a school computer two or more times each week. The length of time the children used the computer at home was generally more than the time they were allowed at school. Equally important to the children was the fact that they had more control over the amount of time and choice of activity that they spent using the computer at home. Seventy per cent of children said that they used their home computer by themselves. At two schools, computer use was structured in ways to allow students to have a computer to themselves, at four schools computers were shared by small groups of students and at three schools computers were sometimes used by single students and small groups. Some children mentioned the availability of assistance at school from teachers and classmates, especially if parents had little computer expertise.

4   ISSUES FOR TEACHER EDUCATION

The above findings raise many issues that need to be addressed both by practising teachers in classrooms and those preparing teachers in pre-service courses. The issues that will be addressed in this paper relate to equity, management of school computing, developing computing skills, and developing home-school links. Within pre-service courses, these issues need to be addressed both in wider contexts such as discussions on the broader issues of equity, on select topics such as gender issues in managing classrooms or specifically within technology contexts.

Equity issues

The equity issues involved in children's access to home computing are complex and likely to become more extensive as the range of affordable technologies increases. Clearly there will always be children in classrooms who have no access to computer technologies in their homes as well as children who only have minimal access to basic equipment. These children are likely to come from families who do not share equally in the social and workplace benefits of computing technologies, nor have access to a range of other literacy processes and artefacts in the home. As computer and communication technologies continue to converge the differences between the 'haves' and the 'have nots' will continue to grow and the impact will be strongly felt in the classrooms.

This problem is not new to schools, much research, policy and curriculum development has occurred around the problems of children's access to print-based literacy processes and artefacts in the home. Various models and programs have been devised to handle these differences. These include compensatory, remedial, 'head start', home-school programmes, parent helper, tutor and training programmes. Practicing and pre-service teachers need to engage in debates about how to respond to these issues at the school and classroom level and what programmes if any they would seek to use.

At the same time as these debates are held, practicing and pre-service teachers need to question the equity issue surrounding the continuing reticence of many classroom teachers to help capitalise on the skills and understandings that some children bring to school. Some of these teachers justify their position on a reverse equity argument that children with computers in their homes would have an unfair advantage. The fallacy of this argument is obvious if once again the analogy is drawn with print-based literacy processes and artefacts: Would any teacher deny children access to books and writing implements in the home, or ignore children who come to school already being able to read? Practicing and pre-service teachers need to develop strategies and processes so that all children within their classroom benefit from the extra skills and understandings that some children bring to class. Similarly when setting homework and project work, teachers need to help children effectively exploit all the resources available to them at home and at school. A necessary corollary would be the improved ability to assess the content and structure as well as the appearance of electronically produced texts.

Managing computer use within the classroom

Many children bring from home a range of attitudes and behaviours that will have a direct impact on the successful use of computers for instructional purposes in the classroom. These include the strong link children have between game playing and computer use. Not only do many children use the language of game playing to describe their tool use of the computer, they are also likely to transfer some of their game playing strategies directly into instructional tasks. In particular many children in the study expressed a preference for working with their own computer at home because they could work by themselves. When designing computer-based instructional activities, teachers need to make explicit to children the nature of the task they are setting, the purpose of making the activity a group or paired activity as well as helping children to develop the skills and attitudes necessary to make the pair or small group work effectively. In this way children will begin to appreciate the differences between various computer uses and adapt their expectations accordingly. Teachers also need to consider the issue of allocating time for children to explore the use of the computer or engage in purposeful tasks on their own.

A further issue that could be explored within a management framework is the notion of maximising children's sense of control over the use of the schools' computers. Strategies need to move beyond rosters and booked computer time to take account of the timely access to computers at the point of need, possibly for extended periods of time. Again these issues are not isolated to use of technologies but are more broadly linked to managing the use of any scarce resources, or in the context of technology-rich schools, training children to accept more responsibility for managing their own learning time.

Skill development

One of the key findings to arise from the study was that neither home nor school (except in isolated cases) have taken the responsibility for the systematic development of the skills and knowledge to effectively and efficiently use computers as information handling and communication tools. Children reported that from time to time, particularly in the early stages of use, parents and teachers did engage in some explicit teaching of hardware and software use. This instruction did not usually go beyond 'getting started'. After this, children used 'watching', 'asking' and 'fiddling' as their main learning strategies. In many cases this meant that children were still using primitive processes to edit and layout their text within a word processor even though they had been regular users for several years. Similarly when children described processes for accessing information from electronic texts such as multimedia encyclopaedia, they rarely described processes that went beyond the keying in of the exact term or title of their search. Practising and pre-service teachers need to debate the need for some form of systematic skill development in a range of areas associated with computer use, and devise and implement programmes which will develop these skills.

Developing the home school links

A final issue that needs to be addressed relates to the school's influence on what is happening in the home. Although socio-economic circumstances played a large role in determining how much and what computing equipment is in the home, there seemed to be little difference in what children did with the equipment they had. Predominantly they played games, and as they get older they completed homework and project work using the computer. As seen by the range of explicit and implicit rules in the homes, parents value the educational role of the computer. Practising and pre-service teachers need to engage families in dialogue about ways to increase the educational potential of the computers in homes.

5   CONCLUSION

The issues raised by this study need to be addressed by teachers and teacher educators. They are complex, and in many cases they parallel issues within print literacy which still have not been fully resolved in theory or in practice. Attention to key issues surrounding equity are of particular importance if education is to play a major role in addressing the growing gap between the technologically affluent and poor families in our societies.

6   REFERENCES

Downes, T., Reddacliff, C. and Moont, S. (1995) *Preliminary Report of Children's Use of Electronic Technologies in the Home.* Faculty of Education, University of Western Sydney, Macarthur, Campbelltown, NSW 2560.

Downes, T., Reddacliff, C. and Moont, S. (1996) *Stage 2 Preliminary Report of Children's Use of Electronic Technologies in the Home.* Faculty of Education, University of Western Sydney, Macarthur, Campbelltown, NSW 2560.

Wheelock, J. (1992) Personal computers, gender and an institutional model of the household, in R. Silverstone and E. Hirsh (eds.) *Consuming technologies: Media and information in domestic spaces.* Routledge, London.

7   BIOGRAPHY

Toni Downes is the Associate Dean of the Faculty of Education at the University of Western Sydney. Her teaching responsibilities include educational computing subjects in the undergraduate and postgraduate courses. Her research interests include information handling skills, children's use of information technologies in the information handling process and more recently, children's use of electronic technologies in their homes. She is co-author of two recent books: *In Control: Young Children Learning with Computers* and *Learning in the Electronic World.*

Section 11: Future scenarios and the challenges they offer

40

Teachers and teacher education facing information and communication technologies

Bernard Cornu
Institut Universitaire de Formation des Maîtres (IUFM)
30, Avenue Marcelin Berthelot, 38100 Grenoble, France

Abstract

Information technology and communication technology are evolving and converging, giving rise to new tools for teaching and learning. Step by step, a new profession is emerging: the teacher of tomorrow. This paper will try to describe what the profession of the teacher of tomorrow will be like. Education now needs for its goals a real generalisation and a real integration of new technologies, but generalisation and integration are possible only if teacher education is redesigned. The paper will outline some elements for teacher education, from experiences in France. It is clearly impossible to provide a new teacher with all the competencies and knowledge he (she) will need throughout his (her) career. Therefore, one must provide new teachers with "basic" competencies and knowledge, and prepare them to evolve and adapt. Consequently, not only the content of the training is important, but the methods used in teacher training play a major role.

Keywords

Communications, future developments, information technology, integration, national policies, teaching methods

1 INTRODUCTION

Education has certainly not been influenced by Information and Communication Technologies (ICT) as much as one might have thought it would be ten years ago. Computers have been put into schools, some curricula have been changed, some teachers have been trained; but all this equipment is underused, and in fact teaching and learning have been little affected by new technologies, and there is generally no real integration of ICT in teaching. At the same time, ICT are developing very rapidly, and influence society more and more. More and more pupils can use a computer or a calculator, but most of the time it is not at school that they learn how to use them! One must prepare for and master this evolution, anticipate what the teacher of tomorrow will be, and adapt teacher education to the new needs.

2   TOWARDS THE TEACHER OF TOMORROW

2.1 Evolutions

Information technologies are changing: computers are more and more powerful, more and more user-friendly, smaller and smaller, cheaper and cheaper. Software meets our needs (or we are creating new needs which meet the new computer facilities!) more and more. Information, whatever its nature, is digitalised (i.e. put into a sequence of 0 and 1): texts, images, pictures, sounds, can now be considered as similar information, which can be processed in similar ways.

Communication technologies are changing at the same time: new communication technologies enable lots of information (i.e. sequences of 0 and 1) to be carried very quickly and at a low price, making possible what was not possible before.

The joint developments of information technologies and communication technologies converge to provide new facilities: Information and Communication Technologies. So, different pieces of equipment are now more and more similar and may merge: a CD-ROM contains all kinds of information (sounds, music, images, video, texts, ...), and TV, computer, radio, record player, telephone, fax, may now appear as a single machine, or are at least closely connected.

This leads to multimedia and network facilities, which are the main results of the convergence between information technologies and communication technologies.

New ICT tools, multimedia and networks, influence education in several ways. They influence the knowledge itself, and the needs for knowledge. They influence the ways one can have access to knowledge, and therefore the status of knowledge itself. They influence teaching, providing a wide field of new possibilities. They influence learning, but a lot of research is necessary in order to understand and master the effects of ICT on learning. Many interesting experiments have been carried out: computers in classrooms, use of multimedia and a great deal of educational software and product development, experimentation, simulation and modelling, networking, video-conference teaching, etc. These features can affect and change the role of the school, the place of the school in knowledge transmission, and therefore change the role of the teacher.

2.2 Generalisation, integration

A lot of experiments and successful innovations have been carried out. They are generally done by volunteers and enthusiastic teachers. It is certainly necessary to continue research and experimentation, but a major problem is now to have ALL teachers involved in information and communication technologies. And what is possible with a few of them is much more difficult with all of them. Generalisation of ICT in teaching is a crucial point for the future, which we must address and solve. It requires a precise study of the obstacles against generalisation, it needs technical and "hardware" actions, in order to simplify the access to technologies and their use in education, and it needs a huge effort in teacher education.

Integration is the second major problem. It is not simply a case of "adding" new technologies to what existed before: adding specialised rooms in schools, adding computers to classrooms, adding a new chapter on technologies to books and courses, adding computer activities to the existing syllabuses and curricula and to lessons. One needs to integrate ICT into education: integrate it into knowledge and subjects (i.e. take into account the evolution of knowledge, of concepts, of subjects), integrate ICT into teaching (i.e. in content and in methods), into learning, integrate ICT into the school, integrate ICT into the profession of the teacher. Once again, teacher education is an essential means in order to develop integration.

2.3   New competencies

Not only do new technologies influence the role of the teacher, but in most countries, social parameters are important: more and more pupils can pursue their studies at a higher level. So, schools and classes are more and more heterogeneous, with pupils at very different levels of skills and capacities. Economic and social problems (unemployment, housing, poverty, social exclusion, delinquency, drug addiction, etc.) all influence what happens in schools, the behaviour of the pupils, and the needs of society with respect to education. Knowledge is more and more complex, and knowledge transmission more and more difficult. The role of school and education is discussed as a major point in most countries: is it only to transmit given knowledge? to accompany each pupil in their quest for knowledge acquisition? to transmit social values? to prepare the citizens of tomorrow and help pupils attain social insertion? to contribute to the solution of social problems?

In any case, the role of a teacher is becoming more and more complex, and more and more diverse. Let us try to list some of the competencies a teacher will need :

-   to master the knowledge to be transmitted, as well as teaching and learning processes.
-   to be able to create and develop his (her) teaching; he (she) must have the competency of a technician and an engineer.
-   to be able to build up his (her) own competencies permanently.
-   to be able to use the results of educational research, and to question research.
-   to transmit the love for learning and an appetite for knowledge to pupils, and to arouse the curiosity of the pupils.
-   to be the guarantor of equity and equality for all pupils.
-   to transmit the fundamental values of society.
-   to prepare and mould the citizens of tomorrow: their judgement, their freedom.
-   to help the pupils to conceptualise, theorise, model, and build abstraction.
-   to prepare the pupils to pass their exams (this is a short term objective, compared to the previous one which is long term focused).
-   to sometimes replace the parents' authority when they fail.
-   to apply and put into action a policy, the educational policy of the Minister.
-   to be an adviser, as well as a leader and a manager.
-   to be an organiser and an evaluator.
-   to be able to work alone (preparing lessons, marking works and examinations).
-   to be able to work in teams, with colleagues (concertation, preparation of lessons, share competencies, reflection, research, etc.).

- to be able to work with the whole class, but also with small groups, and with each pupil individually.
- to be able to work at home, and at his (her) office (but generally schools do not provide offices for teachers! Perhaps they will do so to greater extents in the future).
- to be able to work in a laboratory (laboratories will develop, not only for sciences, but increasingly in every subject, with the help of information and communication technologies).
- to manage the fact that more and more, he (she) will not be the only one to transmit knowledge: he (she) will have to manage the access to knowledge, to help pupils organise the knowledge, hierarchising the knowledge.
- to be able to evolve and adapt.

Such a list leads one to make certain comments. Firstly, it is almost certainly impossible for a teacher to have all these competencies. Secondly, there is a risk of dilution between all these competencies. Thirdly, one must try to determine which competencies can be acquired in initial training and help them to acquire other competencies progressively, whichever competencies need to be acquired in in-service training. A major competency for a teacher will be that of being able to evolve and adapt, throughout their career. In-service training must therefore be considered as an essential part of the profession of a teacher, and no longer as an optional and luxurious activity.

3   TEACHER EDUCATION

3.1 Some principles

Some basic principles must be taken into account in teacher education and training, and especially regarding the integration of information and communication technologies.
- Teaching is a profession, for which one must be prepared, educated and trained. It is not enough to be good at mathematics in order to be a good mathematics teacher!
- The profession of a teacher is an intellectual profession, and a profession of freedom. It is essential to keep thinking, to take into account the diversity of pedagogical strategies.
- Knowledge (disciplines to be taught), human and social sciences, pedagogy and educational concerns, must be well balanced in teacher education.
- Teacher education needs a permanent interaction between theory and practice.
- It is impossible to provide a future teacher with all the competencies and knowledge he (she) needs, for an entire career. There is no "rucksack" for a good teacher! In-service training is an essential component of the profession of a teacher.
- Ability to evolve and adapt is an essential component of the profession of a teacher. This ability must be developed in initial education. Regarding ICT particularly, nobody knows how it will evolve during the next 30 years, and which competencies will be necessary in 20 years!

- Teacher education must include short term aims (such as "recipes" for teaching, or preparation for the first professional moments) and long term aims (more fundamental and theoretical inputs and reflections).
- Training methods are as important as contents. Teachers will generally teach not the way they are told to do, but reproduce the way they were taught. Therefore teacher education methods will change teacher behaviour.
- It is not enough to give courses ABOUT new technologies and their integration into education; ICT must be actually used in teacher education, in all its dimensions and components, and integrated in teacher education contents and methods (similarly, one does not learn collaborative work through courses about collaborative work, but by practicing team work!).
- Future teachers are not only to be taught that it is possible to learn something through ICT. They must themselves actually learn something new through new technologies.
- In teacher education, ICT is both an object and a tool. Indeed, future teachers will have to teach ICT, will have to use ICT, and will have to integrate ICT into their teaching.

3.2   Teacher education in France : the "IUFMs"

In 1990, a reform of teacher education was introduced in France. Before the reform, primary teachers were trained in "Écoles normales", outside the university community. Secondary teachers were trained by universities, but only in subject matter (they gained pedagogical training, provided by inspectors, during the first year of their career). In 1990, new institutions were created: University Institutes for Teacher Education (IUFMs). They train both primary and secondary teachers (student teachers must first undertake 3 years at university, then 2 years at IUFM). Thus primary and secondary teachers have the same level of training, and as a consequence, the same salaries afterwards. In IUFM, education includes that for specific disciplines (primary teachers teach all the disciplines of primary school; secondary teachers generally teach only one discipline), human and social sciences (psychology, sociology, philosophy, etc.), and professional and pedagogical inputs (pedagogy, didactics, etc.). Training includes practice periods in schools, with interaction between theory and practice. IUFMs are independent higher education institutions, similar to universities, which collaborate closely with universities. They also contribute to in-service training, and participate in educational research.

A particularity of France is that teacher recruitment is linked to teacher education. Teachers are recruited by the State, not by schools. The process of being recruited is a result of a competitive examination, which students take at the end of the first year at IUFM. If they succeed, they continue in second year (during which they are paid, as civil servants), and are then given a post.

The French State recruits about 26,000 new teachers every year. Altogether, IUFMs train about 90,000 students.

3.3 Integrating information and communication technologies into teacher education

The integration of ICT into teacher education has been a main concern for IUFMs. They started at a very low point, and had to develop ICT in a great many respects. In 1995, all the IUFMs were asked to elaborate a 4-year plan to include ICT integration.

The content of ICT education for future teachers is based on two aspects of use: ICT as tools; and integration of ICT. We try to avoid too many courses or modules about ICT. We prefer to offer:

-   some courses in order to help the students use and master the tools (word processing, main software, basics for using computers, multimedia, networks, etc.);
-   integration of ICT in the teaching of all other subjects, including the pedagogical use of ICT in each of these subjects.

As a first consequence, we do not need mainly specialists and computer scientists: we need all the staff to practise and integrate ICT in their teaching. This leads to an enormous problem of trainers' training. We are now implementing a trainers' training plan in order to have all our staff trained as soon as possible.

ICT integration in teacher education must include three main components: social and cultural aspects (i.e. how ICT influences society, and which technologies and techniques are available), technical aspects (the ability to use software and hardware as a tool for practising the teacher profession), and pedagogical and didactical aspects (linked to the subjects and knowledge to be taught). It must also be linked with the articulation between theory and practice, which is an essential component of teacher education. So, we are working closely with schools which are equipped and in which there are teachers able to tutor and advise our students in ICT integration.

We want ALL our students to be able to use ICT. It raises issues regarding equipment. Our institute is spending a great deal of money on ICT equipment, trying to do so in a very diverse way: equipping the lecture halls; equipping specialised rooms for new technologies (computers, audio-video, multimedia and networks, computer aided experimentation in sciences, etc.); providing ordinary rooms with minimal equipment; having self-service rooms available to students when they need access; having an ICT corner in libraries with CD-ROMs and software, etc. We also help our students to buy their own equipment: every year, we organise exhibitions with equipment we have selected, and which are offered by companies at a lower price; a bank provides special loans for students in order to buy ICT equipment.

We have installed an internal network (our institute is split into 5 different centres, in 5 different cities), firstly for management purposes, but also for our staff to communicate, and in this way, to start using ICT as a daily, easy and useful tool. And we have started providing access to Internet, despite the fact that in France it is very expensive!

Our project includes the following actions:

-   to integrate ICT into training programmes;
-   to integrate ICT in the "scientific life" of the Institute;
-   to establish a plan for ICT equipment in the Institute;
-   to participate in the production of tools and products (such as CD-ROMs, multimedia tools, etc.);

- to develop an "ICT-library" (teachers are professionals; they need professional tools, and they need the most up-to-date tools; these tools must therefore be available in every teacher education institution);
- to develop networks, inside the Institute and with the exterior; to develop tele-working (among our staff, and with the student teachers);
- to work in collaboration with external partners. In this way, we work together with other IUFMs in France, with the local universities, and with teacher education institutions in several countries. We participate in European projects aimed at developing ICT in teacher education;
- to implement a trainers' training plan;
- to develop research activities in the field of ICT in education and in teacher education.

All these actions are not equally as difficult as each other, and some of them can only be regarded as long term actions. They need not only "good will", but a strong policy, structures in place, and finance.

4   CONCLUSION

ICT seems to develop more quickly in society than in education! It implies new roles for schools: the school is no longer the only place where pupils can learn. Information is now accessible in many other places, through many resources which are outside school. It is a challenge for educational systems to deal with this evolution and to adapt to that which society now needs. Teachers are the main actors of the changes; they must be prepared for their new roles. This makes it necessary to act both in teacher pre- and in-service training. The convergence between information technologies and communication technologies, the convergence between technology development and educational research development, has lead to new tools and to new possibilities for teaching and learning. But certainly more research, experiments and innovations are needed in order for us to progress further, and to solve the two major difficulties: generalisation; and integration.

5   REFERENCES

Cornu, B. (1995) New technologies: integration into education, in D. Watson and D. Tinsley (eds.) *Integrating information technology into Education*. Chapman and Hall, London.
Cornu, B. (1995) Teacher Education and Communication and Information Technologies : Implications for Faculties of Education, in B. Collis, I. Nikolova, and K. Martcheva (eds.) *Information technologies in teacher education*. UNESCO, Paris.

6   BIOGRAPHY

Bernard Cornu is a mathematician at Grenoble University. He studied the influence of computers and informatics on mathematics and its teaching, and also worked in didactics of mathematics. He was the Director of the Institute of Research on Mathematics Teaching (IREM) of Grenoble, and then the Head at the in-service teacher training office (MAFPEN) for the Academy of Grenoble. He contributed to the French reform of initial teacher education, leading to the creation of the University Institutes for Teacher Education (IUFM), in which all primary and secondary teachers, in all disciplines, are trained for two years. Bernard Cornu is the Director of the IUFM of Grenoble, and was until 1994 the Chairman of the 29 IUFMs in France. He is the Chairman of IFIP Working Group 3.1.

41

Converging technologies in teacher education: key issues, key competencies

Paul Nicholson and George Duckett
Deakin Centre for Education and Change
662 Blackburn Road, Clayton Australia 3168

Abstract
While converging technologies have had an enormous impact on industry and commerce, their impact on education is only now beginning to be felt as the Information Super Highway finds its way into ever increasing numbers of classrooms. Its move into schools has not occurred as fast as one might have expected two years ago, a situation common in regard to the general infiltration of new technologies into schools (Cornu, 1995). The reluctance of teachers to change is the major non-economic reason for the low uptake. Students however are keen to experience the new media. The challenge for teacher education is to produce teachers who can adapt this technology to their needs before the technology makes schools themselves irrelevant.

Keywords:
Teacher education, attitudes, future developments, innovation, pedagogy, teaching methods

1 INTRODUCTION

This paper is written in response to the following questions:
1. Will converging technologies and globalisation bring about the death of schools?
2. What role will 'teachers' have in the new, potentially information-rich, virtual environments?
3. How will teachers learn to 'teach' in these environments?
4. How will teachers conduct a 'class' with a virtual, loosely-structured group of learners?

These questions, whilst long standing, are suddenly timely and relevant as the advent of global communications and broadband networks brings rich and varied sources of information into the family home. Globalisation, the emergence of global technology and communication systems controlled by global companies, has the potential to reduce educational diversity and to develop global, corporate, and business oriented models of education. Additionally it creates a significant pressure for educational systems to adopt their current technology by offering images of '...utopian educational futures made available on line' (Kenway, 1995) with the corollary that schools that fail to adopt the technology will have no future. They find themselves driven and transformed by three linked factors (Tinkler, Lepani and Mitchell, 1996):

1. increased competition for increased market share in a global education economy,
2. changing market requirements for services with the shift to a knowledge economy,
3. the transformative impact of information technologies on the structure and organisation of the education industry in responding to these imperatives.

Teacher education, as a 'responding industry', must clearly change, but it must make the kinds of changes that will maximise educational quality in teaching and learning, and not simply respond to the uncritical, consumer-like adoption of the technology for its own sake. The fundamental epistemological battle to be fought is for the belief that the technology on its own is educationally pointless – that only with skilled intervention and guidance from teachers will these new technologies be educationally valuable and viable, a point which Riel (1990) makes strongly in defending Information Technologies from Cuban's comments on the failure of technology to significantly restructure education (Cuban, 1986).

2   PERSPECTIVES

Bigum and Kenway (1996) identify four philosophical and functional perspectives on this issue:

1. *Boosters* (the unequivocal promoters of new information technologies in education),
2. *Anti-schoolers* (to whom schools are unable to be reconstructed or reconfigured using computer technology – they should simply be scrapped),
3. *Critics* (those sceptical about many of the claims advanced for using the new information and communication technologies in education),
4. *Doomsters* (unqualified opponents of the new information and communication technologies).

In this paper we wish to follow a scenario based mainly on assumption that the technology will be omnipresent, and that the boosters and anti-schoolers' perspectives will prevail (Negroponte, 1995; Papert, 1987; Papert, 1993; Schwartz, 1991). In this scenario, a post-industrial world (Toffler, 1980) has rendered schools irrelevant, and, as products of the industrial revolution ...

'... *schools it is argued, are unable to be reconstructed or reconfigured using computer technology. They should simply be scrapped.*' (Bigum and Kenway, 1996; Perelman, 1992).

The potential realities of this outcome are significant in terms of redefining teaching and learning ...

...a totally 'wired' world, one in which classrooms, kids, teachers, the home are all permanently connected to a global computer network. They see such a world offering high quality access to information, remote and world-wide-expert teachers and other learners around the globe. Teachers who have not adapted to this massive shift in the way that schools operate have been discarded. There are no problems in terms of equity and access since the technology has become so affordable and available (Bigum and Kenway, 1996).

3   NATIVES AND IMMIGRANTS

In considering the role of teacher education in this brave new technological world, assuming that it has a role, it is important to consider the likely responses of teachers and students to such a radical systemic change. Already Barlow (1995) has raised serious concerns about the fundamental cultural and technological differences between teachers and students – students who are 'natives' in this environment being taught by 'immigrant' teachers who do not understand the power and potential of the technology. Many teachers are also hesitant to adopt the technology and demonstrate low levels of computer literacy (Mitchell, Paprzycki and Duckett, 1994). For example, while students have rapidly understood, appreciated and assimilated the ease of access to information that the Internet provides into their educational activities, most teachers have not. Teachers frequently find it difficult to comprehend that the school and the family home today are both flooded with masses of unstructured, cheap and uninterpreted information. (However this should not be taken to mean that students *can* actually interpret and organise this material into a coherent cognitive structure.) Teachers have found, to their dismay, that technologically aware (native) students can trivialise cherished, long-standing educational practice with some minimal Internet skills. Such mismatches in competence and knowledge are common in many classrooms today.

Unfortunately the educational future will include both small and large scale cultural clashes between the natives and the immigrants as access to the technology becomes cheaper and more common. In addition to changing schools, teachers themselves will have to be reconstructed to cope with the changed nature of technology, and the purpose of schooling in general.

In the longer term, this will be less of a problem as 'native' students move on to teacher-education institutions (which may then face a serious challenge themselves). While there is a rich literature on the future directions of teacher education, there is little action.

4   THE DEATH OF SCHOOLS?

Schooling as a means of transmitting knowledge appears to be in imminent danger of being bypassed by converging technologies. Already there is evidence of widespread informal learning occurring as students browse the Internet from home, using equipment frequently far in advance of what they have access to at school. A scenario based on this becoming a 'normal' way of learning would see schools and teachers having to radically readapt, changing both purpose and pedagogy. This fundamental contemporary restructure of the pathways to knowledge has led to an ego-centric model of learning rather than an institution-centred model. Comparing the changes from 1900 to today, the reality of this is enormous, yet still schools persist with the belief that it is not happening. Many studies have shown that this is partly due to teacher resistance to change, and to their low levels of computer skills and confidence (Paprzycki, Mitchel and Duckett, 1994).

5   VIRTUAL TEACHING ENVIRONMENTS

Our future teachers will require a very different skill-set from those currently imparted by teacher education institutions. These new competencies will require virtual practicum experiences, conducting on-line classes, as well as the ability to create virtual learning spaces/lessons with enhanced collaborative software environments such as traditional and graphical MUD's and MOO's like Palace (Time Warner, 1996) and rich multimedia bulletin boards and web software tools that are now appearing. Figure 1 shows an example of the environment of a typical virtual classroom (http://www.deakin.edu.au/edu/MSEE/GENII/GENII-Home-Page.html). The teachers challenge is to turn this basic graphic displayed on a computer screen into a productive and rich on-line learning space.

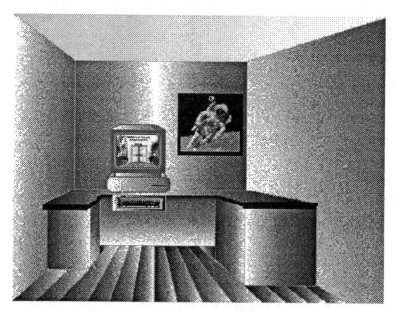

Figure 1 The starting point for a virtual classroom

Even sophisticated graphics, video and speech do nothing to address the pedagogical issues. For example, the more refined 'study' in Figure 2 provides a visual clue to its purpose, but is curiously modelled after a 19th century metaphor, one of the many mixed metaphors found in these environments. However there is no inherent pedagogy in this graphic, other than to suggest it is a place for discussion.

Figure 2 A virtual study based on 19th century models

How will our new teachers gain the knowledge and skills to develop these sorts of environments (or will all future teachers have to be programmers?) How will they acquire competency in their use? And exactly what is an appropriate pedagogy? Is it hard coded into the script, or does the script have to be designed to produce a learning environment in which good pedagogy can occur? These are critical challenges that must be addressed as part of the changing expectations of the education industry.

Treating teaching issues as programming concerns may be quite invalid of course, but the transition from real to virtual teaching environments requires enormous discussion about the design, nature and purpose of teaching. Adopting Barlow's 'critics' stance, the real question is basically how much of the present culture and nature of teaching are we prepared to forgo simply to embrace the technology. The balance sheet of gains and losses needs to be examined very carefully, and not simply from an economic perspective.

6   CHALLENGES

A key question for teacher education institutions is how much emphasis should be placed on these new skills at a time when the majority of teaching is still conducted in a traditional didactic classroom mode. However, the decision may not be theirs to make. For example, Don Hayward (Minister of Education, state of Victoria), predicts that traditional classrooms may be non-existent by the year 2000 (Bushfield, 1996). Ultimately it will be the availability of information outside school - the very institutions set up to pass on information to the next generation - that forces change in teacher education.

Like Papert's time-travelling surgeons (Papert, 1993), our teacher education institutions face becoming irrelevant by failing to understand both the *nature* and *dimensions* of the changes that they face. When IT is included in teacher education courses, it is frequently synonymous with word processing, database and e-mail.

The kinds of competencies that are becoming increasingly significant in the context of a 'wired society' are those that accept its presence, and acknowledge that a major revolution in education practice has, or is, occurring. Typically, the kinds of competencies expected of teachers today should therefore include such things as (NBEET, 1995):

- the use of computer-based services to search and find relevant information in a range of contexts for goal-oriented learning tasks.
- the ability to retrieve information using a variety of media.
- the ability to decode information in a variety of forms - written, statistical, graphic.
- the critical evaluation of information, including the use of systems thinking to explore the interconnectedness of different fields of knowledge in a context dependent manner.
- the use of computer-based services to analyse, present and communicate information to create knowledge and insight.
- the use of information technologies to create/use networks of co-learners in the pursuit of knowledge and information sharing.
- the ability to plan and conduct teaching using a variety of telecommunications environments, including virtual and real-time systems.

Sadly, when we compare these with current practice, there is a major discrepancy. Teacher education programs are still grounded in essentially outmoded models of education. Their failure to adapt in a very short time scale will see their demise and the possible death of schools as we currently conceptualise them. We must act now to ensure that this does not mean the rise of *"corporate edutainment"* as its replacement. The impact on society would be profound and extremely difficult to redress, especially in Western societies where economic discourse dominates the political agenda. At risk is the fundamental tradition of a liberal-egalitarian model of education. Its replacement in a globalised economy would surely give the Cyberspace fantasies of William Gibson some sense of imminent reality - one that many of us would not wish to share.

7   REFERENCES

Barlow, A. (1995) Natives and Immigrants to Information Technology in Education. *AP*, July, 34-36.

Bigum, C. and Kenway, J. (1996) New Information technologies and the ambiguous future of schooling - Some possible scenarios, in A. Hargreaves, A. Leiberman, M. Fullan et al (eds.) *International Handbook of Educational Change*. OISE, Toronto, Canada.

Bushfield, W. (1996, Tuesday February 27) Pupils outdo teachers in new skills. *The Herald Sun*, p. 9.

Cornu, B. (1995) New Technologies: Integration into Education, in D. Watson and D. Tinsley (eds.) *IFIP Transactions A: Integrating Information Technology into Education*, **A-34**, 3-11. North-Holland, Amsterdam.

Cuban, L. (1986) *Teachers and Machines: The Classroom use of Technology since 1920.* Teachers College Press, New York.

Duckett, G. et al (1995) Athena University -VOU and GENII: A Model of Conceptual Change and Collaboration, in J. L. Schnase and E. L. Cunnis (eds.) *CSCL'95: Computer support for collaborative work,* p. 94, Bloomington, Indianna.

Kenway, J. (1995) Reality Bytes: Education, Markets and the Information Super-highway. *The Educational Researcher,* 22, 1, 35-65.

Mitchell, T., Paprzycki, M. and Duckett, G. (1994) Computer Literacy: A Global Perspective, in G. H. Marks (ed.) *Mathematics/Science Education and Technology,* pp. 114-117. AACE, Charlottesville, VA.

NBEET (1995) *Converging Technology, Work and Learning.* National Board of Employment, Education and Training, Canberra, Australia.

Negroponte, N. (1995) *Being Digital.* Knopf, New York.

Papert, S. (1987) Computer Criticism vs. Technocentric Thinking. *Educational Researcher,* 16, 1, 22-30.

Papert, S. (1993) *The Children's Machine: Rethinking School in the Age of the Computer.* Basic Books, New York.

Paprzycki, M., Mitchel, T. and Duckett, G. (1994) *Computer Literacy and Competencies: Preparing Teachers for the Information Superhighway.* Paper presented at the Eighth Annual Southeastern Small College Computing Conference, Furman University, Greenville, South Carolina.

Perelman, L. J. (1992) *School's out: hyperlearning, the new technology.* William Morrow, New York.

Riel, M. M. (1990) Co-operative Learning through Telecommunications, in A. McDougall and C. Dowling (eds.) *Computers in Education: Proceedings of the Fifth World Conference on Computers in Education,* pp. 467-474. Elsevier, Amsterdam.

Schwartz, P. (1991) *The Art of the Long View.* Doubleday, New York.

Time Warner (1996) *PALACE Moo Software.* Time Warner, Los Angeles.

Tinkler, D., Lepani, B. and Mitchell, J. (1996). *Education and Technology Convergence: A survey of Technological Infrastructure in Education and Professional Development and Support of Educators and Trainers in Information and Communication Technologies* (Commissioned Report Number 43). Department of Employment, Education and Training, Canberra, Australia.

Toffler, A. (1980) *The Third Wave.* Bantam Books, New York.

8   BIOGRAPHY

Paul Nicholson taught science and computing in secondary schools before moving to the tertiary sector as a lecturer in educational computing. Since 1988 he has co-ordinated postgraduate computer education courses at Deakin University. His Ph.D. studies are in the use of computer probes and simulations as tools for probing cognition in physics. He is the joint chair of the RICE (Research in Computer Education) group at Deakin University. The group, currently actively involved in major national and international research and development projects, also provides consultancy and training programs to industry. A number of current research projects are focused on the impact of converging technologies on educational practice.

42

Learning to teach at a distance: exploring the role of electronic communication

Michelle Selinger
School of Education
The Open University, UK

Abstract

The Open University is now training the third cohort of PGCE students since its inception in 1994. Approximately 1,100 graduates are trained to teach in primary and secondary schools each year on an 18 month part-time distance taught course. In addition to traditional text based materials, video and audio cassettes, students are loaned an Apple computer for the duration of the course complete with Clarisworks, a Stylewriter printer, a modem and the electronic conferencing system, FirstClass. In this paper some of the issues that have emerged to date will be explored in an attempt to illustrate the potential of this form of communication for teacher education both in traditional institutions and in distance education for beginning teachers and teachers in the early years of their career. These include the establishment of the system, the training and workload implications for staff, and the students' perceptions based on questionnaire data gathered to date.

Keywords

Teacher education, communications, distance learning, open learning, teleconferencing

1   THE COURSE STRUCTURE

The computer conference structure in the Open University Postgraduate Certificate of Education (PGCE) course have been set up to mirror the course structure (see Selinger, 1996; Selinger, 1996a; Selinger and Parker, 1996 for more details). This means that students have the opportunity to participate on a voluntary basis in a range of different electronic groups. They are assigned to a tutor group of 15 students according to whether students are following the primary or secondary line of the course. These tutor groups are led by part-time tutors appointed to the Open University by a regional staff tutor in one of twelve Open University regions in England, Ireland and Wales. Each region has its own conference moderated by the staff tutor. There is also a 'lobby' for all students to contribute to discussion of a general nature and then there are subject conferences for each of the secondary subject lines and a primary conference. Primary students are actively encouraged to participate in the subject conference, thereby encouraging primary/secondary liaison (an atypical feature of a PGCE course). Technical queries are kept separate from the academic discussion in the 'ACS helpdesk'. There is also a 'General Chat' facility within the lobby which is for 'coffee time talk' and a group of students run a 'virtual pub' called 'Ye Olde Curiosity Shoppe' within General Chat.

Two questionnaires have been sent to the first cohort of students who finished the course in 1995. One was returned by about 700 students who completed the course and the other, a more detailed questionnaire, was returned by 300 students. A revised questionnaire will be sent to all second cohort students when they finish the course in July 1996. The results from the second cohort are expected to differ as these students have had more access to FirstClass. The differences have become particularly noticeable after 5 months on-line and are discussed later. The first cohort of students came on-line in February 1995, a year after starting the course. This was for a number of technical and administrative reasons. The second cohort came on-line six months into the course and the third cohort come on-line in April, just two months after the course started, and this is expected to become the norm for future presentations of the course.

2   COMMUNICATION PROTOCOLS AND ISSUES

There is no teaching built into the on-line conferences, but students are strongly encouraged to use the system. In the 1996 on-line presentation structure, students have access initially to tutorial and regional conferences in order to establish a pattern whereby the line of communication meets traditional Open University (OU) protocols, i.e. the tutor is the first point of contact. Having a system which permits ease of access to the course team has meant that the students are using the lobby as a forum for asking questions normally asked of tutors. One dilemma has arisen, which is currently in the process of being discussed and resolved; a single question to the meeting room can prevent the same question being asked in every tutorial group. However, if this happens and is responded to quickly, it soon becomes recognised as an efficient method for dealing with the questions, and the lobby becomes clogged up with queries instead of course-wide discussion and support; the purpose for which it was intended. The dilemma can be resolved by setting up separate sub-conferences in the lobby for course-related enquiries, or to delete any such messages and informing the 'offending' students via their private mailbox that the question must be forwarded to their tutor. There are advantages to the former. The course team are able to resolve any problems very quickly by posting a message to all the students and can then make adjustments to course materials for subsequent presentations of the course.

The ability to ask these questions, however, is important. In the evaluation questionnaire, it was very clear that seeking advice and clarifying instructions for things like the assessment portfolio was a very important factor in the students' use of FirstClass. It may also have contributed to their use of the system. Of the 266 students who responded to the more extended questionnaire and had said they had used

FirstClass, 212 had used it 'for seeking information'. The next most utilised function was 'receiving moral support', with 127 students responding positively to that item.

3   SUBJECT CONFERENCES

Students were asked which conference had been the most valuable. Thirty six per cent reported the subject conferences as being the most useful. This was expected, and was one of the main reasons for setting up the FirstClass system. Secondary students only have access to one or two students following the same subject line in their tutor groups, as they are geographically allocated within either the primary or secondary line. These tutor groups meet together on five occasions throughout the course. Tutor groups in any one of the twelve regional areas of the Open University will also come together at Day Schools on another four occasions, with one seminar during the day allocated to subject issues. The FirstClass subject conferences therefore provide wider and greater access to all students following their line, and to the member of the course team and any tutors who are specialists in that area. Comments about the subject conferences were very positive:

"[I was] able to share information with like minded colleagues";

"We considered the practical teaching of maths and ideas for the classroom";

"Sharing school experience - good to see other students having similar difficulties and for sharing ideas";

"It gave me direct contact with the subject specialist on the course".

4   BULLETIN BOARDS

The bulletin boards, where messages from the course team are posted, and to which part-time tutors and students had read-only access, provide students with important information, changes and clarification of issues, as well as information about forthcoming events in their region or nationally. They also advise students about recent articles in newspapers or relevant TV and radio programmes. There are several bulletin boards: one general; one for each region; one for the primary conference; and one for each of the subject conferences. Many students reported only logging in to get information from the bulletin boards especially when they were in a hurry.

5   STUDENTS' USE OF FIRST CLASS

As stated earlier, the first cohort of students came on-line late in the course, therefore they did not all make full use of the system. Many reported this in their questionnaire responses. FirstClass was introduced almost a year after students had started their course. This was at a time when the last tutor-marked assignments were being written and the final school experience was nearing, so students were feeling very much under pressure. Another 'chore' was not welcomed by many. The reasons given for not making much use of the system were varied. Many gave lack of time (38 students) for the reasons given above, but others ranged from lack of confidence in the value of their contribution, to their lack of skill in using FirstClass or the computer.

"I only posted one message - I felt nervous about the system having never communicated in writing `electronically' before";

"I lacked confidence in writing messages. I felt I had nothing to say";

"I never felt the need to";

"Lack of time. Feeling uncomfortable with computer apart from word processing".

The second cohort started to use FirstClass well before the second school experience and the use of it actually increased as school experience came round. The subject conferences became places to share resources and ideas while the lobby was to offer and gain moral support. This was also true of those in the first cohort of students who used the system. This is just one example:

"Thanks S for the brilliant idea for difficult classes. I tried your method almost verbatim on a horrendously "challenging" class. Only year 8, but all SEN pupils! Double period last thing Monday PM. Followed your system/gave them some "copying out" to do while I went round and assessed them for work which I thought would catch their (limited) imagination. I was delighted at the end of 100 minutes to feel a certain satisfaction. I recommend your tactics to others."

As the students go into their final school experience (referred to in the following messages as SE3), the lobby has been full of postings offering support and sharing concerns:

"I'm experiencing feelings of real terror. SE3 begins tomorrow. It's now a case of fight or flight. I don't fancy fisty-cuffs, so I might instead do a runner! This is crazy. I'm all grown up now! I should be able to handle this. I guess I'm afraid of failure......
Thanks for playing psychoanalyst, Lobby."

"I would just like to thank contributors to 'lobby' for the support that they provide. When I feel really low I read some of the messages and they always manage to cheer me up. It's reassuring to know that there are others who are going through exactly the same emotions. I know one thing, and that is, you're all special people and that's why you're doing what you're doing. Keep fighting and well done so far. I'm starting SE3 tomorrow as well and I'll go ahead knowing that I'm in good company!"

6   ISSUES IN THE COURSE TEAM

The course team, comprising of the PGCE director, 2 deputy directors, the subject and primary specialists and the regional staff tutors, also uses FirstClass to communicate.

This has been particularly beneficial since regional staff tutors are located throughout the UK, therefore face-to-face meetings are expensive both in terms of time and cost, and there are a number of working groups to which they belong which have been set up to support and develop various parts of the programme. The structure of FirstClass enables separate conference areas to be set up, allowing members of each group to discuss issues between meetings, to set up agendas, to prepare joint working papers and to develop ideas. The general on-line area for the course team allows them to explore a range of issues, and there has been much wider opportunity to discuss and debate changes in policy before final decisions are made at course team meetings. The outcomes of use of FirstClass itself have been discussed by the course team. The regional staff tutors find the system valuable, in that contact can be easily made with students and tutors in their region, but they are unsure of how the protocols discussed earlier in this paper should be maintained. It has also increased their workload considerably, as one staff tutor pointed out. The process initiated a discussion that went on for several days, causing many to share their concerns about FirstClass as well as the benefits:

"At the moment I have this love/hate relationship with First Class as well! I love being able to get in touch with you all at the press of a button and feel secure in the fact that people in this conference know me to a greater or lesser degree and know my personality. As a result, consciously or sub-consciously, people will use that information in interpreting what I write.

On the other hand, turning on the machine and seeing a morass of red flags I find extremely stressful. I have to select what I am going to read, otherwise I will be here all night, but so many of those red flags are still there! I begin to feel inadequate! Is everybody else on the team reading all of this?

People can increase my work load at the press of a button and there are subtle in-built assumptions about the speed of reply. More stress!! My workload is increased as students can now reach me direct with the smallest of problems, by-passing their tutors and then feeling aggrieved if I re-direct them back to the tutor. Do I need this aggro and TIAS [Teaching in a second school] problems as well? No!

Although as many of you will know I am not a whiz kid on the computer, I have had a fair amount of experience as an advisory teacher of helping staff and pupils to get e-mail projects between schools and between different countries going. My learning curve is still going on. In terms of First Class, I may not always contribute to the conference, but I do get a lot out of reading the e-mail and will contribute when I have something to say. If I feel like this, I wonder how our less confident students feel!

While I agree that we need to encourage students to contribute, I don't think we should interpret the fact that reading rather than writing e-mails is somehow unsuccessful."

7   TUTOR TRAINING

Certainly the training issue for tutors and students has been reconsidered from time to time, as the benefits of electronic communication are accepted and considered to outweigh the problems. It is now deemed essential that tutors are sufficiently IT confident to use FirstClass, to support their students in coming on-line, and that any new staff members are fully trained through face-to-face, hands-on sessions. The student and tutor handbooks have been updated to offer more support, in an attempt to encourage students to make full use of the system, and tutors are given ideas about how they might encourage students to use the system. The acceptability of FirstClass by the course team, tutors and students alike has increased through usage. As one tutor reported:

"As a tutor I have been able to follow the fortunes of some of my past students, see how they're developing and generally have access to something that has never been available to me before. I think FirstClass should be extended to most if not all OU courses."

8   ALUMNI

What is referred to above is the alumni conference which has been set up for any student who has completed the course and has access to a modem and computer. Many of the students who have stayed on-line have purchased computers from their partner school if they did not want Apple machines. About 100 alumni initially expressed an interest in staying on-line, and a number of others have made contact in the past few months to inform us that they now have a computer and modem and want to join the alumni. Members of this conference were asked what they thought of FirstClass:

"I would say that using FirstClass as an alumni has been like an extension of the PGCE course. There is a constant supply of help and ideas as well as an exchange of views about every issue that faces any teacher not just students and newly qualified teachers. Most of my colleagues at school are only available to me for short times during the day, at lunch or break when they are not involved with other things; so learning from their experience is quite difficult as few have the time to spare and others have no inclination to let others benefit from their experience."

"I only have to log on and I can benefit from the best practice that is taking place in many schools and educational establishments around the country, not just my own; I can gain motivation and insight that other teachers cannot get."

Those who have accessed the system and utilised it fully are aware of the potential to communicate with other teachers and colleagues in the field of education. However, the benefits are not immediately apparent. All the partner schools from the first cohort of PGCE students were contacted and asked if they would like to be part of the alumni conferences. Only 100 schools responded positively, despite the fact they had access to a dedicated computer and modem which they gained as a result of having a student from the Open University. The service has been offered at no cost apart from telephone charges which are mostly at local call rate, yet still less than 50 teachers from these schools are active participants in FirstClass, let alone active contributors (a participant here is defined as someone who reads and/or contributes to messages).

9   SUMMARY

The use of FirstClass has enabled students working at a distance to feel part of a community of Open University students. The debate and discussion that the system has allowed has meant that students have been able to share and express their fears and anxieties as well as their ideas and successes with a large community of others. The openness of this expression has been surprising and has been a factor in the success of the system.

Issues of training and support for staff use are being addressed, and the use of FirstClass is gradually being accepted as part of the normal workload. As more alumni come on-line each year, a growing community of teachers in schools all over the country will be able to communicate about their work, share ideas and resources, support each other through the traumatic early years of their careers, and become a new generation of teachers for whom computer mediated communications will become an expectation and a norm.

There is still much to be found about the ways in which teachers perceive the value of electronic networking. It is clear from the small survey reported here, that it is seen as a possibility by a very few. For others the costs and time are prohibitive when so many other factors challenge their daily routines and pressures. More detailed evaluation and follow-up interviews with cohort 2 students should provide more pieces of the jigsaw. This will enable the electronic community of teachers that could support and encourage long term professional development, from initial teacher education to continuing professional development, to be firmly established as a natural part of teachers' practice.

10   REFERENCES

Selinger, M. (1996) The role of electronic communication in supporting beginning teachers, in *Proceedings of ED-MEDIA/ED-TELECOM 96,* Boston, MA, June 17-22.

Selinger, M. (1996a) Beginning teachers using IT: The Open University model. *Journal for Information Technology in Teacher Education,* April 1996.

Selinger, M. and Parker, B. (1996) Supporting teacher education through distance learning and electronic communications, in *Proceedings of SITE 96 Conference,* Phoenix, Arizona, March 1996.

11   BIOGRAPHY

Michelle Selinger is a lecturer in education at the Open University in the Centre of Research in Teacher Education. She writes distance learning material in the areas of IT across the curriculum and in mathematics education in pre-service teacher education and at masters level. She is a consultant to the UK National Council for Educational Technology. Her research focus is in the use of computer mediated communication as a medium for fostering a critical community of teachers.

43

Research on telematics for teacher education

Antonio J. Osorio
University of Exeter, UK and University of Minho, Portugal
School of Education, Heavitree Road, Exeter, EX1 2LU, UK

Abstract

This paper draws on research being conducted, to find out how telematics, as an educational tool or resource, can be used to enhance the professional development of teachers. After a short literature review, the role of telematics in the context of a teacher education course is analysed. Qualitative data supports illustrations of the value of various types of telematics applications and, finally, a conclusion is presented.

Keywords

Professional development, teacher education, case studies, electronic mail (E-mail), flexible learning, teleconferencing

1   INTRODUCTION

Telematics, and the perspective of the availability of the Information SuperHighways to schools and the educational community generally, are currently under active discussion, raising exciting debates in a number of areas. In the changing times that society and education are experiencing, it raises important questions relating to education and, in particular, to teacher education.

Telematics is a hybrid word increasingly being used to describe the combined use of telecommunications and information technology. Terminology such as electronic communications, or communication and information technology are also often used, as is the word telecommunications. However, the important things to stress are the possibility of communication provision, disregarding location or distance, that such technology offers, with the possibility of a range of data exchange: text, sound, image, video. Telematics applications and services are one more in a series of challenges for teachers, which could provide a valuable opportunity to study how teacher education and teacher educators can promote teachers' continuous professional development. This is the background to the research described, to identify how telematics, as an educational tool or resource, can be used to enhance the professional development of teachers.

The research project described consists of a multiple case study of telematics usage by student teachers in the University of Exeter (UK) and by in-service teachers in Portugal. The study uses various methods of data collection including short questionnaires, interviews, electronic mail (e-mail) and computer conferencing messages, observation of on-line and face-to-face activities, and field notes. Data were analysed using a qualitative approach.

The paper focuses on the Exeter case study, using telematics in initial teacher education by student teachers and tutors involved in a postgraduate certificate in education (PGCE) course. It starts with a short literature review and an overview of the teacher education model of the University of Exeter, which uses a "deliberate approach to learning to teach" (see Harvard, 1994; Jennings, 1994). An analysis of the role of telematics in supporting the development of learning how to teach follows and, subsequently, different types of telematic services and their usefulness for teacher education are illustrated.

2   TELEMATICS: A NEW CHALLENGE FOR TEACHERS

Telematics were already present in our lives in a number of daily routines, but until very recently schools using telematics applications and services were the exception rather than the rule. However, children and students are increasingly using networking, if not at school, at home and in their leisure time. Comparing the 'explosion that was the Internet' with the Klondyke gold rush 100 years ago, Heppell (1996) predicts that 'by the end of 1996 a substantial number of students will be connected' to the Internet in one way or another.

This state of affairs suggests that past calls for a new type of teacher (Gwyn, 1988) are still pertinent. It also implies the need to address issues arising regarding the changing role of the teacher and the need to research and to develop the introduction of communication and information technologies for initial and in-service teacher education.

Research conducted to study the use of telematics for teacher education highlight the potential of the technology and very often raise various issues for further research and development. For example, the following two cases involved student teachers in experiences with the use of telematics applications.

The virtual case competition was piloted by the University of Virginia in the spring of 1994 and included two other American Universities, one Canadian and also a British team from Exeter. Each team had to study a case posted to a mailing list as described by Kent, Herbert and McNergney (1995) who stressed the 'value of technology to those who would educate teachers using case methods.' With the virtual case competition they discovered that 'it might be possible to use telecommunications to stretch far beyond what is possible to do in live settings.'

History student teachers at the University of Ulster (Austin, 1995) used e-mail to develop European awareness as they were given 'an immediate point of comparison in the ways that their own subject was being taught in other countries.' In addition, the student teachers had an opportunity to deal with the 'kind of controversial issues they could expect to come across in the classroom on teaching practice' because the activity they were involved in was an exchange with 16 year old Norwegian high school pupils. Roger Austin also highlights the importance of giving student teachers the opportunity to develop their technical skills. In this case, being able to use electronic mail enabled the student teachers not only to tackle IT 'as one of the cross-curricular themes but also [to employ it] as a practical tool for joint work within a wider Europe.'

Current telematics applications and continuous technological developments such as the future Information SuperHighway offer teacher education an interesting challenge that all involved will have to respond to.

3 THE ROLE OF TELEMATICS IN SUPPORTING LEARNING HOW TO TEACH

After a brief review of various experiences with telematics for teacher education, let us consider what telematics can offer both student teachers and teacher educators. In the University of Exeter context, where, according to recent government guidelines, teacher education has a greater proportion of school-based work, there are four areas where telematics applications can be used, as follows.

3.1 Supporting communication among people

There are a number of communication channels and communication needs among the variety of people involved in a teacher education program. The following list is not exhaustive; it is only an indication of the kind of possible interaction, where telematics applications can play an important role:

- social interaction between students.
- co-ordination interaction among university staff (academics, administrative, technical).
- dissemination of information about a calendar or program of events, i.e. dates and locations of seminar days.
- dissemination of information about Guild of Students' issues.
- co-ordination of dates between tutors and students.
- dissemination of general information.
- co-ordination of interaction between university tutors and school subject and co-tutors.
- sharing of experiences, concerns, anxieties, findings.
- management of library loans and reservations.
- support to the mentor training scheme.
- availability of relevant teaching resources.
- provision of non-confidential information about people.

3.2 Providing access to information resources

For their assessment, University of Exeter PGCE students have to complete nine assessment assignments, which means approximately 18,500 words or equivalent.

Easy remote access to information resources either from the library or from elsewhere through CD-ROM, on-line databases, gopher, ftp or WWW is important.

3.3 Supporting teaching and learning activities

Telematics can provide support for new, flexible, on-line teaching and learning teacher education activities, both during the university-based and school-based work. Examples are:

- face-to-face seminars with on-line 'hands-on' activities.
- on-line seminars, for example, an on-line moderated discussion about special education needs.
- preparation of university assignments, for example, tutor sending comments on a draft version of an assignment.
- organisation of supervisory conferences, for example, sending a file with an agenda of an episode of teaching to a tutor, prior to a supervisory conference.
- asynchronous supervisory conferences.
- synchronous supervisory conferences, for example, discussing a video footage of an episode of teaching over a video conferencing session.

3.4 Providing new teaching methods and resources

Telematics services also provide new teaching resources and simultaneously bring about the need for adaptation in the way teaching is performed and for which student teachers have to be prepared these days. A very short illustration of some new interesting educational activities includes:

- e-mail among different denominational schools, for example, the 'Education for Mutual Understanding' program in Northern Ireland (Cunningham, 1992).
- 'pen pal' exchanges, for example, the 'Logo Pen Pal' conference where students shared Logo programs instead of letters (Mageau, 1990).
- newspaper days, for example, the periodic event on UK Campus 2000.
- electronic data collection and transmission, for example, the 'Globe' international partnership for global learning and observations to benefit the environment.

4   TYPES OF TELEMATICS SERVICES FOR TEACHER EDUCATION

There are various ways of classifying the types of existing telematics services. Services available at the University of Exeter can be organised into four groups. In this section, brief illustrations are given showing how electronic communications have been used to support teaching and learning in initial teacher education.

4.1 Electronic mail for individual communication

For a senior member of staff at the university 'the advantage of e-mail is that [students] can communicate with anyone [and] we encourage them to communicate with each other, we encourage them to communicate for social purposes.' Other purposes for the use of e-mail were also identified by an administrative member of staff who explained how e-mail could be used for delivery of information amongst the various people participating in the teacher education courses: 'information about school placements, course material, careers questionnaire, you know, all sorts of things...'.

Either to contribute to the development of a social dimension or to serve as a means of information delivery, the use of e-mail was not widespread amongst the students, and particularly not when they were in their placement schools. However, evidence collected shows that e-mail was used and has potential for communication exchange in a teacher education context for:

- communication between students (within the university and with colleagues and friends elsewhere).
- communication between tutor and student (for various sorts of purposes, including request-provision of information, assignment supervision, advice and development of 'practical argument').
- communication among tutors (either those at the university or the school tutors, for information sharing and co-ordination messages).

4.2 Computer conferencing for group communication

Computer conferencing has been used in teacher education at the University of Exeter for some time and has employed Exeter local news groups, which provided the 'forum' for new activities and the opportunity to:

- learn about IT and telematics 'skills', such as the use of e-mail and computer conferencing, modem installation and dial up connections.
- discuss the future evolution of IT in schools.
- discuss, meaningfully and in context, educational change issues.

The analysis of posted messages reveals that most of the on-line discussion took place during face-to-face sessions. This fact indicates to some extent inexperienced use of electronic communications, which is understandable amongst beginners. Despite some difficulties such as weak preparation of less technically skilled students, one tutor pointed out: 'If that relies on teachers having imagination to understand the technology enough to develop [it], then I would see it as being vital in terms of where teaching is going, in the next ten years or so.'

4.3 Electronic resourcing

With student teachers spending more time in schools, there are considerable changes in their means of access to bibliographic and educational resources, very often due to distance reasons.

Research conducted among University of Exeter PGCE students, to look at the 'possibilities afforded by the electronic library' (Myhill and Jennings, in press) developed the idea of 'resourcing distance learning in combination with other features such as postal loans'. The importance of resource provision from schools is highlighted as are the resources offered by the university library. In addition, the feasibility of electronic access to information services is established.

This possibility is important because the new information age is increasingly making available educational resources for a wide range of areas. These resources are pursued by student teachers: a technician described PGCE students' queries in an IT room as 'a large majority of it was to do with the teaching, [they] wanted to find out information [using the web] for their teaching. Possibly using it as a resource to prepare their lessons... Possibly as well as books...'.

4.4 Computer desktop and video conferencing

The use of computer desktop conferencing for initial teacher education at the University of Exeter followed various stages, as follows.

Small group teaching practice through desktop conferencing
Student teachers used desktop conferencing (DTC) for a teaching session with a small group of 4 pupils. The student teachers were using a workstation at the university and the children were in their school. The exercise was part of initial experiences to research the educational potential of electronic communications using ISDN. For an introduction to the facilities offered by the DTC software, student teachers used an 'ice breaker' activity where the completion of riddles by the students at the school would allow both the establishment of a working (teaching and learning) relationship and the adaptation to the features of the software (Davis, 1994), prior to mathematics teaching practice.

School-based teacher education through desktop conferencing
After the previous experiences showing the educational potential of DTC for teacher education, the system was used to support school-based teacher education. At an early stage the training of the university tutors and the students on how to use the system was conducted at the university. Subsequently, when the students were already in their school placements, the system was used both for assignment supervision and for supervisory conferences. A tutor describes the use of such technology as 'a much more formal occasion' by comparison with the use of e-mail. She thought that the asynchronous nature of the communication, requiring the 'set up [of] a time and a place and the student to be there' meant that the occasion was 'a very professional time.' She added that the student 'had to do a lot of thinking to prepare for it and therefore the quality of the dialogue during that time was at a much higher level than sometimes when I just go and visit the school.'

School-based teacher education through video conferencing
With developments in the transmission of video over ISDN, the DTC software was enhanced with the video conferencing facility and new experiences were planned to make use of them to support school-based teacher education. Again, there was a period of adaptation for tutors and students to the video conferencing systems. This took place in term 1 of the academic year (95/96) and was followed by supervisory video conferences, where tutors at the university discussed students' agendas, describing episodes of teaching and followed the criteria for argument to promote reflection and, therefore, help students to develop their professional skills/capabilities.

5 CONCLUSION

This paper considers a range of telematics applications that can be used in a range of ways and in a range of roles to support teacher education. Telematics applications provide excellent potential for a more flexible teaching and learning approach, which is increasingly being required of teacher education institutions. Such a potential is strengthened by the availability of different applications, from text communication through e-mail, to multimedia communications via, for example, computer videoconferencing.

To transfer the potential into practice, however, is not a straightforward task, and raises issues that need detailed and further thorough analysis. Simultaneously, it seems important that the teacher education community develops its awareness of the possibilities offered by these technological developments, in order to be able to participate actively in the process, comprehensively, of making the necessary adaptations in the technology and in the design and performance of teaching and learning.

6 REFERENCES

Austin, R. (1995) Using Electronic Mail in Initial Teacher Education to Develop European Awareness. *Journal of Information Technology for Teacher Education*, **4**, 2, 227-35.

Cunningham, J.B. (1992) Electronic Mail in the Context of Education for Mutual Understanding (E.M.U.). *Computer Education*, **February**, 5-7.

Davis, N.E. (1994) ISDN technology in teaching, in R. Mason and P. Bacsich (eds.) *ISDN applications in education and training*. Institute of Electrical Engineers, Stevenage.

Gwyn, R.(1988) Teacher Education and Change: The First Decade of IT. *European Journal of Teacher Education*, **11**, 2-3, 195-205.

Harvard, G.R. (1994) An Integrated Model of How Student Teachers Learn How to Teach, and its Implications for Mentors, in G. Harvard and P. Hodkinson (eds.) *Action and Reflection in Teacher Education*. Ablex Publishing, Norwood, NJ.

Heppell, S. (1996) Strategy in a world on the move. *Times Educational Supplement*, 5.1.96.

Jennings, S. (ed.) (1994) *Cognitive Apprenticeship in Teacher Education*. University of Exeter School of Education, Exeter.

Kent, T.W., Herbert, J.M. and McNergney, R.F. (1995) Telecommunications in Teacher Education: reflections on the first Virtual Team Case Competition. *Journal of Information Technology for Teacher Education*, **4**, 2, 137-48.

Mageau, T. (1990) Telecommunications in the Classroom: four Teachers' Stories. *Teaching and Computers*, **May/June**, 18-24.

Myhill, M. and Jennings, S. (in press) The electronic Library and Distance Resourcing: the Exeter Experience. *Program*.

7 BIOGRAPHY

Antonio Osorio is an IT in Education lecturer in a Portuguese University. Currently he is conducting research for a PhD in the field of Educational Telematics at the University of Exeter School of Education, UK. He is being funded by the Calouste Gulbenkian Foundation Lisbon.

44

What expertise do teachers require to facilitate pupils' self-expression with multimedia?

Hiroyuki Tanaka
Faculty of Education, Osaka Kyoiku University,
4-698-1, Asahigaoka, Kashiwara, Osaka, 582, Japan

Abstract

This paper describes the expertise that teachers need to acquire in order to facilitate pupils' work with multimedia. The central idea behind the argument is that multimedia is a creative tool for children, and that multimedia learning in the near future is expected to be "Learning by Producing". In such a context of creative learning, pupils need to be recognised as multimedia producers, and in order to achieve this situation teachers need to know how to become learning supporters, curriculum developers and multimedia co-ordinators, not just instructors. The necessity for teachers to know the typology of multimedia expression, the features of multimedia expression and programme evaluation is also discussed with some suggestions.

Keywords

Elementary education, teacher education, collaborative learning, curriculum development, multimedia

1   MULTIMEDIA PRODUCTION BY CHILDREN

Before addressing the aspects of expertise that teachers need to acquire in order to facilitate pupils' multimedia expression, it is very important to describe new possibilities for children's learning - that is - children as multimedia producers, and also what literacy they are expected to obtain in the process of producing multimedia products.

Children as multimedia producers

In Information Technology (IT) education there has been a slow but steady shift from computer assisted instruction (CAI) to multimedia assisted communication and production (MACP) (Jacobs, 1992; Tanaka, 1995). Multimedia is becoming not only a teachers' instructional tool but also a creative tool for children. With the help of many user-friendly software packages children are now using multimedia to express their ideas and the information they obtain during their studies. Thus it has become possible for children to experience the role of multimedia producers (Turner and Dipinto, 1992; Kenneth et al, 1994; Tanaka, 1995).

In addition, the collaboration between children is very important because multimedia production requires students to take diverse roles, for example, a writer, a painter, a video editor, an audio mixer, computer programmer and so on (McMahon, 1990; Crook, 1994). For these reasons teachers need to acquire expertise which is different from traditional methodologies of instruction.

Multi-mode expression

Multi-mode expression is a comprehensive way of self-expression which integrates sound, pictures, video and text. A good example of this is a musical. A musical incorporates music, singing, choreography, dancing, scenario, stage lighting, stage set, and so on. Thus it can be said that multi-mode expression as actualised in a musical or a drama has much similarity with multimedia expression (Trowsdale, 1995). When multi-mode expression is created with multimedia, it results in multimedia products in the form of an electric slide show or an animation.

Multimedia literacy

The list below offers a tentative set of multimedia literacy items. These ten literacy items (Tanaka, 1995) can also become educational objectives in instructional planning. Those involved need to:

1. understand the characteristics of multimedia, the various modes of information and their combination patterns.
2. have a basic command of multimedia.
3. select appropriate media and to collect various pieces of information and find the relations between this information using those media.
4. operate data input and information retrieval with a variety of computer peripherals.
5. acquire learning methods and computer literacy through simulated experiences with Hypermedia.
6. give a multimedia presentation making good use of the features of each medium.
7. convey multimedia products made with various computer peripherals to others by computer telecommunication.
8. produce a handmade TV program using a video camera, a video editing system, a sound effecter, a sound mixer, a multimedia computer, and so on.
9. make presentation materials with an interactive video system or Hypermedia.
10. create multimedia products which integrate knowledge, images and emotions.

2   CROSS-CURRICULAR MODEL OF MULTIMEDIA LEARNING

In most in-service training courses for IT use offered by local boards of education, the main topics would tend to focus technological aspects of IT education more than pedagogical considerations for it. However, considering that IT co-ordinators are now being recruited in several technologically advanced countries like the United States, the United Kingdom and Japan, the classroom teachers' role could be changed from that of a technician to that of a pedagogical facilitator in the process of developing the IT curriculum and learning projects (North, 1991; Owston, 1995).

2.1 Isomorphic structure and cross-curricular model

Anderson (1991) pointed out the importance of IT education as a cross-curricular element in terms of the availability of IT to all pupils and the possibility of improving the quality of learning through enhancing common information skills. Fox (1996) discussed some effective ways to incorporate media education (one form of IT education) as a cross-curricular catalyst into the school curriculum.

However there has been little literature so far which has discussed the potential similarity between multimedia learning and cross-curricular activities. In figure 1 such a similarity between the two is illustrated.

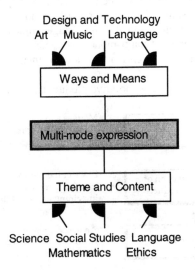

Figure 1 Cross-curricular model for multi-mode expression (Tanaka, 1995)

Educational multi-mode expression is a common activity to both multimedia learning and cross-curricular activities, because multi-mode expression needs both content for inclusion and the means with which to produce outcomes. Such a combination of content and means of multi-mode expression is a typical feature of cross-curricular activities. Thus, when pupils produce multimedia materials, a cross-curricular learning context could help to provide pupils with both of these aspects of expression which are integral elements of multimedia production.

Such a cross-curricular model illustrating the isomorphic structure of multi-mode expression would also be useful to teachers when they were developing an integrated learning unit for pupils' multimedia production through a combination of aspects from different subjects.

2.2 Learning unit model

In order to consider the quality of learning activities and multimedia products, a guideline offering a sequence of productive activities is necessary. After examining the learning unit models adopted in two classroom implementations (Tanaka, 1995), several common features (listed below) were found, and a cross-curricular unit model was constructed according to these features.

1. The model includes a comprehensive sequence of activities, i.e. an appreciation of various multimedia products, image construction of multimedia products, image enrichment by analysis of previous products and research outcomes, creation of scenario and design blueprint, production of parts, assembly of parts and a final stage, i.e. presentation, performance and appreciation.
2. At the fifth stage, 'Production of parts', various expression modes, for example, sounds, pictures, stories are integrated to produce moving images.
3. The first activity stage, 'Appreciation of various multimedia products', stimulates students' interest and the third stage, 'Image enrichment', provides them with good examples of multi-mode expression.
4. The third stage is inserted to enrich the motif or theme with empirical data for students.
5. This model accommodates collaborative production and role assignment.

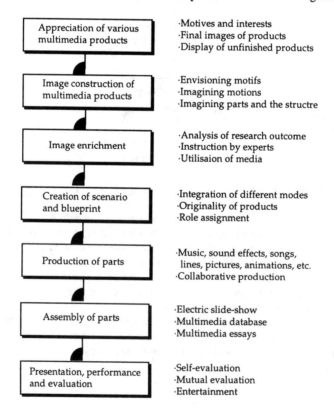

Figure 2 Learning unit model for multi-mode expression (Tanaka, 1995)
Naturally the model is based on the idea of combining the investigation phase (which supports the contents of expression) and also the production phase (which supports the means of expression). This idea of combination was discussed by Innocenti and Ferraris (1988), who made a combination model of the instructional use of a database by showing the necessary linkage between the database creation phase and the investigation phase.

2.3 Typical multimedia learning projects

The provision of pedagogical ideas about typical multimedia projects would make it easier for class teachers to acquire expertise in developing an integrated learning unit with cross-curricular activities for multimedia expression. Here are some examples of project ideas which could function as scaffolding for effective curriculum development.

Let us produce a CD-ROM encyclopaedia
This project could include both investigation about the topics which pupils have in mind and multimedia expression with CD-ROM facilities. These topics might be related to one or several subjects like language, social studies, science, music and art. Pupils' multimedia production would result in a variety of multimedia CD-ROM titles like a multimedia slide-show, a home town database, a botanical database and a computer art gallery respectively.

Let us open our children's TV station
When children select a drama program as a production task, the combination of a language class (in charge of producing scenario), a social studies class (ethics and related laws of broadcasting) and an art and design class (multimedia production) would be very useful. In contrast when they select a news program, the integration could be between language, social studies, art and design, science, etc.

Let us produce an Internet newspaper on the WWW
A tremendous amount of information is being exchanged through Internet. It could be possible for pupils to experience cross-curricular activities related to multimedia newspaper production and to obtain communication skills which could be applied to their future career or everyday community services.

3   FACILITATING ROLES OF TEACHERS

Pedagogical considerations at the level of curriculum development and project construction have been discussed so far. Focusing on these two points specifically from the perspective of teachers' roles will be important when clarifying what expertise teachers require. Multimedia is not only a teacher's tool for efficient instruction, but also a learner's tool for creative learning. It is important for teachers to note that their role is no longer that of an instructor but more that of a supporter for learners. In terms of curriculum development, some teachers in practice might think that it would be a good idea to wait for new curriculum resources to be developed by researchers and publishers. But what is more valuable for the professional development of teachers is that teachers experience a workshop to develop curriculum aspects themselves. The role of a curriculum developer facilitating pupils' multimedia expression should include four aspects:

1. curriculum development for basic training of media literacy.
2. development of a cross-curricular learning unit.
3. emergent curriculum development.
4. specific knowledge about multimedia production, presentation and evaluation.

4   CONCLUSION

The forms of expertise identified above, to be included as a knowledge base in in-service training programmes, is necessary because pedagogical knowledge relating to the educational use of information technology is as necessary as technical knowledge and skills. The subsequent research tasks needed will be to develop effective training methodologies to make this knowledge available for practice. In training workshops it will be important that this knowledge base be utilised with a great deal of flexibility so that teachers can adjust the content to meet the needs of each classroom context. In order to achieve this, a comparative study method using several cases of implementation would be one effective way of identifying and producing possible means of teacher training.

5   REFERENCES

Anderson, J.S.A. (1991) Information technology: a cross-curricular competence for all pupils. *Computers and Education*, **16**, 1, 23-7.

Crook, C. (1994) *Computers and the collaborative experience of learning*. Routledge, London and New York.

Fox, K. (1996) Media education: a rich life in the margins, in R. Webb (ed.) *Cross-curricular primary practice: taking a leadership role*. Falmer Press, London.

Jacobs, G. (1992) Hypermedia and discovery-based learning: a historical perspective. *British Journal of Educational Technology*, **23**, 2, 113-21.

Innocenti, R.D. and Ferraris, M. (1988) Database as a tool for promoting research activities in the classroom: an example in teaching humanities. *Computers and Education*, **12**, 1, 157-62.

McMahon, H. (1990) Collaborating with computers. *Journal of Computer Assisted Learning*, **6**, 149-67.

North, R. (1991) Managing the integration of information technology across the curriculum of the secondary school. *Computers and Education*, **16**, 1, 13-6.

Owston, R.D. (1995) Professional development in transition: a Canadian provincial case study. *Journal of Computer Assisted Learning*, **11**, 13-22.

Tanaka, H. (ed.) (1995) *Multimedia literacy*. Japan Association of Broadcasting Education, Tokyo.

Trowsdale, J. (1995) Exploring the drama and media relationship. *Drama*, **4**, 1, 8-14.

Turner, S.V. and Dipinto, V.M. (1992) Students as Hypermedia authors: Themes emerging from a qualitative study. *Journal of Computing in Education*, **25**, 2, 187-99.

6   BIOGRAPHY

Hiroyati Tanaka is Assistant Professor in the department of Educational Methodology at Osaka Kyoiku University. His teaching responsibilities include educational methodologies across the curriculum and information technology education in the undergraduate and postgraduate courses. His research interests include children's use of multimedia in cross-curricular work and curriculum development for integrated learning. He is author of a recent book entitled 'Multimedia Literacy'.

Reports from the Focus Groups

Focus Groups 1 and 2: How should we teach teachers to change?

Focus Group 1 Participants: Michael O'Duill (UK), Peter Hubwieser (G), Qi Chen (PRC), Herbert Loethe (G), Marta Turcsanyi-Szabo (H), Michal Yerushalmy (IL), Patricia Marzin (FR), Yvonne Buettner (CH), Jean Underwood (UK)
Chair: Brent Robinson (UK) **Rapporteur**: Margaret Cox (UK)
Focus Group 2 Participants: Bruce Rigby (AUS), Raymond Morel (CH), John Oakley (AUS), Phil Nanlohy (AUS), Steffen Friedrich (G), Kay Rye (NZ), Bernard Cornu (FR), David Passig (IL), Ruth Reiz (IL), Andreas Schwill (G), Enrica Lemut (I), Yehuda Huppert (IL), Steve Kennewell (UK), Sindre Rosvik (NOR), Amos Dreyfus (IL), Janet Talmon (IL), Livi Lamir (IL)
Co-chairs: Paul Nicholson (AUS), Michelle Selinger (UK)

Background

This report is the third in a sequence examining the issues influencing the effective use of information technology (IT) in education. The first report (Watson and Tinsley, 1995) examined the issues around the integration of informatics in education. The report from the World Conference on Computers in Education then examined the theoretical basis of IT and effective implementation (Tinsley and van Weert, 1996). This last report continues the theme with a focus on the question "How should we teach teachers to change?" It examines this question from the perspectives of change theory and lessons we have gained from practice.

Introduction

Teachers are expected to change their practice in order to incorporate IT effectively in their teaching and learning. They are expected to be innovative in a system which frequently expects teachers to be resistant to personal or systemic change. Where change is actively promoted, it is expected to take place in an environment which differs vastly from industry and commerce where managers can spend up to 30% of their time in training for technological change within the organisation. Developing support for professional change requires that the external view of education is transformed so that teachers can be regarded as true professionals in the same way as, for example, doctors with an equal expectation of lifelong learning and significant ongoing professional development. The operating theatre of today is very different from that of a century ago. Can we say the same of today's classrooms (Papert, 1993)?

It is important to clarify the systemic imperatives that drive large scale change. For example, what is the rationale for change? Is it focused on the attainment of educational goals or is it driven by economic considerations? Because educational change is affected by the political climate, the goals frequently change, as does the notion of "what is appropriate" at any time. This can be a serious impediment to long term change, or even to ensuring success in the short term. A clear understanding of the nature and purpose of change is essential to breaking the cycle of ignorance

(Underwood, 1996). Teacher education programs need to be based on the mechanisms of change, not just on the educational milestones commonly set by the policy makers or on the perceived immediate needs of teachers.

Change is inhibited because there is no clear conceptual model of the educational benefits of IT. This leads to alternative perspectives, sometimes unrealistic, about classroom practice and appropriate resource levels. There is also a common perception that professional development is not needed because it is assumed that normal classroom pedagogy can be transferred directly to the technological medium. Teacher change is gradual and requires a change of knowledge, teaching strategies and beliefs as well as the acquisition of IT skills (Fullan, 1991).

The Need For Models

To make effective change requires certain knowledge, skills and attitudes to be an effective change agent. Having clear visual and conceptual models can help teachers and others to understand and implement change, and to analyse their changing pedagogy over time. It is important to analyse the entities that change and to identify the intended versus implemented aspects of change. There is a need to link change originating from research with developmental change arising from practice. Research evidence needs to be presented in a forum which is accessible to teachers, and visual models facilitate this. Also, models help in examining innovative processes and experiments already undertaken in pedagogy and outside education. (IT is not a special case.)

Pedagogical and didactic models

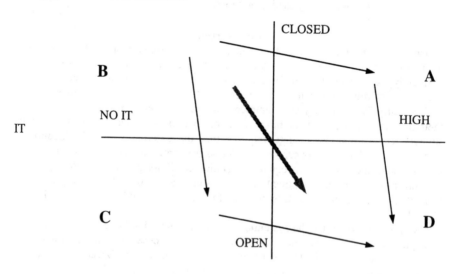

Figure 1 The Oren model - pathways for classroom change with IT

The Oren model in figure 1 indicates pedagogical positions teachers adopt in relation to IT. Some teachers for example might be high IT users and teach in an open-ended way, and would therefore appear in quadrant D. Change is perceived in such a way that teachers at B are often directed towards D, when a move to C or A might be more appropriate. The possible moves are listed in table 1.

Table 1 Transitions in the Oren change model

Change	Meaning
B to D	This is a major shift in two modes at one time. It implies a shift in both pedagogy and in IT usage. It is often too hard to make this concurrent shift in two variables. There are therefore two different pathways in which more gradual change might occur.
B to A	This would represent a IT being used as a tool within a traditional classroom model, for example the use of a graph plotter instead of plotting graphs by hand.
A to D	This represents a change in pedagogy in which classroom activities move into more open ended, problem solving modes and exploration learning instead of completing the traditional classroom exercise
B to C	involves a shift towards problem solving and open ended activities in a traditional classroom.
C to D	involves the uptake of IT to enhance the activities in an open ended classroom.

Note that it is not necessary that Position D always be attained - some teachers can remain in A and be successful teachers using IT.

Conditions for change

The change process is represented by a shift on this map and there are factors which drive this process. But before teachers can move across the map the change process needs a stimulus to occur.

The Oren model in Figure 1 depicts the common expectation that teachers at "B" - traditional classrooms with a conservative curriculum model and no use of IT, are expected to move directly to "D" (the grey arrow), where they are expected to become users of IT in an open-ended curriculum. This requires a change in two dimensions of the model - IT use and pedagogy. This may simply prove too difficult for some to be able to make the change. Perhaps a better way to conceptualise what is expected of teachers is to consider the pathways the model depicts.

For example, some teachers may simply want to make the transition B-A to incorporate IT into their traditional classroom setting, where it acts more as "tool" than a transformative agent. This transition of course is a valid one, and many teachers may wish to stay at that point. Equally, others may follow the transition A-D, where the IT facilitates a change in pedagogy based on pre-existing experience with IT in traditional environments. Similarly the transition B-C-D reflects a situation where a non-IT user adopts a more open curriculum and at some later stage recognises the potential that IT has in developing that type of curriculum to provide new types of learning experiences. The key point of the model is that simultaneous change in too many dimensions may be too hard, and so fail.

A further aspect of the model above is that it could also be used to map the use of IT in a curriculum, with teachers or schools mapping their activities over a year onto the model to see in which areas they fall. This would potentially be a useful tool to help a reflective practitioner to consider their pedagogy.

Educational software embodies a model of learning while other "tool" packages require teachers to impose their own teaching style or model of student learning upon them. To maximise the potential of IT, teachers must look for a match between what IT can do and what they want to happen in educational terms within the classroom. Such an examination might very well prompt teachers to look for new ways of teaching and learning.

The following tools can help teachers and school systems to identify the conditions that need to be changed - exactly what their current practice is, what factors affect it, and what the change means in regard to those items.

The Kiryat model (Figure 2) is a mapping of time, place, group size as they relate to classroom practice. This three-dimensional model can help teachers to conceive of where their practice is located, and what things might be changed to move to a new place in the model. Like the Oren model, this could also be used as the basis of a chronological mapping of practice, so that the diversity of teaching models could be tracked over time.

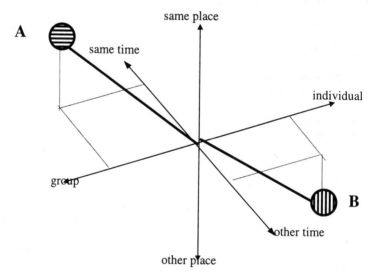

Figure 2 The Kiryat pedagogical model

In this model, various kinds of educational settings are depicted. For example, the circle "A" in figure 1 represents a traditional classroom - all students together in the same place at the same time. Circle "B" represents a "distance-education" student - somewhere else, learning alone, at some other time. In the design of this model, it was assumed that mapping educational goals onto this pedagogical model would lead to further insights into the curriculum and delivery processes being examined as part of planned change processes.

In addition, there was seen to be a need to fully understand the responsibilities of the stakeholders in the change process corresponding to educational principle components - exactly who was going to do what, and why? The sample Anavim grid (Table 2) is an example of the type of analysis that is seen to be an essential component of analysing change processes. The grid's headings are to be altered by each user to suit their needs and are not meant to be definitive. The crosses indicate who assumes responsibility for the elements of change in the left hand column.

Domains	Student	Parent	Teacher	Principal	IT Person	Board	Authority
LEARNING							
-Basic skills							
-Learning Styles	X		X	X		X	
TEACHING							
-Professional development			X	X			
-Curriculum development			X	X		X	X
-Program development			X	X		X	X
-Materials development			X				
IT							
resources	X	X			X		X
-networking	X	X	X	X	X	X	X
ORGANISATION							
-funding				X		X	X
-communication			X	X			
EXTERNAL							
-Community expectations		X	X	X	X	X	X
-Employer expectations		X					
-Vocational pre-requisites		X					
-Policy Framework						X	X
-Technological evolution	X	X	X	X	X	X	X

Table 2 A sample Anavim grid for stakeholder analysis

Change Models
Teachers must also have a firm understanding of the nature of change and how to bring it about effectively. Change often arises because the current situation is problematic and uncomfortable. Tension and conflict may already exist. Certainly as change begins, it is likely that these uncomfortable states will occur (Schon, 1971). Teachers must be prepared to accept that change is uncomfortable: it will involve doubt and uncertainty, risk taking and conflict. Teachers and policy makers should understand the distinct phases of structured change. Change should begin with the identification of teacher needs. Teachers might have existing needs which IT can help satisfy. New needs may also be created by external agencies or by the existence of technology itself. The Concerns Based Adoption Model of Change or CBAM (Louacks and Hall, 1977) offers a structured way of conceiving the origins and process of change.

Not all needs can be satisfied with IT. The technology might not be appropriate or the barriers against using it might be too great. Realistic goal setting is therefore required. Problem solving change models help focus on the need to identify realistic and appropriate goals, paying attention also to potential barriers and catalysts of the intended change. Force field analysis techniques can be useful as a way of assessing the strength of opposition and obstructive barriers.

Attention must also be paid to the likely and expected implications and outcomes of innovation (Consequence Projection) and to the strength and desirability of these

(Significance Evaluation). (For further discussion of these techniques see Eraut, 1991). Sometimes, the intended change is just not worth the effort to be expended. A successful change agent is one who also knows when not to attempt change.

The implementation phase requires a sound perception of who and what will be required to effect the change and where and when the intended actions will take place. While the end result of educational change must ultimately be new behaviour in the classroom, in order to get there teachers will require changes in their knowledge, skills and attitudes. The work of Joyce and Showers (1980), among others, offers a useful taxonomy of the types of support which may be offered to suit the particular demand. Monitoring and evaluation are essential components of any change effort. Goal setting should be accompanied by attention to the way in which the attainment of the goal can be assessed. Performance indicators offer one form of measurement. Observation techniques, surveys and other forms of data collection and analysis can be borrowed from research methodology for the purpose.

Who undertakes the evaluation and for what purpose are other important questions to consider. (For further discussion of this subject see the report of Focus Group 3 which follows.) The evaluation process should be seen as a start as well as a conclusion to any change effort. Change should be a continuous cycle of improvement built upon the ability to be a reflective practitioner. Action research offers a good model of the iterative process involved (see Elliott, 1981).

Change requires recognition of the fact that it cannot take place in isolation and requires co-operation and collaboration with others. Other individuals, institutions and whole systems need to change if individuals are to change. Individuals therefore need to be effective organisational change agents too.

References

Elliott, J. (1981) *Action-Research: a framework for self-evaluation in schools.* Cambridge University Press, Cambridge.

Eraut, M., Pearce, J., Stanley, A. and Steadman, S. (1991) *Whole School IT Development.* Kent IT in Schools Support Team, Sittingbourne.

Fullan, M. (1991) *The New Meaning of Educational Change.* Teachers College Press, New York.

Hall, G. and Louacks, S. (1977) Assessing and facilitating the implementation of innovations: a new approach. *Educational technology*, **17**, 2, 18-21.

Joyce, B.R. and Showers, B. (1980) Improving inservice training: the messages of research. *Educational Leadership*, Feb, 379-85 .

Papert, S. (1996) *The Childrens' Machine.* Basic Books, New York.

Schon, D. (1971) *Beyond the stable state.* Norton, New York.

Tinsley, D. and van Weert, T. (eds.) (1996) *IFIP: Window to the Future; IFIP World Conference Computers in Education VI, WCCE 95 Post Conference Report.* Aston University, Birmingham.

Underwood, J. (1996) Focus Group DG04 Report, in B. Samways and T. van Weert (eds.) op cit.

Watson, D. and Tinsley, D. (eds.) (1995) *Integrating Information Technology in Education.* Chapman and Hall, London.

Focus Group 3: Evaluation in technology-equipped settings

Participants: Lisbeth Appelberg (SW), Doug Brown (UK), Eric Bruillard (FR), Rachel Cohen (FR), Ard Hartsuijker (NE), Joyce Currie Little (USA), Anne McDougall (AUS), Gail Marshall (USA) Zemira Mevarech (IL), Tomas O'Briain (IRE), David Passig (IL), Jim Ridgway, (UK) Bridget Somekh (UK), Hiroyuki Tanaka (JA), Harriet Taylor (USA), Deryn Watson (UK), Menucha Weiss (IL)
Chair: Bridget Somekh
Rapporteur: Gail Marshall

Introduction

Evaluation is a complex and challenging task. In Birmingham, England at the World Conference on Computers in Education '95 the Professional Group studying Evaluation and Assessment of the Use of IT in the Elementary School agreed that "evaluation is a process which uses appropriate methods to consider the process, outcomes, and effects of actions or intentions." It was also agreed that evaluations can be framed in a number of ways including formative, summative, judgmental and non-judgmental.

As it discussed evaluation in schools equipped with technology, the Professional Group also agreed that fundamental differences in epistemologies - constructivism versus behaviourism - lead to different questions being asked, different methods being employed to answer the questions, and different interpretations being applied to the results.

The Birmingham participants also identified factors influencing evaluation and assessment: technology variables (for example, types of hardware and software), school variables (budgets, training patterns, and access, etc.), teacher variables (teachers' capability to implement a technology, teachers' pedagogical and cognitive needs, etc.), and student variables (the cognitive, social, and motivational, etc.). They recommended that each of these factors must be carefully considered when framing evaluations of IT use in school settings.

Since time constraints did not allow the Birmingham Professional Group to examine methods, criteria, indicators, outcomes, and the uses of outcomes, they recommended that further discussion of evaluations in technology-equipped settings was necessary. Thus the work of the Professional Group meeting at the IFIP Joint Working Groups 3.1 and 3.5 held in Israel in June-July, 1996 built on the work of the Birmingham conference and extended the work. However, only four members of the Birmingham Professional Group were members of the Israel group since many of the Birmingham group did not attend the Israel conference. Members of the Israel group represented a cross-section of professional roles, working at many levels of education, from pre-school to postgraduate, and held differing beliefs on the process of evaluation and the interpretation of evaluation results, so the discussion applied to evaluations in many different schools and over a range of national, economic, and political settings.

The Work of the Professional Group Israel 1996

In beginning its discussion of evaluation in technology-equipped settings, the Professional Group identified many key issues that must be considered in designing and conducting evaluations:

- What is the role of the evaluator?
  - There may be many different roles such as: truth teller; data provider; data interpreter; partner; insider/outsider; story-teller; judge; consultant;
  - The evaluator may be more like a scientist enquiring at the cutting edge where there are no definite answers, or more like an engineer intent on improving the production line for a rocket.

- How does the evaluator deal with ethical and moral dilemmas?
  - These dilemmas lead to conflicts about role;
  - Evaluators have responsibility to different stakeholders and interest groups;
  - There must be respect and care for individuals - the evaluator often holds considerable power in a situation where people might lose their jobs as a result of the evaluation.

- Who is the client?
  - The sponsor?
  - The participants?
  - The policy makers?

- What is the purpose of the evaluation?
  - Who do you write the reports for?
  - Evaluations may be mainly concerned with contributing to public knowledge, to the learning of policy makers, to the process of accountability for the spending of public money;
  - In which cases is there a need for answers?
  - There may be (should there be?) a marketing dimension to evaluation;
  - Where do you draw the boundaries around what is being evaluated?
  - Is evaluation in schools sometimes/always a vehicle for teacher development?
  - Evaluations can be a mechanism for support or a vehicle to promote change;
  - Evaluations may measure the attainment of goals (knowledge acquisition, social and moral competence, data literacy, media literacy).

- What is the climate under which evaluation is conducted?
  - Evaluations need to take account of the culture - is it punitive? is there a climate of deficit or of openness?
  - There may not be a culture of asking hard questions.

- How political is the evaluation process?
  - There are implications for the funding of initiatives;
  - Evaluators cannot avoid promoting and institutionalising particular sets of values;
  - There is the naiveté of some clients;
  - There is an issue of co-optation;
  - What effect does the evaluation have on what is taking place?

- What effect does evaluation have on policy and practice?

• What is to be evaluated?
  - What is the question?
  - What is the process of collecting data and/or presenting the results?

    - What curriculum competencies, content, skills, attitudes, expectations and experience should be considered in the evaluation?

• What are the variables that play an important role in the evaluation?
  - The context may be important;
  - Facilities, personnel policies, organisation, resources, access can play a role and are focal points.

• What are the criteria?
  - Who sets the criteria?
  - What types of criteria play a role?

• What is the appropriate methodology?
  - What are the tools?
  - What are the variables we should look at, and how should we formulate them?
  - Have we got the ability to see it all?
  - Does the methodology take into account real learning?
  - How do we tell the difference between what people think they are doing and what they really do?
  - How can we look at technology use without knowing where the teachers are in their planning and teaching?

• What are the outcomes?
  - Do they change the teacher's role?

• Do we need a development of new models?
  - The introduction of technology and the questions raised by technology call for new models of evaluation, and the students as well as the teachers should be regarded as partners in the evaluation process.

• How do we cope with different epistemological assumptions?
  - Differences between constructivists and behaviourists lead to differences in the
    questions asked, the models chosen, and the interpretation of results.

Whilst not exhaustive, the list of questions/issues does highlight the complexity of the evaluation process and bring to light differences in the educational perspectives of the various participants. These differences served to remind us that evaluation is far from a "cookie cutter" process, but, instead, calls for the considerations of many different aspects of a situation in designing, administering, and reporting evaluations in school-based technology settings.

Participants questioned whether non-evaluators were aware of the complexity of the task and aware of the self-scrutiny that many evaluators conduct as part of their professional activity. The analogy of the spider spinning a web and being caught in the web was offered as a metaphor for the situations in which evaluators often find themselves.

The Professional Group stated that evaluation changes what it evaluates. This poses a moral dilemma which discomforted some members of the group. However it was recognised that this can have a positive outcome. For example, questioning teachers and other stakeholders about what has been observed can change teachers' perceptions and future actions. In this way evaluation serves as an important component in the teacher education process. A further development of this approach would be Action Research, in which teachers collaborate with external researchers in a process of data collection, reflection, action planning, and evaluation - a process that repeats the cycle often as each member of the team defines and refines questions, observations, and analyses. In these collaborative evaluations, participating teachers often receive certification as an acknowledgement of their contributions.

It was agreed that framing questions and deciding how to answer those questions was a major concern of evaluators. Techniques such as informal observation, the use of rating scales to assess the level of teachers' interest in using IT, and analysis of video-taped lessons were suggested as useful ways for evaluators to break out of the pattern of administering end-point tests and comparing groups on such outcome measures. In fact, the group rejected the simplicity of the pre-/post-test model as trivial, inadequate, and misleading. In their view such evaluation strategies fail to capture the richness of the problems associated with the introduction, integration, and institutionalisation of IT.

There was general agreement that there is often an important role for teachers, students, parents, and the community to be participants in the evaluation process, and that this often enables them to act directly on the outcomes. It was suggested that children could often take part in evaluation activities and if they were taught some of the evaluation process, that this could have a beneficial effect on their development as learners.

It was also agreed that when we are talking about evaluations in technology-equipped settings we are not just talking about the use of tools; instead we are talking about the process of change, the conditions required for change, and the effects of change. The evaluators, it was agreed, were agents of change and should address the question of the purpose of education as they examine the acts within the educational context.

At that point in the discussion it became clear that it was important to specify the level of analysis - school level, classroom level or student level and whether the problem under investigation was the question of using IT with the current curriculum and evaluating all the aspects of that process or whether the problem was to examine the process of changing the curriculum and thus changing the ways students perform school-based tasks and acquire knowledge. While it was acknowledged that evaluators may now have to address the first set of questions, that increasingly the questions are likely to be directed at why and how the curriculum will be changed as IT's educational potential is more completely explored. Similarly it was agreed that evaluators must inquire about the effects of those changes on the school, the teacher, the student, and all the other stakeholders. It was acknowledged that different questions will follow from different contexts, from the mandate to the evaluators, and from the evaluators' sense of the logic of inquiry.

While acknowledging that there are many levels of the educational scene to be viewed when an evaluation is conducted, some members of the Group cautioned against the tendency to look only at one or other level. Instead, evaluations also need to tackle one or more "strands" vertically by examining the impact of an activity - teacher professional development activities, for example, on government, on school administrators, teachers, and students. Sometimes it will be necessary to examine both levels and strands in the evaluation.

An important question for evaluators concerns the difference between the intended and the attained curriculum. There will always be a difference and many curriculum developers, aware of this difference, contract for evaluations which look for the differences. A major need, the relation between students' performance in technology equipped classes in one subject area and their performance in other subjects areas also equipped with technology, was identified as another area of interest for curriculum developers.

A tension between the consumers of evaluation, policy makers, for example, on the one hand and the participants in the evaluations, teachers and students, for example, or the evaluator on the other hand was noted. The group agreed that at least two perspectives must be considered as evaluations are planned and conducted: (1) the perspective of the sponsoring agency, ministries of education, foundations, community members, which tends to be results oriented and (2) practitioners who will use the evaluation to affirm the value of current practice or use data to inform the process of change. Policy makers say they need to know "the whole picture" and need to know what changes need to take place, while school- and classroom-based clients often say they need data on more specific issues such as the degree to which one or another type of pedagogical activity produces the desired effect on students.

It was pointed out that government documents do not reflect theories of educational practice, but instead propose sets of actions based on instrumental goals - installing a certain number of computers in schools, for example, without considering the educational implications of that process. Nevertheless, it was agreed that the evaluators' duty was to draw on theory in order to create a framework in which the evaluation can be conducted. This raised the question of the evaluators' objectivity. Some members of the Group believed that the evaluator and the evaluation began from a value-free base, while other members of the Group said we all act from one or another belief system and it is the evaluators' responsibility, while acknowledging their own beliefs, to respect the goals and objectives of the situation to be evaluated. In spite of those differences, it was agreed that the work of the evaluator must not be compromised, either by the evaluator or the agency contracting for the evaluation, but that academic freedom to present the data as the situation appears is essential.

The duty of the evaluator to maintain a broad vision of what must be part of the evaluation and what can be accomplished as a result of the evaluation was affirmed by the Group. Similarly, it was agreed that the evaluator must affirm existing good practice and not just assess the extent to which there are deviations from the intended design or variances from good pedagogical practice among those observed. It was also agreed that evaluators must know how to specify when a project has been successful and when it has been a failure, for the failure to acknowledge success may well mean the project can be judged to have failed.

This pointed to the need for the specification of the perspectives of different models and the criteria flowing from those models. It was acknowledged that evaluators are often not trusted because the public-at-large and constituencies within education are not aware of the criteria applied in evaluative situations and may not understand the full import of those criteria as they apply to the models and to the situations. This may mean that continuing professional development for evaluators and consumers of evaluation must include a knowledge of the models which can be applied and a knowledge of the range of criteria applicable to those models. There was a tension within the group on the advisability of setting guidelines for evaluators' professional development, with some members saying that evaluators must answer to themselves and that acting with reflection upon the issues surrounding the evaluation is sufficient. But it was agreed Jim Ridgway's discussion of Vygotsky's work, presented in the conference keynote, on the development of tool use was a fruitful conceptualisation for reflecting on the problem of change in behaviour.

The fundamental division between epistemological views - ministries and other funders typically seeing education in behaviourist terms and practitioners often seeing education in constructivist terms - was seen as a problem and it was suggested that educators must adopt an "instrumentalist" stance when they present their findings. Similarly, the caution was raised that the evaluator must plan how the evaluation reports and summaries will be used, and plan for different levels of description for different audiences, and it was agreed that evaluations cannot be considered as abstractions, but must be thought of in terms of the environments in which they are conducted.

Discussion also addressed the question of whether there would be a revolution or evolution of educational practice as a result of the use of technology in school settings. Some members of the Group said that governments were working to make radical change which was needed, while others said government was seeking revolutionary change in areas where past practices had been *perceived* to fail and there was a danger of losing good practices which do not require technology under the governments' demands for increased student performance.

There were clear cut national differences within the Group, related to differences in cultural patterns, differences in goals for schooling, and differences in the stages of implementation of technology. For example, differences in epistemological perspectives yielded differing views on what questions should be asked and how those questions should be answered. It was acknowledged that these differences were an important part of the educational practice of individual countries, but that those differences should be analysed by evaluators as they set about their work.

It was clear that current evaluation practice must begin to look to the future and devise and use taxonomies of educational objectives that accord with the behaviours that futurists tell us will be developed and applied as a result of our interactions with technology in school settings. Reanalyses of taxonomies such as Bloom's taxonomy of educational objectives have been conducted and they specify how the objectives are enhanced or changed as a result of the technology revolution. Currently many evaluators are working with models and objectives suitable to a factory or small land holding farmer, but the Group agreed that the 21st century tools and challenges call for a re-examination and a re-formulation of the evaluators' tools and methods. Such a re-examination would be a fruitful task for subsequent Professional Group activities.

It was also suggested that subsequent Professional Group activities assume the task of formulating sets of criteria that are applicable to the different stakeholders - ministries of education, teachers, school administrators, and the community at large. Guidelines are also needed on how to educate the stakeholders in acting on the evaluations' findings and recommendations. So the work of the Israel-based

Professional Group on evaluation, while informative and wide-ranging, is far from complete as it applies to the manifold questions and issues facing evaluators in technology-equipped settings.

The Chair and Rapporteur wish to acknowledge the significant contribution made to this report by Rachel Cohen.

Focus Group 4: Internet and teacher education

Participants: Beverly Ferrucci (USA), Klaus-D. Graf (D), Pieter Hogenbirk (NL), Huppert Jehuda (IL), Alnaaz Kassam (CAN), Anton Knierzinger (AUT), Antonio Osorio, UK (P), Ruth Reiz (IL), Wolfgang Weber (D)
Chair: David Squires (UK)
Rapporteur: Toni Downes (AUS)

What facilities does the Internet provide for education?

- The Internet acts as a medium for electronic communication among students, student teachers, teachers, school administrators, educational managers, teacher educators, curriculum developers, researchers, experts in other professions and institutions and the community. It also provides for communications between these groups. The basic facilities include e-mail, discussion groups/news groups, chat facilities.
- It provides access to electronic sources of information, and educational resources and services. The basic facilities include the WWW, FTP and TELNET.

What are some of the possibilities/potential benefits of using the Internet in education?

For pupils Internet use can:

- facilitate the creation of electronic communities where communication process and information access can be combined.
- provide opportunities for classroom walls to be broken down and community isolation to be lessened as children of different ages, from different geographic regions, with different world views and experiences communicate, work together and share resources as they learn. Cross-cultural communication and global education can become a real part of classroom learning.
- support mother-tongue and foreign language learning through access to resources in many languages and communication with people of different language backgrounds.
- facilitate learning and equity by empowering people through access to large amounts of information, to real-time information, electronic resources and remote sites.
- facilitate equity by removing barriers to publication of ideas and information through informal but accessible channels, for example, scientists and children can publish along side each other, dissidents can publish within and beyond their own communities.

- remove some of the spatial and temporal constraints of communication and community building by providing electronic access to people and resources outside the classroom.
- facilitate multiple identities of individuals or 'hide' differences of those communicating, allowing for learners with disabilities, or different cultural, ethnic, social and language backgrounds to communicate safely through the single channel of written text.
- provide a wider range of purposes and audiences for pupils' reading, writing, talking, listening, researching and co-operating.
- provide opportunities for students to use technology for 'real' purposes and in a way that will be increasingly more common in their future lives.
- support experimental learning with pupils having access to 'real-time' data, data from remote sites, or data collected collaboratively over a number of sites.

For teachers the Internet can:
- support teachers in their professional role through communicating with other teachers and access a wide range of educational resources and services.
- support student teachers in their course-work and school-based component through communication with other student teachers, supervising teachers, mentors, university staff and through access to a wide range of educational resources.
- support teachers who are endeavouring to change their modes of teaching to include a resource-based inquiry mode and co-operative learning.
- improve educational management, school administration and dialogue between practitioners, researchers and policy makers through e-mail and discussion group facilities.

What role should the Internet play in education?

A rationale for the use of the Internet in education is the crucial issue in any discussion about its use. However a rationale can only exist within the context of a clear vision of what we are trying to achieve in education or particular levels of education or particular learning communities. As there are many such visions and differences in the political, economic and philosophical environments among and between nations, the notion of single rationale beyond the following points was not considered appropriate.
- The Internet is but a single part of the mosaic of information and communications technologies that are changing the way society functions and have the potential to support teaching and learning.
- The Internet is a new technology that pupils as learners and future citizens must be able to use for a variety of their own and others' purposes.
- The Internet should only be considered as an educational resource within the framework of enhancing learning for pupils of all races, cultures, language background and gender.

A range of tensions exist when considering the Internet as an educational resource. These include tensions:
- between providing support to improve current practices and change current practices.

- about questions of whether this technology is sufficiently revolutionary to change the vision of what education could or should be.
- about whether this technology is sufficiently different from other learning resources that it needs particular attention on its own.
- about whether this technology will increase the gap between rich and poor individuals, communities and nations.

What are some of the policy issues surrounding the use of the Internet in education?

- Many politicians and service providers are presenting unrealistic images of the uses and powers of the Internet. Much of the current hype implies that the Internet can solve many of the complex problems confronting today's classrooms.
- There are many governments who only provide the hardware and infrastructure for schools, few provide resources to create useful educational gateways to quality resources on the Internet, develop curriculum projects, moderate discussion groups, and provide teacher development opportunities.
- Effective Internet use will require a well developed policy framework. Some policy issues include:
- What can be published on the Internet? What is the role of the provider?- quality control, user pays/cost recovery, privacy and copyright, controls on access to the information?
- Equity and access to the information, between nations, between communities, between students.
- What constraints should there be to access to Internet resources - financial, registration for legitimate users, legal, censorship, pedagogical reasons?

What are some of the issues/problems of using the Internet in education?
General

- Educational systems need to create educational resources and environments within the Internet. Teachers need to develop learning environments within which pupils use the Internet in a structured way.
- There is a continuum of teacher use - from teachers who will be independent and enthusiastic users of the Internet, searching and developing their own resources to teachers who will benefit from the resources of the Internet in an 'off-line mode' by using information and curriculum materials developed by intermediaries.
- There are a range of ways that the Internet can be included in the teaching and learning process. These may vary according to the levels of education, the stages of schooling, access to infrastructure, hardware and expertise and the purpose of use:
- as an off-line resource.
- as a filtered resource.
- as an unrestricted resource.
- The use of written electronic texts as sources of information and a medium of communication needs to be balanced with the use of a range of other modes of language use including oral and personal modes.

The Internet as an information platform

- Searching the Internet can be a very time consuming task with many pitfalls. Teachers need to take account of this in terms of time needed and possible frustration.
- There are seldom quality control checks on the information published on the Internet. A critical analysis of the information needs to take account of the accuracy, voracity, bias and recency of the information.
- Education systems have a responsibility to provide a range of systems and services for teachers and classrooms. These include filters to allow pupils and teachers to easily access high quality, relevant and culturally appropriate materials in mother tongue languages.

The Internet as a communication platform

- Discussion groups, forums and "chatting rooms" need to be moderated so that maximum educational value can be gained. Moderators need to lead discussions but also provide expertise or access to expertise, and timely responses.
- Teachers and pupils need new ways of looking at the authoring, publishing and accessing processes. Within the Internet there are so few constraints on what is published that users can receive so much information that they are overwhelmed.

The Internet as a co-operative learning platform

- Co-operative projects require careful planning, targeted publicity and sufficient lead time so that teachers can plan for curriculum integration and access to the necessary resources.
- Teachers also require access to relevant teaching resources, on-line support and moderation of discussion and projects.

As a classroom resource (practical issues)

- Teachers and pupils need skills and new processes to cope with the information demands made more critical by the nature of the Internet, for example, handling too much information and evaluating the quality of information.
- Teachers and pupils need to know what media to use to communicate and to access and publish information. For example, the Internet is an appropriate information source when teachers and pupils need access to immediate/recent or actual/volatile data or data held in remote sites.
- Pupils need access to communication channels and information in their mother tongue at a level of language appropriate to their stage of schooling. In general information on the Internet is text dense and mostly 'adult level'.
- Teachers need time to plan, overcome problems, design or adapt curriculum materials.
- Continually changing technologies and environments cause frustration and barriers for teachers and pupils.
- The management and organisation of the resources within the school is often complex and requires a rethinking of normal practice.

Implications for teacher education

- All teachers should use technology and teach about technology in ways appropriate to their discipline and stage of schooling. ICTs should feature in all teacher education courses - pre-service and in-service.
- Teacher educators, teachers and student teachers as well as pupils need to use ICTs in their own learning in a range of ways for a variety of purposes.
- Teacher educators, teachers and student teachers need to rethink literacy and information handling environments in the light of the wide range of new ICTs.
- Using ICTs in teacher education programmes and classroom learning should be an activity integrated into the curriculum rather than an additional activity to be 'squeezed' into an already overcrowded curriculum. This may involve a reorientation of existing practices.
- In teacher education programmes the emphasis should be on how to use the Internet as one of the ICTs, as a medium, to improve teaching and learning rather than the study of the Internet for its own sake.
- As teacher educators we need to support/prepare teachers and student teachers for independent use of the Internet and its resources as well as for preparation for using services and resources that education systems and other providers have created. Some of the knowledge/skills include:
- basic ICT skills (in the context of a wide range of ICTs skills).
- some simple basic concepts, for example, networks, client-server notion, Internet structure, name conventions, transport mechanisms.
- use of Internet browsers and e-mail facilities.
- information seeking and handling skills and strategies (for example, narrowing searches, filtering irrelevant/poor quality information).
- ICTs awareness and competence skills.
- understanding the various media, their strengths and weakness and cost effectiveness.
- developing critical awareness of when to use which media.
- understanding the nature of multimedia in terms of the cognitive complexities of the information/learning environments rather than the complexities of the media used.
- developing an awareness of the validity of claims made about the Internet.
- pedagogical skills.
- designing classroom environments which use a range of media in a variety of ways.
- using as an off-line resource.
- using as an on-line resource.
- sharing control of learning with the student.
- designing environments which focus on learning processes, shared roles, curriculum goals, project-orientated learning.
- evaluating teaching and assessing learning within the contexts of new ICTs.
- reflect on own role as a teacher/facilitator.
- reorientation of specific subject matter as related to ICTs, for example, use of satellite technology in the study of landforms within geography.

Teacher educators need to develop a wide range of strategies, resources and support for getting teachers started:

- providing teachers/student teachers with personal and professional tools to meet existing needs and problems.
- sharing and creating case studies/success stories.
- providing on-site, integrated support - on-line or personal, peers or external agents.
- Teacher educators need to consider the role of the Internet in traditional forms of teacher education as well as a means of developing new forms of teacher education processes and resources.
- Teacher educators need to support some teachers in developing further knowledge/skills relating to Internet uses so that these teacher can act as leaders within their schools/systems.

The knowledge and skills required include:

- choosing/evaluating service providers and other cost-related resources.
- authoring on WWW.
- acting as moderators of discussions.
- acting as project leaders, curriculum developers.

Glossary

Internet - A network of networks which is based on TCP/IP. The distinguishing feature from other global networks is the developing capacity to handle images and sounds as well as text. Many of the points made in the sections above apply to any global network, not just the Internet.

Information and Communication Technologies (ICTs) - The term is a general one which refers to a range of processes and products related to handling information and communicating. It encompasses paper-based and screen-based media, a range of networked, telecommunications and local environments, and a range of hardware including television, computers, telecommunications and other devices.

Alphabetical List of Conference Participants

A

Lisbeth Appelberg
Department of Child and Youth Education,
    Special Education and Counselling
Umeå University, S-901 87, Umeå, Sweden
Tel +46 90 16 64 44, Fax +46 90 16 65 11
E-mail lisbeth.appelberg@educ.umu.se

B

Amalia Barrios
Escola Superior de Educacao De Lisboa
Avenue Carolina Michaelis De Vasconcecos,
    1500 Lisboa, Portugal
Tel +351 1 714 1878, Fax +351 1 716 6147

**David Benzie (Chair of Programme
    Committee)**
CITE, College of St. Mark and St. John
Derriford Road, Plymouth, PL6 8BH, UK
Tel (0)1752 636804, Fax (0)1752 636823
E-mail 100441.3313@compuserve.com

Doug Brown
Schools Advisory Service, Portland Centre
PO Box 2757, Edgbaston, Birmingham, B17
    8LW, UK
Tel +44 121 235 5303
E-mail dbrown@lea.birmingham.gov.uk

Eric Bruillard
IUFM de Creteil, Route de Brevannej
Bonneuil Cedex, 94861 France
Tel 33 (0) 1 49 56 37 23 ,Fax 33 (0) 1 49 56 37 91
E-mail bruillar@citi2.fr

Yvonne Buettner
Fachstelle Informatik der Lehrerinnen
Postfach, CH-4133 Pratteln, Switzerland
Tel 61 / 821 04 04, Fax 61 / 821 04 00
E-mail ybuettner@mus.ch

C

Qi Chen
Beijing Normal University
Beijing 100875, China
Tel (86 10) 220 8190, Fax (86 10) 201 3929
E-mail chenqi@bnu.edu.cn

Rachel Cohen
I.E.D.P.E., Universite Paris-Nord
72 Rue de l'Est, F-92100 Boulogne, France
Tel +33 1 4825 0319, Fax +33 1 4825 0319
E-mail euroboulogne@citi2.fr

**Bernard Cornu (Vice-Chair of Programme
    Committee)**
Institut Universitaire de Formation des Maîtres
    (IUFM)
30, Avenue Marcelin Berthelot, 38100
    Grenoble, France
Tel +33 76 74 73 70, Fax +33 76 87 19 47
E-mail cornu@grenet.fr

Margaret Cox
School of Education, King's College
Waterloo Road, London, SE1 8WA, UK
Tel 44-(0)-171-872-3126, Fax 44-(0)-171-872-
    3182
E-mail MJ.Cox@kcl.ac.uk

D

Toni Downes
Faculty of Education, University of Western
    Sydney
P.O. Box 555, Campbelltown, New South
    Wales 2560, Australia
Tel +612 7729200, Fax +612 7742390
E-mail t.downes@uws.edu.au

Amos Dreyfus
Hebrew University of Jerusalem, Faculty of
    Agriculture
P.O. Box 12, Rehovot 76100, Israel
Tel 972-8-9481908, Fax 972-8-9473305
E-mail dreyfus@.huji.agri.ac.il

F

Binyamin Feinstein
Hebrew University of Jerusalem, Faculty of
    Agriculture
P.O. Box 12, Rehovot 76100, Israel
Tel 972-8-9481908, Fax 972-8-9473305

Beverly Ferruci
Keene State College
Keene, NH, USA 03435-2001
Tel 603-358-2506, Fax 603-3358-2897
E-mail bferrucc@keene.edu
Steffen Friedrich
Bodenbacher Strasse 135a, D-1277 Dresden,
    Germany
E-mail friedrick@soft1.inf.tu-dresden.de

G

Shahaf Gal (Invited Speaker)
Center for Educational Technology
16 Klausner Street, Ramat-Aviv, Tel-Aviv
    61392, Israel

Shosh Gilad
Centre for Educational Technology
16 Klausner Street, Ramat-Aviv, Tel-Aviv
    61392, Israel

Klaus-D. Graf
Kurstrasse 5, D-14129 Berlin, Germany
Tel +49 (30) 8018451, Fax +49 (30) 838 75
    109

H

Ard Hartsuiker
SLO, P.O. Box 2041
7500 Enschede, The Netherlands

Pieter Hogenbirk
PRINT/VO
Plotterweg 30, 3821 BB Amersfoort, The
    Netherlands
Tel + 31 334534343, Fax +31 334534353
E-mail PRINT@XS4ALL.NL

Peter Hubweiser
Fakultat fur Informatik, Technischen
    Universitat Munchen
D-80290 Munchen, Germany
Tel (089)-2105-8162, Fax -8183,
E-mail hubwiese@informatik.tumuenchen.de

Yehuda Huppert
School of Education - Oranim, University of
    Haifa, Tivon 36910, Israel
E-mail huppert@math.tau.ac.il

K

Alnaaz Kassam
Department of Curriculum, OISE
252 Bloor Street West, Toronto, Ontario, M5S
    1V6, Canada
Tel 923-6641 ext 2607
E-mail alnaazkassam@oise.on.ca

**Yaacov Katz (Chair of Organising
    Committee)**
School of Education
Bar-Ilan University, Ramat-Gan 52900, Israel
Tel +972 3 5318444, Fax +972 3 5353319
E-mail f45410@mvsa.biu.ac.il

Steve Kennewell
University of Wales Swansea, Department of
    Education
Hendrefoelan, Swansea, SA2 7NB, UK
Tel +44 1792 201231 x 2039, Fax +44 1792
    290219
E-mail s.e.kennewell@swansea.ac.uk

**Anton Knierzinger (Vice-Chair of
    Programme Committee)**
Paedagog Akademie
Salesianunweg 3, Linz 4020, Austria
Tel +43 (732) 772666 - 262, Fax +43 (732)
    797306
E-mail kna@mail.padl.ac.at

L

Livi Lanir
Kibbutz Givat Brenner 60948, Israel

Enrica Lemut
IMA, Via de Marini 6, Torre di Francia
16149 Genova, Italy
Tel +39-10-64751, Fax +39-10-6475660
E-mail lemut@ima.ge.cnr.it

Joyce Currie Little
Department of Computer Sciences, Towson
    State University
8000 York Road, Baltimore, MD 21204, USA
Tel 410-830-3783, Fax 410-830-3868
E-mail jclittle@midget.towson.edu

Herbert Loethe
University of Education Ludwigsburg
Postfach, D-71602 Ludwigsburg, Germany
Tel +49-7141-140385, Fax +49-7141-140418
E-mail loethe@ph-ludwigsburg.de

M

Gail Marshall
2393 Broadmont Court
Chesterfield, MO 63017, USA
Tel 314-230-6613, Fax 314-230-3609
E-mail 74055.652@Compuserve.co

Patricia Marzel
IUFM, 30 Avenue Marcelin Berthelot
38100 Grenoble, France

Anne McDougall
Faculty of Education, Monash University
Clayton, Victoria 3168, Australia
Tel +61 3 99052790, Fax +61 3 99052779
E-mail anne.mcdougall@education.monash.edu.au

Zemira Mevarech
School of Education
Bar-Ilan University, Ramat-Gan 52900, Israel
Tel 00972-3-535 702, Fax 00972-3-535 5048
E-mail F45400@BARILAN

Raymond Morel (Member of Programme Committee)
Centre Informatique Pedagogique, P.O. Box 3144, CH 1211 Geneva 3, Switzerland
E-mail morel@uni2a.unige.ch

N

Phil Nanlohy
Faculty of Education, University of Western Sydney
P.O. Box 555, Campbelltown, New South Wales 2560, Australia
Fax +61 2 7721565
E-mail p.nanlohy@uws.edu.au

Paul Nicholson (Member of Programme Committee)
Deakin Centre for Education and Change
662 Blackburn Road, Clayton Australia 3168
Tel +61 3 9244 7286 , Fax +613 9562 8808
E-mail pauln@deakin.edu.au

O

John Oakley
School of Teacher Education, Charles Sturt University
Bathurst, New South Wales 2795, Australia
Tel +61 63 384365, Fax +61 63 384469
E-mail joakley@csu.edu.au

Tomas O'Briain
37 Pineview Avenue
Tallaght, Dublin 24, Ireland
Tel +353 1 2300977
E-mail tobriain@iol.ie

Mícheál Ó Dúill
Logos the Logo User Group
37 Bright Street, Skipton, North Yorkshire, BD23 1QQ, UK

Baruch Offir (Vice-Chair of Organising Committee)
School of Education, Bar-Ilan University
Ramat-Gan 52900, Israel
Tel 03 5318444, Fax 03 5353319

Shimon Ohayon (Co-ordinator on Organising Committee)
School of Education, Bar-Ilan University
Ramat-Gan 52900, Israel

Antonio Osorio
School of Education, University of Exeter
Heavitree Road, Exeter, EX1 2LU, UK
Tel +1392 264781, Fax +1392 264736
E-mail A.J.Osorio@ex.ac.uk

P

Don Passey (Proceedings Editor)
STAC Project, Department of Psychology
Lancaster University, Lancaster, LA1 4YF, UK
Tel +44 1524 593600, Fax +44 1524 841710
E-mail d.passey@lancaster.ac.uk

David Passig (Member of Organising Committee)
School of Education
Bar-Ilan University, Ramat-Gan 52900, Israel
Tel +972 52 782377, Fax +972 3 5353319
E-mail passig@ashur.cc.biu.ac.il

R

Judith Ram
7 Stern Street, Herzlia 46412, Israel

Ruth Reiz
Department of Education in Science and Technology
Technion - Israel Institute of Technology, Haifa 32000, Israel
E-mail rreiz@techunix.technion.ac.il

Jim Ridgway (Invited Speaker)
Department of Psychology
University of Lancaster, Lancaster LA1 4YF,
UK
Tel 01524 593829
E-mail j.ridgway@lancaster.ac.uk

Bruce Rigby
Directorate of School Education
Level 2 Rialto South Tower, 525 Collins
Street, Melbourne, Victoria 3000,
Australia
Tel +61 3 9628 2186, Fax +61 3 9628 2565
E-mail bruce.rigby@dse.vic.gov.au

Brent Robinson
Department of Education
University of Cambridge
17 Trumpington Street, Cambridge, CB2 1QA,
UK
Tel (0)1223 332888, Fax (0)1223 332894

Sindre Rûsvik
Municipal School District Giske Kommune
Øvre Nordstrand, N-6050 Valderoy, Norway
Tel +47 701 82005, Fax +47 701 81286
E-mail sindre@mimer.no

Kay Rye
A. R. P. Ltd
P.O. Box 10, Okato, Taranaki 4652, New
Zealand
Tel +64 6 752 4050
E-mail krye@nzonline. ac. nz

S

Gavriel Salomon (Invited Speaker)
School of Education, Haifa University
Mount Carmel, Haifa 31999, Israel
Tel +972 4 240 767, Fax +972 4 240 911
E-mail gsalomon@research.haifa.ac.il

Brian Samways (Proceedings Editor)
Education IT, Martineau Centre
Balden Road, Harborne, Birmingham, B32
2EH, UK
Tel +44 121 427 4588, Fax +44 121 428 2246
E-mail bsamways@lea.birmingham.gov.uk

Andreas Schwill
Informatik V - Universitaet Potsdam
D-14415 Potsdam, Germany
Tel +49 331977 1044, Fax +49 331977 1720
E-mail schwill@cs.uni-potsdam.de

Michelle Selinger
School of Education, The Open University
Walton Hall, Milton Keynes, M17 6AA, UK
Tel +1908 655983, Fax +1908 652218
E-mail m.s.selinger@open.ac.uk

Bridget Somekh
Scottish Council for Research in Education
15 St. John Street, Edinburgh, EH8 8JR, UK
Tel +44131 557 2944, Fax +44131 556 9454
E-mail b.somekh@ed.ac.uk

David Squires
School of Education, King's College
Waterloo Road, London, SE1 8WA, UK
Tel +44 171 872 3107, Fax +44 171 872 3182
E-mail d.squires@hazel.cc.kcl.ac.uk

T

Janet Talmon
Hebrew University of Jerusalem, Faculty of
Agriculture
P.O. Box 12, Rehovot 76100, Israel
Tel 972-8-9481908, Fax 972-8-9473305

Hiroyuki Tanaka
Faculty of Education, Osaka Kyoiku University,
4-698-1, Asahigaoka, Kashiwara, Osaka, 582,
Japan
Tel +81-729-78-3453, Fax +81-729-78-3366
E-mail hiroyuki@cc.osaka-kyoiku.ac.jp,
hiroyuki.tanaka@kcl.ac.uk

Harriet G. Taylor
EDAF-111 Peabody, Louisiana State
University
Baton Rouge, LA 70803-4121, USA
Tel (504) 388-1356, Fax (504) 388-6918
E-mail taylor@asterix.ednet.lsu.edu
WWW http://obelix.ednet.lsu.edu/~taylor/

Márta Turcsányi-Szabó
Loránd Eötvös University
Department of General Computer Science, 1088
Budapest, Múzeum krt. 6-8., Hungary
Tel/Fax (36-1) 266-5196
E-mail TURCSANYINE@LUDENS.ELTE.HU

U

Jean Underwood
School of Education, University of Leicester
21 University Road, Leicester LE1 7RF, UK
Tel +44 116 252 3679, Fax +44 116 252 3653
E-mail jdu@le.ac.uk

W

Deryn Watson
School of Education, King's College
Waterloo Road, London, SE1 8WA, UK
Tel 44 171 872 3106, Fax 44 171 872 3182
E-mail deryn.watson@kcl.ac.uk

Wolfgang Weber
Landesinstitut fur Schule
Referat Z2, Paradieser Weg 64, D-59494Soest,
        Germany
Tel +49 2921 683235, Fax +49 2921 683388
E-mail 100634.2324@Compuserve.com

Menuha Weiss
The University of Chicago School Mathematics
        Project
The Technion, Technical Institute for Israel
41/18 Hasayfan Street, Ramat Hasharon
        47248, Israel
E-mail weiss@ccsg.tau.ac.il

Y

Michal Yerushalmy
Centre for Educational Technology
School of Education, Haifa University, Mount
        Carmel, Haifa 31999, Israel

INDEX OF CONTRIBUTORS

KEYWORD INDEX